M000286868

To

Marcella

from

Dorothy Juan

Our Great grandmother,
" Satsa C. Trout " was born
1837 in Calhoun, Gordon County
Georgia.

December 1980

Stories of Gordon County and Calhoun, Georgia

VOLUME ONE

By

Jewell B. Reeve

To the Memory

of

Laurens Hillhouse

He molded a brick and planted a tree.
In the red clay hills of Georgia, in the warm white sands of Africa, a building stands, a tree grows — monument and memorial to the skill of his hands and the love in his heart for the beauty of nature.

Copyright 1962 by Mrs. Jewell B. Reeve, Calhoun, Ga.

New Material COPYRIGHT 1979
     By: The Rev. Silas Emmett Lucas, Jr.

SOUTHERN HISTORICAL PRESS
% The Rev. S. Emmett Lucas, Jr.
P. O. Box 738
Easley, South Carolina   29640

ISBN-0-89308-128-0

CHAPTERS

ACKNOWLEDGEMENTS

When I began about five years ago, writing stories about Gordon County's early years, I was only having fun.

Then people began to say "write a book."

The task has not been mine alone. There have been so many helpers that I could not list them all. To them, I am indebted.

First, to Floyd Whittemore, our efficient and courteous Clerk of Court. No matter how busy he was, if I asked about a newspaper volume or a deed book, he always came to my assistance.

To Mina Lusk and Marie Woods, who often left their typewriter to help me find a book.

To the lawyers who never once intimated that I was in the way at the long counter. Col. Paschal even said "we'll make a lawyer of you yet."

To David McCombs who was willing to get down on his knees in the grime of the ancient floor and help me dig 1879 from the bottom of the stack.

To the editors of the Calhoun Newspapers, J. Roy McGinty. J. H. Hobgood and John Hughes, I went to the newspaper office with a story and said to the tall, silver-haired man "I just have to boil over sometimes." "Boil over as often as you like," replied Editor McGinty, "and I'll print it."

To the men in the back with all the mysterious machines. They translated my script with very few errors. One, I remember. I was quoting from one of Minnie C. Harlan's poems, "ever freshening Our Memories." When the paper came out, I read every fisherman's memory." I knew where Frank Dickinson's mind was that spring day.

To R. D. Self and to Dovia Self and Ruth King who did so much of the typing. And my little neighbor, Ann Rhodes, who typed a chapter or two one summer.

To Janette Robbins Gravitt. who has been the typist for the greater part of this book. She refused to accept payment (except for one small check) saying, "you are doing a good work, why shouldn't I help you?"

To my dear departed friend, Harris Reeve Cantrell (Mrs. F. A.), whose wonderful mind was a storehouse of memories of Calhoun and Gordon County. She lifted the memories out, carefully dusted them off and gave them to me pure and clear.

To Maude Ballew Neal, who has spent her entire life in Calhoun. It is to her that I am indebted for many of the stories in this book.

To the people in Plainville, Sugar Valley and Oothcaloga district, especially to the Belwood Community Club. Bea Richardson and Virginia Fuller.

To William E. Bray, of the Yale Divinity School, who gave me permission to use his story of the Bray family.

To the L. A. Lee Publishing Company and Mr. Robinson, of Dalton.

To all the people of Gordon County, my heartfelt thanks for your assistance in this work of writing the story of your ancestors.

Jewell B. Reeve

Calhoun, Georgia

FOREWORD

It was the young Anne Morrow who wrote "I should like to be a dancer, a scarlet Spanish dancer if you please. But he said, just now we're crowded with these Carmens. In a century, or twenty we may want you—There's a place for Quaker maidens—I think I wear my Quaker with a grace."

I would like to be a writer, a brilliant, sparkling writer, if you please. You said, the world is crowded now with these Hemingways, these Frosts and Sandburgs.

I cannot wait a century or twenty. The story of my county must be told.

But, who am I to tell it? My words come from the purple shadows of John's mountain, from the babbling rapids of Snake Creek and from the red dust clouds of country roads. My words are tuned to the musical syllables of the Cherokee and salted with the Colloquialisms of my English and Irish Ancestors.

Let my words be welcome then and I will tell you the story of a beautiful virgin forest where the birds sang a heavenly chorus all day long and the deer fed on little new twigs. I will tell you of a land where the rivers ran clear and the Cherokee paddled his bark canoe. I will tell you of a land stripped of it's ancient trees, or humming mills where bright yellow planks were spewed out and quickly carted away to build my grandfather's house, and his barn, and his store. I will tell you of cleared fields, golden with ripened grain, green with tall corn spikes and white with row on row of cotton ready for the picking.

I will tell you of the men and women who took this raw rugged land, turned up the strong red dirt on the hills, stirred the rich black soil of the lowlands, criss-crossed the country with gravelly roads, suffered through war and desolation and left to you and to me, a place of beauty and wealth and a heritage of courage, endurance and culture.

I would erect a monument to the editors of the county newspapers, Dave Freeman in the 1870s, Henry Chapman in the 1880s, Jim Hall in the 1890s and George Tribble in the early 1900s. Young men they were, and not afraid to speak their pieces.

Did the Methodist parsonage need painting? Dave Freeman said so and, in a short time the parsonage was resplendent in a coat of white paint, with green blinds and a picket fence. Was the cupola on the Baptist church odd-looking? Dave Freeman thought so and soon the Baptist church was undergoing extensive improvements.

"Everyone should contribute to the building of the Episcopal church," wrote Henry Chapman, and "people should go to church more than they do. The Council should either light the streets or remove the scaffolds, wood and rails from the sidewalks and—what's the matter with the county? Too much idleness."

When did the first train run over W & A? Joab Lewis knew. Standing near Wash Lawson's store that spring day of 1847, he saw it arrive. Jim Hall wrote Joab's story in 1896. New Echota was but a dream but Albert Tarvin remembered the reality—he was born there. Jim Hall wrote Albert's story in 1902. Other towns have a cotton mill, why not Calhoun? Surely you mean to see that Calhoun becomes greater in the century than in the last.

George Tribble was "a man like all others subject to mistakes, but he would freely, openly and honestly advocate what he thought was right. The right of a citizen to express his views on marriage, the church, the school and the status of the town and county, to write poetry if he chose—these were George Tribble's "rights."

I would ask of you who so proudly wear the mantle of a Gordon County pioneer, do you know of his struggle with the forces of nature? Of how he fenced his fields and yards, cleared the walks of dog fennel and bridged the ditches that the draining waters of the hills had cut across the streets of his town? Do you know of the I'll Try Club, the Debating Society and the Literary Society and how the members of these clubs advanced the cause of learning until a railway mail clerk was moved to say "we put off more papers and magazines at Calhoun than any place on the W & A"?

Then read the story here, my dears, and ponder your worthiness. I once heard a young minister shout from the pulpit "It isn't what kind of ancestors you had it's what kind of ancestor you're going to BE!"

I would question the new citizen here, why did you choose Calhoun or Gordon County for your home? Was it because of the beautiful churches, attractive homes and fine schools? Or the wide paved streets and neon lights, or the rich farm lands and free-flowing streams?

Then learn here how these things came to be and go scatter flowers on the footprints in the sands of time, footprints left by the Cherokee, by the Confederate soldier and his War Widow, by E. J. Kiser and T. A. Foster, J. M. Harlan and Joel Fain, by T. M. Ellis, the half-bothers Reeve and the Boaz brothers. Learn of the Methodist preachers, the Baptist and Presbyterian preachers, who thundered from the pulpit, prayed in the jails and stormed into the barrooms until evil was swept from the Pine Thicket, the barrooms closed and the darkened windows opened.

And, through it all, see Laurens Hillhouse making brick, digging holes, setting trees, planting shrubbery and serving his Maker, even into a foreign land.

It is for you, the blessed inheritors of all this bounty and for you who have come to partake of our fathers' store of goods, that this book is written.

Jewell B. Reeve

Calhoun, Georgia

CLIMB THE HILLS OF GORDON

Climb the hills of Gordon and look back on her years. Yonder runs the river crystal clear, where the little fawn droops her head to drink and the antlered stag swims the dark green pool. There goes the Cherokee, the skillful hunter in the forest primeval, follow him to Echota; see Sequoyah carving out his symbols; hear the words of wisdom in the Council House; watch the greedy white man at his dirty work; walk the trail of tears.

Hear the hammers pound, listen to the trowel scrape, the white man wants a house, he needs a store of brick; this path shall be the main street, make another there; build a church, the preacher says; the lawyer wants a courthouse.

Stack the brick and mix the concrete, mud is not for rubber wheels; stretch the wires and light the street, for a man does not want to live in the dark.

Take your seat upon the hills of Gordon for time is not finished. Were you there? The historian asks. No, but my father was, you say.

Nero snickered from his balcony while Christians fought the lions, then could think of nothing to do but fiddle while his kingdom burned.

Did Richard III murder the two little princes, his brother's sons? No one knows for sure but Richard wore a crown for not two years.

"I do not believe my grandfather did all those things," she said, "he was too sweet and good!" Yet the church clerk had recorded "fellowship withdrawn because the brother would not abide by the rules of the church as laid down in the 18th chapter of Matthew."

Grandfather, with his gray beard and his kind face, was he never plagued with the fires of youth? The younger Sunday school teacher says to his class of older women "you are so good you are an inspiration to me" and a sly little spirit runs around the room and whispers "were you always so good?"

Sit upon the hills of Gordon and listen to these stories, for the good that men did will live after them and the evil, if any, shall remain interred with their bones.

No polished dandies were these men who moved into the Cherokee lands in the 1840's, but men of brawn and great determination for here was a task momentous, a challenge to the sturdy.

It's 1847, measure the distance from Dawsonville (Calhoun) to the old Tennessee road, divide it into sections, put an overseer over each strip and call every man to work. Build a road from Fairmount to Sonora for roads must go east and west as well as north and south.

Trains run daily from Atlanta to Ross's Landing (Chattanooga), new roads crisscross the land, more families move in every day, they must have a county and a county capital.

"This feller William W. Gordon is a fine man" and Gordon would be a fine name for a county. So Gordon it was.

It's May 27, 1850 and the Justices of the Peace, David Barrett, W. W. Wall, David S. Law, Martin Duke and Wesley Kinman meet to lay out the various districts as the court has organized them.

Snake Creek, the 7th, Dawsonville, Springtown, the 24th, the 23rd, the 6th, and Oothcaloga, these are the districts designated and the names of the men who serve as jurors in the courts run through the years into now: Barrett, King, Kinman, Dillard, Brownlee, Foster, Curtis, Thornbrough, Roff, Fain, Addington, Byrd, Robertson, Brogdon, Miller, Lewis, Gardner, Haynes, Reeve, Ellis, Chastain, Talley, Harlan, Hunt, Barnwell, McConnell, Camp, Starr, Hill, Fuller, Kiker, Fox, Saxon, Wright, Boaz, Pittman, and many others.

Down from the mountains and out from the springs come the creeks and rivers. Can a man always wade? Why some of them are too deep for a horse to ford! Build us some bridges! Tom Bird, Jr. will build one over Saliquoy for $220 and Stephen Jones can make a bridge over Oothcaloga at Longstreet's Mill. Next year James Price and James Collins will build other bridges on these two creeks and in 1855 James Collins will finish the Cedar Creek Bridge.

But the rivers now, who can build a bridge over a river? We just ain't got the time! Ferries, that's the thing! Miller's, Land's, Tanner's, Herrington's, Printup's, Moore's, Fite's, Fork's Ferry, Pine Chapel, Fields', Reel's—these will do for a while.

"The county sure is growing fast, ain't it?" 861 houses, 868 families, (some of the married sons live with their pa's), 2,646 white males, 2,510 white females and 828 negroes.

Lot of churches too. Bethlehem, started in 1837, Corinth in 1848, Plainville (Springtown) in 1849, the Baptist Church south of town in 1822 and Mt. Zion (now Calhoun Presbyterian) in 1847.

Two busy years go by. Gentlemen, the county has grown rapidly. A capital is needed just as the State of Georgia has a capital. Where shall it be? There, at Big Spring? No, here at Dawsonville!

Then that's settled. But, Dawsonville—we honor Mr. Dawson and his general store, seems though a county capital should have a more dignified name.

John C. Calhoun, now, was a famous man—Calhoun that's the name for the capital, everyone agrees, kinda hard though to quit calling it "Dawsonville".

Have you been through Calhoun? Nice little town up in north Georgia. Good schools too. There's the Gordon County Male and Female Seminary at Sugar Valley and the Calhoun Academy run by the trustees W. P. Barney, Martin Duke, D. S. Law, W. H. Dabney, (later present at Secession Convention in Milledgeville in 1861), E. Barker, W. J. Cantrell and W. M. Peeples.

Nice building, too, there on the corner, big and square with an entrance of double doors and a bell tower. Plenty of room for two teachers and a platform for Friday afternoon exercises. Had to make the desks at home though and the chairs are splint-bottomed, but they even have blackboards painted on the walls.

Where will the court meet? Why in a courthouse of course and by 1852 it's finished. Standing there on the high spot in the town, the brick walled building trimmed with green blinds and surrounded by a white picket fence, looks very imposing as it faces the main street that runs westward across the railroad tracks. G. V. Mergerum has supervised it's building and the cost to the county is $5,800.

In the state government during these years of 1851 to 1860, the county's affairs are being handled ably by Thomas Bird, Thomas Mays, Henry McConnell, David Barrett, William P. Fain and John Baugh in the legislature while William H. Dabney, Thomas Bird, James Shellnut and Joel C. Fain are active in the Senate.

Draw a veil across the screen, lower the shades, turn out the lights, let the imagination hold full sway for a horde of invaders moves across the fair new land and the ten year old town faces blue-clad enemies from the North, intent on crushing out the rebellion of their brothers in the South.

They have left Chattanooga! They're at Dalton! At Resaca! Where shall we go? To Sugar Valley? No, they're coming through Snake Creek Gap! Then to the east, pile things in the wagons, load the carts, take to the woods and watch from a distance as fire consumes every house in the village except the ones the invaders are using.

The courthouse and the academy are full of them and most of the records are burned. Barricade yourselves in the depot. Make holes in the wall and shoot a few of them anyway. Useless though, the victors go on to bigger battles and the old men, the women and the children come out of the woods to begin all over again.

A battle may be won, a rebellion can be crushed but never can the spirit of a God-fearing people be conquered.

The hardships of these years of reconstruction are a familiar story to the grandchildren of Confederate soldiers and the rapid recovery of the towns and cities of the South is ever a fascinating saga.

Spend the night upon the hills of Gordon for there are other years to see, there are other tales to sell.

"Does the road wind up-hill all the way?
Yes, to the very end.
Will the day's journey take a whole day long?
From morn 'til night, my friend."

—Christina G. Rossetti.

TURN THE PAGES
OF TIME BACK 100 YEARS

The hot September sun beat down upon the concrete pavement in the streets of Calhoun on a day in 1957, with now and then a cool little breeze to come dancing along setting the leaves aquiver and giving a moments relief from the sun's hot breath.

Traffic on Wall street was heavy and as the lights changed from red to green and green to orange to red, the lines of cars rolled on going north or south, turning right or left around the courthouse, curling and twisting, then straightening, like the swirls and eddies and lines on a map of the ocean's currents.

From his bench on the courthouse lawn, John Lay could watch this hurry and hustle and going and coming that fills a day in the life and times of a small city of the twentieth century. To the right, he could see the newest Lay store with its bright red and white and gold-lettered sign over the modern glass front of a double building, the south half of which once housed another Lay store.

He could see two buildings on the northeast corner of Court and Piedmont where two other stores in the years gone by had carried the Lay name on their sign boards.

Looking south, he could see a two-story building that had been, until recently, the home of the Lay 10 cent store and he knew that just out of sight on a corner of Piedmont was the home of the Lay-Hall Wholesale Grocery Company.

By a mere lift of the eyes, he could look west along Court street, through a leafy green tunnel into the distance where a purple mountain peeped through the trees as if to say "oh yes, little city, I've had my eyes on you for a hundred years or more."

Are you still there? Did you keep your seat upon the hills of Gordon? Then turn the pages of the years and stop at 1857.

There's the courthouse on the same spot, but it isn't the same building. This one is a square red brick with green blinds at the windows and a white picket fence all around the grounds. There's no stock law, you know, and a bunch of pigs could ruin the yard in no time, rooting with their long noses.

The hot September sun of 1857 warms the dust in the streets that were trails of the Cherokee only a few short years ago. Wagons and high-wheeled "carriages" stand at the hitching railings at the side of the courthouse and in front of the stores. The buildings are all one room stores with floored porches and high-topped fronts.

Most of the dwellings in town, too, are of wooden construction, but a few are brick. Claiborne Kinman's house near the intersection of Piedmont and South Wall streets is built of brick as is the Presbyterian church just north of town.

See the wells here and there on the streets? They are used for fire protection as well as to furnish people with drinking water.

In addition to the Presbyterian Church, there are two others, the Baptist Church, down on Piedmont street and the Methodist Church on the corner of Court street and the river road. So, with the Calhoun Academy, one-half mile north of the courthouse, the town is well-supplied with facilities for religious and educational training.

Yes, John Lay in 1857, looks upon the town and finds it a pleasant place to live. He had bought a lot when Calhoun was first laid out, paying $402, and Elias Lay had paid $205 for a lot. The town had grown so fast that by 1854 the city limits had been extended to one-half mile each way from the courthouse.

"Things sure have changed in the last few years" thought John Lay as he sat on his bench in the sunshine. "Why, just ten years there was nothing but woods out Blackwood way and wolves howled around the few houses in the clearing." But the land was good for growing corn and wheat and corn-cribs were bulging and many bushels of wheat were shipped each year.

The pioneers were strong and had gone to work in the wilderness with such a vim that soon they were living as well as any section in the state. Everywhere there were sleek cattle, fat hogs, and fine horses. Much attention was given to horse breeding for everyone rode horseback.

For years men had been going clear to McDaniel's Station to have their corn ground but now there was Longstreet's Mill on Oothcaloga creek. People would come from beyond Snake Creek to the mill and camp all night nearby.

The town has a jail house, too, a two-story red brick, with white-bannistered porches across the front upstairs and down. Sheriff Sam T. King and his family live on the first floor, while the second story, re-inforced with thick logs, is the prisoners' quarters.

If a man needs a lawyer, he can call on Col. W. R. Halford or Col. A. L. Shepherd and the town's newspaper "The Democratic Platform," W. V. Wester, editor, (later "The Georgia Platform" edited by G. J. Fain) keeps the citizens well informed on news of the county, state and nation.

E. R. Sassen, manager of the Calhoun Hotel, furnishes livery for his guests and the neat rigs and high-stepping horses can be seen on pleasant days as the hotel guests drive around town or out the river road.

Dry goods firms are Heyman and Hertzberg, Scott and Arthur, and Wylie and O'Callagan. Another merchant, W. J. Kay, advertises "don't forget to bring along the Rhino for I do not now propose to sell goods on time."

By 1860, John Lay was to see other stores begin business. Brogdon, Brown and Ingles sold mantillas, crockery, saddles, school books, stationery, fancy dress and staple dry goods, jewelry, gold and silver watches "at such prices that cannot fail to give satisfaction." Young, Jackson and Company offered "attractive bargains to cash-paying customers."

Pitts and Johnson have a store on Court street and Grant Hunt's Drug store stands on a corner near the railroad selling Ayer's Pills, Hostetter's Bitters and Dr. McClane's Vermifuge.

Mrs. S. J. Callaway keeps boarders for $9 a month and her table is supplied with the best the market affords.

It's hard to remember the name of the newspaper, it is changed so often. For two years it was called "Valley Register" W. V. Wester editor, then it became "Confederate Flag" published by James N. Scott and James L. White. The paper now has four six-column pages with professional cards filling the front page and a picture of Jefferson Davis draped in a Confederate flag, on another page. An editorial compliments the people on their first observance of Fast day and states that a cause of the war would be removed if trains were forbidden to run on Sunday.

The town is new and the times are rough. In among the stores are several saloons. The fight against liquor had begun in 1852 when the Sons of Temperance No. 161 had been organized, meeting in a courthouse room for which they paid a rent of $20 yearly.

The women cannot vote but they can go to the polling places sing hymns, serve coffee and lemonade and beg their men to vote against liquor.

The Rev. Daniel Ingles, an eloquent Presbyterian preacher, has been holding camp meeting in town. One night he was told that some young men were planning to hold a mock meeting in a saloon and serve the sacraments. Fearlessly, he went to the saloon and said in thundering tones "God, in his wrath, I verily believe, will strike you down this very night, unless you repent!" Shortly after, the leader, while ridiculing sacred things, dropped to the floor dead and the others, terrified, ran to the camp meeting begging for prayers.

It is 1861. War has come to the little town only eleven years old. A proclamation is issued ordering bonds of the county, amounting to $10,000 to be sold for the benefit of the soldiers. It is dated August 5, 1861 and signed by I. N. Buckner, Henry McConnell, John Helton, W. E. Brogdon and Thomas Foster, Justices of the Inferior Court, and J. B. Richards, clerk.

"Ah, a tear! let it drop where the shell did its part
O'er the past, let it fall, as dew from the heart
Ever freshening our memories of warfare that stay
On the old field Manassas and grow in love's way."

—Minnie C. Harlan.

From the old field Manassas, from Gettysburg, from Appamattox they come, those who are left after the shell has done its part. They straggle into town from the north and the south to find Calhoun in ruins. Most of the houses are in ashes and the fine brick Presbyterian Church is a shambles. True, the courthouse stands but most of the records are gone, burned with the homes of the officials who had carried the papers and ledgers home for safe keeping.

"But the bluebirds will sing with the coming of spring
And I feel an old song in my mouth
A song that my lips are a-hungry to sing
In the warm, dim woods of the South."

—Maurice Thompson

In the warm, dim woods, along the banks of the Oostanaula, the men of Calhoun and Gordon County find a song to sing, a song of reunion and reconstruction, but only in the memories of the sons of these men can that song be heard, the song that tunes the wail of a hungry child, the screech of the saw and the pound of the hammer as the tasks of beginning again follow day after day, year after year.

If you listen you can hear the song as it echoes from the hills of Gordon. Hear it as it sings of the valor of men, of the courage of women and how they built a city upon the ashes of the one their fathers had made in the wilderness.

CALHOUN, 1870's

It is 1870. The song has ended it's minor tune and now hums in a major key. The lean years take their place on the pages of Time and the little city faces the future with a smile.

During the war years, the town has had no newspaper and the merchants have advertised in the Dalton paper but now, Elam Christian is publishing The Calhoun Times, using a Washington hand press and printing a pape of four six-column pages.

Other editors of the 1870's are: H. F. Ferguson, W. R. Rankin, Sr., W. C. Rice and D. B. Freeman.

The Courthouse is again the heart of the town and county life and the men who hold the offices in the county government are: Aaron Roff, E. J. Kiker, W. R. Rankin, J. T. Black, T. M. Ellis, M. W. Hall, David W. Neel, John Gresham, Isaac E. Bartlett, W. G. Taylor, W. M. Russell, S. W. Robins, W. H. C. Loyd, W. E. Jones, L. M. Simpson, Thomas J. Norton, Robert C. Mizell, N. J. Boaz, J. H. Arthur, J. W. Marshal and B. R. Bray.

The churches, too, are once more serving the community, now in new buildings on new lots. The Methodist and Baptist churches face each other on Wall Street, north of the Courthouse. The Presbyterians with only a few members have not found the courage to rebuild but when the Rev. J. B. Hillhouse comes to Gordon County in 1873 he has, by the next year, organized a church of fifteen members and is holding services in the Methodist Church.

The Gordon County Agricultural Society conducts a Fair in Calhoun in the Fall of each year when colts, cows, pigs and farm and kitchen products are entered for show.

By 1875, some far-sighted citizen has thought of filing copies of the county paper for the use of posterity and now the facts are there for everyone to see. (Several copies have the name "J. M. Reeve" written across the top).

D. B. Freeman is the editor during 1877 and 1878 and, in his "Town and County News" column, he begins the January issue with "mud." "The Blinding Mud." "Information-mud." The mud and slush make it anything but pleasant underfoot and the county roads are almost impassable.

Umbrellas did the most good yesterday when they were used up. "Well, now that's put on" says a countryman as he watched a young lady reach behind her and gather a handful of skirt as she crosses the muddy street. A woman comes out of a store, stands for a moment on the porch then reaches down, pulls her top skirt over her head and launches out into the rain.

Members of the council, Mark Moore, P. A. Summy, Dr. R. W. Thornton, C. C. Harlan and James W. Jackson, have recommended that footpaths across the streets be graveled.

Wilson and Wilson run a general merchandise store at Shelor and Rankin's old stand, T. M. Ellis has good saddle and buggy horses and new buggies at his livery stable and Marshall and Lee have moved to their old stand in the two-story Young building on the south corner of Court and Wall Streets.

Mr. Henry Harlan is clerking at Foster and Harlan's, which is of course, the oldest business in town since it was established in 1859.

"You never can tell about appearances, said Mr. Atkins, manager of the Calhoun Hotel, "a well-dressed female stopped at my hotel and when she left, numerous household trinkets went too!"

W. M. Dunn, tailor, two doors east of B. M. and C. C. Harlan has the latest New York fashions in concord jeans, cassimeres and cashmerets. The newest dresses are flat behind, the bustle is gone and the ladies can sit down again whenever they choose.

Bob Ransome, postmaster, has returned from New Orleans with a pocketfull of Mardi Gras seed. Mr. Hightower is setting out trees around his hotel, spring has come and lovely woman is seen often on the streets.

Last Sunday, three girls thought they could row a boat on Oothcaloga Pond but the current pushed the boat against the dam where the screaming girls held it until some men rescued them.

During the warm weather, the young people have promenaded the streets and had a lot of fun on a visit to Hibernia Bluff on the river. Women have taken up knitting while visiting and should be able to knit six-finger-lengths while discussing the neighbors' affairs.

Dr. King's drug store advertises toilet soap, hair oil, lily white, bloom of youth and eveything else that goes to make up a woman's toilet.

Although there are three saloons in Calhoun, you seldom see a drunk man but, the other day, two gentlemen who had tasted the "rosy" walked up to a citizen and one of them said "See here (hic) Major (hic) I wish you would tell me which is me, I want to go home!"

A cardinal nose is no longer fashionable and mustaches are worn trailing.

Editor Freeman warns the citizens that it is cyclone time and that everyone may be hurled into eternity before next week. There was a bad storm last Friday, April 27, when out-buildings and fences were blown down but no one was hurt.

Did you hear the debate on the Constitutional Convention? J. A. Gray and T. W. Skelly upheld the affirmative while the winning negative side was argued by E. J. Kiker and S. R. Freeman.

The Literary Society, oganized at the home of Mr. R. J. Wilson. is very active, having thirty members. The ladies and gentlemen are to give a concert at the courthouse, benefit of the Methodist Church. The church looks nice in it's new coat of white paint. The Rev. Mr. Williams is pastor and Miss Mattie Freeman, organist.

The new steamboat, Etowah Bill, launched at Rome, passed yesterday on its way to Carter's landing. Citizens are urged to buy stock in the new Oostanaula-Coosawattee Steamboat Company. "A good suggestion is like a crying baby in church, it should be carried out."

Judge Foster is having his old store house torn away and will erect a nice brick structure running 60 feet on Wall Street and 26 feet on Court Street. The Post Office has moved from Jackson's stand to the corner next to Littlefield's unfinished building and has been established as a money order post office.

Moonlight blue and sorrell green are the new colors, trains are longer and silk stockings with a lace medallion covering the instep are $30 a pair.

When a Gordon County girl accepts a sweetheart she says, "Bein' as it's you, yes." It's fashionable now for bridesmaids to wear hats at Church weddings.

The Baptist Church has purchased one of Mason and Hamlin's finest organs. B. G. Boaz has bought an elegant new parlor organ with 12 stops. It has a powerful tone and the chime of bells adds to the pleasure of the music.

T. M. Ellis has bought a Shoninger piano.

The school situation has not been the best in the world during '77 and '78. Miss Laura Reeve had a private school of 40 pupils for awhile, then Calhoun was without a school. Mrs. T. C. Milner has announced that she will soon open a private school and Miss Lizzie Wilson has opened a school in the building that was lately the Hightower Hotel.

Now comes the announcement that the Rev. J. B. Hillhouse has leased the Calhoun Academy for five years and citizens can feel assured that their children will have a proper education.

During the closing exercises of the Academy in June the following students received high marks: Belle Boaz, latin, grammar and dictionary; Mamie Pitts, arithmetic and dictionary; Bonnie Hillhouse, arithmetic and geography; Lizzie Craig, arithmetic; Minnie Lee and Laura Tanner, spelling.

No telephones yet. Are we to have a new jail? The other day, they were having trouble down at Oothcaloga Mills, the wheel wouldn't turn. Finally, the cause was discovered—the wheel was clogged with eels.

Mr. J. E. Parrott has built a neat walk from the depot to his house, just west of the depot.

The summer of 1878 has been a gay one with picnics at Big Spring, excursions, weekends at the National Hotel in Dalton and at Catoosa Springs. Hotels are open to summer guests in Atlanta, Marietta, Cartersville, Dalton and Chattanooga and the W. & A. Railroad has excursion rates on the Kennesaw Route.

Croquet is popular and a baseball team has been organized. In one of the first games Dalton defeated Calhoun 22-14.

One of our young men bought a red bandanna at a bargain sale, tucked it in his pocket and went to see his girl. The day was hot and walking was most uncomfortable so he dipped the bandanna in a cool stream along the way and bathed his face. His girl met him at the door, eyed him with wonder, then led him to a mirror. His face was very red for more reasons than one and he resolved never again to buy cheap goods.

The Fall season has arrived and Gov. J. E. Brown is at his farm for a rest. Judge John P. King is visiting at the Peter's farm and Gen. John B. Gordon is scheduled to speak at Fairmount.

J. W. Gray, C. O. Boaz, Fred Reeves, Lucius Reeve and J. F. Harkins have left for school at Dahlonega and Senator J. C. Fain and Representative W. R. Rankin are at home from the State Legislature.

Gone but not forgotten is the man who left the door open in January 1879. The cold weather has caused many to break their New Year pledges, swine in immense numbers have frozen to death, the pond is frozen over and the young people have enjoyed the skating, except for bruised noses and sprained limbs.

Christmas was rather dull with only the trees at the two churches. The young people enjoyed firecrackers, old hammerless pistols and army guns and the turkey shoot was exciting—The turkeys were placed in boxes with head sticking through a hole and the good marksman could bag his Christmas bird for ten cents a shot. Dr. King gave an enjoyable little dance and the social masquerade at the Calhoun Hotel was very pleasant but the usual balls and sociables were not given.

J. M. Reeve, clerk of the Board of County Commissioners, has published legal notices that the old private road commencing at John L. Williason's house and running by Morrison's Ferry to Plainville will be established as a public road. There's a new post office at Redbud, a telegraph office at Resaca and a petition for a mail route from Sonora to Fairmount has been circulated.

Calhoun is to have another dram shop and Messers. Roberts and Carter are opening a new barroom. Most of the court cases are for carrying concealed weapons. With the new firm of Fain and Rankin and Col. O. N. Starr, who has recently been admitted to the bar, the town now has seventeen lawyers.

Foster and Harlan have the largest stock of goods since the war at hard time prices and the largest lot of ready-made clothing ever brought to Calhoun. Bustles are back and the material for ladies' hats is a fine French chip. The hats are caught up on one side and covered with roses or on both sides and covered with shirred brocade or satin.

Have you heard the latest slang? "Oh, you're too new, the dust sticks to you!"

Some people are like eggs, too full of themselves to hold anything else so they think only of the hard times and their own troubles but there are people who can be amused by things that happen in town like the other day when a rabbit went tripping down the street with the dogs yapping behind him, and the joke on Col. Fain. The sheriff came to the door and called Col. Fain who, thinking he was needed, was behind the bar before he realized that the room was empty. Court had been dismissed and he didn't know it!

There have been many spring repairs, trees planted, fences remodeled and houses painted. The first fly of the season was chased all over the store by the owner with a potato in the end of a long stocking.

A few years hence the growing trees on the streets will give Calhoun a beauty not excelled in all North Georgia. The public well on Courthouse Street is one of the best in the County.

The flock of geese that runs on the streets is a nuisance!

Eaves and Farley are running a soda fount and will sell soda water, lemonade and cider.

Fishing frolics are all the go and the young people plan a grand ball and supper at Young's building with music from Rome. Isn't it strange how two young men will make the largest parlor seem crowded?

The year's progress in schools has been amazing. The Calhoun Academy has had a fine year under the Rev. J. B. Hillhouse; Mrs. L. E. Messenger and Miss Lizzie Sayre have taught private schools in town, while Miss Fields school at Resaca and Miss Jennie Candler's at Plainville have done excellent work.

The closing exercises at Plainville will have a band from Rome and S. W. Wright from Rome will speak at the Exhibition.

Sonora's exercises begin Thursday with pupils' examinations, continue with speaking Friday morning and the general exhibition Friday night.

The churches have all had good protracted meetings during the summer, the Baptist with Revs. W. M. Dyer, McMurray and Bell, the Methodist with Rev. Underwood in charge, a camp meeting at Liberty Presbyterian and a protracted meeting at New Town Baptist. Organs are little used in the churches now.

Miss Lizzie Wilson has a splendid music class and Mrs. J. E. Parrot's music class gave a cantata, "May Day," at the close of School.

A young man is learning to play the flute and we do not know which to pity, the young man, the flute or the neighbors.

What do you think of the crowd at the post office on Sunday at mail time? It's much bigger than the crowd at church.

The new white mail cars on the W & A are attracting much attention. A new two-cent postal card has come out. It has a stamp at each end, the sender uses one and the return correspondent the other. People beg for postals as they would a match.

The W & A is selling a round trip ticket to Atlanta for $1.60, and 80 residents have gone down to the Fair. Major Aaron Roff has won a $25.00 prize on his cow and Col. Peters was given a number of prizes on ramie, hemp and farm animals.

Mrs. J. C. Fain and Miss Ella Harlan are visiting in Atlanta and Mrs. D. G. Hunt of Dalton and Mark Moore of Rome are visitors to Calhoun.

Mr. C. C. Harlan has bought Judge Foster's new house in the east part of town and will move there soon.

Mr. J. D. Tinsley has just completed a model for a self-coupler on railroad cars. The Cherokee railroad to Cedartown has been completed.

Berry Dorsey gave the boys an oyster supper during the fall season, a rope walker gave an exhibit on a rope stretched from the Calhoun Hotel to a tree and the dance, with excellent music, at the Calhoun Hotel, was attended by everyone and his sister.

It's the fashion to make little girls' dresses out of gay plaid bandannas, ladies hats are pokes with big brims and skirts are cut just to escape the promenade.

John and Polly Lay did not live to see the end of the conflict nor to share in the great task of rebuilding. They saw John Lay leave to join Gist-Walker's Division in 1861 but they could not know that John O. Lay had been called for the last great effort and to see the end at Appamattox, nor that G. W. Lay had served from Stovall's Brigade, nor that Berry Lay did not come home, for John Lay died in 1862 and Polly in 1863, each at the age of 75.

Listen to the pines whispering on the hills of Gordon, for they are tall and they are old. They have seen the years go by and they wait for the years to come.

There was quite a bustle and stir around the post office in town on Saturday in 1875, for that was the day The Calhoun Weekly Times came out.

"Dave Freeman is real handy with words" one man said, "listen to this—'the juvenile mustache sprouting on the average young man's face looks luxuriant and will reach it's second growth in the spring if the frost doesn't get it'."

D. B. Freeman's connection with the paper had begun in February 1873, when he became editor for W. C. Rice, then the proprietor. On January 1, 1874, Mr. Freeman became proprietor and editor.

The first paper in Calhoun was The Democratic Platform, published in 1855 by W. V. Wester. G. J. Fain became editor in 1856 and changed the name to The Georgia Platform, but, from 1858 to 1860, W. V. Wester was again editor, calling his paper The Valley Register. In 1861, James N. Scott and James L. White were publishing a newspaper they called The Confederate Flag.

The first copy of The Calhoun Times, published by Elam Christian, came out on August 12, 1870 but authorities did not realize the importance of saving copies of the paper for future generations, so the earliest volumes stored in the courthouse vaults are dated 1875 and 1876.

A January 1875 issue of The Calhoun Times carries a news item from the Atlanta News which reads—"W. R. Rankin, Sr., who was editor of The Calhoun Times from 1871 to 1873, ran one of the best newspapers in the state. In eight years of perserverance and integrity, he has won fame and a good name and is certainly one of the rising young men of North Georgia."

Years later, Col. Rankin was to say to a group of legislators in Atlanta, "Twenty-two years ago, I got off the train in Calhoun without a cent. I did without breakfast because I wouldn't beg. Before dinner, I got acquainted with a school trustee who invited me to his home for dinner and supper. I asked for the place as school principal, borrowed money to go back to South Carolina for references and, six months later, borrowed money to go back for my wife. Right there in Calhoun I've been ever since. I call myself the pioneer tramp and if a tramp ever comes to town and asks for breakfast, he gets the same breakfast that I have."

A schedule for the W & A trains from Atlanta to Chattanooga is printed in the upper left hand column of the 1875 issues of The Calhoun Times. Law firms are E. J. Kiker and son, Fain and Milner and Rankin and Neal. J. D. Tinsley is the watch-maker and jeweler and Mrs. C. A. Hudgens, Milliner and mantua maker, runs an establishment on Court Street.

Other business firms are J. H. Arthur General Merchandise, Railroad Street; Z. T. Gray, Buggies and Wagons, and J. W. Marshal, groceries, on Railroad Street.

This year Calhoun clamoreth for a good boot and shoe shop. The Calhoun Hotel, Mrs. Skelly, manager, is being improved and painted and Mr. Hightower has purchased lumber to commence improvements at his new quarters on the south side of Wall street. His new hotel is 3-stories high with 15 or more rooms. Mr. Hightower has a sheet iron gong on his back veranda and when he gave it the first shake everyone sought the cellar, thinging a cyclone was coming. It is commonly remarked that Hightower is the most graceful man in town.

One of S. D. Bridgman's patent pumps has been inserted in front of the Calhoun Hotel. Our two excellent hotels are gaining popularity with the traveling public—Mr. Hightower fed 46 people on Monday.

Several droves of mules have been quartered at the livery stable for the past week. The town council has located new and convenient hitching racks at various places in town.

One of the most enjoyable entertainments in Calhoun for some time was the dance at the residence of Mr. Thomas Black. The Virginia Reel was danced to "Hop Up Kitty Puss", "Cottoneye Joe" and "Billy in the Low Ground". The kangaroo hop, pigeon wing and double shuffle were revived from ante bellum days.

Hicks and Ferguson have oranges, lemons, coconuts and candy. Reeves and Malone sell all styles of calicoes and shirting goods at ten cents a yard.

The Gordon County Agricultural Society met and elected O. H. Davis, president, C. A. Harris, secretary, J. W. Swain, vice-president and J. M. Harlan, treasurer.

Mr. B. H. Irwin is showing Indian relics dug up at Chickamauga station, a tomahawk, skull pices, two teeth and a few bones.

The Calhoun Hotel and the roof of the Academy caught fire but the blazes were quickly extinguished by all citizens lending a hand.

Red used as a railroad signal means stop. Same thing on a man's nose.

Heavy rains from Monday night February 22 until Friday night have raised the water courses to the highest level since 1861. The river is higher than in the freshet of 1867. Wheat in the lowlands is drowned, soil from plowed lands washed away and fences ruined. The railroad track is under water and trains cannot pass. Three bridges on Chickamauga creek are gone and water is three feet deep in Ogleby's mill.

Guano and March winds! What next? Spades are trumps, gardening has commenced in a small way and the town cows wear more cheerful countenances.

It is seemingly impossible for any but a pretty face to be under the crown of flowers or wreath of wheat or the dressy silken linings of the new spring bonnets. They have a certain style that reminds of fields and shepherdesses yet are evidently elaborated for carriage and evening wear. The trimming of wide scarfs of cream white maize color is worn around the outside or looped under the brim and fastened with gilt buckles or gold, pearl or steel ornaments. The bonnets are set on the back of the head.

A small party enjoyed a rural hop at Col. Fain's Saturday night and the young people attended the grand ball and supper given by Mr. Robertson of the Couche house at Kingston. The brilliantly lighted hall was hung with cedar in garland wreathes with here and there a spring flower. Prof. Shelfield called the first dance to strains of music from the Rome string band, the floor was soon filled with gay beaux and belles and joy rolled it's sphere in radiant realms until a late hour. There were hardly any Kingston ladies present, a few from Cartersville and more from Rome. Young men should see the propriety of taking more ladies, there were too many stags.

The new marshal has been ordered to move a certain old lady's fence but she keeps a kettle of boiling water and says he "darsent touch it." Up to this time he hasn't.

A post office called Lily Pond has re-opened with Mr. Hambleton as postmaster.

Mr. J. M. Reeve's new building in the north part of town seems ready for the finishing touches and presents a very tasty appearance. Major Aaron Roff is erecting a handsome new barn. The marshall is working on the streets but we need more flowers and shrubs around the places.

Spring courting is the next thing in order. Several people have ordered new gate hinges. Sunday, quite a number of young people in two's were enjoying the delightful features of an evening promenade under a breezy atmosphere. These moonlight nights are lovely but oh, the sufferings of gate hinges!

The little elms set out by the council on Wall street are now in foliage giving attraction to that thoroughfare. The council has also set out two rows of mulberry trees on the common east of the railroad. To Mr. Thomas A. Foster goes the credit for having the Courthouse yard cleaned and the trees trimmed.

Our young men now saunter around in their spring duds and look as gushing as an irish potato leaf that has escaped the cold snap. Blond hair is now called the light fantastic tow. Calhoun has more clever young men and fewer ugly young ladies than any town of its size in the country.

The Calhoun Debating Society is becoming a power in the land. Some of the first year's subjects with the winning side are: Were the Crusades Beneficial to Europe? Negative; Do the Works of Nature Clearly and Unmistakably Prove the Existence of a Supreme Being? Affirmative; Is the Mind of Woman Equal to that of Man? Mistrial; Should women be Allowed to Vote? Thrown out of court.

Ten lots of land lying west and north of the Methodist church were sold at prices from $20 to $29. Mr. M. L. Matthews is erecting a two-story wood shop on the west side of Wall Street south of Court Street. The Mary Carter, recently recanvassed and re-painted, going down the river with 1700 bushels of wheat on board, grounded on shoals at Governor Brown's farm. A small leak was sprung but was repaired after unloading some of the wheat.

Messrs. J. C. Fain, B. G. Boaz and J. T. Black have bought from Mr. Ogleby the Calhoun Mill located on Oothcaloga creek one mile west of town for the price of $18,000.

A handsome little edifice on Wall Street, south of Court Street, is the new headquarters of The Calhoun Times. The old kitchen at J. M. Reeve's burned with most of the kitchen furniture ruined but the new residence was saved.

A number of lots on the west side have been sold and many improvements are to be made. Major Wells will build a tasty house of 8 rooms on the street leading to the river. Mr. Jack Neal will erect a neat residence fronting the lower end of court street. T. M. Ellis will build a commodious residence just opposite and Mr. M. L. Hallum proposes to build on the little eminence on Southern street running to Oothcaloga Mill.

There is a church service somewhere every Sunday. Pastor A. C. Thomas preaches at the Methodist church on First Sundays. He shows great earnestness and is likely to accomplish much during the year.

Rev. James Harkins preaches at the Methodist church on Second Sundays and service is held on Second Sunday night at the Sumberland Presbyterian church by the pastor Rev. Z. M. McGhee. The old school Presbyterians, Rev. J. B. Hillhouse, pastor, have service on third Sundays and the Baptists hold services on fourth Saturday and Sunday with Rev. W. C. Wilkes as pastor.

The Methodist church has new song books and two beautiful new hanging lamps. The organ, used for a time by the Union Sunday School at the Courthouse. has been moved to the Baptist Church where the school will hereafter be held.

Last Sunday was an extremely lovely day and everyone went to church. Mr. Thomas preached one of his most sparkling sermons. The Methodist church raised $13.00 for missions and $10 to complete payments on the magnificent organ now in use.

A sum has been subscribed for improving the Baptist church. The odd-looking steeple is to be torn away and one of more approved pattern erected. The church is in every way commodious and can be made very attractive with a little pains.

Not in the history of Gordon County has there been such religious feeling as has been witnessed this year in the churches of the area. Rev. A. C. Thomas had the first meeting in the Methodist church where his efforts were crowned with golden laurels in the conversion of a score of the worst sinners in town. After three weeks the meeting was carried to the Baptist church and the fire burned on. 125 members were added to the churches, the Sabbath schools increased 100% and ¼ of the towns population professed conversion. The community is thoroughly awakened and the churches have been crowded day and night. Hundreds have sought the hand of mercy.

Rev. W. C. Wilkes baptized 16 new converts at Ogleby's mill Sunday afternoon at 3:30 with hundreds in attendance. Later, he baptized 6 others and at another time, baptized Mr. and Mrs. J. H. Arthur. Rev. A. C. Thomas baptized four by immersion.

At a meeting at Mount Pleasant, 40 were converted. Revs. Tatum and Blanton baptized 40 at Blackwood and meetings are now in progress at Buford's church near McDaniels and at the Sugar Valley Methodist Church.

Calhoun is nearly destitute of barrooms. The Rev. Mr. Wilkes will deliver a lecture Friday night at the Baptist church on what the Bible teaches about temperance. We advise everyone to go out and hear him.

The Academy closed the term with an excellent program, given by: Henry Davenport, John Hall, Eddie Parrott, Willie Fain. Henry Gray, Jospeh Middleton, Milton Fain, Logan Pitts, Robert Hallum, Miss U. Johnson, Mattie Young, Lou Jackson, Maggie Cantrell, Mattie Kiker and Georgia Hicks. Music was furnished by Mrs. Parrott. Lizzie Holmes and Mattie Freeman.

Mr. John Baugh, of Sugar Valley, was found at the bottom of a pit on his farm where he had fallen and broken his neck. Mr. Baugh was generally respected by all his neighbors and at one time served in the legislature.

Jennie, a negro living with the family of Mrs. Malone at Sugar Valley, died on the 23rd of September at the age of 118. She had a vivid mind and could recall events back to the Declaration of Independence.

Cool winds of autumn wail sadly in the ears of the young lover and the tender maiden. Sweet reunions over the front gate will soon be among the things that were and fond memory only will be left to comfort them.

The course of true love never did run smooth. At Sugar Valley lived Miss Tinnie Staggs and Mr. A. C. Shugart who had long entertained feelings for each other, to which the father of the young lady did not give his sanction. Last Sunday, while the family was away, her trunk and fixings were handed out into a vehicle from a back window and the two proceeded a short distance to the home of Rev. W. M. Bridges where the nuptial knot was tied in the presence of a few friends and the twain go on their way rejoicing.

An observer says that the best evidence of a coming court week is to see Kiker lay on that beaver and Dick Tarver wearing a stand-up collar.

A man saw some pigs trying to get out of the way of something and found three rattlesnakes chasing them. 2 got away but he killed one 5 feet and 5½ inches long with thirteen rattles.

Mr. John Abbott killed five large wild turkeys last week. The hard times has swooped down on this country like a hungry man on six buckwheat cakes, covered with sorghum molasses.

The Young building on the South corner of Court and Wall streets was bought by Mr. A Nichols at a bankrupt sale for $2,001. He later sold it to Shelor and Rankin, who improved the building by tearing away the wooden platform and building a raised sidewalk. The store in the west side has a recessed doorway making a showy and handsome front.

The Oothcaloga creek bridge has been finished. The hill on the left is to be cut down and the road on the east raised.

Dr. D. B. Reeve, son of A. W. Reeve, died in Chattanooga at the age of 35. If deeds of charity and mercy on earth constitute treasures in heaven, there will be few richer than Dr. Reeve. The City Council of Chattanooga adopted resolutions on the death of Alderman Reeve.

As the setting sun throws its golden rays upon the leaves of russet brown and delicates tints which yet cling to the trees on the beautiful hill against our village on the west, an evening panorama is presented as enchanting as some of the painted scenery of Switzerland.

Married on the 8th of December in Rome, D. B. Freeman to Miss Callie D. Goodwyne.

When a bit of Sunshine hits ye after passing of a cloud
When a fit of laughter gets ye, And yer spine is feeling' proud
Don't forget to up and fling it at a soul that's feelin' blue
For the minit that ye sling it, It's a boomerang to you.
—Capt. Jack Crawford

Hard times? Well maybe, but Calhoun people are hardly aware of it. There was a big leap year party given by the young ladies at the home of R. F. Wyatt. Mrs. Wyatt prepared the supper with great credit to her culinary skill. One young man, who was not at the party, explained, "It has always been my luck, when I requested a young lady to allow me to call, to receive a reply expressing regret. So I thought, in order to get even, I would regret the first and accept the second request. I'm still lamenting."

The young people met at the home of Mr. W. H. Bonner Friday night for a charade and tableau party. Four young ladies presented "The Old Country Aunt's Visit To The City". "Aunt Betsy and Her Beaux" was done by Miss Fanny Bonner. Mr. Johnny Craig was "Squire Hopper". Miss Lula Bonner gave the best portrayal, that of Joan of Arc at the stake. The young ladies entertained with sweet music during the evening.

The family of Mr. Robert Black, of Plainville, composed of five families left for Texas last week, paying a railroad fare of $700. Anyone want to go to Texas?

Thomas Skelly has commenced the study of law with Col. Mc-Connell. W. J. Reeves Jr. and Mr. C. F. Griffin have returned from medical lectures with sheepskins and M.D. to their names. Success to them.

An old lady of Calhoun wants to know what we are coming to since Calhoun is literally surrounded by steam whistles, two saw mills, one planing mill and a big railroad. It all furnishes too much music for her nervous system.

Col. E. J. Kiker and Tom Milner are attending the Agricultural Convention at Brunswick. Col. Kiker wore his beaver hat, butternut suit of home made jeans with potato vine suspenders and shuck collar. Milner wore the same apparel and carried a piece of garlic in his pocket to show as a cure for gapes in hogs. He also carried an excessive essay, copied from Blackstone's Commentaries, on cross-plowing poor land and training gourds on picket fences.

On their return, they will bring a pocketful of periwinkles to show that they have been there.

Mr. James Gray and Miss Sallie Malone were married on February 10 at the residence of the bride's father. Afterwards, they left for the groom's father's home in the country where a sumptuous dinner awaited them. We congratulate the groom on having secured so excellent a companion.

It's time for garden breaking and fruit trees are in bloom. The new division of our town, called West End, is presenting now very much a pioneer aspect. Several new and convenient domiciles have been erected. It is pluck that is one of the prime essentials that build up town in hard times. Some people are holding up progress by asking high rent and high prices for their lots.

A nice altar is being added to the Methodist Church and the aisles are to be carpeted. The Baptists are making plans to ceil their building. Mark Moore is doing the work and the design includes some elegant arch work. Three lamps, a porcelain pitcher and the organ cover were stolen from the Baptist Church.

Little Hal Davenport almost drowned in the river. He was running on the deck of the Mary Carter when he slipped on a wet plank and fell into the water. A negro man rescued him.

Wall street is looking respectable. The trees set out a few years ago are living and looking well. The recent work of the street force adds to the beauty.

Locals for the paper are scarce. Can't someone swap horses or get up a dog fight?

A number of Atlanta young ladies, accompanying Mr. Richard Peters' family, came up in a handsome coach on the state road last week and spent a few days' enjoyment at Mr. Peters' farm two miles from this place. They returned by train Saturday evening.

"From the budding boughs in the sylvan groves the robins deluge the valley with ecstatic joy, and if the spirit of man becomes despondent, he takes another horn."

Ed. Freeman

Mr. W. H. Bonner brought in a specimen of yellow clover three feet high. Mr. T. M. Brand, of Sugar Valley, has raised 18 pounds of onions on a plot 6 feet by 18 feet, and Mr. W. M. Black has a quarter of an acre of onions, enough to bring tears to the eyes of a nation.

As the season for lemonades and iced drinks approaches, a young man insists that it is HER place to treat. But, would he be willing to receive such cool treatment from the fair sex?

There will be a picnic at Craneater springs next Saturday. General Colquitt and others will be there.

Dom Pedro and his suite passed up the W & A road yesterday and was observed as a great curiosity.

Miss Sallie Young returned home last week from Rome Female College from which institution she received a diploma.

In Mrs. J. E. Parrott's recital, Misses Mamie and Lulie Pitts played and sang several duets. Miss Anna Parrott rendered several difficult pieces in a surprising manner and several other little girls. all under twelve, did well, having studied music only a few months.

Judge Foster is making bricks for a new building at the corner of Court and North Wall streets and a neat little business house has been erected by John P. King on Court street in place of the ungainly looking structure that recently stood there. Mr. A. Littlefield intends finishing up his business house on Railroad street at an early date and the work on John Harkins new residence in the suburbs is progressing vigorously.

The storm Monday proved a blessing to the town by demolishing the old livery stable west of the railroad on Court street.

Calhoun has 2 churches, 12 stores, 2 barrooms, 1 tin shop, 1 harness shop, 3 carriage and wagon shop, 1 blacksmith shop, 1 hotel. 1 livery stable, Telegraph and Express office, 1 newspaper, 1 dentist. 4 physicians, 16 lawyers, 8 carpenters, 1 tailor, 1 millinery, 2 jewelers, 1 high school and several smaller schools, 1 steam mill, and 1 water mill.

The Calhoun Times, now entering its 7th year of publication, will now come out on Saturday instead of Thursday.

A letter from "Little Preacher" compliments the choir of the Baptist Church. He writes "I do not think the choir can be excelled by any choir with so little practice. The church should be pround that they have so many excellent singers."

September has been putting on airs by giving us a foretaste of winter. "Ah, meditative autumn! How with retrospective glance we behold the leaves besprinkling the earth from the giant oaks of the forest; the mud turtle's voice is hushed, the bumble suddenly escapes our gaze and the carpet bagger, disgusted with a Solid South, hies away to climes more congenial to his outraged nature." (Ed. Freeman)

Red parasols are the fashion. Canvass grenadines in rich colors are being worn and buttons for ladies' dresses are larger. Jewelry is worn in profusion by young men and colored shirts are fashionable.

Mrs. J. C. Fain, Prof. J. D. Scott, Col. Thomas C. Milner, B. M.

Harlan, Dr. H. K. Main and Rev. Allen C. Thomas are attending the Centennial at Philadelphia.

The blow of the Mary Carter is no longer heard on the river but a new steamer, christened the H. P. Smith, has been launched at Rome.

Corn shuckings are in order and the corn song rings out on the balmy stillness.

Two pedestrians went through yesterday leading a gray wolf, caught on Lookout Mountain. It was very unruly and needed severe beatings at times.

Bishop Pierce dedicated the new Methodist Church at Resaca on Sunday, Nov. 12, 1876.

The North Georgia Conference appointed Rev. J. M. Dickey to Calhoun and Oothcaloga charges. Rev. P. G. Reynolds to the Gordon Circuit and Rev. A. M. Thigpen as Presiding Elder to the Dalton District.

During Christmas week, no paper will be published.

CALHOUN WAS NEVER MERRIER

It was dusk of an unusually warm day in January, 1880. John came into the kitchen where his mother was washing dishes. "Ma will you clean the lantern chimney for me, Lucy and I are going to the sociable at Mr. Parrott's tonight and I'll need the lantern. The holes in the sidewalks are full of water after last week's hard rains! I wish we could get those street lights they're always talking about!"

Calhoun was never merrier than in this January of 1880. Christmas trade had boomed, hard times were over and everyone was happy.

There had been lots of drunkenness and brawls over the county but the streets of Calhoun had been free of it.

Lucy had come from her home six miles southwest of town to spend the night with a friend. The roads were so bad that the twelve-mile drive twice in one night was not to be considered.

She was wearing a new sorrel green cassimere dress and the tan shawl that she had selected from Foster and Harlan's large stock. (She was so slim that she had to wear three bustles to make her dress stand out.)

Lucy looks good enough to eat, John thought. That green color makes her brown eyes sparkle and her black hair so shiny. Silly though, the way she screams at every dark thing in the street or noise by the walk. She ought to know that it's only the Reeve's cow or the Parrott's pig or some of those geese that are always running around the streets. Nice to walk arm and arm with her in the dancing light of the lantern and think about that day in next September.

Besides Mr. Parrott's sociable, there would be a hop at Mr. Bonner's, one at Jasper Boaz's, a big party and candy-pulling at J. M. Reeve's and the dances at Mr. Boisclair's and J. E. Tinsley's.

The boys are all excited over deer hunting in the mountains.

John Dorsey's party chased a 173 pound buck over three counties for two nights and a day before the dogs finally caught him. Biggest deer we ever saw!

Tramps, a bank of gypsies, book agents and fifteen or twenty drummers in town have given the citizens plenty to talk about. Then, there's the new $5 street tax which is really too much. $3 would have been enough.

The new council, E. J. Kiker, N. J. Boaz, C. W. Wells. W. L. Hines and F. A. Foster, have their work cut out for them in keeping the streets free of dog fennel and the cross walks graveled.

The road overseers are working the roads so the grand jury can get to town without breaking their necks. The courthouse needs repairs there are cracks in the walls and it's dangerous for a crowd to be on the second floor.

Later, the grand jury would recommend that three sets of iron bars at equal distances be put through the walls with good iron braces on the outside and that gutters be provided for the building.

The Oostanaula has been in flood and freight trains had to back up to Calhoun because of damage to the tracks north of town. Water got up in the first floor of Boaz Bros. mill and they had to use a bateau. The ponds are full of ducks and flocks of wild geese fly over now and then.

The Oostanaula bridge needs repairs and McDaniel's bridge is unsafe. Wouldn't it be a good idea to build a bridge at the ferry on the Calhoun-Spring Place road?

Colonels Cantrell, Jervis and Fain and Rankin have refurnished their offices, P. A. Summy has painted his house, the Baptist Church has a new coat of paint, Mrs. Pitts is having her dwelling painted and Major Wells has finished his house off until it looks like a little palace.

It's the season for excursions. The Selma, Rome and Dalton railroad will sell round trip tickets to New Orleans for $20. The S R and D has been sold to the Tennessee, Virginia and Georgia railroad for $1,503,000 and will have air brakes and reclining chairs on all the passenger cars. Thirty-five new engines, 28 of them moguls, have been ordered for the TV & G railroad. The excursion to Little Rock and Fort Smith is $17.40 round trip from Dalton.

The excursion trains to Cincinnati are crowded, one carrying 200 passengers and another 600. B. G. Boaz, J. M. Ballew, A. Roff, R. Peters, J. E. Parrott and C. C. Harlan from Calhoun took the Cincinnati excursion.

The W & A is to have 10 new passenger coaches, there is more freight than the cars can carry and the switch at Calhoun is being extended. W & A business is simply immense.

There are four mails daily and the boys never fail to go to the depot when the passenger trains go through.

A load of bananas passed through last week and people at the stations along the way bought from the cars.

The American Union Telegraph is erecting wires along the W & A and will establish offices at all the stations on the state road.

Sugar Valley has re-established a telegraph office and railroad station.

Calhoun is the most delightful place in North Georgia to visit, at least everybody who stops within its hospitable boundaries says so. There have been many improvements in the last ten years and more are going on all the time.

The people are a church going people but we do think that the church benches should be made stationary, they are always being moved about and its hard for the ladies to get between them. The Rev. Z. M. McGhee, who has been pastor of Liberty Presbyterian Church since its organization ten years ago, has resigned. Half of Calhoun was at Liberty last Sunday.

The Methodist Church has 127, the Baptist, 104 and the colored church 15 members.

Miss Sally Ripley of Adairsville is visiting Miss Lucy Sayre. John (Gray) has shed his grocery suit and donned linens since he's been handling the yard stick. Master Clayton Callaway is clerking

"I'LL TRY CLUB"
LEADS CALHOUN FORWARD IN 1881

"She walks in beauty like the night of cloudless climes and starry skies.

But words are things and a small drop of ink,

Falling like a dew upon a thought, produces that which makes thousands, perhaps millions think." —Lord Byron.

It was the night of the ITC (I'll Try Club) meeting at Mr. Ferguson's and O. N. Starr was concluding his sketch of Lord Byron with quotations from the poet's works.

Other features of the evening's entertainment had been the readings, Stepping Stones by Miss Mattie Kiker, A Face Against the Pane by Mrs. Minnie Harlan and a sermon by B. M. Harlan that brought down the house. Dr. Thornton's contribution to the program was an original poem, He Builds to Low, Who Builds this Side of Heaven.

The early 1880's are years of progress in all fields for the little county seat town of Calhoun. The land, especially the land out Reeves Station way, is rich and the crops are bountiful.

Col. W. R. Rankin will make 300 bushels of wheat on six acres, Col. Peters will harvest 40 bushels an acre on 150 acres. Mr. Z. T. Gray has threshed over 15,000 bushels of wheat and Captain McConnell says that a snake could crawl over his field of oats and a patridge couldn't get through.

John Gray has 10 acres of cotton with stalks 16 inches high, Col. "Is" Kiker brought in an Irish potato weighing 2½ pounds, Mr. Orr Southerland's sweet potato weighed eight pounds and Col. W. H. Bonner has gathered 1,000 watermelons and cantaloupes from 3/4 acre.

A strange looking bug has made its appearance. Irish potato vines are its principal food and it strips all leaves from the vines.

The winter of 1881 has been severe with a 4-inch snow and weather so cold that the kerosene and whiskey froze. Boaz Bros. Mill pond has been frozen thick enough for skating and the roads are so bad that an empty wagon is a load going down hill.

Cold Weather hasn't stopped the parties, for there has been one almost every night with a party at Major Bartlett's, one at N. J. Boaz's, one at Major King's and an enjoyable party near Plainville.

By the way, wouldn't it be a good idea for our Methodist friends to paint the parsonage? Let it always be remembered that it would greatly add to the appearance of the town if the Baptist Church had a new cupola.

Mrs. James Reeve and daughter Miss Carrie, are visiting relatives near Atlanta. John Gordon left last week for a two-months' stay in Florida. Miss Lula Bonner is visiting in Nashville and Miss Jeffie Fain has returned from Spring Place. Miss Ada Swain, a beautiful and accomplished young lady of Oak Hill, is visiting her cousin, Miss Flora Foster.

Calhoun has a crop of pretty girls coming on. We heard one of them said, "I wish the boys would do less courting and more marrying." Fess Cantrell admitted that he got a boss valentine but said that times are too hard for marrying.

A fashionable event of the month was the wedding of W. L. Hines and Miss Lizzie Wilson on Wednesday, February 9. The church was beautifully and tastefully decorated and at 8 o'clock Miss Mattie Henderson began a program of organ music. The attendants entered in pairs: Mr. A. L. Dearing and Miss Marselle Harris of Atlanta; O. N. Starr of Calhoun and Miss Jennie Erwin of Hampton, Ala.; W. F. King of Calhoun and Miss Maggie Jones of Cedartown; E. O. Brown of Calhoun and Miss Gussie King of Atlanta. The young ladies were beautifully dressed which added to their natural charms. Mr. Wilson gave an elegant reception at his home after the wedding.

The weather is delightful and it's a treat to see the ladies out on beautiful afternoons. Ice cream and soda water will soon be in order, straw hats and linen dusters are the rage, the dancing season is over and the fishing mania has broken out.

Church street is perfectly beautiful. People should go to church more than they do. Twice this year the Methodist and Baptist pastors have preached on the same text, read the same verses and used the same illustrations without any knowledge or communication with the other. The Rev. Mr. Tumlin of Cartersville is coming to take the pastorate of the Baptist Church.

Mrs. Minnie Harlan gathered the little folks around the organ to teach them to sing. Older folks looking on wished they were little again.

Mat Robertson, Oliver Starr and Fess Cantrell attended the quarterly meeting at Resaca.

The new council, J. M. Jackson, W. L. Hines, J. D. Tinsley, P. A. Summy and H. F. F Ferguson, should either light the streets or remove the scaffolds, wood and rails that are lying around. Street tax for the year is $2.50.

Calhoun has a new grist mill, now lets have a cotton factory. Marsh and Summy's new family grocery and confection store is doing a good business and there's a new saloon in town. James McElroy sells fine drinks, ale and cider in the main building north of the court house. Messrs. Gray and Wells have a very convenient platform scales which will weigh a whole wagon of cotton at one time.

Master Hal Davenport has opened a news stand, Hines and King and Gray and Wells are building two large guano depots, Dorsey and Gober are ready for business in their new black-smith shop and H. F. Ferguson plans to build a 30 x 40 feet two-story brick store.

Col. Peters has sold his "whirl wind" horse for $300. The young people have enjoyed rides over the streets of Calhoun in Col. Peters' hack.

Bill Arp tells a story of a chestnut post and a gate that was hung by General DeSoto or some fellow and is still standing in Gordon

County.

A post office has been established at Skelly's Station and named Oostanaula. Ressaca is raising funds for a fine academy.

Milton A. Cooley of Sugar Valley died of an accidental gunshot wound received when he returned, tired, from a hunting trip and asked his wife to put the gun away. In some unexplained manner the gun was discharged and Mr. Cooley received a flesh wound in the thigh which he neglected, thinking it not serious.

T. M. Ellis' little daughter was sewing on her doll clothes and left a needle on the floor. Mr. Ellis stepped on the needle and developed an infection which kept him away from the store for several days.

Miss Mattie Sessions of Wilkes County, a daughter of Dr. Sessions who once lived in Calhoun, is visiting in town and a complementary party was given for her at the home of T. M. Ellis.

As nearly all of the young men have left town, the balls will be fewer. Col. F. A. Cantrell, one of our popular young lawyers, has been licensed to practice in the Supreme Court. Jimmie Reeve has entered Crawford High School at Dalton and thinks of making a pill driver. He has been elected president of the Young Men's Debating Society.

Calhoun has a very clever set of young men and the longer you stay here the more you become attached to the place. Benjamin Franklin went courting and his horse took the colic. He said it embarrassed him. When a girl has encouraged a young man for two years then tells him she can only be a sister to him he can, for the first time, see the freckles on her nose.

Mr. Lucius Reeve and Miss Mattie McConnell were married at Social Circle last week. A reception was given for them at the home of Mr. J. M. Reeve in Calhoun, when a feast of many good things was served in a royal manner. The hospitality, the exquisite music and the conversation, both private and general, kept people entertained until a late hour of the night. There was also a dining at Col. Joseph McConnell's for Mr. Reeve and his lady.

Excursion tickets to the Cotton Exposition are $1.80. Have you been to the Exposition? If not, when are you going?

Married on December 15, near Sonora, Mr. F. M. Bolding and Miss Addie Hill and on the 22nd, Miss Nettie Parrott and W. F. Felker.

Logan Pitts said that he killed a squirrel that weighed eight pounds. Little Hackett and Morris McConnell caught a 10-pound opossum and the Rev. N. A. Glenn bagged a fine wild turkey. A packett of firecrackers in the pocket of little Charlie Hunt caught fire and badly frightened the little fellow but his clothes were not set on fire.

You may say what you please, but Calhoun in improving. New brick store houses are going up all the time. A fashionable barber shop has been established at W. D. Fain's old stand north of the Courthouse. T. M. Ellis has moved his grocery store to J. M. Ballew's store house and the Misses Reeves have started a millinery and dressmaking shop. There's a fashionable shoe shop at Plainville run by S. D. Goswick and J. M. Neal has opened a new grocery canned goods and confectionery store in Calhoun.

A bridge of five spans, 120 feet long and 12 feet high is to be built across the Salacoa at M. V. Watt's and another bridge of seven spans, 190 feet long and 12 feet high will be erected across the Oothcaloga at McWhorter's mill. The timbers are all to be of heart pine or white oak.

It rains on the unjust and the just alike—on the just mainly because the unjust have borrowed their umbrellas.

Prof. Gharst, phrenologist, has been doing the town. The lazy club has taken up headquarters at the public well. Isn't it all just too paralyzing!

Young man, now is the time to take your girl sweetbud hunting—and oh, oh, the sweetness that sometimes follows.

Bees humming, strawberries ripe and peach trees loaded with fruit.

J. E. Tinsley, jeweler, has arrived and his multitude of friends welcome him back.

Mr. James M. Douglas plans to enlarge his dwelling and Mr. H. S. Gardner is preparing for heavy rains by putting guttering all around his house. Mr. J. W. Swain has built and painted two elegant rooms in front of his house. Boaz Bros. have bought the lot opposite the hotel and will build a warehouse, J. M. Balliew is improving his neat residence on Court Street and will erect a large brick store between his grocery and Mr. Ferguson's new building.

At Sonora, Boyd and Morrison have made durable and convenient improvements to their storehouse. They have a fine stock of goods and welcome the trade of their friends.

Dorsey and Gober are turning out cowbells with a rush, judging by the musical sounds that we hear.

B. M. Harlan's residence has been completed and for style, convenience and neatness cannot be equaled in Calhoun.

Col. J. E. Parrott was seized with vertigo and fell from the platform of a moving train near Adairsville last week. He was critically ill for a while but is improving now. Mr. J. M. Reeve is improving after a fall across the fence. Misses Mary Prickett and Ophelia Hicks and Mr. Quitman Bailey are quite ill.

There have been many deaths and much sickness during the year. Typhoid has been rampant in the county and small pox on the rage in Atlanta and Chattanooga.

While walking along the road, Mr. William Enlow was attacked by a snake, 15 feet long, with a body half as large as a man's and a head as broad as your hand.

Mr. J. M. Ballew has received a fine billiard table for which he paid $275. Prof. Neale Keefe of Petersburg astonishes everyone by the way he handles a billiard cue.

We wish the Dalton newspaper would give us more information on the subject. They say that Frank and Jesse James are living in Gordon County and we think a story of the family would be interesting reading.

A human skelton was found lying on the street in front of the Methodist Church last Sunday. It caused quite a sensation in town.

• Rev. S. P. Jones of Cartersville preached in Calhoun last week.

An interesting revival is in progress at Bethesda with the pastor, Rev. S. H. Cate, in charge. Rev. D. J. McGhee, of Atlanta, preached at the A. M. E. Church last Sunday.

Gordon County is progressive. There are churches and schools everywhere. The people are thrifty and industrious and in a few years the county will be the garden spot of the state.

Two thousand people attended the Baptist Association at Sugar Valley Last week.

Honor students at Mrs. Fields' school for the year were: Edna Pulliam, Daisy Hughey, Jimmie Hall, Marshall Tinsley, Jennie Ellis, Bertie Fain, F. C. Hicks, Bessie Fain, Maggie Fields, Flora Foster, Charlie Hunt, Agnes Tinsley, Carl Thayer, May Hudgens, Lula Brogdon, Eva Reeves, Mattie Tinsley, Ossie Foster and Eva Cantrell.

The ITC Club is large and is becoming an important factor in developing the social interests of the town. Music for the last meeting was given by Miss Jennie Ellis and Mrs. Parott.

Move up higher on the hills of Gordon for there are others crowding there. Can you see the changing shape of things to come? In the dim shadow of the future they wait while the light of the guiding star grows bright with promise.

CALHOUN'S AGE OF ROMANCE

Taffy is sweet, but the sweetest thing at a taffy-pulling is a sweetheart. W. E. Shelor and Miss Ada Swain were married at home in Springtown Valley in December, 1882 and Mr. Joe Johnson and Miss Lina Barnett of Resaca were maried on December 15.

Calhounites enjoyed Christmas immensely with sociables, dinings and dances. Now it's 1883 and the war on turkey is over. Felix Cantrell, student at Commercial College in Baltimore, ate his Christmas turkey at home.

Messrs. Tommy and Robbie Harbin were up from the university last week. We learn that they stand high in their classes, without a "black mark." Colonel Boaz left yesterday to attend school in Lexington, Kentucky.

Miss Anna Parrott, the charming young lady who controls the telegraph at Adairsville, is gracing our town with her presence. Col. W. J. Cantrell and lady left Tuesday for a month's stay in Florida. Messrs. R. F. Wyatt, A. M. Frix, J. E. Tinsley and D. H. Hornbarger made a flying trip to New York last week.

There are some very pretty girls attending the Academy, we wish that we were a young school teacher. Five of Calhoun's prettiest girls will return this summer with their diplomas. Our girls will sell on a premium for brains and beauty and they don't chew gum! One of our Calhoun beauties is said to resemble Mrs. Langtry, only prettier.

Miss Mattie E. Rembert plans to open a school for girls soon and Mr. C. W. Musgrove is prepared to take a number of Academy board-

Boaz Bros. building (Rankin-Norton house) west of the railroad built 1883

ing students. Miss Mamie Pitts will have charge of the primary department of the Academy.

Trustees of the Sugar Valley High School, N. J. Malone, J. N. Wright, V. H. Haynes, S. J. Chandler, P. L. McCutcheon, M. B. Abbott, W. B. Kennedy and W. M. Bridges, announce that the school will begin the new year in charge of Prof. Janes, with Miss Marion Buford as assistant.

Dr. J. H. Malone, County School Commissioner, states that schools will begin January 1 and run for three months and that there will be no summer or fall schools.

Judging by reports of crimes and misdemeanors in other towns, Calhoun is one of the most moral towns in the state. The calaboose is seldom occupied. Judge Fain sat down on one of our lawyers to the tune of $2.00 for inopportune talking.

In a lengthy article on prohibition a citizen writes: "The movement is based strictly on principle. The sale of 400 gallons of whiskey in Calhoun since January 11, 1883 proves that if the success of prohibition in our grand old Georgia accomplishes nothing but the freedom of the drunkards from the thralldom of the liquid tyrant that alone would be worthy of the effort of every sober Georgian." Our commissioners and city council have put the liquor license at $5,000.

The Woman's Missionary Society of the Baptist Church has asked the men to meet with them on April 22.

The Presbyterians, after much discussion, have decided to build on the old site and work will begin soon. Liberty Church is to be ceiled.

Rev. Mr. Darnall preached three excellent sermons in our churches last week. The Baptists have called the Rev. G. S. Tumlin for another year. He is a good pastor and very popular with his people. The ladies of the Methodist Church are raising money to repair the parsonage. The quilt is almost finished, pay 10 cents and get your name on a square. Rev. J. A. Rosser is pastor of the Methodist Church.

The Colored Baptist Convention met at Carters this year. The colored folks of Calhoun are raising funds to build a Baptist church.

A delegation of Baptist met at the hotel to make plans for raising their share of the $150.000 asked for Mercer University.

Misses Belle Boaz, Ida Harlan, Mrs. Wells, Mrs. B. M. Harlan, Judge Harlan and Col. O. N. Starr attended the North Georgia Conference at Dalton.

This conference represents 1/3 of the 6,609 Methodists in the state. There are 215 traveling preachers, 416 local preachers, 50 lay delegates and 52 lay committeemen. It represents a church property of $844,732 and Emory College and LaGrange, Dalton and Covington Female Colleges.

Uncle Tom Strickland, who stays at the depot, is one of the most systematic fellows we have ever seen, he has been handling freight and baggage for 15 years without a mistake.

The hunting club went out and killed 25 rabbits and 15 birds. Ed Tinsley is the champion shot. Jeff Nance of Resaca, accidentally shot himself in the shoulder while hunting. It became necessary to amputate his arm and he died from the injury.

Squire Joab Lewis reports his section as prosperous. Squire

Lewis has the same pleasant manner and his humor never grows old. Col. Bonner is wearing gold sleeve buttons that he bought when he attended Polk's inauguration more than 35 years ago.

The boys had a fine time in Atlanta but were not impressed with Beecher's speech. His notions of the South don't fit ours.

A young man in Calhoun wants to marry. Any woman who can answer these questions can have him: Would it hurt her hands to wash dishes, sew a button on a shirt or make a pair of britches?

Here's a way to use old post cards—cut in quarter-inch strips, they make good lamplighters. After July 1, letters will be two cents. The president has refused his signature, but the bill has passed both houses. Major Wells, postmaster at Calhoun, has put in a set of new boxes at the post office.

Mr. G. W. Mills has introduced the best patent churn dasher we have ever seen. It is called the self-revolving churn dasher.

Prof. J. H. Legg is teaching a singing school at Rev. Harkins Chapel, two miles west of Calhoun.

Will Hughey will add a soda fount to his confectionery.

Mr. William Bailey says he has read the Bible through 86 times. Mr. Quintus Bailey and Gardner, from Alabama, are visiting their father.

Mrs. Sayre, in the county, has cut down a tree that measured six feet in diameter and made 9000 boards.

There was a meeting at Crane Eater last week for the purpose of establishing a large and fine school. Mr. I. M. Fite is having a grist mill built at Crane Eater and Mrs. M. Cates, of Adairsville, has established a millinery shop there.

Judge Wyly Brogdon has a coffee mill that has been used for 43 years and a wash tub that has been in use for 24 years. Both are in good condition. Col. E. J. Kiker has a Spanish coin dated 1311.

A man from Michigan came through the other day, on his way to Florida—horse back. He had come this far in 30 days. Col. T. C. Milner has bought a pony horse and now travels in style. Mr. C. C. Harlan has a brand new buggy and plans to buy a horse. Our estimable citizen is rather portly and a pony is too small. John Neal has the prettiest pair of horses in the state.

Christmas is just around the corner and the town is making big plans. The band is preparing Christmas Music and has ordered two Jew's harps and a tambourine from Atlanta. There has been a light snow and turkeys and deer are plentiful. The churches are planning suppers and the colored folks will have a tree in their new Baptist chuch.

Mrs. Shelor had a party for Tom and Bob Harbin and there was a royal feast at C. C. Harlan's. There are few places in town where the young people can enjoy themselves more freely than at the home of Mr. Harlan and his lady.

January, 1884, drifted in on a three-inch snow and the boys are coasting on every hillside.

The young ladies met at the college and drew for escorts to the leap year party they are planning. The bubble party at W. L. Hines' was quite a novelty and fully enjoyed.

The Misses Haynes of Sugar Valley were guests at the hotel last week and Miss Belle Boaz is visiting her grandfather at Sugar Valley.

A more reliable set of men than those on the new council could not be found. They are: N. J. Boaz, J. H. Malone, J. D. Tinsley, B. M. Harlan, and T. M. Ellis. The dry ticket was elected at Resaca. We congratulate our friends across the river.

The spring has been stormy. One of the chimneys at the Baptist church was blown down, W. F. King's bay window was demolished by hail and Rome is flooded. The long trestle of the EJV and Georgia Railroad has given way. Many people are building storm pits.

The community is saddened by the death of Mrs. J. M. Reeves. Her life of piety and fidelity has been a great influence for good.

Mr. R. F. Wyatt was thrown from his bicycle and suffered several broken ribs—a bicycle is as dangerous as a mule.

A Cartersville dentist was arrested and placed under bond for kissing a Gordon County girl. He has been guilty of this act several times, and we predict that his career as a dentist is about over.

Calhoun can boast of a round dozen of the prettiest, sweetest and smartest girls in the state and they all have good tongues.

Mr. H. C. Hunt has been ordered by the council to set his fence back and open the street by the Baptist church. The council has passed a law to keep goats and other marauding animals off the streets and have been asked to stop the encroachnts on the pine thicket. A petition has been sent to Judge John P. King asking him not to give his consent to the sale of the pine thicket. Judge King replied that he had not given his consent and never would.

Recent real estate deals in the city are: a lot in the rear of J. N. Kiker's sold to E. J. Kiker for $12, one in the rear of the hotel, to Z. T. Gray for $60.25 and Mrs. Field's property to W. A. J. Robertson for $15.

Uncle Jimmy Dunlop, of Atlanta, was in town Tuesday with a gasoline street lamp which he was trying to sell to the City council. He should visit them on the dark of the moon.

The old fence around the courthouse has been sold and a new picket fence will be erected. The ladies are raising money to build a fence around Chandler cemetery. The pie festival netted $14.00 for this worthy cause.

Mr. J. G. B. Erwin of Fairmount, has sold 12 or 15 Champion harvesters this season. The new steamer Idle Wild was launched at Rome this week and will be a great convenience to the farmers in getting in their produce to market. The mail rider from Cassville to Springplace has quit, a great inconvenience to the people.

The dam at Oothcaloga has been finished and is one of the best in the state.

The town is full of visitors for the commencement at the Gordon County University. The Rev. W. H. Darnall will preach the sermon and the Hon. Seaborn Wright, gifted young orator of Rome, will give the address.

The program to be presented by the students is: Spartacus and the Gladiator, Frank Malone; The Builder of the Ship, Miss Minnie Kindred; A Mother's Fidelity, Miss Jennie Ellis; Goodbye Miss Mattie Tinsley; Modern Anomaly, Willie Rankin; The Dying Soldier, W. B. Haynes; Fashion, Miss Carrie Reeve; The Faithful Lovers, Miss Flora Foster; Spring House Cleaning, Miss Bessie Fain; The Murderer's Secret, Mark A. Matthews; The Faded Jacket of Gray, Milton Fain; Literature, Miss Lucile Malone and The Ship on Fire, Miss Nida Boaz.

Col. O. N. Starr is to deliver the address to the alumni of the North Georgia Agricultural College at Dahlonega.

The hotel has received several applications for board for the summer from south Georgians. Anyone seeking a quiet retreat could do no better than spend the summer in Calhoun.

Misses Jennie Ellis and Georgia Hicks left yesterday to attend a meeting of the grand lodge of the IGGT.

A large crowd attended the meeting of the North Georgia Conference in Calhoun. Rev. J. F. Mixon preached at the Methodist and Rev. E. W. Ballinger at the Baptist churches. Fifty persons were baptized after the revival at Sugar Valley. The city was well represented among the 2,000 people who went to Casey's Camp Ground. Rev. G. S. Tumlin has resigned as pastor of the Baptist Church.

The Baptist Negroes cleared $90 from their recent concert at the Methodist church and the money will be used to repair the church. The colored Methodist church has new benches and has been partly ceiled.

Major Wells, postmaster, has announced that the Sunday mails will not be opened until after church services. There is a new coal stove at the Baptist church and the ladies have put down a new carpet at the Methodist church.

The town has quieted down since the preachers have returned to their homes.

The good people at Skelly's Station held a neighborhood barbecue. Music was furnished by Mr. J. H. Gordon and Dr. Wicker, violins, Prof. J. K. Smith, flute, and little Joe Gordon on the guitar

The boys had an impromptu (no bets) walking match on the walk from the Baptist church to the drug store. The winner walked over 11 miles.

Mr. J. B. Hillhouse has a horse that is 28 years old. During the war he was owned by a Mr. Bishop who drove a nail through his hoof to keep the Yankees from getting him. The horse is lame from the injury but still able to be worked.

Mrs. Boisclair, once of Calhoun, a noble, generous, Christian lady, died in Augusta. Mrs. Harlan died and Mr. William Matthews, age 104, died in Murray County.

It is the law of life. The old are gathered to their father and he young take their places. Trees on the hills of Gordon fall, and saplings spring up from the seeds left by the old trees. And the hills, like the sentinel at Pompeii who stood at his post while the ashes of destruction fell around him, still keep their vigil over the valley of Gordon.

"Over the hills and far away,
A little boy steals from his morning play
And under the blossoming apple tree,
He lies and he dreams of the things to be."

—Eugene Field.

"Isn't it wonderful that the weather is so fine now, after all that sleet in December?"

"Wasn't it cold! Why, the night of the candy pulling at the hotel, we almost fell down six times before we got there!"

"Don't you hope that the weather stays like this until after the wedding! We haven't had a church wedding in so long, it just must be a pretty night. Jennie, you're lucky, no curl papers for you—with that natural wave in your hair, you'll be the prettiest girl in the wedding procession!"

It was the night of the elegant feast that Lucile and Alfred Malone were giving, when the fair hostess was presiding with her usual grace and dignity over a table laden with good things and the conversation was of course, the coming wedding at the Baptist Church, planned by the young people of town, when one of Calhoun's most charming and accomplished young ladies and a promising young attorney were to be married.

Someone mentioned John Sayre's Christmas dinner. "It was a feast fit for the gods," said Alfred. "John is one of the bigesthearted boys in the state and no one can entertain so well as this noble son of a noble sire."

The dinner at the hotel was elegant too. Mr. Haynes has no equal in the hotel line. Notable among social events was the entertainment given by Squire Tinsley for Weldon Tinsley and his wife, the former Miss Georgia Harris of Macon. The table was laden with tempting viands and luscious fruits.

With the pound party at D. B. Clark's Calhoun society has been quite lively, the young people are having a good time.

Boards have been put up at the street corners giving the names of the streets and it's now impossible for anyone to get lost.

Logan Pitts opened a school near P. M. Craig's Monday, J. H. Reeve is studying medicine at the drug store of Reeves and Malone and Joe Littlefield is again handling the yard stick at Gholston's.

The whisky question is the main topic of conversation on the streets. Rev. G. W. Thomas will preach a temperance sermon at the Methodist Church next Sunday. Long articles, discussing both sides of the question, appear in each week's paper. Prohibition was defeated in Floyd County by 400 votes. "Get out and vote the dry ticket" urges Editor H. A. Chapman, of The Calhoun Times.

W. M. Hughey sings the merits of his merchandise in a 12 verse poem ending.

"So when you come to town, the children you must bring
And you'll find that W. M. Hughey keeps next door to
Hines and King."

The snow and cold in February have made the roads almost impassable. A drummer who was in town while the thermometer was down to 7 degrees said, "Well, if this is the sunny south, I'll go back home!"

But April comes to bloom and spring fashions are the flowers as the new lace brocades for warm weather make their appearance at the churches and at sociables. Silk evening gloves are embroidered in soft colors and among the charming novelties are hammered silver belt buckles and gauze ribbons in ecru, deep cream and red, with tiny chenille dots.

Skirts are plain, even little girls' skirts are made without flounces and blouse fronts are made of Irish tatting, while the English style of hair dressing remains. Magnolia Balm is a secret aid to beauty. You can't tell and the lady won't tell.

The TV and G railroad will have elegant through sleepers to Cleveland's inauguration. Col. E. J. Kiker has shaved his beard in honor of a Democratic president. Back in May 1861, he resolved that no razor should go to his face until a Decocratic president was safely in his seat.

W. F. King has set out a row of shade trees in front of his residence, J. M. Kindred has planted trees in his front yard and Dock Dorsey has erected a neat fence around his lot on Rock Street. W. L. Hines has purchased two lots from Mrs. J. P. Prickett, next to the railroad across from B. M. Harlan's and will build this summer.

Z. T. Gray has traded his stock of goods to B. R. Bray for a farm and will retire. John Gray has left the noisy bustle of the city for the quiet retreat of the farm.

The Council has ordered 200 loads of rock to be put on the Mill road, new hitching racks have been put up and new steps, running all across the front, have been built to the courthouse. T. M. Ellis, tax receiver, says that returns show an increase of 10 to 20 thousand dollars in each district.

Miss Florrrie Foster and Miss Hattie Garlington have brought in the first spring flowers and major Roff's garden, in which he takes great pride, is abloom with 50 varieties of roses. See Major Roff about a ticket to the New Orleans Exposition, round trip $8. About 30 people from Calhoun are going in a special car.

Are you going to the concert at the courthouse Friday night? It is to be given by Blind Tom, musical phenomenon of the age and the greatest living natural pianist. Tickets are 25c and 50c with reserve seats at 75c.

Mr. N. H. McGinnis has purchased the Brogdon property, A. M. Blake has offered $700 for the lot known as the Hunt Corner, Mr. W. L. Hines is building on his lots and the Baptists at Adairsville are planning to build a new church west of the railroad.

Judge J. M. Harlan had a Percheron colt in town Saturday. It is a beauty and would take a prize over anything. Col. E. J. Kiker wants a race track around the pine thicket.

The exercises at the Gordon County University, under the direction of Prof. Landrum, Miss Mamie Pitts, Mrs. M. Kindred and Miss Archie Tillett, music teacher, were excellent. Special mention must be made of little Orrie Malone, Fannie Reeve and Kitty Ellis who seemed natural elocutionists. Quite a large party will go to Pine Chapel for the closing exercises.

Boaz and Fite have moved into their new brick warehouse near the depot. It is one of the handsomest buildings in North Georgia. The woodwork is to be oiled and will show the natural grain of the yellow pine.

A skating rink has been opened over Bray's store, admission 10¢. In a contest for the most graceful skater, the prize went to Miss Julia Blassingame, one of nine contestants.

The Negroes have organized a debating society which meets in the Baptist Church.

The two half lots of land belonging to Deliza Watts have been bought by O. N. Starr.

Rev. J. A. McMurray administered the sacrament of baptism to Mrs. F. A. Cantrell and Misses Mary Fite and Mary Neal at Fain's pond last Sunday evening. Revivals are in progress at the Methodist Church, Liberty Presbyterian, Salem and Bethlehem at Sonora.

Rev. J. A. McMurray has resigned as pastor of the Baptist Church and Rev. Edgar Jewell, of Conyers, has been elected to fill the pulpit. Rev. H. S. Henry has accepted a call to Liberty Presbyterian Church.

W. L. Hines has moved into his new residence "Oakley," across the railroad from B. M. Harlan's. It is one of the handsomest dwellings in this part of the state. The ITC will hold the October meeting at Oakley.

J. H. Reeve left Monday to attend the Atlanta Medical College. Jim is a close student and will make a success in his chosen profession.

Dr. Chastine and Family of Plainville, have moved to town and are living in the Kiker house in the rear of the courthouse.

Damage to the county from the high water amounted to $70,000. The steamer, Mitchell, loaded with 53 bales of cotton and farm produce, could not pass under the bridge and was tied up for a week. Later, Gordon County was sued for detaining the steamer. The middle pier of the Oostanaula bridge is unsafe, the rocks are falling out.

Now that Calhoun, Resaca and Atlanta have voted out whiskey, it will have to go out of the state.

Miss Josie Wilkes is organist at the Baptist Church and Miss Lucile Malone, for Sunday school. Seven thousand people attended the Sam Jones tent meeting at Cartersville.

Miss Mamie Pitts will open a private school, Miss Lulie Pitts is teaching music in Mrs. Fields' school at Jonesboro and Miss Josie Wilkes, the new music teacher for the college here is stopping at J. M. Roove's.

Citizens are laying in the winter's supply of coal at 13¢ a bushel.

Dan Cupid has been busy during the year. Married at the residence of A. W. Reeve, Miss Laura Reeve to Mr. Samuel Dillard on the 31 of March. She is one of our most excellent young ladies, always first in works of charity. He is a substantial citizen with hosts of friends. Mr. W. M. Hughey and Miss Jimmy Prickett were married at the residence of the bride's mother. The groom's parents gave a dinner the next day. He is a man of sterling worth, she, a sweet and charming little lady. Mr. C. C. Everett and Miss Leonora Reese were married on Monday at the residence of the bride's brother-in-law, L. T. Lewis.

Mr. J. H. Gordon and Miss Alice Griffin, two of Oostanaula's most popular young people were married on Tuesday. Mr. S. A. Williams and Miss Lizzie Reeve were married at the residence of Mr. Goodwin, 10 miles from Atlanta. Other marriages of interest to Gordon County people were: Mr. Edge, of Sugar Valley and Miss Annie Weaver of Ringgold, Mr. Will Harber and Miss Gorda Wright, of Sugar Valley and Mr. T. M. Owen and Miss Annie Owen of Dry Valley, on the 13th by Rev. J. D. Huckabee.

So ended the pleasant year of 1885, the year of beginning for so many young people. Would the new year of 1886 fulfill the promise of the old? With cowbells ringing, watch parties and prayers the new year comes in. But wait—what does he hold in his hand? A scroll of prophecy written in red! The hill of Gordon are about to witness a cycle of days that will make the year rest in memory as the most momentous period since the days of Dawsonville. The show will open on January 1, 1886. Have your ticket ready, gentlemen.

"WORST BLIZZARD, DEEPEST SNOW" MARK YEAR 1886

Gentlemen, be seated. The show of '86 is about to begin. Mr. Bones, did you read the paper last Thursday? Yes, Mr. Interlocutor, I did and if headlines can set the pace for the months to come, Calhoun should batten down the hatches and double bar the doors.

Killed by an Engine, Roasted Alive, Buried Alive, Moulded in Snow—these are the headlines that tell the state of the nation in January, 1886.

The music and drama column does bring a note of relief as we read that Mrs. Bernhardt is studying the role of Marian Delorme in Victor Hugo's drama of the same name, that Madame Patti is to sing in the Covent Garden and will visit the United States in the spring and that Clara Morris, an actress, travels with a trunk that is 6 feet high and 5 feet wide. She says it is her home.

Schools throughout the county have opened, the Gordon County University in Calhoun, with Prof. Woods as principal, the Coosawattee Seminary, 6 miles each of Resaca, with Profs. Cheyne and Conley in charge, Mrs. C. M. McBrayer's school at Blackwood, Mrs. E. A. Hill's school at Resaca, Pine Chapel with 102 scholars and Dry Valley Seminary in a beautiful and healthy location, 2 miles from Sonora, Miss Jennie Ellis has a school of 50 scholars at Clark's Chapel and it is succeeding well in training the young idea.

The dry ticket for council, N. J. Boaz, W. F. King, J. M. Smith, J. B. Johnson and H. F. Ferguson, was elected and Adairsville will begin the year with a new council, namely, G. A. Veach, B. F. Bibb, W. J. Hillburn, J. P. Dyar and Thomas Tomlinson.

On Monday and Tuesday large blocks of ice came floating down the river, ice on the pond was 3 inches thick and the thermometer stood at 8 degrees below zero. The cold wave sign was posted at the depot and on Friday the blizzard struck. Saturday, the temperature was 3 degrees above zero and a cold wind blew all day. Monday, the thermometer registered 1 degree above while a heavy snow blocked all business activity.

But the sunny south does not leave her children long in the grip of a blizzard, the sun comes out, the ice thaws, the snow begins to melt and the wheels are turning again.

Mr. G. M. Hunt left Monday for Florida where he expects to prospect for a location. Mr. J. H. Fox and lady are visiting in North Carolina.

Col. O. N. Starr has purchased Judge Fain's law office and Cols. Rankin and Milner have purchased the house belonging to Dr. H. K. Main, north of the square. Col. E. J. Kiker is clearing the hill in the rear of his house and plans to start a vineyard.

Mr. Armstead Abbott has purchased the Hall property across from the Times office. Mr. E. W. Keys has moved to Reeves Station.

The contract has been let to build a new stone jail, 27 x 27 feet with a 5 foot hall running the length of the building and 6 cells 9 x 9 feet. The site selected is just south of the old jail. The cost to the taxpayers will be $3,624.

Drs. Reeves and Malone have set out shade trees in front of their drug store. Mr. Haynes moved into his new hotel on Monday and has put up a street lamp in front. Boaz and Fite are moving the guano sheds between the Haynes house and the depot. J. M. Harlan and Co. have received an order from Louisville for a carload of clover seed. Mr. C. P. Floyd has been appointed N. P. and Alfred Malone is the agent for the Singer Sewing Machine Co. with headquarters at the hotel. Mr. E. A. Brown has given the editor a book, "War Scenes on the W & A," written by passenger agent Joe M. Brown which gives a good description of the battles along the W & A railroad.

Plainville burned last Sunday night. Business houses destroyed in the fire were those of Dr. I. N. Huffaker, drugs, Dodd and Sisk, dry goods, and S. D. Goswick's Shoe Shop. The fire was thought to be incendiary after burglary.

A week of reception and dinners followed the marriage in Virginia of Colonel Boaz and his lady. The young couple is housekeeping in the Harkins place next to the Haynes house.

Another marriage of county interest was that of Mr. George Bandy to Miss Ines Warren at Union Church near Resaca, with the Rev. J. T. Simmons performing the ceremony.

Miss Hattie Garlington came up to attend Miss Mamie Pitts' school and is boarding at Mrs. N. E. Pitts.

Mr. Joe Harber of Texas is visiting his parents at Sugar Valley. The Rev. Joe Jones is preaching at Sugar Valley and "whooping up the boys." He seems to be taking in Gordon County but his language is a little rough for the pulpit.

The Gordon County Singing Convention will hold its second annual meeting with the Calhoun churches on the second Sunday in April. Profs. Showalter and Pound will be here.

We would like to see the Council continue the rock work on the mill road to the railroad and suggest that they invest 5¢ in a tin cup for the public well. The well on Railroad street has been repaired and a sewer is being laid from the jail to the big ditch in front of the courthouse. The Council built a fence around the public well but the next morning it was gone. Calhoun must be a no-fence town.

Miss Ida Reeve came home to take Miss Jennie Ellis' school at Clarke's Chapel. Miss Jennie has been elected music teacher at the Gordon County University. It is a good selection and we are glad to see home talent recognized.

April came in with an equinoctial gale after a snow and blizzard in March. The Oostanaula is a vast sea of water, abutments at both ends of the Calhoun bridge have been swept away and Oothcaloga bridge is floating.

This is the flood of '86 when the river is 8 feet higher than in '81 and the high water mark will be a standard for future generations. Water is 6 inches deep in Major Well's house, 2 feet deep in Oothcaloga Mill and 1 foot deep on the river bridge and still rising. This bridge is 4 feet higher than the one that was swept away in 1861 but we fear that it will go.

A boat with three boys in it capsized in the river and the boys had to swim for their lives. One floated three miles downstream. Trains can get no further than Calhoun, water is five feet over the tacks below McDaniel's Station.

Officials estimate that it will cost $1,000 to repair the bridges over the county. The Oostanaula bridge is being crossed by means of ladders at each end. Men leave their teams on the other side and walk across.

During the flood A. M. Graham saw a cow lodged in a tree below Z. T. Gray's place.

Laurens Hillhouse got the bid to rebuild the bridge abutments. The cost will be $22.50 for the north end and $22 for the south end. The county will furnish the materials. In September the bridge would be covered and the roof extended over each end.

The Gordon County University has been reorganized with Prof. H. B. Moss as principal. The children have been allowed too much liberty, principally the fault of the parents. No teacher can control a school without the cooperation of the parents. Let all hands put a shoulder to the wheel and build a good school. There are about 300 children in a four mile radius of Calhoun.

The Social event of the season was the wedding of Miss Ella Harlan and Col. O. N. Starr which took place at the home of Judge J. M. Harlan on Thursday, May 27 with the Rev. G. W. Thomas officiating. Attendants were Col. Trammell Starr, of Spring Place, and Miss Ida Harlan, Mr. E. A. Brown, of Atlanta and Miss Anne Trammell of Dalton, Mr. C. P. Floyd, of Calhoun, and Miss Minnie Graves of Kentucky, Mr. C. N. King of Spring Place, and Miss Minnie Kindred. After the ceremony, the party returned to the hotel for the reception which for elegance and taste could not be excelled in the state. Col. and Mrs. Starr will start housekeeping in the new Wright house on North Wall Street (now the home of Mrs. Hobgood).

The Gordon County University closed with an interesting program of recitations, declamations and music. Recitations were given by Fannie Ellis, Agnes Tinsley, Maude Ballew and Maggie Rankin, Edgar Pittman, Hackett McConnell, Oscar Hunt and Judson Jewell gave declamations and young musicians on the program were May Haynes, Orrie Malone and Kittie Ellis, vocal soloists, Fannie and Kittie Ellis and Maggie and Bessie Thornton played piano duets.

Mrs. C. C. Harlan and Miss Georgia Hicks have worked tirelessly to get a fence built around Chandler Cemetery. The fence, of wire, with iron posts, enclosing a 400 foot square is now in place. There are three small gates and one large one.

Mr. Alfred Nichols, of Sonora, is 80 years old, cuts 100 rails a day and works every day. Jim Reeve is a prescription clerk in an Atlanta drug store. W. L. Hines, whose home "Oakley" burned last fall, will rebuild on the same site. He will use the same house plan, but make the rooms bigger.

Six fine Gordon raised horses were exhibited on the streets Saturday. A well-trained setter sold for $15 and a blind horse for $21.

Up in the Coosawatee district, deer and turkeys are so plentiful that people have to drive them out of their yards.

Mrs. S. E. Willingham has moved to the Cantrell place on Rock street. Mrs. J. D. Tinsley returned Friday from Macon and Miss Aurie Garlington is visiting friends in the city.

Z. T. Gray plans to build a carriage and wagon repository on Railroad Street. Mr. W. F. King and Dr. R. W. Thornton have bought new buggies from M. E. Ellis. They are quite handsome and stylish.

Mike Moll, with his new accordian, furnishes music for the town at all hours of the day and night.

Squire Tinsley owns a clock that was made in 1790. W. M. Hughey has a new peanut roaster and wants the contract to supply the Georgia Legislature. W. L. Hillhouse's recently opened brickyard will burn 1000 brick this week. There's a new tin shop on the old Hall Corner, run by Mr. Hooper.

Col. O. N. Starr plans to build soon on his lot across from the University. H. N. Patrick has bought the Murphree lot in front of Mrs. N. E. Pitts and H. K. Hicks' new building is completed. Col. F. A. Cantrell is improving his residence on N. Wall Street. The original part of his house was built of timbers from Foster and Harlan's wooden store house, that was replaced by the two story brick building on the North corner of Court and Wall Street.

The ITC failed to meet this week. This club, which meets twice a month, has been the life of the town for several years.

Fall fashion notes say that beaded velvet bonnets, with strings 2 or 3 inches wide, are being worn. Applique galleons trim many handsome cloth and wool dresses. Young girls wear mantles shaped like those of ladies of 18. Condor yellow, mermaid pink and liquorice purple are the favorite colors. Bows are set in every conceivable place about a costume. Young ladies generally like to have many bows about.

Friends have been saddened by the deaths of J. E. Parrott and J. M. Reeve during the year. Mr. W. H. McDaniel is out again after a serious illness.

A reception was given for the new Methodist pastor, Rev. R. R. Johnson. The Presbyterians have a new organ and will give a concert to pay for it.

On Friday, December 4 the great snow of '86 began to fall. By Saturday morning the depth was 5 inches, Sunday 10 inches, and on Monday snow covered the ground to a depth of 24 inches. Many small houses were crushed and all business was at a standstill.

Now sit down, Mr. Bones, the show is over. Will this Christmas be one of gaiety or a period of deep gratitude that the worst blizzard, the biggest flood and the deepest snow have come and gone leaving only financial loss in their wake?

Be seated, gentlemen. We will wait for the hour of midnight. We will say farewell to 1886 and greet the new year as he comes in with clean white pages in this book.

THE DISASTERS OF 1888

Mary Bailey came out of Hines and King's store, where she had gone to buy buttons and thread for Mrs. Rankin's dress, crossed the street and stopped by McKnight's drug store to get a bottle of spring tonic for the children.

It was a late afternoon in the spring of 1888, one of those warm March days when it seems that April is hiding behind every tree and May is sitting in the branches, waiting to spill her basket of flowers on the waking earth.

Her purchases made Mary walk slowly up the street thinking that it was restful to have an hour in town, away from the sewing machine. But of course she didn't mind the work, neither did her sister. They were happy to have the children and each other together in the little house on the corner just south of the Academy on College avenue.

Mary paused for a bit in front of the Kiker home to drink in the serene beauty of the scene—the two white churches facing each other across the street with picket fences and tall trees keeping guard and, beyond, the street two-laning around the middle row of trees,

Gordon County Courthouse completed 1889.

then gently curving east to follow the line of the railroad.

The trees would soon be putting out little mouse ears of green. That's when to plant corn, the Indians said. Back in the 60's, Gabe Hunt had dug the trees on Mr. Bob Franklin's place and set them out in 3 rows along the wide street and there they have stood these 20 years, making cool shade in the summer sun and rattling their bones in the winter wind.

As she passed the Methodist Church, Mary was thinking that it would soon be warm enough for Henry Brogdon to plant his flower beds in the church yard—geraniums and 4 o'clocks, pinks and old maids.

Across the street, the rays of the setting sun, falling against the little amber panes of glass in the doors of the Baptist Church, filled the long room with a golden glow and the strains of "How Firm A Foundation" seemed to float in the air and be answered from the Methodist Church with "Amazing Grace How Sweet the Sound." Mary could not know that this would be the last time she would see this familiar and loved scene.

Like Mary Bailey, the people of Calhoun had spent the day of March 19, 1888 in the usual way. The sun went down, twilight came, then the dark. The soft glow of lamplight slipped through the windows of houses all over town. The flickering light of a lantern danced along the street—Mr. Hines had stayed late to work on the books.

Supper is over, the children's lessons done, now one by one the windows darken and the village sleeps. Midnight. The Seth Thomas clock on the parlor mantle quietly ticks the minutes away. A child stirs restlessly, for the night is warm and the covers are heavy.

Somewhere a rooster begins the 3 o'clock call and is answered by another, and another until all the feathered alarm clocks have set the day a-yawning. One old bird, grown fat and lazy, simply nods his head and settles back among the complaining hens as the last echo falls and all is quiet again.

Then, from out of the stillness of the predawn hour, and with the roar of a dozen freight trains, there descends upon Calhoun that black sheep of nature, that sky-demon, spawned by the Vernal Equinox, a cyclone!

Snatched from deep slumber, mothers and fathers try to calm the frightened children whose cries cannot be heard over the roar of the wind, the crash of falling timbers and the crunch of breaking tree limbs. At the Cantrell home on north Wall street, the porch roof comes off and lumbers over into the backyard. Across the street, Mr. Laurens Hillhouse's new house, ready for the weather boarding, is laid flat. Mary Bailey's cottage falls in a clutter of boards and only the sewing machine, supporting the fallen timbers, saves the children from injury.

On the street behind the Methodist Church, the Ellis family sits in frozen terror and listens to the church falling. Across the railroad the roof of Mrs. Willingham's boarding house twists away, in the town square bricks from the courthouse tumble to the ground and shingles fly through the air. At the Ballew home near the center of town, Mrs. Ballew screams to the two little girls, "lie down on the floor"! As they obey, a piece of timber from Hines and Kings' store crashes through the window and comes to rest inches from the baby's head, as she lies in her bed.

Mr. and Mrs. Ballew try to hold the door but it is pushed inward and sets itself neatly against the sewing machine. One little girl cuts her feet on broken glass and Mr. Ballew sustains an ankle injury that keeps him on crutches for weeks.

All the store buildings on the south side of Court street are unroofed and many houses in the south part of town damaged.

As suddenly as it came, the storm is gone. Daylight comes and the dazed people pick their way through the debris to learn the extent of the damage. Weeping women stand over the ruins of dear little white churches. "What will we do without churches", sobs one. Another stoops to pick up a song book caught under a broken pew. A piece of carpet from the Methodist Church hangs on a tree snag. The roof of the Baptist Church is gone, a wall torn away. One pew lies undamaged near the ruins of the Mason and Hamlin organ. (This pew has stood for a number of years in the kitchen of the First Baptist Church.)

Downtown, the men stare in stunned disbelief at the wrecked courthouse. There would be two terms of Superior Court before they could build another one!

But these are the sons and daughters of pioneers, there is for them no idle waiting, they are up and doing. J. C. Harkins, C. C., W. M. Black, Ordinary, J. T. Simmons, T. R., T. M. Ellis, T. C. and W. J. Reeves, county treasurer, begin to remove records and undamaged furnishings from the courthouse to the second story of the Young building, where the August term of court is held. The February 1889 session would be held in the second story of J. B. Johnson's store on the south corner of Railroad and Court Streets.

The congregations of the churches recover from the shock of their loss and begin to make plans for rebuilding. The Methodists hold services in the Presbyterian church while the Baptists meet at th Academy. Stores and houses are repaired and business resumed.

But what of '87? Have you no news of 1887? Is he to roam forever with the lost Lenore in the raven's land of Nevermore? We shall see.

Early on the morning of October 23, 1888, the people of Calhoun are awakened by the shrill continuous blowing of the whistle on the morning freight train. What is it? What's wrong? The town is on fire!

Starting in the newspaper office, the fire spreads until the entire east side of the south block of Court Street and half of the north side are burned. H. A. Chapman's drugstore, M. L. Matthews' and M. E. Ellis' wood shops, Dorsey's blacksmith shop, W. G. Dukes, McGinnis and Gaines and Hick's & Pitt's grocery stores and Reeves and Malone's drugstore are the buildings destroyed. The brick wall of Hines' & Kings' store finally stops the fury of the flames.

While Editor Chapman is negotiating for a new press, a half sheet is printed in Cartersville.

The main features of the single sheet of newsprint are a full account of the fire and the story of an interesting event in Cartersville.

In 1838, a 14 year old boy, who had just moved to town, and his grandfather were passing a house as a pretty little girl of 12 came out. The boy said, "that's my wife". They met at school the next morning, later fell in love and planned to be married as soon as they were grown up. Like Jacob, the boy waited 7 years for his wife. His name was Stephen D. Roberts, hers Elizabeth Emmaline Thompson. Their descendants met at the home of Mr. Starling Roberts in Cartersville on October 23, 1888 to celebrate the golden wedding of Stephen and Elizabeth Roberts.

By November The Calhoun Times is again in regular size. Hicks, Hughey and McGinnis are rebuilding and there will soon be 3 handsome new brick stores in town. Mr. Dorsey is rebuliding, his blacksmith shop. Calhoun cannot be downed, not in 1888!

Judge J. A. Mims has moved into the new Fuller house on the corner of Rock and Railroad streets. Mrs. Ida Johnson is visiting in Cartersville, John Gray, who is with M. C. and J. F. Kiser in Atlanta, is visiting in town, and Miss May Haynes will spend the holidays in Smyrna.

A delegation met to pick the site of Ryals High School but could not decide whether to make the school male, female or mixed. The ladies will give an oyster supper to pay off the debt on the Collegiate Institute in Calhoun.

Saturday was a big day in the cotton market, $20,000 exchanged hands and wagons came from Pickens & Cherokee.

Why kick about taxes? We need a new courthouse and $1 per hundred is not heavy. The city council could do a good work by replanting the trees ruined by the cyclone.

Dr. W. M. Curtiss bought the Curtiss place for $1,560 at an administrator's sale last week.

J. H. Halone, C. S. C., asks that teachers make out another report for October, the first one was lost in the fire.

A tin horn sounds the note of Christmas and the Christmas boys have painted the town red with fireworks and bonfires. Oostanaula sent over a delegation of fantastics. There was little drunkeness.

Southwest corner Court and South Wall streets, from the Courthouse steps the morning after the fire of October 1888.

The Rev. Mark Matthews delivered a temperance address in Atlanta and will conduct special Christmas exercises in Calhoun.

The young men of the town gave a delightful dance at the Calhoun Hotel and the handsome parlors of the Haynes House were crowded for the spelling bee and for the dance given by Mr. and Mrs. Sinclair Mims.

Mr. John B. Boyd and Judge J. M. Harlan attended the Conference in Milledgeville last week. The new Methodist pastor, Rev. Simon Shaw, is a young man without a family and is staying at the Calhoun Hotel.

Mr. J. A. Jackson and Miss Cora Ramsaur were married in Rome and will live at the Calhoun Hotel until Mr. Jackson's house is completed. Invitations have been received to the marriage of Mr. Will Connor and Miss Mattie Tinsley. The couple will live in Birmingham.

Miss Josie Wilkes and Mr. S. K. Dendy, of Seneca, S. C., were married at the home of the bride's mother in Chattanooga, on Tuesday, Nov. 27, 1888 with the Rev. A. H. Mitchell performing the ceremony. Mr. and Mrs. Dendy passed through Calhoun on the way to their home in Seneca. Several friends of Mrs. Dendy, who is well known in Calhoun, met them at the train.

So the disastrous year ends on a note of hope, despite the blackened earth and the wrecked courthouse that still stands on the square in the center of town with the ghost of the cyclone swishing through the dusty halls.

The fire of the spirit glows on unquenchable, and the foundation of the soul is built upon a rock and it shall not be moved though many a stormy wind shall blow.

THE YEAR OF RECOVERY, 1889

The year of 1888 had been a rough one, yet the people of Calhoun had caught the falling star and Christmas was reflected in it's brightness. Signs of disaster still lay about them but, in the burned area, new buildings were going up and the Baptist and Methodist Churches were far along in construction.

The spirit that has born in a shining star still lived in the hearts of a people who could rise above adversity and remember that to share with others is a gift of the Magi.

Mrs. Hines and Mrs. Wilson gave a pleasant dining to a few of their lady friends at Oakley, their pleasant home, on Thursday. Misses Charley Reeve and Kittie Ellis gave entertainments and the young ladies gave a leap year party at the hotel.

Heavy rains ushered in the new year and later in the month, snow fell, but melted rapidly.

Mr. John Logan has moved his mother's family to town and they will reside at the Reeves place. Mr. Haney's family arrived Monday and are residing at the Ballew cottage. Both families are receiving a cordial welcome.

Logan and Haney are adding new teams and a fine carriage to their livery stable. We had a ride behind one of their fast horses and fairly split the wind. Rev. Mark Matthew's livery horse ran away, hit Mrs. Dillard's buggy, dragging Mary Sally several feet, ran down Wall street to Rock street where the buggy stopped against C. O. Boaz's fence, then returned to the stable with one shaft hanging.

One evening two young men had a race on College avenue and, being full of corn juice and thinking the street was full of buggies, ran into the only one there, Judge Harlan's buggy standing in front of O. N. Starr's.

The city council should do something to the walks, there's not a respectable one in town, not even one fit for a pig trail. Also there should be a pump in the public well and the two old engines standing on Railroad street should be moved, the horses might be frightened.

Hicks and Pitts have a new sign and Hines and King are making a partition in their building. They will dissolve partnership and have two store rooms. Mr. Offutt has finished a nice residence on Rock street.

There is a new cover on the public well, a line of sewage is being built on the west side of Wall Street, where Court Street enters and the city council has purchased 15 street lamps. The town is crowded with tourists and is fast getting the reputation of being the best town on the W and A. Calhoun has more enterprise to the square foot than any town of her size. In spite of cyclones and fires, she is forging ahead.

A man named Ellis, living near Adairsville, claims to have one of Jesse James' pistols with nine notches in the handle. Did the James brothers of outlaw fame at one time live in Gordon County?

They may have had relatives here with whom they could have found refuge.

Mr. A. M. Graham has a Colts revolver that was in the first and the last battles of the Civil War.

In the block just north of town, the homegoing citizen quickens his step and walks with a glad heart as he passes the new Methodist Church and looks across the street to the new Baptist Church almost ready for services.

Work on the buildings was suspended during the holidays but now has been reserved. Mr. L. G. Bradbury is painting the Methodist Church. The architect and builder of the church, J. T. Waldrip, yet a young man, has built thirty seven churches and says that this, his latest, is the best of them all. Standing on a slight eminence just north of town, is the pretties little church in North Georgia and our people are rightly proud of it.

The building is forty by sixty feet with two spires in front, one 83 feet, the other 85 feet from the ground. Between the spires and leading to the door is a recess, covered with a neat roof, which greatly adds to the appearance of the front. From the vestibule, you enter the church by a door at either side leading down to the altar. The church is ceiled in sections with beaded pine ceiling, arched toward the center, where a ventilator of beautiful design breaks the monotony of a bare wall.

The church will be seated with comfortable pews. It is one of the handsomest buildings of its kind and catches the admiring glance of all who see it.

The first services in the new church were held in April with the pastor, Rev. Simeon Shaw preaching and the Sunday School was organized in the same month.

Rev. H. C. Morrison would preach the dedication sermon on May 9, 1889, using as his text Matthew 16:16-18.

The collection on this Sunday would be $60, $20 more than the assessment.

The chime bells for the Baptist Church arrived in December 1888 and on January 20, 1889, are in place, their mellow tones calling the people to worship. In later years a member was to say, "no one could ring the bells like Uncle Riley did. He had music in his soul!" (Uncle Riley was church janitor for many years).

The church is as handsome as any edifice in North Georgia and is an ornament to the town. The outside is painted a soft gray with olixt rim and the inside is in several delicate shades. The new pews, ordered from North Carolina, are of ash, very handsome and comfortable, in circular form and, from door to pulpit, are arranged to form two aisles. The church is heated by a furnace.

The Sunday School organization was perfected in April and the Rev. W. W. Dyer conducted the first church service. The dedication of the church was held on Jan. 9, 1889 and the W and A railroad gave special roundtrip rates to Calhoun from nearby towns.

The Rev. D. Hawthorne began the impressive and beautiful service to a packed house using as his text "If this counsel or this work be of men, it will come to naught, but if it be of God, ye cannot overthrow it." Dr. Hawthorne became ill and could not continue. Captain Dyer took the stand and stated that the church was in debt $7000. This amount was soon raised and the church dedicated.

It is a banner year for the Presbyterians too, for their church is receiving the finishing touches as Mr. L. G. Bradbury does the painting and the new chandelier, giving a beautiful light, is installed. The Rev. W. W. Brim D.D., of Canton would preach the dedicatory sermon on Nov. 24, 1889.

A band of 30 little girls from all the churches, called The Lovers of Jesus, has been organized with Rev. Mark Matthews as leader. The group will alternate meetings with the 3 churches. A meeting was held at the Presbyterian church to give prizes to children who had read the Bible through.

W. L. Hillhouse attended the Presbyterian Assembly in Chattanooga, Mr. and Mrs. H. F. Ferguson attended the Baptist Convention in Dalton and in July, a missionary meeting in Dalton had the following representation from Calhoun: Major Aaron Roff, Miss Flora McDaniel, Mrs. B. M. Harlan, Mrs. H. C. Erwin, Misses Ida Harlan, Mary Harlan, Emma Barrett and Lula Brogdon.

Honor students in the school for the past term are: Eva Cantrell, Howard Findley, Pauline Rankin, Nettie Fields, Dora Cantrell, Barrett Boaz, Wilburn Hubbard, Cornelia Cantrell, George Rankin, Henry Tate, Maggie Kiker and Jessie Lewis. Maude Ballew and Grace McConnell received medals in music and the music class presented a beautiful silver card receiver to the music teacher, Mrs. J. I. Ingrahm.

In August, the Confederate Veterans meet to organize with Major G. W. Wells as president, T. M. Ellis is secretary and J. T. Black, J. A. Jarvis, H. C. Hunt and J. H. Bridges appointed to draft by-laws.

Heavy rains have damaged the streets and sidewalks and the ditch across the street needs a bridge. Collections of $2,100,349 have made a good showing after the disasters. The fire alone cost $30,000.

Gordon County needs a race track and the best place for it is in the western part of town. The talk about a clock for the courthouse continues and the county board will either decide to put a clock in the tower or leave it to the bats and owls.

Charters have been granted for 4 new railroads through Gordon County. Surely some of them will be built. The day is not far off when there will be a road through Snake Creek Gap.

Mayor Cantrell is making improvements on his residence & Mr. L. N. Jones is building a residence on College street beyond L. L. Reeves. J. M. Douglas is building a veranda to Hines and King's store with steps going up from the sidewalk in front.

In October, The Calhoun Times office will move to the second story of J. M. Ballew's new brick building on Railroad Street. Hall and Bros. Store has been selected as a depository for the Bible Society. Here you can get Bibles at low prices.

Messrs. Logan and Haney have let the contract for a new livery stable 45 x 90 feet. McGinnis and Fain have laid brick pavements in front of their stores. If other storeowners would do the same, the town would have paved walks without cost to the people.

Dr. Chastine has bought Dr. Malone's drugstore and the Malone family has moved to Atlanta.

H. J. Roff announces the opening of his ice cream parlor where, for 10¢ a serving, you may buy chocolate, almond, tutti-frutti and strawberry ice creams, Roman and Kirsch punch and all flavors of sherbets.

Miss Mamie Pitt's school at McHenry closed with Mary Egan, Nettie and Bessie Fields, Alton McDaniel and Emma Love as honor students.

May Hudgens won the medal in Miss Lulie Pitts' music class. She now has 3 and her superior attainments in the divine art are well known in our music loving little city.

The county Commissioners have passed an act to abolish all ferries and build bridges at the crossing. The Post Office has been cut off from McKnight's drugstore and the entrance is now on Railroad street.

Mr. Dowling, contractor, began the work of tearing down the old courthouse on March 11, 1889. A smoothing plane was found in one of the columns supporting the front, evidently left there by a workman 35 years ago. It is in good condition and cuts as if it had just come from the grindstone.

The contract for the bookshelves and vaults for the Courthouse has been given to R. H. Morrison of Rochester, N. Y. The 400 shelves and files are entirely of metal and there will be no danger of fire. An Atlanta firm has secured the contract for draining the Courthouse for $300. A sewer will run all around the building and empty into the ditch across the front. Mr. Dowling opened a kiln of 160,000 bricks Tuesday, the best in the state, which will be used for the outside of the Courthouse. The county commissioners are making plans for a grand time when the cornerstone is laid.

The Pompeii entertainment in Atlanta was a grand sight. Among Calhoun citizens going to see the spectacle were: J. M. Ballew, Miss Maude Ballew, C. O. Boaz, B. M. Harlan, Dr. W. B. McKnight, Bay Dyer, W. A. Holland, Miss Bessie Fain and Judge J. C. Fain.

Charley Nelson, of Sugar Valley, W. J. Campbell and J. J. McElreath went on an excursion to Texas. Mr. H. C. Byrom has returned from Florida. Dr. and Mrs. J. H. Reeve, of Atlanta, are visiting friends and Col. J. J. Haney and Mr. J. H. Dobbs, of Cartersville, are visiting the family of T. A. Haney.

Captain Joe McConnell, who suffered a stroke 5 years ago, is an invalid from paralysis and nearly blind. To one who knew him 10 years ago as an active and progressive lawyer, his condition brings a feeling of sadness and sympathy. Captain McConnell was one of the Confederacy's bravest soldiers, commanding a company in the 4th Georgia. He was in the night surprise on Fort Steadman & was shot down & left a prisoner. He lost a leg and received 5 other wounds in this battle.

Mr. J. A. Middleton has returned to Nashville, where he has a position on the Daily American, after a visit to relatives. Joe received his first instructions in The Times' office and we are always interested in his progress as a newspaper man.

Plainville shipped over $1000 worth of peaches this summer. The last barroom has gone from Plainville and that village is again free from the vile influence of the whiskey traffic.

Gordon County made enough corn this summer to last 3 years. The streets were packed with cotton wagons Saturday when 150 bales sold at 9½¢. A 16 wagon train of cotton came in from Fairmount on Monday. It made a very impressive sight. The depot at Resaca burned with all contents lost, including 18 bales of cotton and

Stewart's $2000 stock of goods was lost when their store at Redbud burned.

Mr. G. L. Peacock has sold his stock of goods to J. A. Dobbs of Cartersville. Mr. C. C. Harlan has sold his residence to J. B. F. Harrell and will buy a lot and build in the spring. Mr. J. M. Ballew is building another residence on his lot on River street (now the Moody home). Mrs. Mell Cameron has built a handsome cottage at McDaniels and will live there.

Marriages during the year were: Mr. T. G. Brewer and Miss Mollie Bennett, Wednesday, Feb. 20, Mr. E. L. Parrott and Miss Rosa Howard of N. C., Mr. Will Swain and Miss Annie Steele, minister, Rev. J. J. S. Callaway, Mr. W. B. Kiker and Miss Mary Tate at Blue Springs, Mr. J. S. Edge and Miss Mattie E. Graham, at Sugar Valley, Mr. Sam Mansell and Miss Emma Pyrom at Fairmount.

Beloved citizens taken by death were E. W. Engrahm, former editor of The Calhoun Times, W. M. Scott of Plainville and Captain Joe McConnell who died at the home of his sister, Mrs. A. J. Barrett.

Stay now upon the hills of Gordon, Time, and turn backward in your flight. See the years of beginning, the years of war and its aftermath and the period of struggle between evil and good. Bless the religious revival of the 1870s and make note of the eventful 1880s with the biggest flood, the most destructive storm, the deepest snow and the most consuming fire.

Forty years in the valleys of Gordon, living on manna from the fields, casting out the molten calf, reaching for the promised land— may your children rest, O Father Abraham?

Not yet, my son, there are 10 more seals to open, there are 10 more years to spend until the spinning wheels roll in another century.

COURTHOUSE, RAILROAD, BANK, AND A BRASS BAND
(1890-91)

Walk about Zion! Go round about her, consider her palaces and tell it to the generations to come. Walk about the springs in the valleys that run around the hills of Gordon and it shall be said of you "this man was born there."

But do not weep by the rivers of Gordon, nor yet hang your harp on a willow tree for her people have walked in the midst of storm and fire and flood and have triumphed greatly. They have considered the ways of the ant, that she was wise, and the fruit is sweet to taste, but it is not yet time to sit down in the shade of the trees.

The trumpet sounds a stirring call upon the hills for in the valleys the places of her tents must be enlarged.

The telegraph flashes it, every man speaks of it, every mail train on the W & A brings a report of it—it's no moonshine, the Fort Payne and Eastern railroad will be built and it will come from Summerville through Snake Creek Gap to Calhoun and on to Fairmount and Gainesville.

An old engine from the Central road has been standing on the sidetrack for several weeks and the boys say it is for the Calhoun-Fairmount road.

Let our people see that the railroad is not diverted from its original course. Calhoun has lost several enterprises in the last few

Calhoun, looking north from Doughty building. Foster building right foreground Hill house warehouse, left background, 1892.

years through the indifference of her citizens. Last week, W. R. Rankin, T. M. Ward, M. V. Watts, J. M. Harlan, H. C. Erwin, W. E. Ferguson, W. A. J. Robertson, N. J. Boaz, J. O. Fain, and H. A. Chapman were appointed to the railroad committee.

Calhoun is to have a bank. A northern gentleman was in town recently and proposed to put in $15,000 if Calhoun would raise $10,000. A bill granting a charter has already passed the senate.

The newly organized brass band is under the direction of J. C. House, of Dayton, Tennessee, would be employed to instruct the band. The popular drama, "Cast Upon the World" will be given for benefit of the band and the first concert is scheduled for Christmas week.

The workmen are putting the finishing touches on the new courthouse. Mr. H. M. Wentz, of Chattanooga, who did the graining on window and door facings and wainscoting, finished his work and left on Monday.

Mr. W. H. Parkins, architect, and Mr. W. F. Dowling, contractor, will meet the County Board on January 15 and turn over the new courthouse complete and ready for occupancy. The architectural design and symmetrical proportions of this handsome structure please the eye from every point of view. The arrangement is perfect and a more complete courthouse cannot be found in the state.

Entrance through the vestibule of the tower, which rises to 96 feet on the left hand corner, leads you into a hall running across the front to the stairway in the round tower on the right. Directly through the center is a 10 foot wide hall from which doors open into the various offices.

Passing under the arch on the left, we find a room which may be used for ladies attending court. The rear staircase leads to the jury room. From the front, we climb winding stairs to the courtroom handsomely frescoed and lighted by large windows.

The traverse jury room is on the right and a door behind the judges stand, hidden by a screen, leads to the grand jury room and the judge's private office, all finished in oak and cherry. The tower room on the second floor has a witness room, above this, a belfry and, still higher, a place for a clock.

The building, to which Mr. Dowling has given his personal attention, is strong and substantial from foundation to roof. The Commissioners decided to build wooden steps instead of stone and the contract was given to W. L. Hillhouse for $85.

The County Treasurer, C. C. Harlan, says that the courthouse, costing $14,000 was paid for with cash and the county is out of debt. Superior Court will meet in the new courthouse for the first time in February and if the grand jury will recommend a clock for the tower and the commissioners will put it in, the building will be complete and without a rival in the state. The commissioners are having the old trees cut, the grounds cleared, and the ditch in front filled. The city council is working on sewers, but what about pavements?

Holiday visitors to town were: Miss Laura Wells, an accomplished young lady of Powhatan, Arkansas, guest of her cousin, Miss Nettie Wells on River Street, Prof. F. Johnson and daughter, Miss Kathleen, visiting Mrs. J. A. Dobbs, Mr. Will Rankin, assistant state librarian, Charley Hunt and Jim Boaz from Atlanta.

Mr. H. L. Hall has moved to the house recently purchased of Mr. W. G. Fuller on Rock Street (now Line Street) where he has a comfortable home. Mrs. N. E. Pitts has bought the lot on the north corner of Rock and College Streets from Mr. L. L. Reeve. Mr. M. L. Foster and family have moved to town and are living next to L. L. Reeve. Mr. Maddox, a carpenter and his family, from Resaca, are occupying the Hunt house next to the Baptist church.

Mr. Sinclair Mims is building a neat four room cottage on Mill Street near the gin and B. M. Harlan is making improvements on his house in "Gilt Edge." T. M. Ellis plans to add another story to his house. J. M. Ballew will build two cottages on River Street and J. M. Harlan will erect a handsome two story brick building just below his present stand.

Logan and Haney have added fifteen horses and several new buggies to their livery stable.

New picket fences at G. M. Hunt's and W. F. King's and new window blinds and fences at the Methodist parsonage add much to the appearance of the streets.

Mr. and Mrs. F. L. Dyar gave a delightful entertainment at their new home near the railroad in honor of Mrs. Dyar's sister, Miss Mary Benson.

Mr. Harvey Barrett and sister, Miss Emma, gave a pleasant entertainment Wednesday to a party of young people from town.

The spring term of the Collegiate Institute will begin Monday, January 27. Miss Lulie Pitts has been elected by the trustees to the music department at the college. Miss Lulie has taught music for several years and her pupils always make rapid progress.

Miss Mamie Pitts left Sunday to begin teaching in the public schools of West End, near Atlanta. Miss Mamie is a most accomplished teacher and we congratulate the school. Mr. E. M. Dyer has been elected principal of the Sumach school. Miss Charley Reeve left last week for Brunswick, Georgia where she has accepted a position in the schools as music teacher. She is one of our most popular young ladies and the young people will miss her from social gatherings.

The Cherokee Presbytery will meet at Marietta to receive Mr. John Temple Graves of Rome, and Mr. Mark Matthews, of Calhoun, into the ministry.

Rev. W. M. Dyer at the Baptist and Rev. L. P. Winter at the Methodist churches are preaching able and interesting sermons. The Baptist pastor was assisted in a series of meetings by Rev. B. M. Pack of S. C. The colored Methodists will soon begin to rebuild their church which was destroyed by the cyclone two years ago.

Captain W. M. Dyer and J. A. Hall are attending the Baptist Convention in Texas and will tour the state before returning home. Rev. L. P. Winter, Mrs. L. R. Wilson and Miss Julia McDaniel attended the state Sunday School Convention at Thomasville. Major A. Roff and Misses Emma Barrett, Nettie Wells, and Nettie McDaniel were delegates to the International Sunday School Association at Pittsburgh, Pennsylvania.

Vandals are breaking out the street lamps. Two Calhoun boys were fined two dollars by the Resaca Council for swinging the trains.

Dorse Bonner is in charge of J. M. Ballew's billiard table since he bought a half interest and the ten pin alley over Fain and Turner's store is enjoying a liberal patronage.

Calhoun has had summer visitors for a number of years. This summer's guests at the Calhoun Hotel are: Mr. H. J. DeBondio and wife, Miss Adele DeBondio, Miss Armide DeBondio and Mr. W. De-Bondio of New Orleans.

Uncle Billy Bailey, now 81, came to Calhoun long before the Indians left and had many dealings with them, trading goods for furs, gold, silver and other precious metals, of which they seemed to have an inexhaustible supply. He says that to tell the location of the metals was punished with death and, try as he would, he could never learn the location, except for a nod toward the Oostanaula river. He tried them with whiskey, making them drunk, with presents, and all the persuasive power of his nature, but they departed with their secret and no man has ever been able to locate the hidden treasure.

Tim Haney claims to have found a lead mine of immense proportions near town and the ore is free from dirt but he has locked the secret within his breast and refuses to divulge the location.

Confederate veterans have organized an Association, called Camp Joe McConnell. In August, they met, 500 strong, in Calhoun.

The 8th Battalion line formed in front of the Calhoun Hotel, headed by the Marietta Silver Cornet Band, and marched to the Grove where they heard addresses by Col. John W. Gray of Adairsville, Col. S. P. Mattox, of Dalton, and Col. W. R. Rankin and Judge J. C. Fain of Calhoun. The veterans partook of a big feast prepared by the ladies of Calhoun and vicinity. The next meeting will be at Resaca in August, 1891.

T. A. Haney recently bought the Harlan place from J. B. F. Harrell and the Fite and Tinsley places from N. J. Boaz. He sold his interest in the livery stable to Mrs. S. E. Haynes and first planned to enter the oil business, later buying an interest in W. F. King's store. King and Haney have made many improvements in their store.

The church was beautifully decorated about the pulpit and chancel for the wedding of Mr. Logan Pitts and Miss Flora McDaniel. At 8:30, the father and mother of the bride walked down the aisle and took their places at the right. The minister then took his place, followed by the ushers, Mr. J. W. Logan and Dr. R. M. Harbin, who stood on either side of center.

The flower girls, Misses Lucy Freeman and Virgin McDaniel came in, then the bride and groom. Rev. Mark Matthews performed the ceremony, assisted by Rev. L. P. Winter. After the wedding, an elegant reception was given at the home of the groom's mother.

Another summer wedding of interest was that of Mr. T. W. Harbin and Miss Ida Harlan which took place at the home of the bride's father, Judge J. M. Harlan on Wednesday, June 25. Attendants were: Mr. G. I. Harlan and Miss Lula Brogdon, Dr. R. M. Harbin, and Miss Stella Ewing, Mr. Tom Ewing, and Miss Mattie Boyd, Dr. W. B. McKnight, and Miss Stella Munsey. The wedding party stood in a semi-circle with the bride and groom in the center. The ministers were Revs. L. P. Winter and M. A. Matthews. After the ceremony, the guests were invited into the dining room where an elegant feast was spread before them. Mr. and Mrs. Harbin took the train for South Carolina to visit relatives of the groom.

Tom Harbin is one of the foremost young men of the county. Educated at the State University, he returned to the farm of Dr. W. R. Harbin which he has managed with great success.

Miss Ida Harlan, a most excellent young lady, was educated at Shorter College, graduating with honor. She has that womanly grace and charm of manner which win for her friends in every circle. May their lucky star always be in the ascendant.

Judge Lewis announces that the semi-annual Singing Convention will be held at Fairmount the third Saturday and Sunday in July.

The L & N has bought the W & A railroad for $35,000 per month for twenty-nine years.

For the September term of court, Mr. J. H. Brownlee, of Plainville, is foreman of the grand jury. We hope that Gordon County will never again have four murder trials in one week, as in this term of court.

Whitfield County went dry this year, now Gordon is the only county on the W & A where whiskey can legally be sold.

John Logan and Col. E. J. Kiker say they will each give $100 toward the building of a race track. A few more like these will build the finest race track in the state. Col. Kiker has sold his Percheron stallion, Fandango, to Mr. Bates, of Murray County and Dr. Harbin has sold his fine young horse to a gentleman in Atlanta.

Mr. L. L. Reeves big white bull dog went mad and took in the town, biting dogs owned by Mrs. Foster, Mrs. Matthews, W. D. Fain, G. W. Wells, J. C. Harkins, P. N. Beard, J. M. Ballew and Bud Turner. When last seen, the dog was headed toward the river.

Mr. H. J. Roff has given up his position with the Shellman house at Cartersville and returned to Calhoun to reside. He will establish a chicken farm on ten acres of ground near town, and will raise chickens for the market, using incubators.

Mr. and Mrs. H. A. Chapman left Tuesday to attend the Press Association at Augusta. Later, they will visit Tampa, Key West, and Havana.

The steamer, John T. Warlick, received three passengers for Rome at this place last week.

Dr. J. H. Malone will return to Calhoun, having purchased Dr. W. B. McKnight's drug store. We welcome the doctor to his old home.

Mr. James A. Hall, now serving as city reporter on the Rome Tribune, is adding lustre to that department of the paper.

E. M. Dyer, H. J. Barrett and Will Watts have been admitted to the bar.

The Aramanthine literary society has been organized to meet each Friday afternoon at the Calhoun Collegiate Institute, with Miss Maggie Thornton as president, Miss Julia McDaniel, as secretary and Miss Fannie Ellis as vice-president. The school is progressing nicely and will soon have all modern school aids; charts, globes, maps, numeral frames, arithmetical blocks, etc.

A cooking club, the S. L. D., has been organized and will meet twice a month when each member brings a dish. The motive is to improve the members' cooking. The words for which the letters stand are a complete mystery. The young men are sour and call them Selfish Little Devils. But, in December, these same young men tendered a grand banquet to the S. L. D. club at the Calhoun Hotel when all Calhoun society attended. In the brilliantly illuminated dining room, graceful vines were festooned about the chandeliers and the festal board was laden with dainties rich in profusion. "To Young Men, Their Trials" was the toast given by Col. H. P. Barrett, with response by Miss Maude McDaniel. "Our Women" by Rev. M. A. Matthews with response by Miss Bessie Fain followed the first toast.

The next week, the S. L. D. Club met to adopt a pledge to keep the name a secret and to admit no new members.

Mr. J. A. Fields took out of the water wheel at the mill one day 195 pounds of eels and on another day, 165 pounds.

An election is to be held on whether the hog should be allowed privileges of the town. Two or three hundred hogs on the streets are a nuisance. A town ordinance to confine the cows goes into effect next week.

A bill to start public schools has passed the Legislature. M. E. Ellis, secretary of the Council, says that the taxable property is $200,-000.

Calhoun received 185 bales of cotton Wednesday. To handle that many is a big day's work for a town of this size.

Rev. Simeon Shaw, a former pastor of the Methodist Church, is now a missionary in Japan.

A disturbing report is going around that there was a republican on the Committee sent to the Democratic Convention. This was stoutly denied by county officials.

1891

The Farmers' Alliance is a leading organization in this year of 1891 and The Calhoun Times becomes the official organ of the Alliance. H. A. Chapman begins the year as proprietor but, in January, sells the paper to W. W. Wilson, J. A. Hall, and J. W. Ingram.

At the Ocala, Florida meeting, the Alliance had adopted a platform asking for abolition of national banks, insisting that Congress pass laws to prevent dealing in futures and condemning the silver bill passed by Congress. A demand for passage of a law prohibiting alien ownership and rigid governmental control of all public communications and transportation, together with a petition not to build up one industry at the expense of another formed other planks in the platform.

But the question uppermost in the minds of Calhoun citizens was whether to have public schools or not and M. E. Ellis, secretary of the City Council, had set January 5 as election day.

Editor H. A. Chapman is concerned over the lack of houses in town and the fact that rents are higher here than in either Dalton or Cartersville.

The Postmistress, Mrs. Ida Johntson, was almost ousted by a Republican last week but W. R. Rankin, J. M. Ballew, and E. J. Kiker went down to Atlanta and persuaded the Republican to take another job and the popular Postmistress stayed on. Later, Miss Edith Ransome became her assistant.

While the men are occupied with weighty questions, the women find time to visit and entertain. Miss Dessie Taylor, of Atlanta, is the guest of Mrs. G. M. Hunt, Miss Laura Haynes is visiting in Smithville and Miss Cora Turley, of Knoxville, is Mrs. Ida Johnston's visitor.

Miss May Haynes left last week to visit Miss Charley Reeve in Brunswick.

Mr. J. M. Wright is back from Texas. He was delighted with the state but likes Georgia better.

Misses Lucy Freeman and Maude Ballew entertained their friends at Mr. C. C. Harlan's.

Mr. and Mrs. F. L. Dyar gave a royal feast in honor of their guests, Misses Benson and Parham Monday evening. The supper was indeed a feast for the gods and was enjoyed by a large party of young people.

The Sugar Valley Methodist Church, beautifully decorated, was the scene of a brilliant wedding on December 31, 1890, when Mr. John F. Harris and Miss Martha Cooley were married with Rev. Mark Matthews performing the ceremony. Mr. John Cooley and Miss May Harris and Mr. Lee Cooley and Miss Maggie Thornton were the attendants.

The groom came in with Mr. Charley Herrington and the bride with her sister, Miss Georgia Cooley. The wedding party returned to the home of the bride's mother, Mrs. Cooley, where a sumptuous repast was served.

The couple will make their home in Selma, Alabama. The groom is one of Gordon County's most industrious young men and the bride one of Sugar Valley's prettiest and most accomplished young ladies.

Mrs. H. B. McEntyre is visiting her father, Mr. Y. J. Malone at Sugar Valley. Mr. and Mrs. McEntyre were recently married by Rev. M. A. Matthews.

Calhoun is the leading woman's rights city of the South—what other place has got a S.L.D. (Sweet Little Darlings) Society? The young men are thinking of organizing a Bachelors' Protective Union and the S.L.D. is thinking of forming an emmigration association.

The S.L.D. Club had an especial dress affair Tuesday night at J. B. Boyd's which surpassed anything ever attempted by the club. The S.L.D. continues to grow and the young men expect much from this organization.

Prof. J. C. House, W. B. Haynes and Lucius Frix made a pedestrian tour to Resaca Sunday.

Tuesday was sale day and an unusually large crowd was in town to see the Foster building on the north corner of Court and Broad Streets bought by Col. W. G. Foster for $3,750. The building has been occupied for a number of years by J. M. Harlan and Co.

Stock is being sold for the Fort Payne and Eastern railroad company and the bank is an assured fact.

We cannot afford brick pavements. We couldn't afford street lights two years ago, but we did. Everyone knows that our sidewalks would not take the prize at the World's Fair. There is no place for any kind of entertainment. It is hoped that some public spirited citizen will soon move.

He who is willing to join his neighbors in a public enterprise is more to be desired than he who painteth the town red or wears the frock coat on Sunday. If the people of Calhoun don't build up Calhoun, who will?

The Grand Jury finds that the records are neatly and correctly kept but that the burnt room at the jail should be replaced and bars and locks put in good order.

The roads are in a bad condition and the county needs a better system of road work. Wanted—a new road law, any kind.

Also, there is a lack of comfortable school buildings and the Grand Jury recommends that citizens in the various districts get together and build houses.

Mr. C. C. Harlan, County Treasurer, reports that the county has collected $10,880.75 from liquor, jail, road, and office fees and from cotton sold.

Mr. J. N. Kiker now talks across the mountain to laborers on his farm by telephone and Mr. B. M. Harlan has run a line from his store to his house.

The W & A railroad announces that no more passengers will be allowed on freights. This has knocked the way-freight connection with the Rome express at Kingston in the head.

The W & A fare has been changed to three cents a mile. The fare to Atlanta is now $2.30 and to Chattanooga $1.80. The depot has been improved by moving the ticket office nearer the front and making a waiting room of the old office.

Keep your eye on the Cornet Band. It still surprises Calhounites by improvements. Prof. J. C. House, who has directed the band for three months left last week for Wisconsin.

Calhoun is a hummer any way you put it.

Mr. J. E. Curtiss has commenced the manufacture of wagons and buggies. W. L. Hillhouse and J. H. Legg have formed a building and contracting business and M. M. Caldwell and Co. of Chattanooga have opened a dry goods store in J. N. Patrick's glass front store.

Mr. L. R. Pitts will in the near future commence erection of a handsome residence on the corner of Rock Street (Line) and College Avenue. Hillhouse and Legg are building an elegant residence on Broad Street, opposite N. H. McGinnis' new house, for H. K. Hicks and also a residence for E. J. Simmons.

Mr. L. G. Bradbury is doing some of the finest painting ever seen on N. H. McGinnis' house. Some of the rooms are finished in hard varnish, very beautiful.

J. M. Ballew will improve the recently purchased old Gresham house. F. L. Dyar will build on the lot below Boaz's building and Col. F. A. Cantrell has bought the lot next to C. O. Boaz.

Mr. J. H. Legg will build an elegant five room dwelling on his lot next to J. M. Neal's residence. Mr. W. J. McDaniel has bought the Pulliam house and the lot adjoining the Methodist church. J. B. F. Harrell will erect a fine residence on the lot next to the Baptist church and Mr. J. C. Harkins plans to remodel.

If anything under the sun keeps a town growing, it is men who are not afraid to put their money in real estate. The future of Calhoun cannot be contemplated without a sense of extreme satisfaction. Look back five years to a ramshackle crossroads village and compare the energetic and ambitious young city of today. An entirely new and costly system of public buildings has taken the place of rotten and decayed pretenses. There are stronger, better, more city-like dwellings everywhere. Five years ago, there was no cotton market, now 4500 bales a season are sold. Calhoun has gone through some great conflicts, but has come out nerved for greater conflicts and hungry for greater victories. We want no boom. We will have none. We want the same honest, persevering work that we have been having. (Ed. J. A. Hall).

Mr. B. M. Blackburn writes in the Atlanta Constitution "Glorious Calhoun, the coming City of North Georgia, rich and rare in possibilities, with the most refined and cultured people."

The men who hurt a town are those who oppose improvements, never push their business, run down the town to strangers or envy their neighbors' prosperity.

County schools are in good shape. Prof. Dickey began the term in Calhoun with 100 scholars but resigned in September because of ill health and returned to his home in Sugar Valley. Bannie Hillhouse has a flourishing school at Sugar Valley and Miss Fannie Fields is teaching a school near Oothcaloga mills.

Mrs. W. L. Hines has resumed her music class. All who are interested in instruction on piano, organ, or guitar, please see her.

"What has become of the Calhoun Collegiate Institute? A charter was granted in 1884 for twenty years for educational purposes only. The Institute belongs to the people. The trustees have employed a man to teach in the building. He calls it The Calhoun High School and proposes to prepare pupils for college. Have the trustees a right to degrade the school in this manner?"

Signed "Populi".

The owls have a delightful place in the clock tower.

The city has received a load of terra cotta pipe from Chattanooga and will put a force of hands to work laying sewers throughout the city. The thirteen new gasoline lamps will be put in the business section and the old oil lamps scattered over the city. New brick pavements are being laid.

The Council recently called a meeting to discuss violations of the beer laws. A burning temperance sermon, preached by Rev. M. A. Matthews at Ringgold, was printed in "The New South," Ringgold newspaper, last week. Townspeople, greatly stirred, said that Matthews was scathing them like the burning efforts of Sam Jones.

A whiskey law, passed by the Legislature and signed by Governor Northern, will stop the sale of whiskey in all parts of Gordon County.

What will be done with the owl holes in the courthouse tower?

Did you ever—hear F. A. Cantrell sing a solo? See anybody go to sleep in church?

Do you know—who the two young ladies are who have been proposed to? Who the young lady is who stirs up a racket in the cooking club?

They say—that John Logan is trying to buy him a dwelling house. That T. A. Haney has a recipe for reducing his children's board bill.

Pay your store bills, your preacher, and your subscription.

Do you wear pants? Get them at Hall Bros. Do you wear a straw hat? Get one at Hall Bros.

Dr. J. H. Malone's drug store was robbed. The window was broken out with a large lump of coal and $100 worth of goods taken. Robbers also visited Ferguson's store, taking money and valuable papers and setting a fire in the back of the building. Except for the quick work of the bucket brigade, Calhoun might have repeated the sad experience of 1888 when half the town was burned.

Henry Roff is having great success with his incubated chickens.

Dink Offutt has a fine blooded horse for sale. You can buy him cheap.

Jinks Fain's fine blooded horse is ahead of all movers. He can do a mile in 1:10.

Si Tweedle has returned to his home in Sugar Valley after several months in South Georgia. John Linn, who has been living in Texas for several years is now living in Gordon County.

CHURCH CALENDAR

Presbyterian—Mark A. Matthews, Pastor
Services on 4th Sundays
Sunday School Superintendent, W. L. Hillhouse
Baptist—Rev. B. M. Pack Pastor
Services on 2nd and 4th Sundays
Sunday School Superintendent, W. L. Hines
Methodist—L. P. Winter, Pastor
Services on 1st and 3rd Sundays
Sunday School Superintendent, T. M. Ellis

The Christian Endeavor Society with 25 members meets alternately with the three churches.

A beautiful new chandelier has been received at the Baptist church. The pastor preached a strong and pointed sermon Sunday.

There were 75 converts in a meeting at Blackwood when Revs. Pitts and Austin were preaching.

Mr. T. A. Haney attended the Sam Jones meeting in Cartersville Sunday. Everybody in town is thinking of going.

Misses Julia McDaniel and Mary Hill and Major Aaron Roff and Prof. A. E. Lashley left Tuesday for Columbus to attend the State Sunday School Convention.

The Conference of the Ladies Missionary Society met at the Methodist church here. A committee met all trains and carried the delegates to the homes assigned to them. On Friday night, the Conference members were entertained by the Calhoun Society and the children of the church. Miss Emma Barrett gave the address of welcome with response by Mrs. W. A. Robertson of Dalton. The District Secretary, Miss Hattie M. Gibbons, was introduced by Mrs. B. M. Harlan. Miss Belle Bennett, of Scarritt College, and Miss Mattie Jones, a missionary to Brazil, were the featured speakers.

During the Stanton tent revival, there were 100 conversions and 50 joined the church. It was a great thing for Calhoun.

The Calhoun Times carried a picture in a recent issue of the popular young pastor of the Presbyterian church, Rev. Mark A. Matthews. The broad high brow, crowned with waving dark hair, the thin, delicate-featured face picture the high intellect that was to lead Mark Matthews on to become the pastor of the biggest Presbyterian church in the world at Seattle, Wash.

He is said to resemble Dr. J. B. Hawthorne, a distinguished Atlanta minister. Many years ago, Mark Matthews threw himself into the work of the ministry and is widely known at an age when most men are selecting a calling. He owns an extensive library. He speaks fluently and eloquently, sometimes using a manuscript, but often using none. Numerous and flattering calls have come to this young minister, but he has decided to stay in Calhoun at least another year.

The bank charter has been accepted and subscription books opened with a capital stock of $25,000. Directors of the bank are D. Livermore, D. H. Livermore, N. J. Boaz, B. G. Boaz, H. F. Ferguson, and J. H. Gordon. The new bank will occupy, for the first month, the north room in the Boaz building near the railroad, one of the best in Calhoun. (Rankin-Norton house) The bank is one of the safest and best equipped in North Georgia. A time lock of the most improved style has been put on the vault.

Now for that City Clock.

When will Calhoun ever have enough houses for her people to live in?

Mr. J. H. Doughty, of Texas, has formed a real estate agency with offices in the Harrell building.

Mr. F. L. Dyar now rides in a handsome new turnout.

Straw rides, picnics to Barnesley's Gardens and camps at Co-hutta Springs keep the young people entertained during the summer months. An ice cream supper, given by Misses Fannie and Kittie Ellis to their friends, a tea and croquet party at the home of Miss Minnie Clark, the Donkey Party at Miss Bertha Norton's, Mrs. W. L. Hines' party for the little folks and a tea at Miss Lulie Pitts home were features of the summer social season.

Master Eugene Doughty entertained at the Calhoun Hotel Friday. Misses Bertha Norton and Naoba Cary had a Japanese tea at the Haynes House. Lanterns made the place look like a museum of Jiddo. The hostesses wore Japanese costumes and served ice cream. The Oriental napkins were decorated with strange birds, frogs, and dragons.

Dr. Will Darnell and Miss Mary Garlington will be united in marriage this evening, June 25th at the residence of the bride's mother. Dr. Darnell is a successful physician at Center, Alabama. Miss Garlington is one of Gordon County's most popular belles.

Mrs. T. A. Haney and children are visiting in Cartersville and visitors to Calhoun are Dr. Johnson and Mr. Jesse Johnson of Resaca, W. M. Peeples of Fairmount, J. B. Brownlee of Plainville, and Mr. Alfred Malone of Atlanta.

Mr. and Mrs. Z. T. Gray have returned from a visit to their son, Col. J. A. Gray, in New York. Mrs. W. G. Connor of Birmingham and Mrs. J. E. Tinsley of Hawkinsville are the guests of Mr. and Mrs. J. D. Tinsley.

Mrs. A. L. Hines and son, Richard, have returned from an extended visit to relatives in Statesboro, North Carolina.

Miss Lily Roe has returned from a visit to her aunt at Eads, Tennessee.

Two crates of fine oil paintings received at Hall Bros.

All wool jeans at Halls for 25c.

A well-aimed shot gun applied to a melancholy dog at midnight is what we call a howling success.

Ere long we'll gwie a chestnut hunting o'er the hills of autumn brown.

Mrs. G. W. Wells is dead. She had, while ill herself, nursed a dying friend. Beyond the vale of human sorrow and human griefs, the flower of a pure and beautiful life blooms again, enriched in celestial fragrance in a nobler, fairer garden.

Calhoun is much too large a city now to use wagons to carry the dead to the cemetery. We need an undertaking establishment.

All persons interested in Fain Cemetery will meet at Hines and King's store to talk over improvements.

Describing his trip to Lake Ponchetrain, W. B. Haynes writes. "a blue-eyed nymph and I were tripping smoothly on the pebbly path, the mocking bird was chirping your name. Ah, the melodious chord, the sweet lullaby, wafted by summer breezes, billowed by golden atmosphere, murmur to me like a Southern sunny dream, on the silvery, lucid waves of the lake and we could discern the hues of nature on her dreamy lull of magnetic recluse".

Plans for Mr. D. H. Livermore's new house, erected on the lot bought from C. C. Harlan, were drawn by a New York architect. Work was started in July and now, in October, it stands finished, a beauty, and one of the finest residences in the city.

Broad Street, in the vicinity of the churches, is fast becoming noted for its stately residences. Mr. and Mrs. C. C. Harlan are domiciled in their new house which is one of the handsomest buildings in North Georgia.

Mr. W. L. Hillhouse has about completed his new warehouse and is doing a rushing business. The W & A railroad would complete a side track to the warehouse by next year.

Honorables J. M. Harlan and J. H. Swain are at home after a long and tedious session of the Legislature.

Rev. Ben L. Hunt of Walker County was in the city Tuesday.

Mr. and Mrs. B. M. Harlan celebrated their tin wedding Tuesday night, receiving numerous tin presents. Calhoun has seen but few finer tables and more sumptuous feasts than the elegant supper served at 9 o'clock. Afterwards the company repaired to the parlor for conversation and social reunion.

Get your Christmas oranges at D. Westfield's

Cards are out for a high dinner to be given by the Y M D Club in honor of the young ladies of Calhoun at the Haynes House on December 23rd. This dinner is supposed to outswell all the previous swells in Calhoun.

Mr. Chas. P. Nelson, of Sugar Valley, and Miss Mattie Kay, of McHenry, will be united in marriage at the residence of the bride's father, Mr. W. M. Kay. The ceremony will be performed by the Rev. J. J. S. Calloway, of Dalton. It will be a rather quiet wedding with only a few relatives present. Mr. Nelson and Miss Kay are well known and have lots of friends who are extending best wishes.

Mr. Lee Cooley and Miss May Harris were married on Sunday, December 27, with Rev. J. W. Gober performing the ceremony.

Social events of the Christmas season were: a Christmas tree at J. H. Legg's, sociables at the Haynes House and the Calhoun Hotel, a dinner at Mrs. R. L. McWhorter's at McHenry, a sociable at the home of Misses Fannie and Kittie Ellis and a dinner at the Resaca home of Miss Emma Hill when the guests from Calhoun were Mr. and Mrs. J. W. Logan, Miss Laura Haynes, W. B. Haynes, and G. L. Harlan.

Mr. W. H. McDaniel has moved his family to town and is domiciled in the house recently vacated by Rev. B. M. Pack.

Hackett McConnell has gone to visit in Alabama.

Miss Mary Boaz left Monday for LaGrange to resume her studies in the Southern Female College of that city.

THE DOUGHTY BUILDING, OUTLAWS AND WHITE CAPS

Wanted — bids to furnish and lay brick for a three story building in Calhoun. For further particulars see H. J. Doughty. When erected on the Reeves and Malone corner, this will be the finest building in the city.

Progress of work on the Doughty building, the marauding gang of outlaws and midnight stalking White Caps are the news features that headline the Calhoun Times as the new editors, John H. Harkins and W. W. Wilson, take over in March of 1892.

The heavy snow in January was followed by rain and the Oostanaula River rose. However, few expected a flood like that of 1886. For a while it looked as if the wagon bridge across the river would be swept away but it was tied with ropes and men were stationed on the bridge to keep off logs and driftwood. Trains were pulled over the trestle below town by three freight engines.

A pleasant pound party at the country home of Mr. P. M. Craig and a leap year party at the home of T. M. Ellis enlivened the spirits of the young people.

An entertaining singing was given by Miss Sallie Rice at Fairmount.

Miss Edna Pulliam left Monday for Fairmount to take charge of the music class.

Mr. Henry Pittman, a popular musician, sang in the Fairmount church Sunday.

Mr. D. T. Tanner found on the street in Calhoun an old copper Canadian coin dated 1861.

The spring term of the Collegiate Institute will be in charge of Prof. J. J. S. Callaway with Miss Mattie Boyd and Miss Louise Willis as assistants. Prof. Callaway and family are located in the Boaz brick building.

Miss Azile Jones is teaching at Resaca and Miss Fields has a school at Boston Grove near Resaca.

Mr. W. C. Mitchell, of Blackton, Alabama, and Miss Mattie Hyde were married at Sugar Valley on Wednesday, January 20 by the Rev. J. W. Gober.

Mrs. Eliza Garlington of Reeves Station died in January at the age of 92. She was well known, being related to some of the most prominent families in this section.

John W. Gray died at his home after a brief illness of heart trouble. He was born in 1861 and had lived all his life in Gordon County except for two years in Atlanta. He was married to Miss Lucy Sayre about 12 years ago and they have four interesting children.

Mr. Damascus Reeves, of St. Louis, arrived last week to spend some time with Mr. and Mrs. A. W. Reeves who are quite ill. Mr. A. W. Reeves died at the residence of Mrs. Dillard later in the year.

Revs. J. J. S. Callaway and M. A. Matthews conducted the funeral. Mr. Reeves came to this section in 1838, helped to lay the W & A railroad and was active in building in Calhoun and Gordon County.

Mr. James M. Kay, 78, died at Salem and Col. E. J. Kiker is very sick with the terrible grippe.

Bailiff James Kell, 70 years old, of Gordon Superior Court, has been a bailiff longer than he can remember. He has never worn a pair of boots, never bought a suit of clothes, and never had on a collar or neck tie. He is a great smoker and his pipe is his constant companion.

Rev. John C. Rogers and wife, of Quitman, have moved to Calhoun. Mr. Rogers is a Baptist of the old school and will preach at Harmony Sunday.

The fine river plantation of J. N. F. Neal has been sold to Mr. Joseph F. Allison, of Cartersville.

Mr. J. E. Curtiss is occupying his handsome new residence on Wall Street and Mr. J. H. Legg has moved into his new house on River Street.

Two tintypes for 25c at the Calhoun Photo Gallery.

Mr. W. F. King will at once begin erection of a handsome new dwelling on the lot recently purchased from Col. F. A. Cantrell. This lot is the prettiest location in town, being on the line of beautiful water oaks running north from the Baptist Church. In June Mr. A. B. Gregg of Dalton would complete this residence and an elegant one for W. R. Rankin.

Mr. N. H. McGinnis is finishing an elegant hall and office apartments over his brick store. The stairway will run up from the front entrance of the store.

All right, gentlemen, we are quite ready for that sidewalk!

Calhoun is growing; can't you tell it? Calhoun is booming; don't you know it? She is fast becoming a town of beautiful residences and in a short time has earned for herself recognition as one of the most rapidly growing little cities on the W & A.

Calhoun is to have a fire engine. The bucket brigade is a thing of the past. The powerful engine is mounted on a four wheel carriage that has two brass lanterns, a sixty gallon copper tank and a force pump. Three men can set the engine, lay off 100 feet of hose and have it working in one minute. There is also a hook and ladder wagon, carrying a 16 foot roof ladder, an extension ladder, two pipe poles, twelve buckets, and one lantern.

Town officials built a temporary house down near the depot, to be used as a fire test for the engine. Later the citizens voted against buying the engine, so the bucket brigade continues to function.

At 2 o'clock Friday morning, pistol shots and cries of "Fire!" roused most of Calhoun's people from their dreaming. The beautiful little home of Mr. Matt Ellis was in flames. Most of the furniture was saved but valuable papers were lost with the house.

In the hour after midnight on a Wednesday in September, the engineer on train No. 13 discovered fire at the beautiful residence of W. G. Fuller. The whistle on the section engine joined that of No. 13 but no one roused. Trainsmen broke down the door and found Mr. Fuller and his two little boys sleeping soundly. Swinging their lanterns, the men yelled, "Get up quick, your house is burning up!"

then grabbed the boys, bed and all and rushed out. Most of the things were saved but the beautiful old house that stood for several decades in the grove of trees is gone.

Calhoun has acquired a hard reputation in the country and Mark A. Matthews speaks out in a lengthy article defending the little city. "I am tired", writes the Rev. Matthews, "of the ignorant spirit that abuses our beloved town. You simpleton you, the town is what you make it! Calhoun has produced more noble sons and daughters than any town her size. Her intellectual, musical, artistical, and moral talent is great. He is the basest of base who does not love and work for his own home, his native town."

O. C. Engeram, in resigning from the council said, "I didn't like the way things were going. We were not doing our duty."

Our quitting man has quit quitting.

Hon. T. W. Skelly, Calhoun's brilliant orator, will give the Commencement address at Pine Chapel and will speak at Mt. Pleasant Children's Day program.

Prof. Ernest Neal, of Sonoraville, went to Atlanta last week and took part in the reading entertainment at the Fifth Baptist Church. Prof. Neal, a young man of no ordinary ability, will also give an address at the Sunday School Convention in Gordon County.

Rev. M. A. Matthews, pastor of the Presbyterian Church, will deliver a special sermon at 7:00 P M Sunday when he will touch up the officers, blind tigers, and barrooms, etc.

Some men are blessed with a spirit of extreme politeness. One of Calhoun's brilliant attorneys walked down main street and tipped his $5 Stetson to a dummy in front of the millinery store.

Gents underwear $1 — fine shoes $1.50 at Hall Bros.

Col. W. R. Rankin, matchless orator and one of Democracy's purest sons, delivered an address at a political meeting at Sonoraville. Calhoun's splendid brass band, with Henry Roff as leader, gave the citizens a real treat by rendering five or six pieces of choice music.

Prof. C. D. Smith, of Cartersville, is coming to instruct the band for three months.

The W & A is rushing work on the bridge at Resaca. Trains come to a full halt, then proceed at four miles an hour.

Mr. J. M. Neal shipped 15,600 eggs last week and still has on hand 4800.

Two large wild turkeys, weighing 22½ pounds and 15½ pounds, were killed in the county last week and a blue crane, measuring 6½ feet from wing tip to wing tip, was killed on the mill lakes by Cam Jackson.

140 dozen boxes of matches at 10c per dozen — the last I will be able to get — W. M. Hughey.

W. L. Hillhouse's mammoth brick warehouse is doing a rushing business. Farmers know that Calhoun is a good market and Rome no longer gets the thousands of bales of cotton that once were sold there.

Mr. W. L. Hillhouse is improving the sidewalk in front of his house. Laurens, never idle, is always enterprising. Mr. J. M. Ballew is laying a brick sidewalk in front of his residence. By fall, all the principal walks in town would be paved with brick. The walks are smooth, wide and beautiful. One imagines he is in Marietta or on Whitehall. The brick came from Rome.

A new postoffice called Fambro has been established with Jeff French as Postmaster.

White Caps are stalking abroad in the midnight land. They are active in the County but are not thought to be Gordon County men. Thirty White Caps rode through Calhoun Friday night. At Redbud, they whipped four negroes and forced Bailiff Hallum to whip two. They applied the lash to a trifling no good white man and Sugar Valley was threatened by Whitfield County White Caps. Ginners were forbidden to run their gins until cotton was 10c a pound. The gins were shut down for a week.

Fifteen White Caps appeared at the home of Bob McClure, east of town, fired both barrels of a shotgun through the pine front door, then broke down the door and threw turpentine balls in to light up the room. The balls fell on the bed where the children were sleeping and set the bed on fire. McClure was shot and whipped.

The affair was a great surprise to everyone for McClure, a good industrious man, had lived around town for four years, at one time working for Judge Fain. Much indignation was felt among the white people of the community. Later it was learned that the White Caps were really after another negro who had been staying at McClure's.

The Gordon County Teacher's Institute, recently organized, met in Calhoun for five days last week. Over sixty teachers from Bartow Whitfield, and Gordon Counties attended. Prof. W. Harper, Supt. of Americus schools, was in charge of the Institute. Other lecturers were Profs. Dickey, Fulton, Neal, and Kinnamon, Mrs. Fields, Mrs. Floyd, and Miss Mamie Pitts.

The spring term of the Calhoun Collegiate Institute closed without a commencement. Rev. Callaway, principal of the Institute, was, during the school term, accused of unjustly punishing a student. A resolution sustaining him, signed by E. J. Kiker, O. C. Engram, W. D. Fain, C. C. Harlan, and B. G. Boaz, was adopted and printed in the county paper. Mr. E. E. Johnston was elected principal of the Institute to begin with the fall term, but in November he was to resign because of ill health. Prof. Woods, of Sugar Valley, was elected to succeed Prof. Johnson.

Parties of young people go often to Barnsley's Garden, where the serpentine walks, flowers and fountains make it an ideal place to dream away a summer day.

Chaperoned by Mr. and Mrs. C. P. Nelson and Mr. and Mrs. Will Harbour, a group of Sugar Valley young people enjoyed a picnic in The Pocket, that picturesque valley lying between John's and Harn's Mountains in the western part of Gordon County. Members of the picnic party were: Misses Edna Bell, Ettie Chandler, Agnes Moss, Battie Black, Ida Warren, Stella Haynes, Hattie Wright, of Rome, Messers Frank and Will Swain, Tom Steele, Milton Wright, Oscar Haynes, Lawrence Cooper, and Captain Ivey of the L & N Railroad.

Miss Cora Abbott, of Sugar Valley, left Sunday for an extended visit with friends in Rome and Cedartown.

Mr. J. W. Barrett, of Dalton, spent several days in the city last week as the guest of relatives.

Mr. W. F. Dew, who has been absent from the county for about eight years, arrived in the city last Friday night from Puamo, Michigan.

Miss Viola Wright, a beautiful and accomplished young lady of Rome, is visiting friends in Calhoun.

Mr. and Mrs. Livermore, of Springfield, N. Y. are visiting their son, Mr. D. Howard Livermore, president of our flourishing bank.

Mr. Newton Legg, son of J. H. Legg of our city, is fast coming to the front as a brick mason. He is a young man, in the business only a short while, yet his work will show up with more experienced men.

In April, the Gordon County Singing Convention, met at the Calhoun Baptist Church. Song leaders were Prof. W. H. Alexander, E. W. Keys, A. M. Kay, W. H. Pittman, Joab Lewis, John Harris, J. A. Coley, and Charley Mosteller. Organists were Mrs. W. L. Hines, Mrs. Ida Jhonson, Misses Lulie Pitts, Edna Pulliam, Mary Kay, Lula Brogdon, and May Hudgins. The Fall Convention would be at the Methodist Church.

The Saturday night young men's prayer meeting was an occasion of real spiritual powers. It was a manifest enthusiasm that means much for the uplifting of our fair little city.

Saturday and Sunday were grand days at historic old Shiloh Church at Fairmount. The new building, clean and beautiful, rose from the ashes and presented itself for dedication. Rev. E. M. Stanton, the pastor, had a solemn right to be happy.

The Centennial of Missions has been observed by all Baptist Churches of the County during 1892.

Sunday morning, August the 21, the clouds had winged their way to other climes and the dawn was roseate with crimson kisses that the jolly old king of day was throwing at that queenly old matron, Mother Earth. Everybody was going to the Tabernacle meeting at Wesley Chapel. Calhoun went in wagons, buggies, jump gullies, horse and mule back, and one man was trying to get an ox.

Bishop Fitzgerald preached to a congregation of 2500, dedicating the tabernacle. The collection at the service was $130. W. W. Campbell, W. H. Hardy, J. H. Harmon, R. F. Ellis, and George W. Stewart were members of the building committee. The detailed report of the dedication service was written by Neal Keefe.

Rev. Mark A. Matthews preached on "Indifference" at the Presbyterian Church.

A Children's Centennial service at the Baptist church was highly delightful to all with its recitations and sweet songs. On a Sunday in October, Columbus Day would be observed at the Methodist Church when 400 years of American history were briefly reviewed with special reference to the Christian work that marks these centuries.

Mr. R. S. Abbott is furnishing fruit to Calhoun — peaches, pears, plums, and apples from one of the best orchards in Gordon County and John Wylie, colored, is furnishing the town with delicious country melons.

The family of Joab Lewis held a reunion at his home "Ingleside" in honor of Mrs. Lewis' 63rd birthday. Thirty relatives enjoyed the dinner on the lawn at 1:30. The presents were numerous.

The little son of Mr. J. C. Bolding was bitten by a rattlesnake but recovered after treatment by Dr. Chastain. Mr. George Thornbrough killed 76 snakes at New Town. Funny thing, they were all in one place.

Drs. W. M. Willingham, and R. L. Dudley have returned from

Chattanooga full-fledged M. D's Dr. Willingham was valedictorian of his class.

Mrs. O. N. Starr and her handsome little son, Trammell, visited in Dalton last week.

Mrs. J. M. Harlan and her daughters, Mrs. Starr and Mrs. Harbin were thrown from the buggy by a contrary horse that backed the buggy into the ditch in front of Col. Starr's house. Mrs. Starr was hurt. Miss Maude Ballew jumped from her buggy and suffered a sprained arm when her horse became frightened at a fast train.

Mrs. H. P. Barrett left Friday for Powhatan, Arkansas for a month's visit with her parents.

Miss Lula Brogdon, one of the county's most popular and attractive young ladies, left yesterday to attend Centennary Female College at Cleveland, Tennessee.

Miss Eva Cantrell left for Rome to enter the Conservatory of Music. Mr. Will Hall will enter Mercer and Miss Lucile Dudley writes a glowing account of Rock College at Athens.

Little Miss Janie Boaz, who is attending school at Tunnel Hill spent last Sunday at her home in Calhoun.

I have a beautiful line of millinery goods — Mrs. G. M. Hunt.

Mr. J. O. Middleton, a recent graduate of Vanderbilt Law School, is to make Calhoun his home. He will be associated with Col. W. R. Rankin.

Miss Estelle Wright, a most charming young lady of Rome, is visiting friends at Sugar Valley.

Mr. M. C. Tinsley left Monday to accept a position in Cartersville with Baker, the jeweler.

Mr. John H. Todd and mother of LaGrange are stopping at the Calhoun Hotel for a few days.

Mr. W. T. Wilson and wife of Atlanta are at the Calhoun Hotel. Mr. Wilson is a wealthy young man and speaks of buying a farm in Gordon County where he plans to raise stock.

Shoes at Engrams — 35c to $6 a pair.

Victory! the most glorious ever achieved! Grover Cleveland is president of the United States and the country is safe.

Calhoun is a hummin.

Just on a regular boom
Since Grover was elected
And Bennie met his doom.

Col. Rankin, Representative, came in in regular Nancy Hanks in the recent election.

Are you going to the State Fair at Macon?

Handkerchiefs at 1c and the largest stock of shoes at Hall Bros.

New stock being received at King's Kash Store.

King and Haney dissolved partnership September 13, 1892.

Mr. Stephen King, father of W. F. King, died at Cave Springs in September.

Mr. A. H. Chastain has bought his brothers drug store (Dr. G. L. Chastain).

Miss Bay Hall has gone to Rutledge to visit relatives.

A distinguished visitor to Calhoun is Mrs. W. H. Felton, of Cartersville. She is the guest of W. L. Hines.

Many of our people have been ill during the summer. Newton and Boaz Legg have had typhoid fever, the two little children of

Mr. J. B. Addington have been very sick and Mr. Thomas Moss has been ill. G. A. and H. L. Hall are out after an illness. There are rumors of cholera about the country and everyone is urged to clean up his premises. The best disinfectant for a sick room is burnt coffee.

Westview is just now one of the most promising of Calhoun's suburbs. Mr. J. N. F. Neal has recently moved into his handsome new residence in Westview. (Oostanaula Road).

The big barbecue stand was beautifully decorated by Misses May Hudgens, Laura Matthews, Fannie Ellis, Edith Ransome, Bessie Thornton, and Azile and Lizzie Jones for the big political rally when Hon. J. W. Harris spoke and Gov. Northern was present.

Mr. J. B. Addington and family spent last week with relatives in Waleska, Georgia.

I have the finest china ware and crockery ever shown in Calhoun. — L. P. Roebuck.

Neal Keefe is sure of a mail route. He has bought a $12 mule.

Mr. J. B. Thornbrough is using a pocketbook bought in 1835.

Mr. L. P. Roebuck dropped his pocketbook containing $55 in cash and $450 in notes in the well. A negro went down and got it.

D. H. Livermore, the bank president, has purchased a handsome steed, a bicycle. He may now be seen whirling through the streets on his way to and from the bank.

500 ladies' and children's hats at reduced prices — Mrs. T. M. Ellis.

Mrs. R. J. Nesbitt of Gwinnett County is visiting her son, Claude, near town.

Carpenter Stanton has built a handsome new residence on River Street for Mr. J. M. Ballew. Mr. John King now occupies it.

Resaca has erected more buildings this year than ever in its history.

At King's Kash store, henriettas, shawls, ladies' underwear, men's clothing.

Dr. F. L. Malone left last week to locate in Tilton. Dr. Malone is a fine physician and Tilton is fortunate to have him.

The Calhoun set attended the baptizing at Sugar Valley Sunday when thirty-eight converts were baptized.

Mr. A. H. Chastain is a relic collector. He has a book that was bound in London in 1657.

Rosser Thomas, the handsome and popular tobacco drummer is in town.

Mrs. G. M. Hunt, Mrs. C. C. Harlan, and Miss Lucille Freeman have returned from White Path, the beautiful mountain resort.

In the parlor of the Haynes House, Mr. Emmett Mattox, of Cartersville, delighted a large crowd of young folks with music on harp, guitar, and piano.

Bedsteads $1.25 to $15 at Ferguson and Doughty's.

Rev. J. A. Smith, of Cave Springs, has been elected as pastor of the Baptist church. He is a minister of considerable ability.

The ladies of the Methodist Church will have a supper at McGinnis Hall. The price is 25c and there will be tables for two. Pretty girls, wearing white caps and aprons, will be at the door.

The Y M D Club will give the annual dinner on December 23rd.

"Baby Ruth" is the name of the handsome new doll in W. M. Hughey's window.

Mr. J. H. Henderson is having a neat residence built on his lot in the northern part of town.

Seedless raisins, prunes, dates, currants, and citron at Westfield's

The new steamer, Resaca, made its first voyage last Saturday and will make regular runs from Rome to Carters.

The county has been greatly disturbed by the existence of an organized gang of outlaws. They robbed the post office at Little Row, and committed other serious crimes. There's a $2500 reward for their capture.

Sheriff Noah McGinnis got word that the gang was hiding at a house in Plainville. He and his deputies surrounded the house and a furious gun battle took place as the officers tried to break up and capture the gang. In the gun fire, Sheriff McGinnis received a serious wound that later caused his death. Rev. Mark A. Matthews preached the funeral. Thus was buried our brave and gallant sheriff whose loss to the county is irreparable.

The gang was finally captured and carried to Atlanta to be tried for the robbery at Little Row. In June of 1893, a member of the gang would be tried for the murder of Sheriff McGinnis and sentenced to life imprisonment. The trial would last three days and A. W. Fite, Solicitor General, would make one of the most powerful speeches ever heard for the conviction. Later in the year the outlaw escaped but was recaptured.

A citizen was hunting in the woods one day when he heard a bullet whiz by his head. Dropping to the ground he looked up to see one of the outlaws firing at him. He returned the fire and the outlaw fled. He was seen again near Dew's Pond. "It's a funny thing", wrote the editor of the county paper "that the outlaw is being seen so often yet nothing is done about it."

The outlaw was described as carrying a Winchester rifle over his shoulder and wearing a big pistol on each hip.

It's a beauty! The H. J. Doughty building on the south corner of Wall and Court Streets, begun last June, has just been completed and is indeed a handsome structure.

Calhoun is justly proud of this handsome building, this ornament. No business house in Marietta, Dalton, Cartersville or on the W & A can rival this one in beauty and elegance.

The building is a three story brick 25 feet in width and 70 feet long. The plate glass front has iron columns. A decidedly attractive iron balcony extends from the second floor front over the wall on Courthouse Street. On the front of the building is a marble slab bearing the name "H. J. Doughty" and on the east wide another slab is engraved "W. L. Hillhouse, Builder".

The cornice, giving the appearance of oolitic stone, which crowns the front, north, and east on top is attractive indeed. A flag with stars and stripes floats in the breeze above the cornice which was manufactured and placed by J. B. Johnson, the tinner, of Rome.

The interior is finished up beautifully. Robert Koehne, with twenty years experience in Europe and Rome, did the painting. Mr. J. F. Field, of Greenville, Tennessee and Messers Joel H. Legg and Thomas Cantrell, of our city, did the woodwork.

The second story, reached by a stairway at the rear, is to be fitted up as a theatrical hall or opera house. The third story will house the Masonic Hall and be fitted up in a most elegant manner.

The building cost several thousand dollars and is complete in every particular. Mr. Doughty was a poor young man who, 35 years ago, married a daughter of Mr. Abel Burch, one of our county's most honored citizens, and started for the West to "grow up".

Sure enough, he grew. He amassed a fortune. A little over a year ago, he came from the Lone Star state to Calhoun. Mr. Doughty is an entertaining public-spirited man.

Hall Bros. will occupy the first floor of the Doughty Building. We congratulate them. Light, convenient, beautiful, it is one of the most desirable stores in North Georgia.

The story of this firm's growth and development is full of interest and shows how pluck and perserverance can succeed over obstacles. In the Fall of 1885, Mr. H. L. Hall left the farm and came

Doughty Building 1892

to Calhoun and entered business in a small way, the capital invested being the proceeds of a one-horse crop.

The first year was one of trial and disappointment. He stuck and hoped on. "I was too poor to leave", he said.

He was joined by his brother, James A. in the fall of 1887. Gradually the business grew. Money commenced to flow and in a few years the firm was on the road to prosperity. In 1888, James left the store and entered journalism in Rome. Later, G. A. took his place.

Everything the firm touched prospered and they began to look for new quarters. The handsome Doughty building was secured and Hall Bros. will make its headquarters there for all kinds of goods. They have thousands of friends, all over North Georgia who will rejoice in their success.

About a year ago, J. S., the youngest brother, was placed with a leading wholesale house in Chattanooga and keeps his brothers advised of the latest in styles and prices.

When Cupid goes traveling, he never looks to see whether he has enough money in his pocket to pay expenses. But travel he does. Mr. B. F. Silks and Miss Elda Darnell were married by Rev. W. T. Hamby at her home July 17. General Marvin Green and Miss Nancy J. Roberts were married in November and Mr. James Riddick and Miss Pearl Borders were married at Redbud.

Miss Laura Matthews gave an old maid party.

Mr. F. M. Boaz, of Sugar Valley, has sold his residence to A. M. Bridges and brother, and will leave for Texas.

Mr. Joseph Whitfield, aged citizen, died of cancer of the eye. Prof. J. I. Ingraham, at one time principal of the Calhoun Collegiate Institute, died at Washington, Ga. and was buried in Chandler Cemetery.

A stock law and a law against throwing trash on the streets have been passed.

Our night marshal, M. E. Ellis, is the right man in the right place. Little meanness can be done that he doesn't know it.

CALHOUN—TOWN MADE BY A CYCLONE
1893

Out from the hills of Gordon and across the valleys beyond swells the cry, "Build, Build, Build!" Back from the west where the sun goes down and dreams lie waiting Horn mountain flings back the challenge "build! build! build!"

"Build," you say? Why, we have built. Don't you see the new courthouse on the square? And the Doughty building on the corner? And a dozen new houses? Aren't you satisfied? "Build" the echoes answer.

"I didn't want to go" wrote Trox Bankston, of Ringgold. "I wasn't a church member nor a Christian. But, because of my work in the Sunday School, my pastor insisted that I attend the Sunday School Convention in Calhoun.

"With each turn of the wheel as the train rolled southward, my apprehension grew as I thought of the hours ahead. What if my hostess asked me to ask the blessing!

"But, with my arrival in Calhoun, all my dark thoughts vanished as if by magic before the cordiality of such a people.

"Several friends invited me to their homes, but I went to the Calhoun Hotel as the guest of Dr. Harbin.

"The last time I was here I toured the city with Prof. Ingrahm. Calhoun had been almost totally wrecked by a cyclone. But now, I should design Calhoun the most modern city in North Georgia. Of the present homes, 75% are modern in every style of architecture. The houses show considerable artistic taste, and from the pretty yards, the air is laden with exotics as it fans your brow. The churches are handsome, standing as monuments to the Christian people who inhabit the town.

"The business houses are large and the merchants carry a large stock. Best of all are the hospitable people. The men are sociable, their wives are charming, and the sons and daughters add to at attractiveness of these delightful places.

"Calhoun is the only town I ever knew that was made by a cyclone."

The hospitality of these sociable men, charming women, and attractive sons and daughters is never more evident than at Christmas time when special church services, banquets, and parties fill the holidays with activity.

At the banquet given by Oothcaloga Lodge No. 154, addresses were made by Worshipful Master T. M. Ellis, Col. W. R. Rankin, and Rev. Mark A. Matthews.

On Christmas day, Rev. M. A. Matthews had dinner prepared and carried to the prisoners in the jail. He stood in the dark hall and offered a beautiful prayer as the prisoners wept bitterly.

Of course, the main feature of the season is the dinner given by the Y M D Club at the Calhoun Hotel.

MENU

Soups

Mock turtle and Consomme

Sago with Queen Olives

Fish

Columbia River Salmon, a la Hollandaise with mashed potatoes.

Lobster salad with mayonnaise dressing.

Meats

Christmas Turkey - Cleveland Dressing

Baked Sweet Potatoes - Cranberry Sauce and Celery

French Boiled Ham   Spaghetti with Cheese

and Stewed Tomatoes

Entrees

Oyster Patties   Rice Croquettes   Vanilla Sauce

Desserts

Orange Meringue Pie, Mince Pie, assorted nuts,

raisins, oranges.

Java coffee, crackers, Roquefort and Switzer cheese.

The after dinner speeches were highly entertaining. G. A. Hall spoke on "People You Meet," J. O. Middleton's topic was "Recollections of Leap Year," W. L. Hillhouse told of "The Sorrows of Bachelorhood" and Rev. M. A. Matthews honored "Woman" in his brilliant style of speaking.

The costumes worn by the ladies were notably handsome.

Not to be outdone by the young men, the S L D Club entertained friends at the home of Major G. W. Wells. The parlor and dining room were beautifully decorated with greens, ivy, and mistletoe. At 11 o'clock a sumptuous feast was served.

Rev. Matthews preached one of his most eloquent and entertaining sermons at the Presbyterian Church on "Waters of Joy." The church was beautifully and appropriately decorated and the music sweet and charming.

A sermon by Pastor Smith and beautiful music at the Baptist Church commemorated the Christmas season and, on Sunday night, the Methodist Church was well filled to hear Rev. W. T. Hamby's brilliant and entertaining sermon on "The First Christmas. It's Proper Observance Today."

The new postage stamps are beauties. Have you seen them?

R. L. Land, popular and clever star route man, has moved to town.

Mr. C. C. Harlan is back with J. M. Harlan selling hardware since resigning his position at the bank. Mr. Joe B. Gordon, of Oostanaula is now employed at the bank.

A chair at the home of Mr. Frank Smith has been in the family for 120 years.

Miss Marian Brownlee, of Plainville, is visiting her sister, Mrs. A. M. Frix.

Pull for Calhoun. Don't wait until next year to begin, either.

A cotton factory. How does that sound for Calhoun? It is astonishing that such an industry has not long been established here. It is being seriously considered by far-sighted men. LaFayette has a flourishing cotton mill. Why not Calhoun?

Snow is ten inches deep, the pond is frozen 5 or 6 inches thick, and for once in 50 years, the Oostanaula is frozen. The temperature stood at 4 degrees below 0 Saturday.

Robed in garments of white, Horn Mountain, 5 miles west of Calhoun, presents a picture pleasing and grandly beautiful.

G. L. Chastain, M. D., advertises that he has secured the medicine and instruments for extracting teeth without being painful to the patient.

Clay Dyar, 3 year old son of Mr. and Mrs. F. L .Dyar, almost died of membranous croup. Dr. Harbin, assisted by Drs. Malone and Chastain, performed a dangerous operation, cutting into the windpipe and inserting a silver tube. Clay is improving rapidly.

Earl Hughey, son of W. M. Hughey, died of membranous croup.

Col. James Rogers died at the age of 88. He was born in Tennessee, graduated from the University of Virginia, and joined General Nelson's battalion for the Indian War in Florida. He was on the Governor's staff at Milledgeville. His sons are Thomas and Newton. Col. Rogers is buried in Salem churchyard.

Mr. H. J. Roff will assist Judge Harbin in the ordinary's office. That clock! Will we get it this year? We must have it by some hook or crook.

Mr. A. H. Chastain, popular and clever propietor of Calhoun's flourishing drug store, and Miss Ella M. Bowie, of McCool, Mississippi, were married Sunday, February the 19th. They are now visiting Mr. Chastain's parents at LaFayette.

"Grandmother Hildegarde's Legacy" will be produced by Calhoun talent at the Opera House. Rev. Charles Lane, D. D. of Atlanta, will lecture for the benefit of the Presbyterian Church and Conroy's Novelty Company will play two nights at Doughty Opera House.

Church attendance is good for these wintry days. Calhoun is far above the average in this respect.

In a letter to the local paper, Rev. M. A. Matthews asks that the grand jury "keep our new courthouse clean. It is sometimes a disgrace. Stop the blind tigers and look into these stores with screens, find out why they are there."

Some rude boys entered the Calhoun Collegiate Institute. Books and desks were torn up and the rooms and the piano scribbled and written over.

The Oostanaula is out of banks. Samuel Davis, Newton Legg, and Robert Koehne were out in a boat and overturned. Hearing their wild shrieking, kicking, and splashing, Pat Wyatt went to investigate and rescued the boys.

Messers Kiker, Matthews, Skelly, Middleton, Harrell, Hamby, and Dr. Harbin have organized a debating society and the U and D Literary Society is active with Col. J. O. Middleton, president, W. J. McDaniel vice-president, and Miss Azile Jones, secretary.

We fear that the Calhoun Cornet Band has breathed its last. It will never do to give up now, boys.

Ryals High School, at Sugar Valley, is flourishing, with 150 scholars under Prof. Brinson, his daughter. Miss Annie, and Miss Lida Farris as music teacher. Ryals is located on the E T V and Ga. railroad. Pure water, mountain air and board in good families for $8 to $10 a month, less in the dormitories, make it a most desirable place to send your children.

The Times is proud of Hubert, Sugar Valley correspondent. He is in every way a first class news gatherer.

"Uncle" Tim Haney is having a neat four room dwelling erected just beyond Oothcaloga Mills, on the Rome road.

W. G. Fuller's house, begun in October 1892, has been completed and is an ornament to the town.

Mr. J. N. Ballew has had four of his residences in West Calhoun painted handsomely.

Oothcaloga Mills, with John A. Fields, head miller, ships meal to South Georgia, Alabama, and North Carolina.

A new bakery is in full blast. Squire Hooper is turning out some excellent bread. J. B. Buffington runs the meat market.

Several new street lamps have been bought. Other improvements are, a temporary wire fence around the park area, old trees in the park dug up, blue grass planted, water oaks and elms set out, and the walks graveled. The streets are in apple pie order, no holes to fall in or rocks to stumble over. The old public well on Railroad Street has been filled and another dug further west, inside the park.

Dong! the city clock will soon be pealing out.

On June the 2nd, the city clock is here. Mr. M. D. Bradley, representative of the Seth Thomas Company is now having the big time piece placed in the tower. Calhoun is the only town on the W & A, save Marietta, to have a town clock. The myriads of sparrows are now homeless.

The Quarterly Conference met Monday, April 3rd, and licensed Dr. George L. Chastain to preach the Gospel. This was a genuine surprise to many of his friends. He has kept the matter perfectly quiet. Dr. Chastain is one of our most consecrated men and we wish him success in his labors. His first sermon, preached at Watsonville, 5 miles east of Calhoun, was well delivered and one of rare interest.

The Presbyterian Church has a new bell, an excellent one of beautiful tone. The galleries at the church have been seated and an overflow crowd is expected next Sunday to hear Rev. Mark Matthews' farewell sermon. He has been called to the First Presbyterian Church of Dalton.

Rev. Matthews would conduct a summer revival in Atlanta which would result in 150 conversions. He can draw crowds as few can. The family of M. L. Matthews has moved to Dalton after 40 years of living in Calhoun.

Dr. Buttolph is the new pastor of the Presbyterian Church.

A brilliant wedding at the church was that of Mr. George F. Ransome and Miss Elizabeth Fox Jones. The decorations were marvels of beauty and artistic taste, due to the efforts of H. J. Roff and Misses Georgia and Azile Jones. To the strains of Mendelsohn's Wedding March, played by Mrs. W. L. Hines, two sweet and beautifully dressed children, Artis Robinson and Julia Ballew, holding daisies in their hands, came in. Next came Mr. D. E. Jones of Marietta and Miss Laura Matthews, followed by Mr. C. H. Barnes of Cartersville and Miss Edith Ransome. The best man, Mr. C. A. Deimer of Nashville, entered with the maid of honor, Miss Nannie Jones. Each bridesmaid carried daisies and the men wore buttonhole daisies. The bride and groom came in and stood under a great bell of flowers where Rev. M. A. Matthews performed the ceremony.

The bride, a picture of youthful beauty and grace rarely beheld, wore white silk and her veil was caught up in the back with a brooch of diamonds. The maid of honor wore white dotted swiss and ribbon trim. Ushers were John Crawford and Percy Howard.

After a repast at the home of the bride's mother, the couple left for a honeymoon in New Orleans and Memphis.

Mr. T. W. Harbin, ordinary, says that the sale of marriage licenses is slow.

Prof. J. T. McEntire, of Blue Springs, called last week. He is a most pleasant gentleman and conducts one of the most flourishing schools in the county.

The millinery store of Mrs. T. M. Ellis is one of the most taste-fully arranged establishments we have seen.

Dr. M. J. Dudley and his wife, of Sonoraville, will leave April 3rd for an extended trip through Texas. Mr. Ben Watts, of Fairmount, has given out his Texas trip.

Mr. Doughty has sold his bank stock and will spend several months in the west.

H. J. Doughty, J. G. F. Harrell, and W. L. Hillhouse are gentlemen who have done much for the upbuilding of Calhoun.

The Easter program at the Methodist church was excellent. The music by the choir was very sweet and several little girls, Bessie and Willie Harkins, Lucy Freeman, Marie Harlan, Virgin McDaniel, Maggie Kiker, Lucile Ballew, and Ida Vernon, gave excellent recitations.

The Sunday School Convention at Wesley Chapel, with over 1000 present, was presided over by Rev. M. A. Matthews. The congregation sang All Hail the Power and Prof. Ernest Neal gave the welcome address. Prof. Neal is a gifted gentleman, well known to the public, an eloquent and entertaining speaker. Miss Lulie Pitts responded and her speech was all that could be expected from this gifted daughter of Gordon County.

The Baptists had a reunion at Doughty building. They filled the Hall and partly filled the Masonic Hall on the third floor.

A very good ladies' slipper for 35¢ - light weight summer shirts - Hall Bros.

Newton Legg, 17 years old, is in the front ranks as a brick mason. He has erected, for the Haynes House, a chimney with eight fireplaces, four in each story, and he did the work in twelve days, laying 10,000 bricks. The Haynes House has recently added six new rooms.

The Haynes House has 24 boarders. Mr. F. B. Lippett and family, of Savannah, have arrived to spend the summer.

Miss Aurie and Nell Malone, of Atlanta, are up to spend the summer with their father, Dr. J. H. Malone, at the Calhoun Hotel.

Guests at the Haynes House are entertained by Mr. Joe Gordon with guitar music and at the Calhoun Hotel by Mr. C. W. Davis on the violin.

L. J. Omohundro Music Company of Chattanooga, is placing many fine pianos and organs in Gordon County. Col. F. A. Cantrell has purchased an elegant upright piano, Mr. C. C. Harlan is the owner of a new Haines upright, and there's a new piano at Ryals High School.

W. M. Hughey is the sole agent for the Etowah Ice Company.

Dr. R. W. Thornton, accompanied by his charming daughter, Miss Bessie, and Miss Fannie Ellis, left Tuesday for Atlanta to attend the Dental Association.

Mr. and Mrs. T. M. Ellis received a telegram from Dr. J. H. Reeve in Atlanta saying that his little son, Tommie, is dangerously ill with pneumonia, Mr. and Mrs. Ellis left at once for Atlanta. Mr. Ellis returned Saturday. The boy is much better but Mrs. Ellis will remain for a few days longer.

Misses Sudie Shelor and Sunia Wright of our community, are visiting relatives in Seneca and Walhalla, South Carolina.

The Calhoun Band will furnish music for Adairsville High School Friday night.

Fairmount College has an enrollment of 224 with an average attendance of 200. There are 100 boarding students. This year's graduates are Arthur Ramsaur, Alda Findley, John P. Clower, Maud Erwin, Bammie and Lillie Fuller. Medals were given first to Meta Dodd, second to Arthur Ramsaur, and others receiving medals for excellence were Lillian Hunt, Minnie Jones, Lawrence Neal, Harlan Erwin, Mary Hudgins, and Master Geise Peeples, of Atlanta. Prof. Sharp is principal of Fairmount College.

At Ryals High School, Rev. Charles Wright, of Chattanooga, preached the commencement sermon. On Monday night, the songs, recitations, and calisthenic drills were directed by Miss Annie Brinson. The young men were trained in declamation by Prof. Brinson and there was not a bobble, nor a break.

The young ladies contested for a beautiful gold medal. Special mention must be made of Janie Everett, Lois Abbott, Della Bridges, Johnnie Crawford, Cora Abbott, Ida Warren, Unie Abbott, Lester Frix, Ada Abbott, and Stella Haynes. Such rare talent is bound to reach a greater boundary than Gordon County.

Tuesday night's program of music, plays, tableau, and a tambourine drill by the young ladies was grand beyond description. Master Ed Norrell brought down the house with "A Yankee in Love." Medals went to Zela Lutes, Johnnie Crawford, and Della Bridges.

The Calhoun Collegiate Institute closed with a commencement of plays, recitations, declamations, and music.

A most entertaining event was the concert given by the Calhoun young people. A flute solo "Marble Halls," by Judge Habersham of Atlanta, delighted the audience and "Old Folks at Home" sung by Misses Aurie Malone, Azile Jones, Lulie Pitts, and May Hudgins, Mrs. T. W. Harbin, Mrs. C. C. Harlan, Messers J. O. Middleton, T. W. Skelly, J. M. Harkins, H. J. Roff, Frank Malone and Prof. Ernest Neal was most impressive.

Then followed a duet by Misses Lucile Freeman and Lulie Pitts and a solo "Love's Sorrow" by Miss Aurie Malone. The treat of the evening was a pantomime by Prof. Ernest Neal. He has a wonderful dramatic power under any circumstances. The pantomime was of a well known Georgia politician making a stump speech. Prof Neal's encore was an irish potato speech in accuracy of brogue and delivery.

Beautiful and substantial, the new bank building stands, up in Attorney's Row. Built of pressed brick, with iron columns in a glass front, it is handsome and dashy in appearance. The building is owned by Hon. W. R. Rankin, the Bank of Calhoun, and Dr. J. H. Malone. The right corner is occupied by Col. Rankin's law office, the middle room by the bank, and the left room by J. N. Neal, Hardware. The bank's 6000 pound safe, in an iron and brick vault, is absolutely burglar proof. Calhoun and Gordon County should be proud that they have one of the most elegant and conveniently arranged banking institutions in North Georgia.

Years later, when this building was razed to make room for the cream brick structure on the Northwest corner of Court and Wall Streets, the boys of the town were hired to clean the brick. They had to buy their own hatchets. "I broke mine" related Tom Banks David, "and it also broke my heart."

Mr. L. D. Hillhouse has bought the residence of A. S. Tatum, up in "Gilt Edge," the most beautiful and desirable section of the city.

The pine thicket, in the west side of twon, is to be cut up into city lots and sold. In 1850 John P. King deeded half of the thicket to the town and half to his son. It is the son's half that is to be made into a residence section.

Dr. W. M. Curtiss, well to do druggist of Atlanta arrived with his family last week to spend part of the summer at his farm near Calhoun.

The finest jersey cow in the country is owned by Mr. D. H. Livermore. She gives five gallons of milk a day.

Mr. J. N. Kiker is digging for water on the top of Mt. Alto. One well reached a depth of 87 feet and another 75 feet—but no water.

Mr. H. L. Hall and family and Miss Bay spent last week at the old Hall homestead on the river.

Mr. O. C. Lewis, of Atlanta, is visiting his father, Squire Joab.

Mr. James A. Hall is in town with a disabled foot. He is now writing for the Constitution with a style like the famous M. Quad's.

There will be a Christian Harmony singing at Blue Springs Sunday.

Miller Erwin says that Murray County has better horses and better water than any place he has ever visited, also the prettiest young ladies in the world. Now, Miller, say "the prettiest young lady."

Tomlinson, the photographer, has a number of large size views of the courthouse, the best and most perfect ever made of this handsome building. Go get one.

There's a new drug store in the Post Office building, established by Dr. J. H. Reeve. Dr. Reeve is a Gordon County boy, born and raised near Calhoun. Twelve years age, he went to Atlanta to medical school. After graduation he located in Atlanta where he built up a general practice. He was elected by the general council to the high and responsible position of physician in the Fifth Ward.

Prof. Ernest Neal, newly elected principal of the Collegiate Institute, has moved to town and is occupying the B. G. Boaz residence on Wall Street (now the Kay home).

A. B. Gregg has just completed a two story residence for L. R. Pitts on the beautiful lot just north of the Baptist church. It is one of the handsomest in the city.

The Dalton District Conference met at the Methodist church for three days. It was an occasion long to be remembered. Reports came from eighteen circuits and missions on 5000 Sunday School workers. What an army this, engaged in the study of God's word!

A strained hush upon the audience evidenced the presence of the Divine Spirit as the minister spoke against Sabbath desecrations. All day singings, the "come and bring yer dinner" kind, were scathingly criticized and condemned as damaging to the Sunday Schools.

Ministers preaching were Revs. M. D. Smith, A. A. Quillian, H. C. Morrison D. D., and G. J. Orr.

At 11 o'clock Saturday, Dr. Warren A. Candler, the brainy, consecrated president of Emory College, preached a sermon of remarkable power.

Sunday A. M. at 9 o'clock, a love feast was conducted by Rev. J. E. England. Dr. Candler preached again at 11 o'clock and Dr. Morrison preached at the Baptist Church. Street services were held in front of Dr. Chastain's drug store at 6:00 p.m. Sunday.

"Do you wish your boy or girl to be a scoffer, a skeptic, an atheist? Then train his intellect and neglect his morals. Do you wish him to become a crank? Then unduly exercise his emotional nature. But if you would have him become a useful citizen, a well-rounded character, a man who can both feel and think the truth, who can theorize and put into practice, then subject him to that education which brings about these proper conditions. Send your children to our home school."

—Ernest Neal, Principal

Mr. J. L. O. Sutherland has one of the finest 35 acre fields of bottom corn found in the country. No storm cloud could ever shine blacker. The field will yield 50 bushels to the acre.

The bridge below Boaz' mill was finished by Contractor Ed Lewis last week. It is a splendid structure, of the best timber and workmanship.

Prof. W. P. Dodd, J. G. B. Erwin, J. A. Dorroh, and Arthur Ramsaur were all at home in Fairmount for the meeting Saturday and Sunday.

Messengers from a number of Baptist churches met at Bethlehem Sunday and organized the Gordon County Baptist Sunday School Convention. Rev. A. H. Rice was elected president, J. W. Swain and Mr. Dillard vice-presidents, and Miss Nellie Willingham, secretary. The next session will be held at the Calhoun church. There are 27 Baptist churches in Gordon County and all have Sunday Schools.

The Missionary Baptist Church, organized at Reeves Station, on Saturday before the second Sunday in March, 1892, was dedicated Sunday, August 13, 1893 by Rev. W. H. Cooper, of Cedartown.

There will be no service at the Methodist church Sunday, but there will be a bush arbor meeting where Clark Chapel once stood at the forks of the road beyond Mr. James Clarke's on the Sugar Valley and Resaca roads.

The Episcopal church, begun in August, was completed in September. Messers Pike Bros. were the contractors and Mr. W. G. Sutherland, of LaGrange, supervisor. Rector Craighill will conduct services Sunday, September the 10th at 11 o'clock. Dr. Barrett lectured at Doughty Hall on the Passion Play at Oberammagrau for the benefit of the Episcopal Church.

Two miles east of the little village of Plainville may be seen the prettiest sight in the world, the young peach orchard of Mr. James C. Brownlee—10,000 young Elberta trees, covering 50 acres of mountain land. He plans to plant 100 acres—think of it! Each acre will net Mr. Brownlee $150. Mr. Milam Gunn, a nighbor, has 40 acres. The people of Plainville are abandoning cotton raising for fruit.

Rev. W. A. Nix, of Sonoraville, has returned from Texas with a petrified tooth, probably a mastodon, that he found on the Red River. It is as large as one's fist and as hard as a rock.

The depot is being repaired. The ticket office is being moved to the front of the building and the former office space will be made into a waiting room.

Engineer Charles Barrett astonished the natives driving through Calhoun on 240 pulling the Velvet Vestibule. He was 30 minutes late and came through Calhoun almost as fast as 240 could turn a wheel. The train, Velvet Vestibule, leaves Atlanta at 10:30 a.m. every day for Chicago, pulling a baggage car, two elegant coaches, and a Pullman. The trains go too fast through town, 40 miles an hour is dangerous to the citizens.

A good iron U. S. mail box has been placed near the depot for the convenience of the hotel guests.

Ten thousand young ladies wanted—at my emporium to see my stock of millinery and goods.—Mrs. F. L. Hicks.

Cicero Stevenson, weight 250 pounds, rode a burro through the streets Saturday causing much laughter.

A man tried to hold up Jimmy Clark in the river bridge as he went home from Church Sunday night but his horse ran the man down and kept going. Congratulations, Jimmy!

Some twenty years later, Phil Reeve, returning from Sugar Valley, ran a man down in the same bridge. His grey horse, Ben, could never stand the whip so when the holdup was attempted, one flick sent Ben bounding out of the bridge. Congratulations, Phil!

Col. E. J. Kiker's horse, a pacer, won the race at Cartersville at 2:10.

Mr. John Miller found 90 blue catfish in his river basket, totaling 80 pounds. Oostanaula fishermen will have to take a back seat.

A young man of Little Row, J B. House, age 14, took up a collection to buy an organ for the church. A Calhoun lawyer gave him a donation. Being unable to get up enough money to buy the organ, J. B. a year later, gave the lawyer back his money. Said the lawyer "that boy will make a man!"

At the ice cream festival at Doughty Hall, Miss Maude Neal

View of Calhoun from Mt. Pisgah, 1890's.

received a beautiful cake, raffled at 5¢ a vote, as the most popular young lady present.

T. M. Ellis, Tax Receiver, reports returns of $2,500,000 for the year 1893.

The people have been saddened by the deaths of Mrs. C. C. Harlan and Mrs. W. F. King who have been ill so long. Grief pervaded Calhoun when Mrs. J. M. Harlan, 63, died only a few hours after the death of Mrs. C. C. Harlan.

Mr. J. J. Haney, father of T. A. Haney, died at his home in Cartersville.

Grandma McGinnis, 86, died. She was the mother of nine children, among them our late lamented sheriff, Noah H. A good old soul for 60 years she was a member of the Baptist church.

Other loved citizens taken by death were Mrs. Bob Prater, age 59, and Mrs. Jane Kiker, aged mother of E. J. Kiker and Mrs. Z. T. Gray. She had lived here 43 years and had 13 children, 24 grandchildren, and 39 great grandchildren.

W. A. J. Robertson died December 30, 1893. He was married to the former Rutha Hudgins and had eight children. Resolutions on his death were written by Samuel Dillard and Rev. A. H. Rice.

HARD TIMES, SPELLING BEES, AND GREAT SERMONS
(1894)

Hard times come again. This is the 1894 New Year's greeting from the editors of The Calhoun Times. But spelling bees are inexpensive entertaining and the one at Doughty Hall was well attended. Rev. J. W. Smith and Col. Starr served as captains and Prof. Neal was master of ceremonies. Your editor disgraced himself on "buoyancy," and Dr. Harbin couldn't spell "cemetery." When "opthalmic" was given out, Col. Starr turned red in the face, stammered, and missed.

When County School Commissioner McDaniel missed "lief," Rev. J. W. Smith was left standing alone, thus winning the Spelling Bee.

Large congregations assembled at the M. E. Church to hear Dr. Henry Darnell preach two of his best sermons. Mr. Hamby tendered the use of his church because it was thought the Presbyterian Church would not accommodate the crowd that would want to hear this gifted preacher. The spacious building was filled at both services.

"Self Against God" will be the topic of the sermon by the pastor at the Methodist church next Sunday. The cold wave, hard times, an a spirit of chronic grumbling will be discussed.

The full context of a sermon preached by Rev. Mark Matthews, pastor of the Dalton Presbyterian Church, fills a page of the paper. Rev. Matthews concludes, "Worlds may give way and lights may fade but my Saviour shall outlast them all. You may pluck every star and world and throw them at my feet. Unfold every treasure of earth. Give the flowers of all climes. Bring the choirs of the universe. Give them all and I turn with disdain from them all and prefer my precious Saviour."

In his sermon on the Resurrection, the Rev. W. T. Hamby, pastor of the Methodist Church said, "The Gate of the City of God flies wide open and the doors are lifted high and the matchless spirit of our Emanuel sweeps through the gate of pearl and toward the mediatorial throne. Heaven is elated. The great broadway of Jerusalem is lined with the spirits of just men and women made perfect. Let us 'behold the man' until the high ideal of Christianity be reproduced in us here."

The ladies of the Methodist Church gave a supper at Doughty's Hall. A fine cake, donated by Mrs. W. G. Fuller, was given to the young lady voted the most popular. Miss Edith Ransome and Miss Minnie Shands tied for the honor.

Bethesda and Mt. Pleasant Churches have organized a Singing Society which will meet at Bethesda every second Sunday, and at Mt. Pleasant every third Sunday. C. H. Lewis is president and E. Borders, vice-president.

Out at Farmville, the new church near Mr. Jeff Brown's will go by the name of Antioch. Rev. H. N. Harden is the pastor.

The Blue Springs Baptist Church was dedicated the second Sunday in July, 1894, by Bro. Scarborough of Atlanta, Corresponding Secretary of the Home Mission Board.

Dr. J. A. Johnson preached an able and interesting sermon at Resaca Monday night.

J. M. and W. W. Ballew recently bought the Boaz mill for $8300. Notice—all persons are warned not to trade, buy, or transfer two notes of $375 each given me in payment for Ryals High School building and lot. They were lost or stolen and I will give a reward for their return.—M. B. Abbott.

M. D. Kimbrough, over 80, died in January. He came to Gordon County before the Indians left and was a teacher among them, with headquarters at New Echota. He owned one of the finest farms on the Coosawattee.

Mr. Henry Addington is visiting his daughter, Mrs. J. H. Legg and his son, J. B. Mr. Addington, 76 years of age, has been a J. P. for 40 years and no ruling of his has ever been reversed.

Mr. and Mrs. L. R. Pitts entertained friends in their new home one evening last week. The conversation was sparkling and the refreshments delightful.

Misses Dora and Minnie Fuller entertained at their home near town Thursday evening. At 11 o'clock the guests were conducted to the spacious dining room where an excellent supper was served.

The ladies of the Baptist Church will serve sandwiches at the Doughty building during court week.

An injunction has been filed by the John P. King heirs and the town council to keep the County Commissioners from cutting timber from the common west of the railroad.

Telegrams are out for the coldest weather of the winter.

School at Little Row is flourishing under Miss Lizzie Johnson. Miss Lula Brogdon has 54 scholars at Decora. Miss Bessie Fain is teaching a school at Crane Eater.

There are 59 schools in Gordon County. Teachers' salaries and other expenses for last year amounted to $10,426.34.

The negroes are trying to secure suitable grounds for a school. Money will be furnished by Northern Philanthropists. The building will be better than the one used by the whites.

In the "Reeves Ripples" we note that Miss Aurie Garlington has returned from Center, Alabama where she visited her sister last week.

Mr. Booth, of Atlanta, is here on a visit to his sister, Mrs. Ernest Neal.

Miss Orrie Malone gave a Valentine party in honor of Miss Minnie Shands Wednesday evening. The parlors were elaborately decorated with ferns and flowers. Games, instrumental and vocal music, and dancing entertained the guests during the evening. When refreshments were served, each young gentlemen was required to give a list of the ingredients in the pies cooked by the young ladies.

Present at this lovely affair were: Misses Azile Jones, Lulie Pitts, May Hudgins, Eva Cantrell, Beulah Willingham, Ruby Freeman, Nettie Wells, Lola McWhorter, Laura Haynes, Allie Rankin, and Minnie Shands; Messrs Cantrell, Skelly, Haynes, G. A. and J. S. Hall, Berry Boaz, F. L. Malone, W. H. Bonner, Watts, Hillhouse, Harbin, Middleton, and Mr. and Mrs. D. H. Livermore.

Messers Miller and Smith, two engineers, were here Monday in consultation with the city council as to the cost of a system of water works. They examined the spring on the Fain place and said that it would furnish an ample supply of water, and that they could build a plant for $7000. In addition to the convenience of running water in the house, a water system would bring a reduction in insurance rates. The citizens are unanimous for the water system, but the council took no action on it at their next meeting.

Mr. David Westfield and Miss Ida Fox were married on a Sunday afternoon in March at the home of Mr. John Fox. The Rev. Mr. Dorsey officiated. The bride is the daughter of one of the county's most prosperous farmers and the groom a prosperous merchant of this place.

Mr. Steele King and Miss Ida White were married at the home of the bride in February. After the wedding, a bountiful feast was served.

People who want only nice things said of them in the newspapers should say and do nothing but nice things.

Quite a number of young people attended the croquet party Saturday at he home of Mr. and Mrs. Fuller at Fairmount. A group of Fairmount young people picnicked at Big Springs last week Several couples from Calhoun joined them.

A new railroad is to be built from Cumberland Gap through Spring Place and Fairmount to Cartersville.

Don't ask us for credit, it makes us tired. Hall Bros.

David Brown was given $50 against the W & A railroad for being carried past the station at Resaca. Mrs. Enlow was awarded $625 for being carried past the depot at Calhoun and put off at Jackson's Crossing below town.

Revenue officers captured a wshiskey wagon up near Pine Chapel Sunday at daylight. A barrel of white lightning was found hidden under fodder. The men were arrested.

Forty carloads of oranges and cabbages passed through here Monday.

Gov. Evans is expected to make an address here Monday.

Mrs. Caroline Brownlee, 71, of Plainville, died in March. She was the mother of James and John Brownlee, Mrs. A. M. Frix, Mrs. Royster Bray and Mrs. Mark A. Moore.

The Calhoun Dramatic Club cleared nearly $40 in performances at the schoolhouse. The Club will put on a show at Dalton for the benefit of the Confederate Cemetery. Their next performance will be "The Spy of Gettysburg."

The Dalton Banjo and Mandolin Club will give a performance in Calhoun Friday evening.

Prof. Neal will go to Atlanta Friday to participate in an entertainment for the benefit of the Walker Street Church.

The old engine, The General, which was captured by Andrews' Raiders during the war and has been on exhibition at the World's Fair, passed through yesterday on the way to Atlanta from Chicago. It was one of the greatest curiosities at the Fair. Thousands saw it.

There were over a dozen extra trains on the W & A Monday. Freight business has increased immensely. There was a wreck at the Courthouse street crossing at 2 o'clock yesterday morning. Several cars were torn to splinters and the engine badly damaged but no one was hurt.

In July the E.T.V. and Ga. railroad was sold to the highest bidder for $3,500,500. It was bought by Mr. Sam Spencer, president of the New Southern Railroad Co.

G. W. Manning has begun a shoe factory in Calhoun and will sell fine handmade shoes at cost.

J. N. Kiker has traded his place for the old Kiker home across from the Baptist church. One Saturday night Mr. Kiker heard a noise in the kitchen. He took his pistol, went in, found a mad dog and killed it.

Mrs. Melvinia Moss, 43, wife of W. H. Moss of near Resaca, died of typhoid in April and was buried at Sugar Valley. Mrs. Moss, a lovable character, was the daughter of Squire Eli T. Haynes. She was the mother of six children and had a large circle of friends.

Dr. Harbin will read a paper on trepanning at the medical convention in Atlanta next week.

The bank has just put up an awning against old Sol's rays.

A jolly crowd of Romans came up the river in a flatboat towed by the steamer Tony this week. They will go to the mouth of the Connesauga and float back down to Rome, hunting and fishing as they go.

Calhoun is taking on city ways. Hall Bros. have installed an elevator in the Doughty building and opened up a stock of goods on the second floor.

While returning from Sugar Valley last Tuesday night, Prof. Neal's buggy accidentally overturned and Mrs. Neal was severely bruised.

Mr. and Mrs. J. W. Logan, Mr. and Mrs. Sinc Mims, Miss Laura Haynes, and Mr. Dorse Bonner went out to the Bonner farm Friday evening for a moonlight picnic.

The Calhoun Collegiate Institute closed with brilliant exercises. On Sunday, Dr. Bays, of Knoxville, preached a sermon of great force and beauty. Col. Trammell Starr, who gave the annual address, impressed the audience as a gifted orator and thinker.

Recitations and songs on Monday night and a Flag drill, plays, dialogues, and music on Tuesday night closed the three day program of the Institute.

Graduates were: Maggie Rankin, Maude Ballew, Birdie Fields, Nellie Fields, and Minnie Fuller.

A little work would improve the school building. A good school deserves a good house.

Mrs. W. R. Rankin, accompanied by her son, George, and daughter, Mamie, left last Thursday to visit relatives in South Carolina.

They say—that Tim Haney went to Sugar Valley on an electioneering tour the other day and stood around all day without telling anyone he was a candidate.

Calhoun has lost three valued citizens in the last few months. Dr. Harbin is now located in Rome, Mr. J. O. Middleton has gone to Nashville to practice law, and Mr. D. H. Livermore has resigned as cashier of the bank and will go to Atlanta where he has purchased stock in a bank and will serve as vice-president.

Mr. Livermore will keep his place as president of the Calhoun Bank. Col. O. N. Starr has been elected cashier.

The Atlanta Chert paving company will run a railroad line from the Southern at Sugar Valley to their mines in Baugh mountain.

An elderly lady said the other day, "this world is getting better, women are parting their hair in the middle."

Messers Mark Griffin and Will Huffaker, two of Plainville's most popular and handsome young men, attended the entertainment at the Academy Friday night.

A great many people complain about the bad taste of the public well. It stands open day and night and nothing could preven the falling in of a big, fine, large dog or cat.

Ask John Garlington if he has learned the way to Resaca yet.

Miss Robbie Garlington left Saturday for Rome where she will enter college.

Misses Nannie and Sallie Swain visited Mrs. J. E. Swain Sunday.

Mr. W. B. Bridges, of Blanche, Alabama is visiting his father, Mr. J. H. Bridges at Sugar Valley and Mr. M. J. Griffin visited his best girl there. Mr. and Mrs. R. L. Norrell went to Rome Thursday. Mr. T. N. Austin and family have moved from Sugar Valley, to Selma, Alabama.

An amusing incident happened in a dry goods store the other day. A stylishly dressed young lady, who had the stamp of an upto-date girl, entered and in a very I-know-it-all manner asked to see some gentlemen's shirts. "What number?" the clerk politely inquired. A look of blank dismay passed over her face and she stood still for a minute as if stunned.

Then, with a look that Edison might have had when he made his phonograph work for the first time she said, "Oh, about a thirty-two" and the merchant went back toward the shirt department softly whistling to himself "Two Little Girls in Blue."

Years later, when this story was read to Jeanette Reeve Owen (Mrs. R. R.) she said, "It was me. Cousin Bessie Thornton and her beau, Mr. Warlick, the merchant, had been fussing. She dressed me up in her clothes and hired me with candy to go to the store and ask to buy a shirt. I was about five years old."

On Sunday, May 6, Mr. L. N. Legg was married to Miss Minnie Moss of Cash. The ceremony was performed at Preacher Huckabee's. The wedding was a great surprise to all as both parties are in their teens. But Cupid catches the young as well as the old and these young people have the best wishes of their friends.

Mr. J. O. Middleton and Miss Minnie Shands of Clinton, S. C. were married at the home of the bride's parents, Dr. and Mrs. W. A. Shands, on May 2 at 9:00 a.m. The couple returned to Calhoun where a reception was given by the I T C at the home of Dr. J. H. Malone. Calhoun's elite gathered and joy was unconfined where youth and beauty meet to chase the glowing hours with flying feet.

J. H. Legg and son have purchased the interest in the brickyard belonging to Mr. Jervis and•will run same. They have begun work on a new 62 foot brick store on Railroad Street for H. J. Doughty.

Mr. and Mrs. Boulineau, of Folsom, entertained a party of their friends last Saturday evening. Nice music by Misses Ida Littlefield, Stella Osburn, and Josie Boulineau and also nice singing filled the evening hours.

A movment is on foot to build a college at Fairmount. Situated at the foot of Ramsaur mountains, this beautiful and healthy valley is richly productive and the community is moral and intelligent.

Mr. Ben Chastain, who has been with the Wrought Iron Range Co. has returned to Calhoun.

Rev. Gus Thomas, the funny Dutchman, is delivering his famous lecture "From Germany to the Bush Arbor" in many communities of Gordon, including Adairsville and Sugar Valley, for the benefit of the schools and churches.

Small talk from the highways and the hedges — Sheriff Fain shot a blue crane with a pistol at 100 yards. The bird measured five feet from wing tip to wing tip.

A barn at the Brown farm burned last week. Four horses, 125 bushels of corn, and 1000 bundles of fodder, belonging to G. T. Fite, were destroyed.

Misses Emma and Mattie Hill entertained a few of their friends most enjoyably at their home in Resaca Thursday night Calhoun was represented by Miss Laura Haynes, Col. Will Watts, W. B. Haynes, and Howard Findley.

Mr. and Mrs. G. T. Fite entertained a group of young people at their home on the river. Mr. and Mrs. Fite certainly understand the art of entertaining. A more hospitable and clever family is not to be found in the state.

Mrs. J. M. Ballew died Saturday morning after a short illness. She was an excellent Christian lady and the sympathies of the entire community go to the family. She left four children, one an infant only a few days old.

A few miles up river from Calhoun, where a high bank faces an abrupt turn in the river, can be found some clods of dross from some kind of ore. Old citizens say that an old Indian had a forge there when the red men lived here and dug a valuable ore from some secret mine. Near this place some Indians sunk their pots in the river before they left for the West.

In 1838 soldiers came to arrest this old Indian. He plunged into the stream, swam to the opposite shore, and ran up stream reaching a sand bar. When he looked upon the river where his boat had glided and saw the woods where he had spent so many happy hunting days, it was too much for his spirit. He fired his own rifle into his heart and fell dead. The soldiers found his body, scooped out a grave on the bank, and marked it with a pen of logs.

New Town—Messers Joe Hall and George Thornbrough and Misses Fannie and Ada Burch visited Riverside Sunday and report a pleasant time.

Married on a Monday in November, Mr. Robert Prater and Mrs. L. A. Roebuck. Some of the girls look very red. They had set their caps for Mr. Prater. He has two sons, so cheer up, girls.

Decora—Mr. Will Canada tied himself for life last week to one of Mr. Pink Greeson's daughters. Come on down, boys, that's the way the world goes.

Mr. G. T. Fite wears on his vest six bright buttons made of silver dimes coined in 1835. They were originally owned by Mr. Fite's grandfather in North Carolina and then by Peter Fite. They will be handed down to Mr. Fite's children and on.

In the darkness of Sunday night, Mr. John Garlington drove his buggy into a post near the Haynes and Mr. Poole and Miss Ruby Freeman ran into a post near F. L. Dyars. No one was seriously hurt.

Henry Dobson and Bob Wadkins, of Clark's Chapel, went to Rome last week on business.

The marriage is announced for Thursday evening of Mr. Mark Griffin and Miss Stella Haynes, of Sugar Valley, at the home of the bride's father, Squire Haynes. It will be a notable affair. The young people are well known and have many friends whose best wishes attend them.

Dock Dorsey sleeps a last long sleep His big heart made him always ready to do anything for a friend. His good nature kept him poor. His was a life worn out and spent in service for others and a nature which felt nothing but kindness.

On Saturday, September 1, when splendor filled the Western horizon and all earth seemed to resound with the sweet melodies of the beautiful mocking bird, we wended our way over the picturesque country to the home of R. F. Patman. "Tis a lovely place and needs only the magic wand waved over it to make it one of the most noted summer resorts in Gordon.

The grounds were neatly cleaned, seats fixed, and a stand made for the organ. Mrs. Hines and others played and Messers Cantrell and Mabre and Miss Wood sang. At 12 o'clock dinner was served down at the spring and the afternoon spent playing croquet and eating melons.

Mrs. H. A. Chapman, of Cartersville, is visiting her father, M:. N. J. Boaz.

Miss M. C. Craig, of Lawrenceville, who, for some weeks past has been visiting Mrs. N. E. Pitts, returned home last week.

Rev. Jesse Hunt, the new principal of Ryals High School, filled the Baptist Church pulpit here last Sunday for Rev. J. W. Smith.

News in General—by Neal Keefe. Miss Sallie Rice, of Sonoraville, visited the Erwins at Fairmount last week. John says that rice is above par.

Dr. Fields, of Cherokee County, has cast his lot with the people of Dry Valley and is now permanently located at Farmville. The doctor is a young man and comes to the people highly recommended as a physician.

Dr. Dudley's old grey horse, Fred, died at the age of 22. Peace to his ashes.

A Sunday School was organized Sunday at Stewart's schoolhouse. Rev. H. N. Hardin was elected superintendent.

Mrs. M. L. Foster, of Redbud, spent several days in Dalton this week.

Miss Grace McConnell has entered the Collegiate Institute at this place and is boarding with the family of Prof. Neal.

Mrs. B. M. Park and Mr. J. H. Norrell, of Rome, were visiting friends and relatives at Sugar Valley last week.

Colima—Mr. T. A. Hopper is attending school at Walesca. Miss Minnie Jones spent last week with friends and relatives in Calhoun. Mr. Gus Robertson and wife, of Dalton, accompanied by a sister of Mrs. Robertson, spent last Sunday at the Robertson home near Redbud.

Col. M. J. Griffin spent Sunday in the city and Mr. E. C. Peters of Atlanta was at the Peters' farm for the day.

Mr. L. G. Bradbury, veteran painter, left last week to spend the winter in Florida.

Mike Frix, for a little exercise, left last Sunday morning for Dalton on his bicycle, making the trip in four hours.

Mr. L. B. Stowers has a vine with 84 gourds on it. Mr. Lee Erwin wins with 117 gourds on his vine.

The melodrama "Capitola" was given by the Calhoun Dramatic Club in September. Characters in the play were represented by Prof. Neal, Mrs. Neal, Paul Callahan, W. Hightower, Orrie Malone, and R. Froman. Newsboys were Lumpkin Fain, Linton Eliot, Joe Gray, and Gallaher Neal.

A string band, under the direction of Miss Laura Haynes, furnished music during the evening. Members of the band are: Miss Laura Haynes, violin, Miss Dora Fuller, piano, Mr. Joe Gordon, violin, Mr. W. B. Haynes, guitar, and Mr. E. L. Parrott, cello.

"Mountain Boy" writes from Carters, "Dear Editor, I will write you a few dots."

Lee Mansel, Taylor Hunter, Charley Ross, and Bert Woodruff, of Printups, went to the Morrison Camp meeting last week.

"Pocket" items—Rev. G. C. Garrison preached Saturday and Sunday. The pulpit was filled Sunday night by Rev. L. J. Metcalf. His discourse was a little scattering, just enought so to hit everyone in the house.

There was a double secret wedding Sunday evening, September 23, near the bridge on the Sugar Valley road. Mr. E. S. Cooley and Miss Lester Frix and Mr. A. S. Cooley and Miss Ida Frix, two brothers and two sisters, were united in marriage. May the fates weave for these young people a happy future.

Night hawks are again abroad. They put in their work Tuesday night when a street light in front of the Baptist church was broken and two or three trees in front of D. H. Livermore's torn up.

Judge T. W. Harbin and D. H. Livermore exchanged residences Saturady, October 28. Judge Harbin gave his residence (now the home of Miss Sallie Kimbrough) and $1,400 for that of Mr. Livermore.

A 14 year old boy, son of Mr. Pew, living on Dr. Reeves' place near town, had his eyes blown out one day last week. He had carried a pound of powder into the field where the hands were picking cotton and, to have some fun, boys smoking cigarettes put ashes on the powder.

Mr. Shelor Wright, of Reeves, had his clothes caught in some machinery and was thrown several feet. His arm was mangled and he received a severe gash in the face. Mr. Wright was treated by Dr. Harbin.

Mr. Alton McDaniel, our efficient "devil" took a notion to visit his brother at McDaniel's Station Saturday. For some reason, the train left him. Not to be outdone, he shouldered his air rifle and took off down the track after the passenger train and reached the Station in time for supper, minus a pair of shoes.

On November the 4th, in Sugar Valley, the nuptials of Miss May Abbott and Mr. John Hilley were solemnized at the home of the bride's parents. Mr. and Mrs. Hilley left immediately for their home in Blockton, Alabama.

Mr. George Bandy is building a new house at Blue Springs.

J. W. Logan went to Dalton last week and bought a closed carriage for his livery.

Our friend, John Ray, of Cash, has joined the Knights of the Grip. He represents a tobacco firm of Winston, N. C. Success to you, John, in your new field.

Rev. W. T. Hamby, pastor of the M. E. Church, was moved by the conference to Winder, Georgia.

Mr. Jim Murphy, of Bartow, has accepted a position with L. P. Roebuck.

Property is pretty cheap in Little Row (Curryville). A house and lot sold at a sheriff's sale bought only $13.

Prof. E. Neal and little son, Jule, left the early part of last week for Florida where they will spend several weeks.

Memorial services were held Sunday at the Methodist church for Mrs. W. F. King, Mrs. J. M. Ballew, and Frank Hamby, young son of Rev. W. T. Hamby.

"It is well that we cannot understand the mysteries of immortality. The lily bud does not expose the golden secret that lies within its folded petals. Some day it shall be revealed and we shall know and see it is well."—Minnie C. Harlan.

FAST TRAINS AND BEAUTIFUL WOMEN IN NINETY-FIVE

The Dixie Humer broke the record from Chicago to Atlanta in January, 1895, making the 769 mile run in 17 hours and 6 minutes.

Charley Barrett was at the throttle on the run from Chattanooga to Atlanta and made it in 2 hours and 59 minutes. A large crowd had gathered at the depot to witness the passing train, but nothing was visible but a puff of smoke as 240 swept majestically by on her run against time to the city of Atlanta.

The Nebraska train for the Western sufferers, all decorated with streamers, passed through this place last Wednesday morning at 1:30.

Beautiful women in lovely attire graced the lamp-lit parlor and filled the rooms with silvertoned laughter on Thursday evening when Mr. and Mrs. McWhorter of McDaniel's Station, gave a party for their daughter, Lola.

Miss Lillie Armstrong was elegantly attired in cream albatross becomingly trimmed in blue silk.

Miss Aurie Garlington wore an exquisite gown of cream which brought out her beauty to great advantage.

Miss Willie Royster wore a dainty toilet of pink silk, trimmed with lace and ribbon, in which her graceful figure was much admired.

Miss Kate Swain was lovely in a fashionable gown of white wool, handsomely trimmed in lace and silk.

Miss Janie Royster's artistic gown was of yellow and black.

Misses Maggie and Bessie Fields were becomingly lressed in cream.

Miss Kate Royster was lovely in white wool combined with silk and cord, and Miss Antoinette Rogers was handsome in a toilet of pink.

The gentlemen present were: T. F. Foster, Frank and Will Swain, John and Jeter Garlington, Oscar Hunt, John Crawford, John Sisk, and Eddie McWhorter.

Mr. F. L. Hicks and estimable lady gave a dining to a few friends last week.

Miss Kittie Ellis, C. B. Thayer, C. W. Hunt, Miss Georgia Jones, E. L. Kiker, Miss Fannie Ellis, Innis Jones, Miss Maggie Rankin, and P. D. Howard formed a group of young people stayng up to watch the New Year in.

Miss Maggie Thornton's guests at an elegant supper were: Misses Julia McDaniel, May Hudgins, Lulie Pitts, Maude McDaniel, Azilee Jones, Fannie Ellis, Nettie Wells, and Aurie Malone; Messers, W. B. Haynes, T. W. Skelly, W. P. M. Watts, J. A. Hall, G. A. Hall, W. H. Bonner, W. L. Hillhouse, H. T. Findley, and Mr. and Mrs. Sinclair Mims.

One of the grandest events of the season was the 4 o'clock tea given at he Haynes House by Mrs. J. W. Logan for Mrs. Orvell Keith of Atlanta. Guests were Mrs. L. P. Wilson, Mrs. Fred Lockrane, Mrs. Ovell Keith, Misses Julia McDaniel. Nettie Wells, and Laura Haynes.

Rev. J. W. Smith, pastor of the Baptist Church, has accepted a call to a church in Savannah and Rev. A. Rice of Sonoraville, has been elected to the pastorate of the church here.

Rev. J. B. Craighill, pastor of the Episcopal Church, writes a note of thanks to the young people of Calhoun for helping to raise money to pay off the debt on the organ.

The Sunday School at Wesley Chapel is flourishing with W. S. Harris, superintendent, and Bob Bohannon, secretary, Dr. W. A. Borders, song leader, and Miss Sudie Ellis, organist.

The newly elected council gave a beef stew at the restaurant last Monday night to their friends.

Miss May Hudgins left last Saturday for Buff, Georgia, where she has accepted a position as music teacher at the residence of H. C. Byrom.

Mr. J. M. Neal shipped 5 carloads of peas to New Orleans this week.

Mr. J. C. Bolding who, for some years, has been running a blacksmith shop at Crane Eater, has moved to this place and is now running a shop back of John Logan's livery stable.

Neal Keefe writes of Fairmount and the beautiful new college being erected there. The bright brainy men who represent the beautiful valley are its sponsors. They are: W. C. Loyd, W. M. Peeples, R. L. Strickland, Doctor Vaughn, M. V. Watts, Durrah Bros., Crawford Strickland, Floyd England, Squire Kay, Ben and Lee Jones, H. Johnson, John G. B. Erwin, H. C. Erwin, and Thomas Carter.

Last Wednesday was a gala day for the Haynes House—they had 24 people.

Mr. Butler Hayes and family have moved to Farmville for the present year.

The school at Sonoraville has over 100 scholars. Prof. Fulton and Miss Cora Pittman are the teachers, Miss Jessie Head and Miss Emma Stewart have 70 in school at Red Bud and Resaca. Prof. R. H. Earle of Marietta is principal of the school. Citizens should consider themselves fortunate in securing the services of so competent a teacher.

Mr. Juan Field is amply prepared to furnish all his friends with good horses and fine turnouts from his newly opened livery business.

Mr. John Linn and Mr. Nabers killed 34 rabbits during the snow. They are not worried about the price of meat going up.

Reeves Station—Christmas is over now. It is time for the farmers to begin making their crops. Make all the fertilizer you can at home, clean out ditches, and cut sprouts.

Hurrah for Democracy! Old Gordon is still in it yet and we hope she will stay in for many years.

A large deer passed through our village a few mornings ago while we were eating breakfast. We all jumped up and took after him, bareheaded and without anything, but as he was not as easily caught as some of our dears, we soon gave up the chase.

We can now boast of a first class hotel and an excellent string band which meets at Foster's Hall once a week.

Miss Florence Thomas gave a sociable to a few friends last Saturday evening.

The Calhoun Times gives hints to housekeepers on how to build a smoke house and cure meat. A one horse crop that will make money is outlined as follows:

150 bushels of corn at 50¢	$ 75
250 bushels of corn	125
6 bales of cotton at 6¢	360
2 barrels of syrup	25
50 bushels of potatoes	25
40 bushels of peas	30
40 tons of peavine hay	600
5 stacks of corn fodder	30
2 hogs 500 pounds	40

Don't call your colt Joe, it sounds too much like whoa. Call him Jacob and he will always think you are ordering an advance.

Blue Springs—Miss Rilla Strain and Mr. Fred Kendrick were married in a quiet wedding at Squire Haynes'.

The old time square dance given by Uncle Willis Mote Christmas night was enjoyed by a large crowd and the party at the home of Misses Florence and Blanche Lacey last Thursday night was much enjoyed.

The style of dress for this year is costly in lavishness and splendor. Muffs are enormous. In furs, victorines in quaint new shapes are being made in sealskin, chinchilla, skunk, and caracul. Dresses are made with mutton sleeves and, for night, with lace ruffles and very low necks. Waists are tiny, skirts long and gracefully flared, and some have long ribbons looped in bows to the hem. Large, elegant fans are carried.

By the will of the late Joseph E. Brown, his river plantation near Crane Eater, estimated at $14,000, was left to his son, Elisha B. Brown.

Hicks and Pitts have dissolved partnership. Pitts has moved across the street and Mr. Lyman Craig is associated with him. Mr. Hick and son, F. L., will continue business in the Hicks-Pitts building.

The coldest wave in years struck like a ton of bricks last week. The back water is covered with thick ice. The Poplar Springs correspondent writes, "We have had quite a grand scene of late. 'Twas the back water frozen over for several days. One day was a hissing, rumbling noise, accompanied by the fall of waters, when the ice broke and began floating away. As I write, the little steamer, Tony, is plying her way down the waters to Rome."

Sonoraville—Grandma Bolding is visiting Squire F. M. Bolding.

Miss Lucille Dudley had the misfortune to lose her canary bird. Its death was supposed to be from chloroform in the air of the room where the cage was hanging.

Mr. John Erwin, Jr., informs us that he will go to Cartersville to study law under Solicitor General Fite.

Editor Hall, of the Calhoun Times, gives instructions to his county correspondents: Do not give opinions. Remember who, what, why, when, where, and how. Always be brief. Don't criticize anything or anybody. Such items as "guess who has a wart on ihs nose" are not news.

Long faces, long coats, and long accounts don't pay.

In the paper this week is a picture of a work of the first American iron casting. It is the picture of a kettle on a crane, cast by the Sangors Iron works at Lynn, Massachusetts in 1642. The kettle was given to Thomas Hudson, younger brother of Hendrick Hudson, and is now on display at the World's Columbian Exposition at Chicago.

A new and attractive sign has been put up at the New York Racket Store here by Nash, the painter.

Sheriff Dan Durham has moved into the old jail and Deputy Dave Johnson will move into W. D. Fain's house. Mr. Fain will move to his farm.

Make your boys work while they are growing up. Don't be afraid of hurting their feelings. Better do that than have them hurt your feelings and your pocketbook when they grow up.

Two mailboxes have been located downtown since the Post Office has been moved to the T. M. Ellis building. One box remains at the depot.

Veach's Avenue, the pretty street in Adairsville just opened and running west of the railroad, has undergone an excellent syetem of sewerage and sidewalks are to be made in the spring.

Both schools in Adairsville are well patronized.

Dr. Borders' well in Bartow had 22 feet of water in it the other day but in 24 hours only 10 feet remained. The U. S. Weather observer says it beat him.

The newly made roads, made by convict labor, have not been damaged by the high water. The thousands of cubic yards of dirt stood the pressure of water without repairs to be made.

There are several excellent lady violinists in Adairsville who have regular assemblies and render pleasing selections.

At Hall Bros. racoon 4 x 4 sheeting 4½¢ calico remnants 4¢ ladies ladies and gents black hose 5¢, all wool jeans 20¢.

Uncle Thomas Addington owns a waistcoat used in the Revolutionary war by a kinsman. 140 years old, it is made of unfinished silk and the buttons are handmade.

Do women know—that a small round mirror upon which to set a jar of one variety of flowers, chrysanthemums, roses, or tulips, is a prettier centerpiece than any amount of embroidery?

Mrs. Jones, 76, died at the home of her daughter, Mrs. J. H. Bridges, in Sugar Valley, on January 19th. She lived a Christian life and as she lived so she died.

Willie, the 6 year old son of Mr. and Mrs. J. T. McEntyre died on January 28.

Miss Annie Bellows is teaching music at Ryals High School. The building caught fire in February and if it had not been for Messers Braden, Norrell and Griffin who discovered the fire and put it out, we would not have a school building.

John Herrington gave a card party to a few of his friends one night last week.

Mr. J. T. Norton, according to the Union Hill dots, gave a wood chopping Monday morning. The boys cut 30 cords of wood in half a day. Mrs. Norton had a sumptuous dinner and everyone enjoyed the dance that night. "Miss Pearl" proved herself a perfect gem in entertaining those that did not care to participate in the dance.

Thirty years after the Civil War, memories are still green and stories still worth the telling. This is how a Gordon County lady fooled the Yankees. She had a lot of fine meat in the smokehouse and when she heard the Yankees were coming, she put the meat in the front yard and sprinkled it with soda, then with flour. Soon a greenish look spread over it. Suddenly the yard was full of blue coats. They asked, "What's the matter with the meat?" "I do not know", said the Gordon County lady, "the rebels were here last night and fixed it up." The Yankees left it alone as if each piece had been soaked in strychnine.

F. M. Green has an interesting relic which he brought home from the battle of the Wilderness. It was found in a field from which the Yankees had been driven. The relic is an old fashioned folding pocket, made by an Ohio girl and sent to her sweetheart. It held a love letter from the girl to the soldier, a gold pen, a needle and two spools of thread. The pocket was strapped to an old fashioned valise, against which a hickory shirt was strapped. A minnie ball had cut holes in the shirt and lodged in the valise.

The soldier's name was W. P. Hibbard, Company H. First Ohio Regiment. Mr. Green has advertised the relic in a northern paper and will try to find descendants of the soldier.

T. J. Brown of Decora has a fine collection of relics, a spoon and a fork used by Union soldiers, a cavalry belt buckle, and copy of general order No. 18, Army of Tennessee, which was issued April 27, 1865 and is signed by Joseph E. Johnston. The order sets forth the conditions of surrender and how the army is to be disbanded and the men sent home.

"Ah, the pathos, the heroism, the sublime glory of that time! Yes, a nation glorious in its defeat, glorious in its unequal contest with mighty odds. Many of those old boys who wore the gray and faced bullets at Chickamauga and Resaca and marched with Joseph E. Johnston through Calhoun are living in Gordon County today. God bless them."

—James A. Hall.

New officers of the bank are: W. R. Rankin, J. M. Harlan, O. N. Starr, D. H. Livermore, W. L. Hines, and J. C. Dayton, directors, Mr. Livermore, president, O. N. Starr, cashier, and Berry Boaz, assistant.

Mr. Claud Nesbitt caught 7 wild turkeys in his pen near Resaca last week.

Mr. W. F. Lay has a small and highly finished Indian tomahawk. It was picked up in a field near Clark Chapel. The tomahawk with a small blade is made of the best steel and superbly mounted with ornaments of silver.

Mr. Will King, of Cash, has 2 octagon shaped gold quarters, coined in 1855.

The Florida exhibit car, stopping at Calhoun and Adairsville, contains a display of tropical fruits and flowers.

Mr. John Crawford and Miss Bessie Hudgins were married in a pleasant home ceremony performed by Rev. B. H. Trammell. They have the best wishes of the community.

Judge Fain died in his office chair Wednesday, March 13, at 2:30 o'clock. The funeral at the Baptist Church was conducted by Rev. B. H. Trammell. Col. I. J. McCamy and Col. J. E. Shumate of Dalton spoke feelingly of his life and characteristics and Dr. R. W. Thornton read an original poem of 8 verses eulogizing the Judge.

One verse read,
"Thou hast lain down the burdens of both peace and war
And folded the mantle of both carnage and state
And rested thine armor with laurels and honors
To mingle thy dust with the good and the great."

Mr. H. J. Doughty has bought the old T. W. Harbin home from Mr. Livermore. (home of Miss Sallie Kimbrough, 1958)

Mrs. G. M. Hunt went to Atlanta last week to purchase a large stock of spring millinery.

Miss Sallie Rice, beautiful and accomplished daughter of Rev. A. H. Rice, visited in town Saturday, to the delight of her many friends here.

City authorities are having the lot below Ferguson's building cleaned off and it will be sown in blue grass. Old trees have been trimmed, new ones set out, and the street opened up from the Ferguson Building to the other street at Fuller's Crossing. (Railroad Street to Line), which adds greatly to the appearance of the town and, when completed, Calhoun will present to the view of the passengers on the railroad a most pleasant and thrifty appearance.

Don't forget to clean off your back yard and use an abundance of lime about your premises. A little attention in this way may save sickness in your family.

Major Roff has put up a new wire fence in front of his home.

Dr. Gambrell, president of Mercer, has offered free scholarships to students of Ryals High School, an honor that only a few schools have received.

Mrs. T. W. Harbin, who has been dangerously ill, has passed the crisis and her physicians believe her recovery certain.

Misses Ida Warren and Janie Everett, two attractive young ladies of Sugar Valley, visited the Misses Ellis last week.

Calhoun stores are filled with elegant spring goods, bright new straw hats, tan shoes, and pretty spring styles of clothing and dress goods. People are buying rapidly and the merchants are happy.

A marriage which created some surprise in Calhoun Sunday afternoon was that of Mr. J. G. B. Erwin, Jr. of Fairmount and Miss Sallie Rice of Sonoraville. The marriage took place at the home of Rev. B. H. Trammell who performed the ceremony and the happy couple left on the northbound train for Tilton where Mr. Erwin is engaged in teaching. May they live long and prosper are the wishes of their friends.

Lon Chastain has two old books that would interest the relic hunter. One is "A Treatise on Philosophical Furnaces" published in London in 1651. The other is a ledger captured by the Confederates from General Dodge's Division of the Federal Army at Pulaski, Tennessee. In it are recorded all kinds of army orders signed by Grant, Thomas, and other generals.

Slippers 45¢ a pair at Hall Brothers.

Our new sheriff, Dan Durham, and deputy, Dave Johnson, deserve much credit for the fact that the courthouse is the best kept in years.

Cicero Curtiss, who has been clerking in Alabama has returned to Calhoun.

Mr. Wade Shelor, of Reeves, is now connected with Hall Brothers. He is an excellent young man and will doubtless prove a valuable addition to Calhoun's business circles.

Mr. G. S. King has about completed his new house at Little Row and the young people are looking forward to a quilting and a dance soon.

Through the kindness of Mr. Henry Pittman of Igo we have been permitted to examine several copies of Calhoun's first newspaper, The Georgia Platform. The oldest copy was dated July 1, 1858 and was a seven column, four page sheet. G. B. Fain was the Editor and Proprietor and the subscription price was $2. The content of the paper was mostly long political articles. E. R. Sassen wa smanager of the hotel. Lawyers cards were, W. H. Dabney, G. J. Fain, W. V. Wester, J. E. Parrott, Phillips and Halford, M. J. Crawford, and T. J. Stokes.

A card for B. J. Hutchins, Resident Ambrotypist was listed. He made photographs, but why this high-sounding title?

Other copies of the paper were dated a year later when the name was The Democratic Platform and W. V. Wester was the Editor. War was coming and a nervous excitement was the tone of the paper. There were red-hot articles on the Southern Opposition Party and the Black Republican Party. Notable was the utter absence of news and no local news at all. But, in its day, The Democratic Platform was one of Georgia's best edited journals.

Mrs. Rebecca Lay of Sugar Valley brought in a copy of The Valley Register, February 27, 1861. The inaugural address of Jefferson is printed and, on other pages, an account of the departure of Captain Walker who carried away a company of volunteers, seventeen of them from Calhoun.

There is a farewell article from David Wylie who announces he has enlisted in the regular army. There are also many bitter political articles.

A copy of The Confederate Flag, dated March 12, 1862, is among Mr. Lay's papers. Scott and White were the proprietors. War was a fearful reality. There were Yankees at Cumberland Gap, gun boats on the Tennessee and Federals at Tuscumbia, Alabama.

The Whiskey Proclamation of Governor Joseph E. Brown is very strong. He says that the amount of whiskey manufactured in the state is fearful, he commands its stoppage and urges the conversion of still metal into cannons.

This year Editor James A. Hall has been writing a series of articles on the history of Gordon County. He begins with the visit of DeSoto in 1540.

DeSoto crossed the Etowah in Cherokee County and followed the Pine Log Mountains to the old Indian village of Connesauga (at Carter's Quarter). He was met there by 20 Indians, each carrying a basket of mulberries and plums and nuts.

The company rested at Connesauga where they found everything needed for the horses and the men, then marched down river to the city of Chiaha (Rome).

As told in The Portugese Chronicles, "the trees grew in the fields without planting or dressing. Five days before he came to Chiaha, DeSoto was met by 15 Indians, laden with maize, which the Cacique had sent. They had 20 barns full of it and all things else were at his service. The Cacique voided his own house in which he lodged and received the Governor with much joy."

"In the town was much butter in gourds, melted like oils. They said it was the fat of bears."

"All up and down the river were rich meadows and luxuriant fields of grain, dotted with stately walnuts. The Indians greatly feared the whites."

A few years ago a well-preserved coat of mail was dug out of the Coosa River at Rome.

Mr. Hall continues the county history with the well known story of missionaries at New Echota, tells of the arrest of S. A. Worcester, and states that his house is still standing at New Echota with the library shelves still in place.

In 1848 Cartersville had a population of 150, Cassville 900, and Dalton 1500, but there was no Calhoun.

After Gordon County was organized in 1850, Mr. John P. King had the hotel built and a big brick store stood where Logan's livery stable now stands (1895).

By 1851, houses were going up on all sides and new citizens were coming in. Major Roff, one of the first comers, operated a saw mill at Oothcaloga Mill. He built the original building where the Haynes House now stands (site of Daves Warehouse 1958) and sawed lumber for nearly all the buildings of the place.

Colonel W. C. Cantrell, W. M. Peeples, and J. A. Mims were also here at the start.

The first Superior Court was held in Calhoun in November 1850.

While John P. King owned the land, he would allow no liquor in the village. A man named Wash Lawson built a little liquor house on a lot, that is now the farm of Mr. Gordon Fuller. The first saloon was located where Mrs. Jones now lives. (Mrs. King's home on King Street, 1958). Soon after the town was started saloons spring up everywhere.

When the state road to the Oostanaula was constructed, a party of Irish blasters was put to work just above where Resaca now stands. It was expected at once that a town would grow up there, which it did and the Irishmen named it Dublin.

John Howard owned the land where the town was being built and sold lots to all comers. Among the first citizens was Thomas Norton.

A powerful lumber company began operations in the vicinity and moved the town across the river.

The depot was built by a man named Cowan who also made the brick.

When the soldiers returned from the Mexican war, they named the town Resaca from the Mexican name, Resaca de la Palma.

Among the first citizens of Resaca were J. A. Fite, W. H. Smith, and J. W. Hill.

Today, May 1, 1895, Calhoun, Plainville, and Lily Pond will vote on the fence or no fence question. (Victory for the no fence).

Ice cream in 5 minutes from the Wonder Freezer at J. M. Harlan's.

Awnings are being put up in front of the Gray building, and the barber shop on Railroad Street. The street looks quite different now. A long shed covers the walk and the fellows have all the shade they need to play checkers.

Calhoun has a new citizen. Dr .McClain, of Acworth, has located here to practice his profession. But in August Dr. McClain moved to Tilton and the people regretted losing his family.

J. C. Johnson is having a picket fence put up around the property bought from Mrs. Freeman. He will improve the old brick residence and when it is fitted up in good shape, will move into it.

An elegant office is being fitted up for the agent at the N. C.

and St. L. depot and the depot is being painted a dark red.

Uncle Balis Greene, 84, is one of the oldest citizens of Gordon County, having come here before the Indians left. He entered the army and helped gather up the Indians and move them to Ross's Landing, (Chattanooga). He was with the garrison at Fort Buffington, which stood in Mr. Prater's field. General Scott liked him and offered him $100 a month to be his bodyguard and go to Washington. Mr. Greene had a wife and children whom he could not leave in the wilds of Georgia so declined the offer. Mr. Greene has never been sick and has used tobacco and coffee as long as he can remember. He voted for Harrison he said "because I knew his granddaddy".

The commencement at Fairmount College begins June 1 and will run through June 5. Saturday is the day for the Primary exhibit and program by the little folks and the sermon will be preached Sunday by the Rev. L. H. Harris of Emory.

Monday, the young ladies' contest for the B. H. Trammell medal and the young men for the J. M. Veach medal. The H. J. Adams and the Sam P. Jones Literary Societies will debate.

Judge John A. Akin, of Cartersville, will deliver the address Tuesday and students will contest for the J. A. Sharp and W. P. Hammond gold medals.

The week's program will conclude with the drama "Handy Andy" tableau and pantomimes.

Mr. Robert Crutchfield of the Wrought Iron Range Company stopped over with friends Monday. Later in the year Mr. Crutchfield was to move his family from North Carolina to Calhoun, buying from Mr. John Simpson the residence where Dr. Hightower was residing. Dr. Hightower would move to the H. J. Doughty residence and the Crutchfield family would stay at the Haynes House until repairs on the house were completed.

One of the oldest and most interesting darkies in Gordon County is Uncle Dick Garlington, 89. He came with the first settlers and has always lived in the county. He comes up occasionally to talk about old times. Uncle Dick belongs to a class of old time darkies now almost extinct.

Blue Springs has 50 folks and 2 stores. The new Baptist church has 100 members.

Mr. J. Q. Everett and Mr. W. F. Tarvin together have shipped 132 crates of huckleberries to Cincinnati and other Northern towns.

Fair Sugar Valley! I don't think Sugar Valley was ever intended for anything but a land of fair summer dreams. So restful, so reposeful. I stopped there today and had a good dinner at the hotel run by Mrs. W. P. Hill, where everything is done to make guests comfortable and happy.

Blitch is the railroad agent and telegraph operator. He is also a farmer, geologist, mineralogist, philosopher, and romanticist.

Across the street Haynes, genial and irrepressible, the wit of Sugar Valley, is winding up the affairs of Dr. A. B. Frix, whose untimely death was such a loss to the community.

Most contented man is Graham, postmaster and merchant, happy, handsome, and fat. There's no mail on Sundays so he goes a-sparking.

Genial and clever W. F. Tarvin is conducting a lively retail business. A good citizen, he is happy and prosperous.

Dr. H. S. Smith has arrived to take Dr. Frixes place.

Mr. Dickey, a young man of fine business qualities, is doing good work for The Tribune.

J. Q. Everett has added livery to his merchandise business. He has put up several barrels of huckleberry wine, samples of which he will show at the Exhibition.

Ryals and Dickey schools are prosperous. For the natural picturesqueness of beauty and its surroundings, Sugar Valley has no rival in all this beautiful North Georgia region (M. M. Folsom in The Rome Tribune).

Miss Rosa White left Resaca last week to resume her duties as teacher in the Holly Creek School.

Col. F. A. Cantrell and family will leave this week for a visit of several weeks at Salt Lake City and other places in the Rocky Mountains. They will return in September.

Some boys did a great deal of damage on Professor Neal's farm near town pulling up corn stalks, breaking tools, etc. Several boys were arrested but since no conclusive proof could be secured, they were released.

Col. O. N. Starr is having improvements made on his house. Albert Gregg of Dalton is doing the work.

A large number of friends gathered at the home of the bride's mother to witness the marriage of Miss May Hudgins to Col. Thomas Skelly. The ceremony was performed by Rev. B. H. Trammell. G. A. Hall and Miss Nettie Wells, W. L. Hillhouse and Miss Lida Thomason, H. T. Tinsley and Miss Viola Wright, and J. S. Hall and Miss Laura Haynes were the attendants. After the wedding, the guests enjoyed a bountiful feast at the home of the groom's mother. Both of these young people are popular in Calhoun and their many friends over the county extend best wishes.

For two weeks, a carload of peaches a day has been shipped from Plainville to Cincinnati, Chicago, and Columbus, Ohio. The price is $1.50 a crate.

The name of Little Row was changed to Curryville in honor of Hon. David W. Curry, prominent Rome druggist, in August of this year.

In a big business deal this week, Hall Bros. bought out the Racket Store from the proprietors, Ferguson and Doughty.

Miss Ora Hunt, of Polk County, a niece of W. F. King, is spending a couple of weeks with her friend, Miss Lula Brogdon. The two young ladies were formerly classmates at Dalton Female Seminary.

There is a rumor going around that the City Council of Calhoun will arrest all boys under 20 years of age who are found on the streets after 9 o'clock at night.

J. B. F. Harrell and J. C. Brownlee have made a real estate deal. Harrell gets Brownlee's farm at Plainville, all of the 260 acre place except the Brownlee residence, and 40 acres. Mr. Brownlee gets 5 houses and lots in Calhoun. The cash value on both sides was $3,500.

There was a bad runaway Monday morning. The two-horse team of V. H. Bentley, standing with a load of corn near the public well, became frightened and ran down the street. The wagon team, going at a rapid rate, ran into D. Westfield's dray in front of Malone's drugstore. The dray was badly knocked about and the mule thrown and seriously hurt. The wagon tongue was broken out. The runaway caused much excitement and the street was soon filled with people.

Several years ago, the town was full of dog weed but now very little of it can be seen. Since the cattle are kept up, other grass has had a chance to grow and choke it out.

J. S. Allison has just completed his home near Crane Eater where he has one of the most complete water works to be found on private property. The creek nearby drives a wheel which operates a pump and, by this means, hot and cold water is supplied to every room in the house and to the yard, garden, and stables.

R. L. Crutchfield has bought an interest in D. Westfield's mercantile business.

Work was started on J. M. Neal's new brick store in September. The building was planned and will be erected by Newt Legg.

Mr. G. T. Fite has just completed a commodious barn on the brown farm.

E. H. Taylor is erecting a wagon yard in the rear of the Calhoun Hotel which he recently bought.

Miss Ida Warren of Sugar Valley is clerking at E. H. Taylor's store. Her friends wish her success.

The merchants are decorating the county with attractive signs.

Mrs. T. M. Ellis has sold her millinery business to Miss Hood.

The Columbian Liberty Bell was exhibited in Calhoun last week to a big crowd. A company of young ladies rang the bell, speeches were made, and a stake driven in the ground to dedicate and mark the spot where the bell stood.

Last Saturday three wagons of Illinois immigrants on the way to Governor Northern's colony in South Georgia passed through Calhoun looking dusty and travel worn. They expect to reach the colony in about two weeks. Numerous wagons would come through later in the year on the way to the new colony.

Two bicyclists from Louisville passed through on Tuesday.

Northern travelers on the W & A frequently say that Calhoun has one of the most attractive depots in Georgia.

J. G. B. Erwin, Jr., a young man of fine promise is reading law at Colonel Starr's office and boarding at Dr. Hightower's.

Mr. Matt Robertson came in from Kansas last week to visit his family. His brother, W. A., came down from Dalton to see him.

Murray wants $1800 from Gordon for constructing the iron bridge across the Coosawattee at Carter's.

Rev. M. A. Mathews, formerly pastor of the Calhoun Presbyterian Church, will leave Dalton and go to Jackson, Tennessee to serve as pastor of the church there.

There was no preaching anywhere in Calhoun Sunday.

Rev. Quillian is the new pastor of the Methodist Church.

Howard Findley, only 20 years old, and a young man full of promise, died in October. His death is mourned by a host of friends and relatives. The funeral was conducted by Rev. E. M. Dyer of Dalton.

Judge J. W. Stanton, one of our oldest and best citizens died at Igo. Originally from Tennessee, he represented Gordon in the Legislature and was instrumental in reducing the $7 a day pay to legislators, which he felt was too high.

An interesting marriage occurred Tuesday night at the home of T. M. Ellis when Miss Fannie Ellis was wed to Mr. T. N. Austin of Plainville. After the ceremony they left for Sugar Valley where an elegant banquet was served at the home of the groom's parents.

The presents were numerous and elegant. Mr. Austin is highly esteemed and Miss Fannie, possessed of rare gifts of personality, has long been a leading figure in Calhoun circles.

Another home wedding of interest was that of Miss Daisy Hughey to Mr. Paris Williams.

FIRST TRAIN TO CALHOUN

"Here she comes!" the shout went up, and around the curve she came, long iron arms working furiously, high wheels spinning, smoke pouring from a stack that looked for the world like a wash pot stuck on top of a spreadout stove pipe—here she comes, the first train to Calhoun.

"Good Lord," cried a woman, "look at that thar thing! Don't you know it's tired? Look how it puffs and blows!"

Puffing smoke and blowing steam, the little engine slowed, and stopped along side Mr. Lawson's store.

The crowd rushed together around the train, the men curious to see what made it run, the women excited over the gay red and green and tan passenger cars.

Folks had come in from Big Spring, Paine Bailey's mill, Gideon's Crossing, Chandlers and everywhere else to see the first train come in over the long, narrow, twisting tracks, completed this year after about ten years of hard work.

W. G. Cantrell—he had been a tailor for the Cherokee Nation in the 1830s was there, Professor Kimbrough, teacher to the Cherokee, was there. A. W. Reeve was certainly standing by with a feeling of pride for he had helped to lay the rails. Sixteen year old E. J. Kiker was there.

Joab Lewis was there, for it was he who told the story in 1896 to Editor Jim Hall of the Calhoun Times.

"The engine was very small," Uncle Joab said, "compared to the one in use today. The train was in charge of Major Wallace, Colonel Richard Peters and Major Dooley. There was no Calhoun, only a little log store run by a Mr. Lawson."

From that day, in the spring of 1847, when the little engine— Was it The General? or The Texas? or the Yonah?—puffed into Dawsonville to the days of 1850, when the State built Oothcalooga Depot, and the Legislature created Gordon County, and through the war years, the railroad had been the life line of North Georgia. As its service expanded, so grew the towns along the way.

Now, in 1896, the place once called Dawsonville or Oothcalooga Depot is Calhoun, a town of 2000 inhabitants.

People of the country had made merry during the Christmas holidays. Mr. and Mrs. H. B. Herrington regally entertained a number of friends at their home near town Tuesday. It would be a hard matter to find a better dinner anywhere than at Henry Herrington's.

At Adairsville, the Christmas tree at the Baptist Church Tuesday night was well laden with lovely gifts. Mrs. Reuben Gaines gave a delightful reception from 1:00 o'clock to 3:00 o'clock in honor of her granddaughter little Ethel Gaines.

Friday night, the Adairsville Clue Club gave a winter dinner. The schoolhouse was decorated to resemble a forest. At 10:00 o'clock, an elegant dinner was served and the guests enjoyed delightful music from guitar and phonoharp.

Mr. Sam Boston, of Cash and Miss Fannie Ferguson were married at Watsonville on December 21, at 3 o'clock. May they live a long and happy life is our wish.

Schools throughout the country continue to be of prime importance to the citizens. Prof. D. E. Green, of Dexter, Georgia, has been elected principal of Ryals High School at Sugar Valley. He will be assisted by Mrs. Coffee and Miss Annie Bellows music teacher. The upper story of Ryals is to be furnished for teachers to live.

The Normal Academy at Rocky Creek is under the management of Prof. L. C. Calbeck, and Miss Minnie Camp. These teachers are well equipped and the school will be a success.

Prof. Dickey, of Sugar Valley, goes to Rome this week as principal of East End Academy. Tom Hopper is assisting Mr. Doss in the school at Redbud and Miss Nellie Littlefield of Adairsville, is teaching at The Glade. She has a fine school and all are pleased with her as a teacher.

Prof. Mill's school at Belcher's schoolhouse, Folsom, has 76 scholars. Mr. and Mrs. B. T. Cantrell are in charge of the Coosawattee High School and rent is free in the dormitories.

The school at Sonoraville is under Prof. Royster and daughter, Miss Willie. We have a handsome building and efficient teachers. Let us unite to make this the most succesful year in history.

The bridge across the Oostanaula has finally been repaired by the County Commissioners. Printup's, Fite's and Fork's ferries are all free now. The new ferry boat at Johnson's Ferry has been needed for sometime.

Dr. W. H. Darnell has been elected pastor of the Presbyterian church. He is highly esteemed by all. Preaching at Liberty Presbyterian Church has been changed to third Saturday and Sunday. Rev. W. M. McGhee, of Chattanooga, is pastor of this church.

Miss Maude Rooker, of Resaca, is visiting in town.

J. G. B. Erwin, Jr. has moved into the house lately occupied by W. W. Wilson.

Improvements on the old Pulliam brick residence, home of J. C. Johnson, have been completed and it is now one of the most elegant homes in town.

The marriage of Mr. Bartow Bridges and Miss Cora Abbott occurred Monday afternoon at 2 o'clock, January 27, at the home of the bride's father Mr. M. B. Abbott of Sugar Valley. It was a very quiet affair and only the immediate families of the participants were present. The ceremony was performed by the Rev. J. J. S. Callaway. Immediately after the ceremony, the happy couple left, via Chattanooga, for their future home at Blue Pond Alabama. Miss Abbott is a young lady of many rare gifts and accomplishments and enjoys the esteem of a wide circle of friends. Mr. Bridges is an excellent young man who is engaged in a successful lumber business in Alabama. The best wishes of their many friends go with the young couple. (My parents J. B. R.)

Beginning next Monday, February 10, the mail route from Oostanaula to Everett Springs will be changed to daily mail.

S. F. Boston has moved into his new dwelling near Gum Springs.

Wade Shelor will leave for Nashville to take a course in one of the leading business college of that city. Mr. Shelor, who has been with Hall Bros. for some time, possesses fine business qualities and his future is full of promise.

Drs. Hightower and McClain formed a partnership early in the year but later dissolved the partnership and Dr. Hightower moved into his elegant new office in the Harlan building.

A no-fence law is the latest subject for discussion at Red Bud. Dr. Langford was called last week to attend Mrs. Wm. Adams, of Fambro, who is very low with lagrippe and heart trouble.

Prof. E. Neal recently purchased the old Methodist parsonage near the Academy, is making improvements and will move in soon.

The new Postmistress, Miss Bessie Fain, takes charge of the Calhoun Post Office next week. Mrs. C. C. Harlan has resigned. She was one of the best the town ever had and her long period of service was one of entire satisfaction. Miss Edith Ransome will continue as assistant.

Damascus church will shortly organize a Bible Class to meet on Sunday afternoon. Rev. M. C. Hooper is the new pastor of this church.

Dr. J. H. Reeve and family, of Atlanta, have moved to Calhoun. The doctor will engage in the practice of his profession here with office in the Post Office building. For the present, the doctor's family has moved into the residence of T. M. Ellis.

Mrs. W. J. Hall has moved into the Boaz place on the hill, recently vacated by R. C. Mizell.

The Grand Jury was organized yesterday with Major A. W. Wells as foreman. The body is composed of excellent citizens and will doubtless do good work.

Mr. A. M. Graham is exhibiting four mad stones of various sizes, a large gray one and others smaller and darker. They were sent from Alabama by his son, W. H. In these days of hydrophobia, the stone will probably be much in demand.

Come a running by hokey—two spools of soft finish thread 5 cents to close out at Taylor's.

Messers J. G. B. Erwin, Jr. and Lee Godfrey were admitted to the bar during court and are now ready to practice. Both stood creditable examinations and are bound to do well.

The subject of cutting the pine thicket is again under discussion. In 1884, John P. King had written to Major Aaron Roff, "I believe the commons should remain under control of the town." On May 1, 1850, Mr. King had written, "I care little about the location of the county seat for the new county of Gordon, believing it, however, for the interest of the railroad and the county, should be placed at Oothcalooga. I will give the county land for public purposes and one half the proceeds from business lots to be laid off."

Captain Andrews and his famous boat, Sapolio, the 14 foot craft in which he crossed the Atlantic, attracted attention on the streets of Calhoun Tuesday. It's a great advertising scheme to name a boat for something you want to sell, then after the ocean has been crossed, to put the boat on wheels and drive it all over the country.

The Calhoun Times this week carries pictures of the two citizens running for the State Senate, O. N. Starr and J. H. Gordon. With smooth, young faces practically disguised by long drooping mustaches, it's hard to tell which is Col. Starr and which is Mr. Gordon.

Mr. Gordon is described as a levelheaded and successful business man and Col. Starr, is a successful lawyer who has made his own way.

Two new school houses grace the countryside of Gordon, one at Crane Eater and one at Boston Grove.

G. H. Gardner, of Lilly Pond, received a severe electrical shock last week. He was standing near the railroad, waiting to exchange mail with a train nearly due and received the shock when lightning struck a telegraph pole one half mile away.

Through the kindness of J. B. Henson, of Rocky Creek, the editor has examined a copy of The Cassville Standard, printed June 16, 1853. There was no paper in Calhoun at that time and advertising was done in the Cassville paper. Cards of Jones and Crawford and J. D. Phillips Attorneys and an ad for John A. O'Shield, fashionable tailor, with office near Peeples' Store, filled spaces in the paper. A new carriage factory was advertised by Matthews and Milholm, located the second door from The Gordon House.

Valley Springs—A ladies missionary Society was organized at Salem in March. It meets on Saturday at 10 a.m. the last meeting, two pieces, read by Miss Lola McWhorter and Miss Sidnie Johnston, both entertained and edified the ladies.

Mr. W. F. King and Miss Annie H. Saxon were married Wednesday, April 15, at the home of the bride's father, Col. Robert Saxon, at Grassdale, Ga. It was a quiet wedding with the ceremony being performed by Rev. W. T. Bell. The bride and groom came to Calhoun on the train, where the many friends of Mr. King extend congratulations. Mr. and Mrs. L. R. Pitts gave an elegant reception for Mr. and Mrs. King. Quite a large crowd was present and the occasion was greatly enjoyed. The refreshments served rendered the evening most delightful.

The Gordon County Singing Convention met at Resaca this year. Joab Lewis is president, S. T. Eskew, vice president and E. W. Keys, secretary.

A Young Peoples Union was organized at the Baptist Church Saturday night. Geraldus Fuller was elected president, Walter Hightower, secretary and Mrs. N. W. Ballew, treasurer. The Union meets on Wednesday nights for social and religious instruction.

The ladies of Sugar Valley have had the Baptist church painted. Mr. Nash superintended the work.

Mrs. W. B. Harbour and Misses Agnes Moss and Viola McCutcheon are visiting friends and relatives in Rome.

A group of young people from Reeves Station, Oostanaula and Sugar Valley picnicked in the Pocket Saturday.

The Calhoun Sunday Schools joined for a picnic in Peter's Grove. Why can't Calhoun have a first class School building? The present Academy is an eye sore to people and a bad advertisement to strangers. Let's get a good building.

Water in the public well has a very disagreeble odor and taste. If it cannot be improved, the well should be abandoned and a new one dug. See that your wells are cleaned out and that no surface drainage gets in.

It is Commencement time at Ryals High School, Fairmount College, Everett Spring Academy and The Calhoun Collegiate Institute. Prof. L. C. Calbeck, who came here recently from Indiana, will conduct a five weeks normal school at Ryals this summer. Prof. E. Neal is conducting a normal school at Blue Ridge this week. Rev. Aquils Chamblee, of Canton, will prach at Sugar Valley, Saturday, June 6, and at Calhoun, Sunday, June 7.

Eugene Doughty and Dorse Bonner started to Atlanta on their bicycles, but got tired and boarded the train at Emerson.

Wagons continue to pass through, going to Fitzgerald and others are going back north, taking homesick citizens.

Mark Lewis and Jim Murphy have opened a new store, dealing in groceries and general merchandise, on Railroad street.

The bank directors declared a semi-annual dividend of 3½ per cent this month.

Calhoun is the best town in Georgia and has the best bank.

The town has presented quite a lively and prosperous appearance during the past week. Work on the Harlan building is going ahead and painters are at work on the Hill Livery Stable, on Mims and Kinmans Store and on S. Mims residence.

Mrs. Ernest Neal is prepared to take several boarders at reasonable rates. Teachers in attendance at the Institute will find this a desirable home near the Academy, with neat rooms and good table board.

Rev. Mr. Bell, a Chinese student at Emory, gave a lecture on China, which was highly entertaining, at the Methodist Church.

Rev. A. S. Tatum was in town Wednesday, shaking hands with friends. He has written a book called Gems of Short Sermons. Rev. Tatum is just from Fitzgerald and says that the Yankee town is doing well and he thinks it will make a fine city.

Dr. R. H. Johnson, of Toledo, Ohio, is spending several weeks at the Haynes House. He is thinking of locating in Calhoun, and says a good many people in his section are thinking of coming south.

For many years, the Haynes House has been one of the best and most popular hotels on the W & A. Here you find first class board, nice, pleasant rooms and homelike accommodations. W. B. Haynes is a born hotel man.

Thursday was a rushing day at Oothcalooga Mills. Over 100 wagons unloaded and over 1000 bushels of grain were handled. W. W. Ballew is making a great success with the mills.

Uncle Tom Strickland is retiring as porter at the W & A depot. Nearly as long as anyone remembers, he has been a familiar figure about the place. He began work on October 17, 1868, under Mr. Parrott. Uncle Tom has never had a row with anyone, has never been in court and never sued. He owns a good home in the southern part of town, where he and his wife live. What a worthy example is his life and character!

The marriage of Miss Nina Gordon and Mr. Will Wilkerson occurred at the Oostanaula Baptist Church Tuesday. The ceremony was performed by Dr. R. B. Headden, of Rome. After the very elegant wedding, a bountiful feast was served at the home of the bride's father, Captain J. B. Gordon. The couple will make their home in Rome.

Cards are out for the wedding of Mr. M. D. Pate and Miss Ida Warren which will take place at the Sugar Valley Baptist Church, Wednesday September 9, at 8 p.m. The couple will leave for Atlanta to spend some time. Both are well known and have the best wishes of their many friends.

A big revival has been in progress at Antioch church, four miles east of Calhoun. Eleven were baptized Sunday by the Rev. W. V. Hall, who conducted the meeting, assisted by Rev. Long.

Charlie Hunt's wonderful slot machine is attracting a lot of attention. Called the Hunt Vending Machine, it is a tall 8 Cylinder machine, set in a strong frame, brilliantly decorated and illuminated with electricity. Drop in a nickel and it gives a choice of seven articles in cubicle boxes and even returns the nickel if no boxes are there.

Charlie spent a year an a half and $1000 on his invention. D. H. Livermore, W. W. Ballew and C. W. Hunt formed the Hunt Vending Machine Company with a stock of $11,000. In November, big headlines in an Atlanta paper proclaimed, The Wonder of Atlanta. "Charlie Hunt's Vending Machine causes a sensation on the street and draws crowds that blocked the sidewalk. The mayor has ordered it moved."

Buy yourself a few good books and learn something these long winter nights. Anybody can be well-informed if they try. Ignorance this day and time is utterly without excuse.

Hon. O. N. Starr was elected by a 1200 majority. We will have an able, conscientious and untiring representative in the next legislature.

Calhoun is growing fast. All vacant houses have been occupied and we need more houses.

Tolbert and Watts have moved into their new stand in the Foster building. An elegant new front is being put in the building. E. L. Parrott is erecting an attractive cottage below the depot. J. C. Johnson has got his new corn mill in operation at his gin and is running day and night. J. B. Addington's store building is being moved nearer the side walk and a new foundation is being built. Oothcalooga Mill has made important improvements.

After the resignation of Rev. A. H. Rice as pastor of the Baptist Church, Rev. J. F. Cox was elected to succeed him. Mr. Rice has served the church faithfully and well and carries with him the esteem of not only the church, but the community, as well.

Pound parties at the home of H. C. Hunt and Mrs. F. L. Hicks were enjoyed by the young people.

The Gordon County Baptist Association was organized at Bethesda, October 31. Rev. John Row was elected moderator and Mr. Julius Putney, clerk. The object of the Association is to embrace all Baptist Churches in the country.

From a New York newspaper, The Calhoun Times prints a story about Maurice Thompson.

Mr. Thompson, on a visit to his native town of Calhoun, was standing in front of the drug store whittling on a piece of wood.

"Who is that feller yander?" asked a citizen.

"Why, that's Maurice Thompson!" Was the reply.

"Hit may be so, but hit don't look reasonable."

"Not reasonable?"

"No, why he used ter go fishin' with me!"

Blackwood Springs—We have a flourishing blacksmith shop at this place. Mr. David Barrett attended Sunday School at Salem last Sunday. Mr. White begins his writing school at this place November 16.

Mr. G. T. Fite, of Crane Eater has an Indian relic found on the river near the site of an old Indian town. It is a round stone ball, weighing 2½ pounds. It evidently was dressed by a long and arduous labor. Mr. Fite also has an iron skillet that is 100 years old.

Mr. D. Everhart Jones and Miss Nettie Wells are to be married at the Methodist Church, Thursday, November 26, at 4 p.m. They will leave at once for their home in Atlanta. A brilliant reception for the attendants and a few friends will be given at the bride's home on

Wednesday evening before the wedding.

Married on November 29, Mr. Lee Barrett and Miss May Kinman by Rev. J. P. Jones. She is a Christian, beautiful and social and will adorn the home of her chosen companion. He is lauded most by those who know him best. Both are members of Salem Church.

Three young fellows went to W. M. Hughey's store Saturday night and bought merchandise with bright new nickels. Later, when the money was found to be counterfeit, the fellows had skipped town.

Resaca—there was a singing at Miss Ethel Edwards home. Miss Maude Rooker is visiting in Calhoun and Miss Mattie Hill is in Atlanta.

Igo—H. B. Owen, of Calhoun, is a visitor here. Col. R. L. Strickland will spend the winter in Florida. Mrs. Foster and little son, of Petersburg, were bruised in a runaway. The horse became frightened and ran into a wagon, turning the buggy over.

Misses Royster and Smith, of Sonoraville, have returned from Rock College at Athens.

Dr. R. E. Cason has moved into his new office in the Harlan building. Mr. A. Hill has moved from Resaca to Calhoun and is occupying the M. E. Ellis house, which he has bought. Mr. Ellis is living in the Mims house near Gray and Mims gin.

King Montgomery came down river from his home to Calhoun the other day and, on the way, killed 2 wild geese, 13 squirrels, 8 partridges and 1 duck. King is an expert huntsman.

Printups—Mose Keys, of Calhoun, was over last Sunday. We presume he is charmed by the beautiful mountain scenery, he comes so often. In February of 1897, Mr. Keys was married to Miss Kate Prichard, one of Cedar Creek's sweetest girls, at the residence of Sidney Van Dyke. Squire T. J. Champion performed the ceremony. In April of 1897, Mrs. Katie Keys died of typhoid.

Two Scotchmen entertained the town with bagpipe music one day this week.

Quite a number of families in Gordon County have moved to Lindale to work in the big cotton mills there. If Calhoun had a mill, our population would be doubled.

Decora—married on last Wednesday, J. C. Fite, of this place, to Miss Tabbie Foster of Petersburg, by Rev. G. L. Chastain of Tunnel Hill. We wish for the newly married couple a prosperous and happy life.

Start right and keep right, advises Editor Hall, as The Calhoun Times begins the year of 1897, by printing a full context of the bill to establish public schools in Gordon County.

Mrs. C. C. Harlan gave a party for her guests, Misses Mona and Christie Chunn, Lyda Saxon and Ora Best of Grassdale. Mrs. L. R. Pitts entertained delightfully for the young ladies and gentlemen during the Christmas season.

Mrs. Bettie Lay will open a first class boarding house for school pupils and others in the B. G. Boaz house.

Mr. Ben Chastain and Miss Odessa Brown were married at the home of the bride's father, Thursday night with Rev. C. Quillian officiating. Both are well known and enjoy a wide circle of friends. She is a lady of remarkable intellectual attainments. He is a member of the Drug firm of Chastain Bros.

There was an elegant Christmas dinner at the home of Mr. and

Mrs. J. H. Gordon, near Oostanaula. There are few more properous or clever farmers than Mr. Gordon and no home where hospitality is more generous.

Mr. S. N. Wallace has leased the Calhoun Hotel and will make a specialty of local patronage. Col. Rankin is building a brick store on the Davenport lot. At Resaca, Mr. J. D. Johnson's beautiful residence has been completed and the family has moved in.

Harry Ellis has bought an interest in Henry Roff's business and they will conduct a restaurant in conjunction with their market.

The United States is in the grip of a blizzard and there is extremely cold weather everywhere. Snow balling and sleigh riding is the order of the day at New Town.

Grippe and pneumonia are sweeping the country and have been severely felt in Gordon. Uncle Tom Strickland, over 60 and a porter at the Depot for 16 years died.

Judge J. A. Mims, 82, died Friday night. He had lived in Gordon County for 21 years. The family had refugeed to Terrell County from 1863 until 1870. Judge Mims was a Primitive Baptist preacher of great force and earnestness and pastor of Harmony for more than 20 years.

The Calhoun Normal College is in charge of Prof. Humphreys, Miss Julia McDaniel and Mrs. Hill. The Editor visited the college and was shown through the various departments. There are over 150 pupils in the college. The best of methods and the most perfect decorum prevail.

At 9 o'clock, there is a chapel service then an hour for recitation. In Prof. Humphreys' room, the pupils are drilled in arithmetic, back and forth, up and down. Prof. Humphreys is one of the ablest educators in the State, schooled in the most modern methods.

In the public school department, Mrs. E. A. Hill, one of Gordon's most efficient instructors, uses a unique method of teaching. A string of small objects is hung on the wall and the small tots are required to spell the name of each. For example, a writing pen and a clothes pin are hung side by side.

Upstairs, in the preparatory department, Miss Julia McDaniel, known as a most faithful and conscientious instructor, presides in up-to-date methods. Here you find an excellent example of map drawing in gaography. In the room formerly known as the music room, a new teacher, Prof. Brewer, teaches higher math and science in the mornings, while, in the afternoons, Miss Azile Jones, widely known as a capable and energetic teacher, looks after a number of classes in different branches. This room also houses the library of 200 volumes.

The Methodist Church is to be moved further down towards J. N. Kiker's lot to make room for an elegant new 2 story parsonage. Mr. Gregg, of Dalton, has the contract and Mr. Alf Prater will move the church. While the church was being moved, the Baptist and Methodist would have Sunday School and Church services in the Baptist Church.

There's a fine school of 52 scholars at Red Bud under Prof. Wilson and here, Miss Mary Gilbert has a fine music class.

New Town School is under Prof. Robertson. Prof. Bell has purchased a 21 inch bell for the school at Decora.

Ryals High School of 130 pupils, at Sugar Valley, has a new dormitory. Prof. Green is the principal, assisted by Miss Lucy Callaway and Miss Mary Fite, music teacher. Miss Ada Abbott, a former student at Ryals, is teaching at Cave Spring.

The Literary Club has been reorganized at this school with Paul Fite, president, Sam Owen, vice president, Andrew Norrell, secretary and Ray M. Fite, censor.

The La Centum Literary Society at Coosawattee Seminary, elected Mr. Sam Borders, president, R. F. Sloan, vice president and Miss Nannie Byrom, secretary.

Alton McDaniel, of Calhoun, contributes dialect stories to the Corinth Mississippi Herald and other papers. His little piece, Gwine Back to Georgia, is quite musical, in fact, one of Corinth's musicians has set it to music. McDaniel bids fair to rival Joel C. Harris or Frank M. Stanton.

Mr. Earl Boston, of Cash, accompanied by Prof. Sharp and Milton Fuller, of Fairmount, and Mr. Mansell of Plainville, took the 2:45 a.m. train at Plainville, for Rome, then drove 14 miles by private conveyance to the home of Mr. Matthews, where Mr. Boston and Miss Mary Matthews were married by Prof. Sharp. They came to Plainville on the 11:00 a.m. train.

The subject of Waterworks for Calhoun is being widely discussed in March of 1897. The town could get water from the spring at the fish pond and build a reservoir on Mt. Pisgah at a cost of approximately $18.000. The matter rests with the citizens.

The Editor looked over the records of the ITC, popular club of the 1880s. It was a grouping of brilliant and genial spirits. The scholarly written minutes were penned by Misses Ida Reeve, Belle Boaz, Mamie and Lulie Pitts and Harris Reeve. The minutes tell of brilliant gatherings in cozy drawing rooms and the literary efforts of Cols. Starr and F. A. Cantrell and of H. A. Chapman and W. A. Robertson.

Charley Barrett, in his career as a locomotive engineer, has been one of the swiftest on the road. For more than 30 years, he has held the throttle on the W & A. There have been all sorts of accidents, but he has never killed a passenger. His engine, 240, is regarded as a pet. Charley said "I have killed 2500 or more hogs and cattle. everyone of which was a full-blooded jersey!"

Quite a diversion was created at the Singing Convention at Oostanaula last Sunday. Mr. Nabors and Miss Strain conceived the idea that married life was preferable to single blessedness, rode a short distance down the road and were joined in wedlock.

Mr. Charlie Herrington and Miss Annie Dodd were married at the bride's home near Plainville by Rev. Clayton Quillian.

The Confederate Cemetery at Resaca has been greatly improved. General Evans, a distinguished soldier and statesman, is coming to deliver an address at the exercises on Saturday, May 15, at the cemetery.

King and Pitts have just received a fine assortment of lawns, lapalettes, organdies and percales.

Gus Hall is advertising umbrellas at 63¢. Old ladies low-cut shoes and all styles in fine lace shoes, $1.25 and up. Men's Alpaca coats, 98¢. Oatmeal, 2 packages 8¢, good coffee 8 pounds $1.00, pine buckets 10¢.

Two bicyclists passed through from Galveston, Texas, via New Orleans, Atlanta, Cincinatti, Nashville and Chicago.

Mr. Conquest Knight's horse was standing on a street in town the other day, hitched to a one horse wagon and in the wagon was a pig in a box. The horse became frightened and ran out Crane Eater road to Harmony Spring 2½ miles from town, before being stopped. Nothing was broken and the pig was still in the box. Charley Hunt chased the horse on his bicycle and overtook him a short distance from town but could not stop him at once.

G. M. Hunt died on Saturday night, May 29, at 8 p.m. after an illness of only a few days. He was born 65 years ago in North Carolina and came here as a child. He served through the war, then spent a short time in Missouri.

For 30 years, Mr. Hunt has been a familiar figure about town and, for the last 7 years, has been associated with Dr. J. H. Malone in the drug business. He leaves his wife and one son, Charles, brothers H. C. and Dr. D. G. of Rome. Dr. Malone said, "I have never known a man who had a higher sense of honor than he."

Messers Julian F. Hurt and Wooten McVay have established a seed farm at Colima. They will grow turnip, okra, mustard and pepper seeds and onion sets, also seed oats, corn and wheat. The seed will be shipped to New Orleans and New York.

The Gordon County Nursery is run by C. J. Wright, of Reeves Station. He has 6 acres of strawberries in 18 varieties and will have 500,000 plants ready for Fall setting. The nursery also grows peach trees. 11,000 crates of peaches were shipped from Plainville this year.

Julius Strain says that he is going to thresh out all the wheat in the county. He says that he not only proposes to knock out wheat but also beans and friend chicken and you can tell by Julius' looks that he can do that very thing.

Col. E. J. Kiker is dead. After only a short illness, he died of pneumonia Monday night, June 7. Col. Kiker was born in Mecklenburg, S. C., Feb. 24, 1831, and moved to what is now Gordon County in 1844. He lost an arm at Fredericksburg, Dec. 13, 1862, and he was honorably discharged. He returned to Calhoun, entered the Commissary Dept. and served to the end of the war. He studied law with Col. W. J. Cantrell and was elected Ordinary in 1877. When the county court was organized in 1884, he was appointed by Governor M. C. Daniel as Judge of the court and served until 1886. Col. Kiker was prominent in public affairs, a true friend, a kind husband and father. He leaves a son, John N., two daughters ,Mrs. R. F. Wyatt and Mrs. G. L. Chastain, his wife and little son, E. J., Jr., 3 years old. He leaves a nice estate and is insured for $2000. He was laid to rest in Fain Cemetery, with services conducted by Rev. Clayton Quillian, pastor of the Methodist Church.

The oldest apple tree in this section is on Col. O. N. Starr's place. L. N. Jones says he has known the tree for 60 years and it must have been 5 or 6 years old when he first saw it. The tree has been bearing constantly for over half a century and now has 10 bushels of apples on it. It is 5 feet 6 inches in diameter with a 33 foot spread of branches.

Dr. J. H. Malone has purchased the lot next to the Methodist Church. Formerly owned by J. N. Kiker, it is one of the most desirable lots in town (Home of R. R. Owens 1917 - 1959).

J. M. Ballew recently remodeled and   painted the old Black residence.

W. B. Haynes has erected several large sample rooms at his

hotel.

Tom Brown, of Tilton, has bought from Dink Offutt, the vacant lot between L. P. Pitts and W. F. King and will erect an elegant residence.

The city has received a car load of crushed limestone from Chickamauga to be used on the park walks.

Two of the finest buggies ever seen in Calhoun were received last week by Harlan and Harlan. One was driven the next day by King Montgomery who feels able to ride regardless of weather.

Fain Cemetery is greatly improved. A large force of hands under M. E. Ellis has cleaned the land, laid off streets and graded lots. Trustees are B. M. Harlan, W. H. McDaniel and M. E. Ellis.

At 10 o'clock next Sunday, Prof. L. C. Calbeck and Miss Mosie Owen will be married at the Methodist Church in Decora. Rev. John W. Bole will perform the ceremony. These young people have the best wishes and congratulations of their many friends.

A wheeling epidemic has struck Calhoun and there are new riders every day, among them Lizzie Johnson, Julia and Maude Ballew. (Miss Maude says that they wore black satin bloomers. She and Julia kept their bicycles in the back hall and one day, on a dare, rode them through the hall and down the front steps.) Miss Edith Ransome and the County School Commissioners W. J. Mc-Daniel were also two of the riders.

An order prohibiting the riding bicycles on the side walks, has been passed by the council.

Coca Cola and other cold drinks at Taylor's Fount.

Rev. Mark A. Matthews came in Saturday afternoon and spent Sunday and Monday in town. Sunday morning he preached a sermon of great force and eloquence at the Baptist Church, to a packed house. His health is greatly improved after his vacation. His friends are glad to see him looking well. He will return to Jackson, Tenn. by next Sunday.

A citizen writes "the town has a $6000 jail and a 15 cent school. All that is wanted is a commodious, modern building that will accommodate the present needs in a decent manner. Many county communities have better buildings than Calhoun." The citizens of Gum Springs are erecting a commodious building.

Uncle Bob Butler, once a slave in the family of Mrs. Skelly, died in September at the age of 66. A union force approached Resaca, Mrs. Skelly sent Bob with a wagon of 2 mules, 2 gold watches and a lot of silver to South Carolina. After the war, the Skellys did not hear from him for a while, but oe day Bob came in and told them that he had sold the wagon and team and buried the money and silver. He dug it up after the war and brought it all to Mrs. Skelly. She gave him half the money. All his life Bob remained devoted to her family.

Miss Bessie Fain, eldest daughter of Judge Fain and Post Mistrees at Calhoun for several years, died of typhoid. Mr. Sam Davis has been appointed Postmaster.

Pearl hunting in the rivers and creeks of North Georgia is an exciting new hobby for the men and boys. Jack Bennett, who lives on John's Creek, has sold $180 worth of pearls taken from the Oostanaula river. Squire S. J. Simm's little son found $40 worth. The pearls grow inside the shells of mussels. An expert comes up and shows how to tell valuable pearls.

An interesting Thanksgiving program was presented by students at the Normal College - Song, America, by the school; Scripture and prayer by Dr. Darnell; Song, Revive Us Again, by the school. Scripture Response by the Junior Class; Thanksgiving recitations were given by Veda Haney, Trammell Starr, Will Tinsley, Ida Harlan and Clyde Haulbrook.

Rev. M. S. Williams was sent by the Conference as pastor of the Methodist Church for 1898.

RESERVOIR ON THE MOUNTAIN

Progressive citizens had been, for several years, agitating the question of a water works system for Calhoun. Fire protection, reduction in insurance rates, water power for such things as fans and other light machinery are some of the values mentioned.

Other projects that are being pushed by prominent men are the building of a new school house, the establishment of a cotton mill and the installation of a telephone exchange. The years of 1898 and 1899 were to see these plans well on the way to completion.

On March 26, 1898, an election for an issue of bonds to build the water works system is to be held. Now let every man who believes in the up building of the town give the good cause his support.

The powerhouse will be built on the H. L. Hall place. Water will be pumped from a reservoir on top of Kiker Mountain in the rear of the jail. The main pipe line will lead down past the courthouse where converging lines will carry water through the rest of the town.

The election resulted in 128 to 6 in favor of the bonds.

Guild and Co. of Chattanooga secured the contract for building the water works and began work in June. By late summer, the reservoir was completed and turned over to the town.

Big plans for town improvement were made. A fountain for the park, set where the paths converge and planted with ferns and sub tropical plants, was suggested.

Two fire companies, supplied with a reel and 500 feet of hose, were organized. Henry Roff, Henry Humphries, Neal Keefe, J. W. Nipper, Alton McDaniel, Charlie Carter, Richard Hines, Paul Callahan, George Rankin and Lumpkin Fain formed the fire companies. These men also organized a brass band with G. Harwell as Director.

The town first bought a hose cart from Dalton, but it was an antiquated affair and was not accepted. The town wanted a modern reel.

Dr. and Mrs. W. C. Darnell, after spending a week with the latter's mother, Mrs. A. A. Garlington, at Reeve's Station, returned to their home in Centre, Ala., last Friday. Services at the Baptist Church in Reeves Station were held on Christmas Day and on Sunday. Not an intoxicated man was seen during the holidays. The Steamer, Connesauga, passed up river last week with a hunting party from Rome.

Prof. J. A. Sharp, president of the College at Fairmount, went to Cartersville one day recently and bought a fine top buggy. On being questioned as to his extravagance, he said he was a scrub no longer.

Prof. Sharp writes a long article for The Times defending the college, refuting criticisms, and says that he will be there for his fifth year unless the Bishop moves him.

Mr. Henry Dobson and Miss Jessie Roe were married Tuesday, Dec. 23, 1897 at the home of Dr. Johnson, who performed the ceremony.

Another marriage of interest occurring during January of 1898, was that of Miss Sudie Shelor and Dr. G. W. Gardner, of Greenwood, S. C., at the residence of Mr. T. W. Harbin. The bride is one of Calhoun's most charming and accomplished young ladies. The Baptist Church loses a shining star out of its galaxy of workers. The groom is a prominent South Carolina Divine and editor of the Greenwood Journal and of the S. C. Baptist.

Mr. Herbert Bradshaw and Miss Antionette Rogers were married Sunday afternoon, February 12, at the home of the bride's father. It was the 22nd anniversary of her parents and the 50th anniversary of her grandparents.

Invitations are out to the marriage of Miss Edith Ransome to Mr. Clifford Barnes, February 23 at the Methodist Church. Miss Lola McWhorter and Rev. L. E. Roberts were married this month at her home in McDaniels.

Mr. Joe French has accepted a position with W. L. Hines for the present year. Mr. French is a clever young fellow and will prove a valuable man to Mr. Hines' house.

A happy family reunion occurred at the home of Dr. J. H. Malone on December 26, 1897. Alfred was up from Rome, Tom, from Atlanta. Paul and Frank were here; also Mr. and Mrs. James A. Gray, from New York and Mr. and Mrs. C. D. Meadows and children, from Atlanta.

The contest, sponsored by Harlan and Harlan, for a little Buck stove, ended December 24. The stove went to Aileen Dyar, little daughter of Mr. and Mrs. F. L. Dyar. We had no idea so many people read The Calhoun Times. A total of 2000 coupons was collected by the children.

The colored Masons of Mt. Carmel Lodge No. 11, met in the Hall and elected officers for 1898. J. B. Wilson was elected Worshipful Master, J. C. Campbell, Senior Warden, A. H. Hunt, Junior Warden, Joe Jackson, Secretary, J. K. Smith, Treasurer, J. W. Wilmart and H. Wooliff, Junior Deacons, M. L. Aber and J. W. Wyley, Masters of Ceremony and W. M. Campbell, Tyler.

A. M. Graham brought in a copy of The Valley Register, dated June 28, 1859. The principal part of the paper was devoted to politics. There was a tone of red hot beligerency about all of the publications advertised. Papers mentioned were The South Countryman, Marietta, and The Cherokee Baptist Field and Fireside, Augusta.

There was an advertisement for Blackwood's Scottish Magazine, The London Quarterly and Edinburg Review, but not a word of local news.

The world moves on and the matter of newspapers has moved a long, long way since 1859.

Mr. J. A. Carter, the Dalton furniture man has rented the store occupied by J. B. Addington and will open a general furniture and undertaking establishment. The house, which is to open soon, will be run by Mr. Newsome and Mr. Carter's sons. Mr. Addington will move to Acworth. He has many friends who regret to see him leave.

The school at Cash, under Professors G. C. Walker and J. C. Huffstettler, has 125 scholars.

The colored citizens have elected as school trustees, W. S. Swann, J. H. Hamilton, H. Lockett, J. Lay, O. L. Murphy, Charles Frix, who will serve as treasurer, and A. H. Hunt, secretary.

Nicholsville school is flourishing under Miss Lula Brogdon as teacher, Plainville school has over 100 scholars. The school at Weldon's Bend had a wood chopping and a big dinner recently.

Starr Institute presented brilliant exercises of recitations, plays, reviews of studies and organ music.

From The Normal College Notes, Calhoun—never in the history of Calhoun do we need a new building more than now.

The Literary Society gave this interesting program last week: An Original Story, Miss Clyde Haulbrook, Reading, Miss Carry Walker, Biographical Sketch of Longfellow, Miss Mamie Rankin, Recitation, Miss Marie Harlan, Reproduction of "Mary's Little Lamb," Miss Virginia McDaniel, Biographical Sketch of Charles Dickens, Miss Ida Hightower, Anecdotes, Miss Maude Harris.

Alton McDaniel, Reporter

Alton McDaniel went to Atlanta in May to seek a position but was back at Hall's after 2 weeks. Alton continues to write and a ten verse poem of his was published in a late issue of The Atlanta Constitution. One verse reads—

A common sort O' critter
I like to shoot with pistols
And be like Diamond Dick
And carry great big razors
And call myself a brick.

J. H. Legg and Son have the contract for building Tom Brown's new residence. This elegant residence, completed in August, would be one of the most commodious and magnificent house in Calhoun. Quite a notable addition to the splendid street on which it stands (Dr. Billings' home).

Mayor Hillhouse is having excavations dug to plant trees on all the main streets of town. With every new house build, trees are laid low. Probably no community in the world ever showed a greater disregard for the use of nature's greatest blessings than this. Succeeding generations will plant and dig and water for years to get shade trees where we cut them down in an hour.

A petition is being circulated to allow a driving track to be placed around the pine thicket, and another to exclude dogs from all houses of worship in town. So far, 30 signatures, among them some of the most prominent citizens of the town, have been secured for the second petition.

Mr. John Harkins has purchased the gramophone from a Rankin's Book Store. It is a wonderful machine, speaks and recites in a most perfect manner.

At the administrator's sale of Col. E. J. Kiker's estate, W. L. Hillhouse bought a half interest in the Field's farm 2 miles north of town, for $350. Mrs. Kiker bought the homeplace and Mrs. G. L. Chastain, the Chastain place. Col. O. N. Starr bought the law office, T. M. Ellis, the barn lot and J. W. Logan, the vacant lots in the lower part of town.

Henry McDaniel has resigned his position at the Depot and entered the Normal College. Willie Brown takes his place as Messenger.

Rev. M. Y. Williams, the eloquent Divine, delighted his hearers Sunday with 2 of the most impressive sermons heard in some time. Calhoun is fortunate in having the best preachers in North

Georgia this year. They are all learned and eloquent.

Several Calhounites went to Rome to hear Hon. William J. Bryan. All were pleased with the address of this great Democratic leader.

The ladies of the Baptist Church have had the house thoroughly renovated and new carpet laid on the aisles. The carpet was bought from Carter and Co. and these clever gentlemen put it down free of charge.

In a half-page advertisement, Carter and Co. list Parlor Suites, $20 and up, brand new pianos, $200, Fiddles, $1 and up, Banjos, $2.15 and up, sewing machines, including Singer, $5 to $50, coffins from $2.50 up, 2 free hearses.

The colored citizens have purchased instruments for a string band. Will Harbour, Monroe Ellison, John Mangum West, Tom and John Frix are members of the band.

Jimmie Lay, son of Mrs. J. B. Lay, happened to a painful, though not serious, accident Sunday afternoon. He had climbed into a dogwood tree to gather flowers and fell 15 feet on his back. He was unconscious for sometime and grave fears were expressed as to the extent of his injuries. However, he has made a complete recovery.

War in Cuba! The United States has called for 200,000 volunteers —the headlines continue through the summer weeks. The Spanish Fleet has been located off the Cuban coast and Admiral Dewey reports a strict blockade of Manila—86,000 volunteers are camping in Chicamauga Park. By July, rumors of peace would be flooding the country and, in September, headlines would jubilate The War is Over!

Mr. G. W. Hunt and others interested in bicycling have worked faithfully to build a race track on the commons facing the railroad. The race track opened on April 27, with a grand celebration. Cyclists from Rome and Dalton entered the race.

Myriads of hanging Japanese lanterns and oil lamps gave the grounds a Kalaidescopic appearance. Refreshments were served from 8 to 12 o'clock and from 11 to 12 a reception at the residence of Mrs. G. W. Hunt complimented visiting and local wheel men.

Dr. J. H. Reeve has moved into his new home, two doors north of the college and opposite Col. Rankin's residence. This is one of the prettiest houses in town and is an ornament to College Ave. Dr. and Mrs. Reeve gave the young people a delightful entertainment Tuesday night.

Mr. J. A. Hall, publisher of The Calhoun Times, and Miss Viola Wright were married Wednesday afternoon at 3 o'clock at the home of the bride's father, Mr. J. N. Wright, in North Rome. The ceremony was performed by Dr. R. B. Headden, pastor of the First Baptist Church, in the presence of the immediate relatives and close friends.

The closing exercises at the College began with an address by Col. Rankin. Programs of music, recitations, drills and tableaux continued for two days. The Unfinished Song, recitation by Ida Harlan, an instrumental duet by Ellis and Jeanette Reeve, a recitation by Clay Dyar, an essay by Miss Nell Malone, a vocal duet by Lucille Ballew and Bernice Tate, an address by Mrs. Felton and a cantata, Fairyland, were some of the features of the exercise.

Heavy rains during the summer have enabled river steamers

to resume trips on the Oostanaula.

Monday, July 4, will be a big day in Calhoun. Old Glory will be unfurled from a 50 foot flag staff in Railroad Park. There will be races in the bicycle park, and a concert by the Gum Springs Brass Band will complete the day's program. After the day was over the total indebtedness was found to be $20. The town held an ice cream festival and cake contest to pay off the indebtedness. The cake was donated by Miss Orrie Malone and a spirited contest between Miss Minnie Dyar, of Calhoun, and Miss Mittie Peacock, of Albany, resulted in a victory for Miss Dyar.

Mr. J. E. Griffin and Miss Una Abbott were married Wednesday at the home of the bride's father, Mr. M. B. Abbott, in Sugar Valley. Mr. Joe Herrington was best man and Miss Bolding, maid of honor. Rev. J. W. Smith officiated. The couple left immediately for the home of Hon. J. J. Griffin at Oostanaula, where they will reside.

Hall Bros., after many years of business in Calhoun, have sold out to Westfield and Kay.

Mr. J. T. Black is putting in a new flour mill at Oothcalooga Mills and there is talk of a cotton mill for Calhoun. Mr. J. B. F. Harrell will deed a site for the mill if one is located here.

C. W. Hunt has established a bath house over J. M. Ballew's store. Pay him a visit. Nothing makes a man feel better than a good bath.

Carter and Co. have a brand new dray.

In October, The Calhoun Times goes to ten pages.

The millinery stores are putting on a gorgeous display of new Fall hats. One hat is a creation of white and cream plumes and a chenille dotted scarf. Others are trimmed in quills and wings. Dainty French bonnets are high in front to reveal the charming face of the wearer.

There are large Gainsboroughs and small toques. Lovely for a blonde is a true turquoise blue with rich plumes of cream sweeping back from a bunch of aigrettes in front. A graceful scarf of blue velvet, with white polka dots, edged with a Frenchy ruffles of black satin ribbon, the end falling over the hair, is caught at the back with a steel buckle.

A circulating library has been started by the Kindergarten Association. Mrs. B. M. Harlan is the president, Mrs. W. J. McDaniel, vice president, Mrs. F. L. Dayar, recording secretary and Mrs. W. L. Hines, treasurer and librarian.

Rev. S. A. Harris is the new pastor at the Methodist Church.

MYSTERY OF THE GLASS DAGGER AND MANGUM

"The Glass Dagger." There it was in plain print, after every item in the personal column of The Calhoun Times for January 5, 1899. No one could find out why "The Glass Dagger" was laced through the locals nor what the three words meant.

Timid souls began to hurry home before dark and imaginative ones began to feel that perhaps someone would be found one dark night with a dagger in his back.

The mystery was not solved until the next week, when the Editor announced that he was beginning the publication, in serial form, of a thrilling detective story called, "The Glass Dagger."

There is not room here for a reprint of the story. You must go to the Courthouse and read it for yourself in the yellowed old papers.

Mangum is gone. Wonder where he is? Mangum, a unique character, drifted in about a year ago and spent his time mending shoes, umbrellas and clocks and most anything. He spoke with a rasping Northern accent and said he was from Ohio.

Mangum was a great church man and attended all of the services. He didn't like dogs at church. He stood at the church door with a big stick and if any dog tried to enter, the stick got in its effective work. He put up a sign, "Notiss-no admission for dogs." A born debater, he argued scripture or anything and got mad if opposed.

The boys around town worried him and accused him of being a Spanish spy during the war. Mangum left town last November.

A leading event of the season was the marriage of Mr. W. P. Dodd and Miss Louie Hightower which occurred at the bride's home in a quiet wedding ceremony performed by Rev. John F. Cox. Mr. Dodd is a leading lawyer of Calhoun and his bride is the daughter of Dr. and Mrs. G. H. Hightower. An elegant dinner was served after the marriage and the couple spent the rest of the week visiting relatives in Fairmount.

Bonnie Kate Barnett, little daughter of Mr. and Mrs. S. M. Barnett, of Resaca, won the big prize doll at J. T. Alexander and Co. on Christmas Eve. The contest excited wide-spread interest and a large number of coupons was collected.

The streets of Calhoun have been crowded with wagons and the stores with shoppers. After a trip to town, a Reeves Station man remarked "Well, I think I'll take er chaw er tobacker now. Couldn't find no room ter spit in Calhoun."

Miss Maggie McWhorter and O. H. Fields were married at Mc-Henry. Rev. McGhee performed the ceremony in the presence of a few friends and the family. After refreshments were served, the bride and groom left on the 7:30 train and went immediately to the groom's home, already furnished. He holds a responsible position on the W & A and she is a highly esteemed young woman.

A surprise marriage last week was that of Mr. Henry Roff and Miss Mary Kay, at the residence of Esquire W. D. Fain. The couple left to reside with Mr. and Mrs. John W. Crawford at McHenry. Both are well known in town and county.

The long-standing mystery of the letters YMD has been solved! The Young Men's Dining Club had the annual dinner at the Calhoun Hotel, but because of bad weather only a few members were present to partake of the good things with which the table was laden. But the SLD Club of Young Women will go down in history as the Selfish Little Devils or The Sweet Little Darlings for they would never reveal the name of the Club.

The big task of the year is—a modern school building. Other projects in sight are, a cotton mill, a crate mill and a canning factory.

Last Monday saw the greatest opening of any Calhoun School when 200 pupils enrolled. A notable fact is that a great many boys and men from surrounding districts come and go each day. The people are greatly indebted to Prof. Humphries and his assistants.

At the college from McHenry are: Josephine and Judie McWhorter, Clyde Adocock, Tommie Sutherland, A. L. Bray and Miss Mary Black, Charlie Mason from Crane Eater and Eckles McClain from Acworth.

The county school term has been cut from 6 months to 4½ months.

A notable wedding was that of Miss Orrie Malone and Mr. Julian Hurt, Wednesday, January 4, at 1:30 at the home of the bride's father, Dr. J. H. Malone. The rooms were darkened and beautifully decorated for the occasion. The wedding march was played by Mrs. W. L. Hines and the ceremony performed by Dr. W. H. Darnell in his usual eloquent manner. After an elegant luncheon the couple left for the groom's home at Colima.

She is one of Calhoun's most popular young ladies, always pleasant and full of life. He is one of North Georgia's leading young men, a member of an old and distinguished family. Full of energy and perserverance, he is, in every way, an ideal companion for the bride he has won.

Sunday was an ideal Spring day. The warm sunshine covered the earth with a drowsy mantle of dreams and everybody who could leave home went for a walk. Rev. John F. Cox treated the congregation at the Baptist church to two excellent discourses, morning and evening.

Efforts are being made to establish a telephone Exchange in Calhoun. Mr. F. L. Dyar is working on it and has secured a list of 35 subscribers. Lines would run to Crane Eater, Red Bud, Cash, Sonoraville, Fairmount and other places. Later, a line would run to Rome and people could call up Rome, Atlanta, LaGrange and Columbus.

In May, the council would pass an ordinance granting a license to F. L. Dyar to erect poles and wire on the streets of Calhoun and to maintain a telephone Exchange.

M. E. Cook wants names for the 3 grades of flour to be ground at his new steam mill, now almost ready. Send in a name and you'll be famous and maybe get a free sack of flour. When the mill was started in March, the best grade of flour was called Mt. Alto, the second, Victor and the third, Cook's Early Breakfast.

Mrs. Doughty has completed an elegant new cottage for her son, Eugene. It is one of the most neatly furnished and conveniently arranged homes in town. J. H. Legg and son never did a better job.

The best material was used and the inside was finished in hard oil. The rooms are all wainscoted in hard oil pine. Elegant mantels and grates are used throughout the house and it is elegantly furnished. (1959, home of Mrs. Story, N. Wall St.) Mrs. Doughty will continue to board at H. F. Ferguson's.

Dr. and Mrs. W. A. Richards and family arrived on Tuesday and are occupying the house made vacant by Dr. Hightower. Dr. Richards and family are receiving a warm welcome to Calhoun. Soon after coming to Calhoun, Dr. Richards bought the Calhoun Hotel and immediately began making improvements, enlarging the building to 30 well-furnished rooms and in November, opened for business with Mr. John Harkins as manager.

Since taking up the practice of medicine here, Dr. Richards has grown rapidly in popularity and is now one of the busiest doctors in town. He is a man of pleasing address and makes friends easily and rapidly.

Dr. G. M. Hightower and family left Tuesday night, January 4, on the 11 o'clock train for Dalton, to make their future home. Perhaps no one has moved away from Calhoun during many years whose departure is so universally regretted as that of Dr. Hightower. He is not only an able and experienced physician but a most pleasant and affable gentleman. His kindly nature, general and sympathetic turn greatly enhance him to suffering humanity wherever met. He is a graduate of Georgia Electric Medical College and has been engaged in practice for 18 years, with special attention to chronic diseases. The best wishes of the people of Calhoun go with him.

Blue Springs—W. R. Lacey and daughter, Miss Blance, and Miss Pearl Strain spent Sunday with the family of R. S. Prichard. Lula Kirby gave a singing, Saturday night. The school children had an interesting spelling match at J. A. Strain's, Saturday night. In a spelling match on Friday, the girls beat the boys. The boys said they couldn't do it again. Miss Leila Strain invited them to her home for another spelling match, and the girls won again. Misses Ila Kirby and Pearl Mote gained the victory.

Will Whittemore, who has been attending school at Athens, has accepted the School at this place. Mrs. Josephine Trimble has entered her children in school at Fairmount. The children of Mr. H. C. Byrom are also attending school at Fairmount.

Prof. and Mrs. Neal are at Jefferson where Prof. Neal is principal of Martin Institute.

Mr. and Mrs. John Logan have been in Atlanta. They will move into their new residence on Mill Street (Daves home, Rome road) at once. The work of refinishing and re-arranging the house has been completed.

Col. W. S. Johnson, one of Calhoun's oldest lawyers, died in February at his home near town and was buried at Chandler's Cemetery. He was born June 29, 1828 in North Carolina and moved to Bartow in 1848, coming here before the town was founded. He married Miss Chandler, daughter of Mr. Abraham Chandler, for whom Chandler Cemetery was named. Before the war, Mr. Johnson was a farmer, then a Methodist preacher and finally a lawyer. He was one of the best read and posted lawyers in town. Having read extensively in literature, he was an interesting conversationalist. He leaves a large family of children.

The Oostanaula is overflowing and the country is at war with

The Phillipines.

Frank Malone and Frank Wyatt, both working in Havana, write interesting letters to the home paper.

The Council is to pass an ordinance prohibiting the use of the drinking fountain in front of the courthouse for any but drinking purposes. The water is free for drinking but not to be carried away in buckets or pitchers.

Sunday night, February 12, a blizzard struck Calhoun. The wind howled all night and the temperature was 8 degrees below 0 in front of Dr. Malone's drug store.

Resaca has shipped over 3000 rabbits since January 1.

B. R. Bray has purchased the McDaniel and Black business on Railroad Street.

B. M. Harlan plans to remodel his residence. The house will be raised to a second story and a new roof added. It will be one of the most modern and attractive houses in town. (Bond home today.)

"Fences suit me" writes Uncle Joab Lewis, "No old sows running around eating up your little chickens. No old cow or sheep bells ringing around your house at night keeping you awake. I don't believe there should be any such law." (As the stock law.)

In the summer, the Editor wrote "A pleasant sight now greets the travelers along the country roads. Green crops grow luxuriantly out to the road's edge, where once unsightly fences stood."

The Evergreen Baptist Church, located on the property of H. C. Byrom, has been the center of a theological storm and has been enjoined from the use of the name. The bitter warfare is over the Greek translation of the Bible. Rev. Newt Blalock came from Tennessee to the church about a year ago and tried to drill local preachers and laity in Greek. Then the trouble began.

It is said theat Rev. B. F. Bright, pastor of the church, has adopted the opinions of Blalock and so have a considerable portion of the members.

R. G. Parker and Matthew Couch opposed this faction and the church is divided. Charges were preferred against Parker and his group is enjoined from use of the name Evergreen Baptist Church.

The Bright-Blalock faction claimed that the Bible is wrong and needed correction. In March the case was dismissed by Judge Fite and Bright was advised to turn the books over to the Parker faction. The Bright faction is now out of the church.

Richard Hines' new trombone is a great addition to the Band. Several other new instruments are to be bought soon.

Post Offices at Igo, Fambro and Coosewattee have been discontinued for lack of enough business.

The millinery stores are a blaze of glory with laces and trimmings on hats of all shapes in a dazling array of color. The window decorations are beautiful and the interiors of the stores present a scene to delight the feminine heart.

Miss Minnie Hood shows an effective hat of white chiffon, trimmed with graceful loops of the same, with ferns and two flowing white plumes in front and a rhinestone buckle and two full blown roses in the back. On another hat, in black and pink, an aigrette gave height.

Seen at Mrs. Hick's, a white shepherdess hat attracted attention as did a black sailor trimmed with long graceful loops of shaded blue ribbon, held by a pearl buckle. The back was finished with bunches of pink crushed roses.

Man tries to kill Miss Kimbrough! The man, here to be name-less, came into the yard and asked Miss Kimbrough to marry him. Indignantly she cried "I'll do nothing of the sort!" Pulling a gun he said, "I'll make you marry me!" Screaming, the young girl ran toward a man working nearby. This man had no gun, but he picked up a pole and stopped the intruder who turned and ran into the woods. Miss Kimbrough is one of the most esteemed young ladies in the county and every man in the community is out looking for the man who would thus endanger her life.

Misses Maude Ballew and Kittie Ellis were elected as sponsors by the Fire Co. for the tournament in Rome. Maids of honor are Misses Etta Cameron and Nell Malone.

An unusual sign on the front of Charley Hunt's bath and bicycle house catches the eye. It is the wheel of a bicycle, operated by the wind, as a windmill and appears very close to perpetual motion.

T. J. Alexander and Co. have put in something new, a gas light known as the acetylene system. As bright as any gas light, the gas is generated by a large tank and conveyed to the jets by pipes. There are 12 lights and the store makes a unique appearance in Calhoun.

No death caused more profound sorrow than that of Mrs. F. L. Hicks on Monday, April 17. She was widely known and highly esteemed, having come to Calhoun in 1891 to enter the Millinery business. She sold her business about 1 year ago.

W. A. Sloan can tell the story of how it feels to drown. Last week, his oxen and cart went off the ferry. As the oxen swam ashore he tried to catch the tail of one but failed and was swept down stream and lost consciousness. His son, Jim and a man took his body out of the water and brought him back to life.

A relic of the battle of Resaca was found last week. It is a gold watch charm engraved "J. C. Breckenridge, Louisville 1860."

Another relic of the Resaca battlefield is owned by Mr. Bud Brookshire. It is a block of red talque. On one side is engraved "USET Co.," on the other, a brass-colored design in neat and artistic tracing. What the thing was used for is a mystery. Old Soldiers don't know.

An old coin was plowed up by Freeman Roach the other day. Made of either gold or copper, it is the size of a copper cent and bears the American Eagle, surrounded by a Latin inscription on one side and the face and name of George Washington on the other. There is no date on the coin.

The fence around the Haynes house has been painted. The City Council's new lawn mower for the park is here. New verandas and other improvements have been added to the residence of T. F. Tomlinson.

The Calhoun Band gave the first summer concert Saturday afternoon and rendered excellent music.

The Georgia monument on the Chickamauga battlefield will be dedicated on May 5. A special train will run and the fare will be $1.50 round trip.

Eighty four year old Major Roff, in Atlanta to attend the Inter-national Sunday School Convention, was interviewed by a reporter on an Atlanta paper.

Major Roff is a native of New York. His father moved to

Augusta, Ga., in 1819. Then, the only way to Savannah from Augusta was by steamboat. A stage coach ran through the woods to what was to be 25 years later, Atlanta.

"I have hunted squirrels where the Kimball House now stands" said Major Roff, "and washed in the branch that used to run where the Union Depot is."

Major Roff was present at the organization of the Sunday School Convention after the war. "Oh Yes" he said "I remembered being here. The Georgia Association of the Sunday School was organized in a room across from the Kimball House."

There are 1200 delegates in Atlanta for the Convention and the number of visitors is enormous.

A fire at Springplace on May 10, took the lives of Dr. L. C. Bagwell, his 3 children and an old lady housekeeper.

Dr. Malone is dead. Ill for several days with neuralgia of the heart and attended by Drs. Richards and McClain, he passed away Tuesday, May 9 at 8 o'clock.

Dr. Malone was a graduate of Mercer and Jefferson Medical College at Pittsburgh. He married Miss Sarah Dickson, member of an old and distinguished family which dates to Cromwell, at Ringgold. Soon after his marriage he came to Calhoun. His family refugeed to Terrell County during the war and he entered the Confederate Service, being stationed at Anderson.

After the war, he returned to Calhoun where he spent the rest of his life, except for a few years in Atlanta. He was in the drug business with Dr. D. A. Hunt and, later, with Dr. W. J. Reeves until the death of Dr. Reeves in 1887. The funeral was conducted by Dr. W. D. Darnall.

In a champion debate between Mercer University and the University of Georgia, Mercer will be represented by Mark Bolding, H. F. Lawson and W. F. George.

Mark Bolding, a Calhoun boy, won over 7 of the best orators at Mercer. He will represent the college in the oratorical contest between Mercer, the University of Georgia and Georgia Tech. contesting for the $50 award and a gold medal given by John Temple Graves.

Mark won this contest. He has made a brilliant record at Mercer since 1896.

Refreshing shower bath at Hunt's Bath Parlors 15 cents—open until 12 p.m. Saturdays. Friday afternoons are observed for the ladies with Mrs. G. M. Hunt in charge.

Charley has put in a cooling fan at the Bath House. It is run by a water motor.

"Talking about fine strawberries," said Lon Chastain, "I have got the finest I ever saw. Why many of them will weigh a pound and it don't take a great many to do it, either."

Captain A. M. Graham knows the value of trees. Instead of butchering the forest around his home, he has converted it into stately and magnificent groves and his home is one of the most attractive in the county. (Sixty years later, this house on the Sugar Valley road was torn down and the timbers used to build a house on the Oostanaula road for Mr. Barton, a modern residence is to be erected by John Bruce on the elevated site just north of the old place, where the stately groves once stood.)

Colonel and Mrs. Starr have returned from a week's visit to

Washington. "One of the most impressive things about the place,"
said Colonel Starr, "was the shade trees lining the streets and in all
the parks."

H. C. Byron brought in an issue of The Calhoun Times, dated
August 26, 1870. E. R. Sassen was the hotel manager and G. R. Boaz
ran the livery stable. There was not much local news. Fairmount was
soon to have a sale of lots. Butter was 20¢, hams 18¢, corn $1.00,
flour from wagons 3¢, meal from $1.00 to $1.10 and salt $2.40 per
sack.

About 1500 people attended The Times picnic at Dew's Pond.
The Starr Band provided music for the occasion. Will Reeves is
leader of the Band and members are: R. W. Smith, M. S. Collins, Z.
O. Reeves, S. P. Collins, W. L. Ray, George Collins, A. O. Collins,
D. D. Pass, W. E. Rowland, J. A. Smith and J. L. Reeves. Neal Keefe
had arranged the band stand. Editor J. A. Hall introduced Mr. Keefe
as the oldest correspondent of The Times. He began in 1879. Squire
Joab Lewis spoke on the early history of Gordon County and Calhoun. Another speaker was W. L. Hines. A picture of the group was
made by T. F. Tomlinson, photographer.

A Missionary and Sunday School Institute will be held at the
Baptist Church on July 5. Ministers to be present are: Drs. Landrum
and Jamison, from Atlanta, Dr. R. B. Headden, from Rome, A. W.
Bealer, Cartersville, E. M. Dyer, Acworth, A. H. Rice, Cass Station,
Revs. Buford, Hunt, Wright, Keith and others.

A big land sale marked the beginning of a new era for Calhoun
and opened for settlement the only vacant property in the city
limits. The J. G. Harkins tract on the west side was cut up in lots
50 by 200 feet and sold to the highest bidder.

Of the 54 lots, the average price was $250. Some brought $56,
others less than $20. Buyers were: Dr. J. A. Johnson, G. T. Fite, S.
M. Davis, J. F. Field, J. T. Sutherland, C. E. Cook, F. L. Hicks,
W. A. Sloan, Joe Campbell and others. The sale was put on by Fitz
Simmons and Phillips.

Fairmount College has two buildings, the college proper and
the Stanton Memorial building. The Stanton building is of splendid
structure with memorial tablets at the entrance. The music and art
rooms and the library are on the lower floor. The upper floor is a
girls hall, furnished with two heaters and easy chairs. The hall is
fine for society meetings, piano recitals and elocution drills. Professor
J. A. Sharp is president of the college and the students member 240.

July 4 will be a big day in Calhoun. The parade will assemble
at the pine thicket at 9 o'clock. A $5.00 prize will be given for the
most unique costume.

It will be one of the most picturesque aggregations ever seen
anywhere. After this parade, there will be a floral parade, with a
prize for the most artistically decorated conveyance. At 11 o'clock, a
6 hour walking match will take place. At 1:00 p.m. the races are
scheduled. In the foot race, the runners will place their shoes at a
50 yard mark, run to them, put them on and race to the 100 yard
mark.

Buy a lot in the Chastain addition—¼ in cash, the balance in
installments. Easy, isn't it?

The Chastain lots went fast. Calhoun is the leading boom town of
North Georgia. The lots, measuring 50 x 210 feet and selling for an
average of $29, brought a total of $1,163. Buyers were, Major Aaron

Roff, Squire V. M. Watts, H. P. Barrett, John Hood, H. K. Hicks, Col. W. B. Rankin and R. H. Land.

This sale marks an important era in the city's life and extends Broad Street straight through to the pauper farm.

Three lots were sold for Mrs. G. M. Hunt, between her house and Col. Starr's. Two were bought by J. W. Logan and one by V. W. Bentley at prices of $25 and $165.

If the ladies would organize a town improvement club it might do much towards beautifying the streets. The club could preserve trees and plant others. Calhoun needs toning up and the ladies are the ones to do it.

Now for more houses. Calhoun needs 100 more. A few good houses costing $1000, could be rented for $8 per month.

The school building question is being agitated anew. Prominent citizens have been interviewed and opinions published in the paper. The majority agree that the old building ought to be torn down and a good one be put up. Others think that the existing building should be improved.

Later a mass meeting was held at the Courthouse with T. M. Ellis presiding. J. E. Watts, F. L. Malone, Prof. A. L. Brewer and B. M. Harlan were appointed as a committee to canvas the town. The Calhoun Band furnished music for the meeting.

At an election in October, the school bonds carried by a majority of 31⅓ votes. The total number of votes cast was 131, 83 for and 43 against.

The band has purchased a new cornet and plans an excursion to Chattanooga on August 25. The railroad will have several passenger coaches on the side track here a day in advance of the big excursion. Have a nice trip and aid the boys of the Band and the Fire Company, see Lookout Mountain, Missionary Ridge, Chickamauga Park and other battlefields.

Miss Maude Ballew and Mr. John Neal were married at 4 o'clock in the Methodist Church. Rev. S. A. Harris, assisted by Dr. W. H. Darnell, performed the ceremony. The flower girls, Julia Ballew and Carrie Walker entered first, followed by Misses Nannie Rhodes and Pearl Ballew. The attendants were: Miss Lucile Ballew and Mr. Clyde Rawlins, of Rome, Miss Etta Cameron and Mr. G. M. Fuller, Miss Kittie Ellis and Mr. W. B. Haynes, Miss Alma Hall and Mr. W. E. Bonner, Miss Willie Harkins and Mr. T. J. Alexander, Miss Leila Neal and Mr. Frank Alexander, Miss Bessie Hunt was maid of honor and Mr. Richard Hines, best man. Ushers were Leslie White, Will Haney and Henry McDaniel.

The church was tastefully decorated and the scene presented was one of profound beauty and impressive solemnity. Mrs. W. L. Hines played the wedding march in her usual inimitable way. The couple took the 4:49 train for St. Simons and points in North Carolina. After their return they will be at home at the Haynes House. Both have lived in Calhoun all their lives, are favorites in social circles and have hosts of friends.

The school reunion at Decora was a grand success. At 9 o'clock, the Starr Band arrived in their new Band wagon, which is a credit to any Band.

Prof. Humphries, principal in 1881-85, now of Calhoun, Prof. C. M. Conley, Rocky Springs, Prof. S. G. Fulton, Cash, J. T. Lemon and L. O. Calbick, Pleasant Valley and J. A. McClain, Decora, were the former principals present.

Rev. D. T. Davis led in prayer and Prof. J. M. Christian, of Cash, made a welcome address spicy with wit and humor. Miss Lula Brogdon read an essay on the history of the school.

Mr. G. C. Fite of Crane Eater, spoke on "War" and gave us some of the horrors of war and the pleasures of peace. Miss May Harris read an essay on "School Days." J. E. Pinion, of Resaca ,gave a spicy speech on "How to Court" and Mrs. T. W. Harbin, of Calhoun, rendered a good solo, with Miss Mary Fite at the organ.

Prof. Huffstettler made the welcome address at the big Crane Eater picnic. Charles Fite gave a declamation, "America," Robert Miller declaimed "Back from the War" and Miss Bertha Douglas recited "The Moneyless Man."

Dinner was served from a table 60 feet long and other smaller tables. Rev. S. A. Harris returned thanks and delivered an address at 1:30. The Sunday School lemonade stand took in $30. The committee is grateful to Mt. Pleasant Church for the use of their organ.

While Rev. J. H. Barton and daughter, Allie, were ill with fever at Farmville, 37 hands, neighbors and friends, went into his field with 18 plows and 19 hoe hands and worked his crop. Such a good deed will never be forgotten by his distressed family.

The Excursion to Atlanta ticket for the Georgia State Fair on August 7 will be $1.50 round trip.

Calhoun needs a good dairy. Few people would keep cows if they could buy milk and butter regularly. It is troublesome and costly to keep cows in town.

Something new in Calhoun! Alexander's big cash sale is advertised in a full page spread.

Send your order for fresh bread every day to Standford's Bakery on Railroad Street—5 cents a loaf. Also fresh barbecue every day at Stanford's.

The horse attached to Ellis and Austin's dray ran away Saturday morning, completely wrecking the dray and damaging a buggy near the Courthouse. One of H. P. Barrett's Horses, attached to a wagon, ran away Thursday. He circled the business portion of town, then ran into Horton's stable without doing any damage.

Earl Keys and Porter McArthur, while working on the Calhoun Hotel, fell when a second story scaffold gave way. Both were badly hurt but rapidly recovered and will be back at work soon.

Logan and Dover have bought out C. E. Cook's new mill. Mr. Cook will return to Blue Springs where he has extensive farming and orchard interests. Mr. Dover will move to town.

Dr. G. W. Mills, of Tunnel Hill, was in town last week. He thinks of moving here.

An interesting old paper, the Wester County, N. Y. Gazette, was brought in by Mrs. H. F. Ferguson. The paper, a prized possession of Mrs. Ferguson's family for many years, printed with a heavy black mourning border, gives an account of George Washington's death, January 4, 1800.

The Calhoun Normal College opened in September with a large attendance. Prof. Brewer is the principal. He is an able and efficient young educator, but what can he do, with the house and equipment given him!

Misses Jane Duke and Idema Hughes came in Monday to take the

Primary department and are boarding at H. F. Ferguson's.

Prof. J. T. McEntire has charge of the school at McHenry, which opened Monday with a flattering attendance. Prof. McEntire is a good teacher and the people are assured of a good school.

There has been an increase in the tax returns for 1899, $192, 162 over 1898. The Grand Jury recommends a school of 5 months, 3 in the winter and 2 in the summer.

Calhoun's taxable property is $300,000. School bonds will be $1.50 per $1000.

A new steel road scrape was seen on the street today. Six mules were hitched to the machine and, though all the hands were untrained, it did excellent work. Only a few minutes were required to make a ditch on the side of the road and convey all the dirt to the middle leaving the track well-rounded in the center.

The unloading of R. B. Maynard's big traction engine from a flat car was an interesting sight and was witnessed by a big crowd. Heavy timbers were placed against the end of the car, the steam was turned on and the big engine rolled itself off the car. Mr. Maynard has lately moved a sawmill from Tilton to McHenry.

The people of The Pocket have a new Post Office which bears the euphonious and poetical name of Zone. Torrid or Frigid?

A big brick works is to be erected by Legg and Son, at once, just north of town. Arrangements have been made with the railroad for sidetrack. The best machinery will be used, extensive sheds and dry kilns will be built and a large force of hands employed.

Captain and Mrs. John B. Gordon celebrated their Golden Wedding Anniversary on Saturday, August 26. A table 50 feet long had been set up in the yard and one of the most magnificent dinners ever served in North Georgia was enjoyed by the 8 living of 14 children, by 22 grandchildren and by friends. Two fat gobblers, a pig and a ham, ice cream and cold drings were part of the menu.

Rev. C. E. Wright, friend of Captain Gordon's family for 28 years, gave a life history of the family.—John B. Gordon and Miss Isabelle Wright were united in marriage 50 years ago in Forsyth County.

Captain Gordon came from South Carolina in early childhood and located in Tennessee. He has always been in the first rank of useful citizens. He spent 2 years of the 1850s digging in the gold fields of California. Both he and Mrs. Gordon are noble specimens of physical health and strength, with cool heads and honest hearts.

Rev. J. A. Sharp orders The Calhoun Times sent to his new address at Young Harris. Dr. J. B. Game is the new president of Fairmount College. His Co-worker is Prof. Odom. J. G. B. Erwin, Sr. writes a long letter to the paper urging support of the College and stating that there is danger of it's being made a district school.

Rev. L. E. Roberts, new pastor of the Baptist church, came up from Rockmart this week and is living in the Doughty house just vacated by Fred McDaniel.

Big hotel deal—the Haynes House has been leased to J. V. Alexander, present leasee of the Calhoun Hotel. Mr. Haynes will continue to board at the Haynes House, but the rest of the family will live with Mr. and Mrs. J. W. Logan.

Mr. Haynes' retirement means a great loss to Calhoun and the traveling public. There have been few more popular hotel men than

W. B. Haynes.

The Calhoun Hotel will be closed for repairs.

Tickets to the Sam Jones meeting at Cartersville are 90 cents and back.

A familiar figure about town is Uncle Clem Strickland, the mattress maker. He is sought often from other counties and, to date, has made 112 mattresses this year.

Nine people in Mr. Frix's family, all the family except Mr. Frix and one son, were baptized at the same time, at Union Grove Church, near Blackwood, by Rev. Mr. Mealor.

Seven cent cotton! Mr. J. B. Watts paid seven cents for several bales Saturday—the highest price in years.

Big Cotton Mill to be built here—A mass meeting in October made the mill a certainty. Dr. M. J. Dudley, of Sonoraville, was made chairman. Speeches were made by Cols. Starr and Rankin. Committees from each district were appointed. From Sonoraville, Dr. M. J. Dudley, S. C. Houch, N. W. Tate; Fairmount, H. G. Findley, Mr. M. V. Watts, J. G. B. Erwin, Sr.; Calhoun, O. N. Starr, W. R. Rankin, T. W. Harbin, W. G. Fuller, J. A. Hall; Lilly Pond, B. L. McWhorter, W. D. Stewart, E. C. Anderson, T. E. McCullum; Plainville, J. C. Brownlee, N. A. Dodd, J. N. Huffaker; Oostanaula, J. H. Gordon, O. Calbeck, W. F. Mansell; Resaca, Samuel Barnett, W. A. Ward, T. J. Norton; Sugar Valley, J. W. Hill, Jr., H. B. Herrington, V. H. Haynes; 8th District, G. L. Harlan, H. C. Byrom, J. N. Thompson, Joe Lewis; Coosawattee, L. C. Mitchell, John Montgomery, B. Y. Pulliam; 24 District, J. A. Hurton, Jr., Julian Hurt, Jr., J. W. Ashworth; 7th District, C. H. Lewis, J. M. Robertson, W. M. Trimmier.

Pigeons were about to take full charge of the Courthouse tower and the Baptist belfry. They had collected on the hands of the city clock and stopped it. Friday afternoon after business hours, citizens arrived with shotguns, marched into the open street in front of the courthouse and opened fire on the astonished pigeons. The shots brought crowds of people around and many birds were killed.

Bob Poarch, crossing the railroad in a wagon, was hit by a slow-moving southbound train. He was thrown high in the air and his wagon knocked in all directions. He fell in the middle of the street and suffered only bruises. The team was not hurt.

A $50 silk patch work quilt is to be given away, by Miss Minnie Hood, to anyone buying $10 worth of goods.

The Fall openings of Millinery show hats of unusually graceful design. The tall lady is remembered in Gainsboroughs and the petite girl will be very attractive in toques and turbans.

One Gainsborough of castor and black is finished in front with an immense bow of tucked velvet, lined with black velvet, against which is nestled a bunch of violets and dainty bows of baby ribbon, held in place by a silver buckle.

The Misses were enthusiastic over a chic chapeau in automobile red, turban effect, trimmed with a handsome bird.

Millinery openings have become popular in Calhoun and this one caused much comment.

He sleeps in peace—the soul of Clayton Quillian has gone to it's reward. Calhoun never had a minister more loved by all classes. He died of typhoid.

Reuben Gaines is dead. Born in Laurens District, S.C., August 4, 1815, he married Miss Elizabeth Walker in 1836, and moved to Geor-

gia. Eight children were born to them, five of whom are living;
James and Lewis, at Kingston, Henry, at Adairsville, Pinkney and
Mrs. Susan Grey, in Texas.

One of the most remarkable men in calhoun is Col. W. J. Cantrell. He is far past three score and ten, Hale and hearty, he comes to
his office daily, to look after business.

The Golden Wedding Anniversary of Mr. and Mrs. John W. Gray,
of Adairsville, was celebrated in a brilliant reception, at their home.
The decorations, in autumn leaves, cut flowers and potted plants,
were beautiful. The dining room was in yellow, with a frieze of yellow
autumn leaves. Pictures of the couple were on the mantel, with the
dates in yellow satin figures and letters.

Mrs. Gray was a picture of gentle dignity, with her daughter,
Miss Jo, and granddaughter fluttering about.

Mr. and Mrs. Gray had four children. Living are, Mrs. William
Trimble, Adairsville, Col. J. R. Gray, Atlanta and Miss Josephine
Gray.

Col. Gray's father settled in Adairsville in 1833, coming from
South Carolina. His stand was secured from the Indians.

Col. Gray had his sword shot from him at Chickamauga and was
lightly wounded at Atlanta. He was elected to the Legislature in 1870.

Clay Dyar had a party on his tenth birthday. His guests were:
Trammell Starr, Jasper Boaz, Gordon Fuller, Van Buren Watts, Ellis
Reeves; Misses Aileen Dyar, Annie Mae Logan, Mabel Hall, Ida Harlan, Susie Harlan, Mary Hill Vernon, Minnie Dyar, Kate Alexander
and Julia Ballew. The party was a great success and highly enjoyed
by the little folks.

Rev. S. A. Harris, preached two eloquent and impresive sermons
at the Methodist church Sunday. This was his last Saturday before
Conference. He has proven himself an excellent preacher. An ex-
emplary christian man, he made friends with everybody.

Mr. Ed Jackson has bought an interest in the furniture business
of Jackson and Griffin, the new firm that bought the business of
J. S. Hall & Co. Mr. Jackson will have charge of the store and he
and Mrs. Jackson have moved into the Henderson house. (Home of
Mrs. Y. A. Henderson, 1959.)

A hoodoo doctor was tried before J. D. Tinsley last week. He had
been selling queer medicine and charms. Had sold one woman a
bottle of liquid and told her to pour it onto her husband's head at
night and he would never desert her.

SPRINGTOWN PEACHES
AND PLAINVILLE BRICK

Two miles east of the little Village of Plainville is the prettiest sight in the world—ten thousand peach trees in bloom on Mr. J. C. Brownlee's 50 acre mountain orchard. Mr. Brownlee intends to plant 100 acres in trees. Think of it, 20,000 peach trees! This was in 1893. But Milam Gunn, a nurseryman from Tennessee, was the pioneer in the peach orchard business for it was he who persuaded Mr. Brownlee to plant peach trees on his mountain land. In 1889, Plainville had shipped over $1000 worth of peaches and by 1893, the people of the vicinity were abandoning cotton growing for that of fruit. Mr. Gunn

COWART HOUSE AT PLAINVILLE

This house was built by Mr. Aspasio Earl, in the year of 1833. The timbers were cut from the farm, and hauled by ox cart 26 miles to Kingston, Georgia to the nearest saw mill, hauled back and hand-dressed. The house consisted of four rooms, 18 feet by 18 feet and a 12-foot open hall-way.

The house is ceiled with 12-inch heart pine planks. The square nails used in construction were made in a Plainville blacksmith shop, by Mr. Dink Smith, Sr., as were the door hinges.

All framing and sills were hand hewn and put together with wooden pegs. The inside doors had string-lift latches for fastening, also hand-made.

The chimney was built of brick made of clay on Mr. Earl's farm. The house was sold to Mr. John Henry Dodd in 1880, who sold it to Mr. J. P. Hammond in 1899. Mr. Hammond's daughter, Jennie, married Lee Cowart the same year moved into the house and resided there until the death of Mr. Cowart in 1936.

The Earls, Hammonds and Dodds, deceased, are all buried in the cemetery on land given from the Earl property.

This property now belongs to Mrs. Ben Miller, daughter of Lee and Jennie Cowart, and to Ronald Taylor, grandson of Lee and Jennie Cowart.

The house was torn down in 1960 and the timbers sold to Mr. Hazelwood who used it to build a house on the Zack Boswell farm.

Ronald Taylor is building a modern brick house where the Earl house stood.

sold $6000 worth of peaches in 1893 with a net gain of $3000 and Mr. Brownlee cleared $150 to $250 an acre on his orchard. The fruit, of the Elberta variety, was large and delicious and commanded a ready market in the north.

The year of 1893 was an eventful one for Plainville in another way—the last bar room disappeared from the village and the people were once more free, from the vile influence of the liquor traffic.

The story of Plainville, however, does not begin with peaches in 1889 or in 1893. History, for Plainville, goes back to that day in 1850 when Gordon County was created and Springtown was laid out as Militia district No. 1,055, beginning at the southeast corner of lot No. 84, running due north to the northeast corner of lot No. 296 in the 14th district, 3rd section; thence due west to the Oostanaula River; thence running with the river to the Floyd County line, precinct to be at John Lay's house, on the Rome road.

Springtown's first road commissioners were Samuel T. King, J. P., Joel Fain and Thomas Durham. Others serving as road commissioners and road reviewers during the years 1850-1855 were Alexander Cameron, Jerry Robbins, Robert Black, Esq. Spencer B. Crow, James Lay, John Henry Dodd, Elias Putnam, Dennis Miller, Aaron Roff and H. M. Camp, Esq.

The name of James Brownlee appears on the Grand Jury list, for 1859, Samuel T. King was Sheriff from 1855 to 1858 and Joel Fain was Tax Receiver in 1850-51.

Militia District No. 1,055 was laid out by the Justice of the Inferior Court, lines were drawn on a piece of paper by surveyors but the inside story of Springtown begins in the records of the Unity Baptist Church.

Sometime prior to 1849, a group of people had migrated from Switzer, Spartanburg County, S. C. where they had been members of Unity, a church organized in 1818 in a building that was erected by Quakers about the time of the American Revolution.

The story is beautifully told in a brochure entitled Unity and One Hundred Years, prepared for the Church's Centennial by Starr Miller, descendant of Springtown pioneers and now a Dean of Tift College at Forsyth.

"To our forefathers" writes Mr. Miller, "the home was a sacred institution. In that home was respect and reverence. The Bible was law and the Golden Rule was a pillar. Fully realizing that the family, the church, the school and the State are organizations which are called institutions of civilization, our forefather established all of these."

At the organizational meeting on March 10, 1849, the clerk recorded:

"We, the Presbytery, being called upon by the herinafter, named members in Springtown Valley for the purpose of constituting them into a church. According to the request, we met on Saturday before the second Sabbath in March, 1849 and, after duly examining them, we found them orthodox in faith and proceeded to constitute them into a church and pronounced them Unity Baptist Church of Christ.

Hezikiah Glover
Jacob Tate
S. G. Hamilton
Presbytery."

Charter members were John Floyd, Sarah Floyd, David Floyd,

Margarett Floyd, J. F. Reynolds, A. C. Hay, Matildy Hay, Nancy Reynolds, Spencer M. Scott, Ellender Scott, L. M. Wofford, May Crossley, Young Scott and Sara Scott.

Like all pioneers, the congregation of Unity moved several times. The first building was located on the Rome road, at Franklin Cemetery, which is still church property. The next move was to a place now known as the Will Climer farm, a little north of Plainville. Unity left a cemetery here too—Scott Cemetery, also under the care of the church today. The third building stood just east of the village where Thomas Hopper lives now.

Mrs. Ada Scott Corley, 93 years old in 1959, joined the church in this building in 1885 and was baptized by Preacher Brooks at Moore's ferry. Mrs. Docia Floyd was another convert, baptized at this time. Mrs. Fanny Scott, who died in 1948 at the age of 99 and was the mother of Mrs. Corley, also joined the church here.

The present building was completed in 1888. Among the leaders of that day were, Marion Floyd, Pink Floyd, Mose Scott, Miles Scott and Than Dodd. A. S. Tatum was the preacher.

The fourth site selected for Unity was a lot adjoining the fifteen year old Academy where the two buildings stood side by side until 1909 when the School was moved and the church purchased the property.

The foundation of the 1888 structure was laid by a contractor from Rome. William Miller, C. A. Boswell, William Hester and C. R. Mostellar, builder of the steeple, were the carpenters.

From 1879 to 1895, Unity was a member of the Cherokee Baptist Association but joined the Gordon County Association as a charter member in 1897 when the big Cherokee Association was broken up into smaller ones.

Unity was strict with her members, reminding them often of the misdeeds of man and the need for repentance and forgiveness. As late as 1925, according to Mr. Miller's history, the following resolution was adopted; "Inasmuch as it is being rumored that a number of our members are living inconsistently with the teachings of God's Word; being guilty of profanity; taking the name of God in Vain; excessive drinking of intoxicating spirits; dancing and allowing dancing in their homes, which is termed reveling by the Scriptures; absenting themselves from the church and continuing to treat it with absolute contempt and many other violations of God's Word. Therefore, be it resolved that in the future, those continuing in the practice of such will be dealt with according to the teachings of the New Testament."

Amusing? Then the Ten Commandments are amusing. Out of date? Then the Bible is out of date.

The church purchased an organ in 1903, probably the first used. In early church services, the preacher would read a line of the hymn. the deacon with a musical ear would heist the tune lead the congregation in singing the line. Some churches were split in two over the question of whether to buy an organ. A few members were turned out of the church for wanting to profane the divine services with an instrument.

For baptismal rites, Moore's ferry and Ship Island on the Oostanaula and Whatley's bridge on Whatley Creek have been favorite places for Unity Church. Baptisms were postponed in 1912 because of the condition of the river after a drouth.

Among pastors of Unity's early days were: Revs. Hezekiah Glover, Billy King, Cates, Brooks, A. S. Tatum and W. A. King. From 1901 to 1949, pastors were, E. Culpepper, A. H. Lattimer, J. M. Barnett, M. L. Keith, Gordon Ezell, J. H. Wyatt, J. F. Hodges, C. S. Henderson, J. M. Cook, Paul Sayne, H. P. Bell, G. D. Legg, J. T. Roberts, H. L. Wright, W. G. Cutts, Garner, Buice and Henry Holland.

About 1955, the church was brickveneered and otherwise remodeled. While at work on the building the men found in the attic a crockery churn through which the stovepipe had been run as fire protection.

Reed organs became obsolete and churches began to use pianos. Perhaps the next important project for Unity will be the purchase of an electronic organ.

Heated by natural gas, lighted with electricity and cornered by paved streets, Unity Baptist Church, granddaughter of the American Revolution, marches with the ages and continues to be a guiding light to the Floyds and the Scotts and the many others whose names have been added to the rolls throughout the years.

Unity was built by Scotts and Floyds but Autrys, Blankenships, Goswicks and Moore led the membership list of Plainville Methodist Church. There's a sprinkling of Millers and some of the Floyds went over to the Methodists, probably through marriage. Boswells married Floyds, Millers married Boswells and Scotts—Oh, I'm lost. Anyway, no one married his cousin.

It was Miriam Blankenship, generally acknowledged as one of the best First Grade teachers in the county and for over 20 years a teacher in the junior department of the Sunday School, who compiled the history of the Methodist church.

Mt. Pisgah, the first Methodist church in the vicinity, Miss Blankenship relates, was located one and one half miles north of Plainville between the farms of William Zuber and Clement Arnold, now known as the Hester and Grizzle farms. Here, ancestors of Plainville Methodist attended services in the early 1850s. Another Methodist church, known as Gilgal, stood one mile south of the village near the Morrow cemetery in the Anthony community on the Southern Railroad. Rev. Whitfield Anthony was pastor there at one time.

These two congregations came together in 1868 to form the Plainville Methodist Church. The same year, David Sisk and Katharine Sisk deeded to J. M. Ellis, W. Hughen, David Sisk, James McCool and Clement Arnold, trustees, a tract of land described as "in the county of Gordon and State of Georgia aforesaid bounded as follows, to wit, lot No. 142, 24th district, 3rd section of originally Cherokee but now Gordon County, as follows: beginning at the post oak tree in the north side of Dodd ferry road opposite W. Hughen's Mill, running from thence 16 rods to a pine stump corner, thence west 20 rods to a stake corner, thence south 16 rods to the Dodd ferry road, thence east along the road 20 rods to the beginning corner, containing and laid out for 20 acres of land." The price paid for the lot was $20.

The church was named Union Grove Methodist Church, derived from the fact that the churches were united and built in a grove of pine trees. The pastorate was in the Floyd Spring circuit until 1891 when it was placed in the Adairsville charge. Miss Beulah Hydle recalled that the last four pastors of the church, when it was on the Floyd Spring circuit, were Sappington, Brown, Perryman and Murdock and that in those days chairs were brought from the wagons and placed in the aisles to accommodate the large crowds.

The church built in 1905 was the second for Union Grove and Sunday School rooms were added in 1947. Through the years, the church has been well organized in all the activities of the Methodist Conference.

A building fund, to continue over a period of 10 years, was begun in 1950. A cigar box was passed to each class on Sundays and continued to make it's rounds for 6 years. Appropriately ,the first sermon preached in the new sanctuary was entitled Faith in Peculiar Places.

Rev. Arvil Allen, student pastor in 1955, began to encourage the congregation to make definite plans for the building program. Then the question of whether to build or to remodel took precedence, finally ending in the decision to build. Mrs. Leonard Fuller, Millard Coulter and Raymond Blankenship were appointed as building committee, plans were drawn by Mr. Herman Tichler, of Rome, and the program was under way. Construction on the Educational Unit began in 1956.

With new plans came a new vision of the church as at least a half station. Men, women, boys and girls went to work and in July 1956, the first Methodist parsonage family ever to reside in Plainville with it's hundred years of Methodism moved into the community. Rev. and Mrs. James Snell, with their eleven months old daughter, Viki, moved from Atlanta into the lovely new parsonage just across the street from the church.

In June 1956, the church left the Adairsville charge, the Oostanaula church came in from the Rome circuit and the Plainville charge was born.

The next year, the old church was moved from the property and a ground-breaking ceremony took place. Contractors for both units were Mr. Thad Cagle, of Plainville, and Mr. Bill Johnson, of Calhoun. On January 26, 1958, the first service was held in the beautiful new Sanctuary with it's stained glass windows, handsome pulpit furniture, candlesticks, Baptismal bowl, kneeling cushion, lectern scarf, communion table, cross, pulpit Bible, two chair pews and Salman's Head of Christ, all given in memory of departed loved ones or in honor of those living.

Plainville Methodist Church was selected by the Town and County commission of the North Georgia Conference as the church of the year in 1957 and was chosen as District church of the year in 1956 and again in 1959.

Some of the well-known names in Methodism connected with Plainville church either in the pastor, presiding elder or Bishop relationship are, Lester Rumble, McHowery Elrod, W. T. Irvine, J. F. Yarborough, S. A. Harris, Frank Quillian, J. R. Turner, A. M. Pierce, J. S. Thrailkill, C. M. Lipham, Peter Manning, H. C. Stratton, Wm. H. Gardner, W. A. Candler, V. W. Darlington, W. B. Beachamp, W. N. Ainsworth and Arthur J. Moore.

The road leads to Rome but you enter Springtown Valley after you cross the Oothcaloga creek bridge and you turn to the right in Springtown, now Scottsville, to reach Plainville.

One afternoon, I rode through Springtown Valley, with Bernard and Mignon Franklin. Bernard, a noted raconteur of Grandpa stories, has recently retired from the office of Postmaster, at Calhoun, after

17 years of service and is devoting his time to farming and cattle raising. A veteran of the World War I, he was several times commander of Paul Gwin Post of the American Legion and member of the National Guard, rising from First Sergeant to the rank of Captain which he held for 12 years.

Our first Grandpa story was the one about Colonel R. M. Young and the first thresher to be brought to Gordon County. It was set up in the field that is now the site of the Gordon County Hospital and the Housing Unit. The machine would not work and Mr. Young said there was something wrong with it and he would have to send the thresher back. Grandpa Franklin said that he knew as soon as he saw it that the men had set the machine with the teeth going the wrong way, but he wouldn't tell Mr. Young.

After we crossed Oothcaloga Creek bridge, we stopped a little beyond the Dean Hayes home and, motioning to the house across the road, Bernard said "that is where John Lay lived in 1838." Grandpa Bill Franklin and John's son Jim were 16 years old at the time. The precinct house in 1850, however, was at the site of the two story house, known today as the Norman Miller place—where the twin silos are. Like those of most of the pioneers, John Lay's house was built of logs. One room of it, probably the kitchen, still stands out behind the big house.

John gave the farm to his son Jim who sold it to Mr. Shelor. Milam Gunn built the present structure for Mr. Shelor at a cost of $1500. Calvin Wright married one of the Shelor girls and so came into possession of the place.

"They grew up with the Indians" Bernard said, in relating stories of the Lay, Franklin and Robbins men and others of their time. In fact, an Indian named Bear lived in the neighborhood. Jim Lay's association with the Cherokees accounts for the attire that he was wearing the day Grandpa Franklin went over to buy the mules. It was a summer day and the Georgia sun was pouring out it's heating rays in full power. "Ain't you thirsty?" Jim asked. Grandpa replied that he sure was, so the two men went down to the spring. "Drink all you want" Jim said, "for I'm going to cool off." After Grandpa had relieved his thirst with a long cool drink from the gourd dipper, Ji mremoved his sole garment, an ankle-length shirt, and lay down in the spring, his head resting on a projecting root.

Grandpa thought "now's the time to talk him out of the mules," so he brought forth his trading tactics and soon convinced the cool and comfortable Jim that he didn't need the pair of big black mules after all.

Just beyond the Lay house, you turn to the left and follow a winding country road through the Durham, Swain, Kinman and Bray acres until you come to the Jerry Robbins house perched on top of one of the little hills that are set around like sand dunes piled up by the ocean waves. Jerry came to Gordon County in 1834 and bought the place in 1835 for $300. His son Steve, said that the apple trees growing there were supposed to be 100 years old then. Jerry first built the house on another lot but, the next morning, tore it down and re-built it on the present site.

On the way to the Robbins place, Zeke Swain's house sits in a curve of the road, deserted and empty, it's paneless windows looking at you forlornly, but the peeling cedars and the scraggby boxwoods, attest to the fact that the place was, a hundred years ago, a stately and beloved home.

When Bernard's Grandpa Sayre came to Gordon County, he bought the Robbins place and it was from her home there that Lizzie Sayre left to conduct a private School at Dr. King's. It wasn't far from the Franklin place on the Rome road to the Sayre home as Bob Franklin soon discovered. Lucy Sayre traveled the dusty road to town to flirt with the handsome John Gray as he handled the yard stick in a dry goods store. John always wore white linens for the summer trade.

Lizzie Sayre became Mrs. Bob Franklin and Lucy Sayre married John Gray.

Jerry Robbins owned slaves, so did the Kings and Jim Lay had lots of them. A woman belonging to the King family disappeared one day. As the search went on for her, someone saw one of Jerry's negroes, Dan Robbins, going into a cave in the hills. Dan admitted that he had furnished the cave and moved in with the King slave. When called upon by the authorities to "tell the truth about that woman," he said "I didn't steal her from Mr. King, Gus Lay stole her. She always did like me better'n him so I stole her from him."

Dan was persuaded to tell the story to the Jury and insist that Gus Lay was the culprit because Jim Lay would not allow his negroes to be whipped but Jerry Robbins would let them "beat the hide off of Dan."

The crystal singing stream that waters the meadows all around is called Robbins Creek. Bernard owns many of the surrounding acres and has an attractive, comfortable cabin, set against a hill where he and his friends go for "circle" meetings and the Franklin daughters, with their husbands spend pleasant, restful weekends. But Mignon says it is so quiet out there that she can't sleep.

Alexander Cameron, another of Springtown's 1851 Road Commissioners, lived in the house that still sits looking into the corner of the Rome and Reeves Station roads. One day, when Grandpa Franklin stopped at a blacksmith shop across the road to have his horse shod he asked about a group of men busy around a wagon and mule that were standing in the Cameron field. "They are burying a man out there," he was told. Tom Brown now owns the Cameron farm.

When the precinct was moved from John Lay's house to one nearer Calhoun, a man who ran a still back on the hill was expected to furnish the liquor for election day. His hound dog, Trail, fell in the Vat and drowned. When the fact became known one man got all the others to agree not to drink "his old Trail liquor." However, the owner of the dog-flavored wiskey carried his jars to the Election. The instigator of the boycott could not long endure the sight of the untouched spirits and blurted "Trail or no Trail, give me a pint!"

Three men owned practically all of Reeves Station, Mr. Fuller, with 600 acres, Osborn Reeves had 1000 and the Garlington's 600 acres. Jesse Swain, too, was a Reeves Station pioneer. His house is the one across the railroad from the depot, and the big house a little beyond the Station is the Dennis Miller home.

Mose Foster ran a store at Reeves in the early days and lived in the house that is now the Fite home. O. A. Mims was a resident of the Station and built the Swain house and store across the railroad. The Mims men were Primitive Baptist preachers and O. A. was tax collector for many years. Roland Hayes picked peaches for Floyd Mims and sang as he worked. Reeves Station men would fish all night and at dawn the entire community would enjoy a fish-fry breakfast.

The Garlington farm was purchased by the Adventist Church sometime before 1920 and was then known as the Hurlbert farm. Later the farm became Scott Sanitorium and is now being converted into a school.

As the years advanced and Dennis Miller (his wife was Margaret Pickard) began to be weak in body but remained sound in mind, and wanting his sons to live in peace after his death, made a pact with Grandpa Franklin who signed a note agreeing to buy the land, and with Jim Lay for the negroes. After Dennis' death the boys fussed anyway, so Mr. Franklin and Mr. Lay tore up the papers they were holding.

When Mr. Fuller came to Reeves in the 1830s, he found that he could buy all the land down to the river for $400, but said it was too much money. He went to Dahlonega and worked in the gold mines for a few years, then came back to Reeves and paid $400 for 600 acres.

Henry H. Dobson was another extensive land holder of the 1850s and owned the Roland Hayes place on the Rome and Dalton road. The Gordons owned the place at one time and Dr. Hansard lived there at a later date.

One day in 1853 Henry Dobson was on his way to Calhoun to attend a land sale. He carried his money ,about $500 in gold and $14 in silver, in a buckskin bag. Crossing Miller's ferry, where the bridge is now, he rode past the field where a man was building a boat on the creek, just where it runs into the river. When Uncle Henry got to the Rome road, he discovered that his money bag was missing. He went back to the ferry, carefully examining every foot of the way. Sure that he lost the bag after he had crossed the river, he questioned the man at the creek who declared he had not seen the money.

The next morning the man who was building the boat, woke up early with a severe pain in his side and died.

For days and weeks Mr. Dobson had slaves hunting for the money that was never found. In 1913, a negro boy plowed up a shower of gold pieces in the field near the ferry and the mystery of 60 years was solved for here was Uncle Henry Dobson's money, $485 in $2, $5, and $10 gold pieces. The silver was missing. People surmised that the buckskin bag of money had been hidden in a stump and the man with the boat died before he could use the gold or tell anyone about it. The tree stump rotted, soil was repeatedly washed over the spot and there the gold lay until a plow point uncovered the hoard over half a century later.

When Grandpa Franklin planned to build his house everyone told him "you'll die if you don't build on a hill." So he built on a hill, and carried or hauled water up that hill. On Sunday, while Mrs. Franklin and the children, escorted by the negroes, had gone to church at Rush's Chapel, Grandpa went down to the low place at the foot of the hill, found a spring and cleared it out. When Mrs. Franklin came home, he took her down the hill, showed her the spring and told her that he was tired of toting water for the family and 30 negroes. The next morning he moved his house to the spring.

The Franklin house on the Rome road, now the home of Mr. and Mrs. Alec Franklin, was the Robert Black place. Grandpa Franklin bought the property when the Black family, 33 members in all, left for Texas in 1876. Mattie Franklin Hicks and Eva Thomas live in two little white houses back among the Franklin trees. The Thomases are fairly new comers to Springtown Valley, having come there in the 1880s. Jess Shelor's house faced the old road and now turns it's back on the paved highway. The Wade house stands at the left on the other side of the bridge near Liberty Church.

Austin Seminary, finishing School for Calhoun and Gordon County girls in the 1880s, stood across from the junction of the Plainville road and State 53. Dr. King was the original owner of this land and, later, Mr. Henley lived there and used Austin Seminary for a barn.

Springtown Valley, full of springs and fertile of land, was a fertile field for the Cumberland Presbyterians and the belief that the Bible is the sole rule of faith and conduct. With their Que Sera Sera they set to work, fully believing that the whiskey-drinking men of Springtown could be redeemed. Though the deeds were recorded in 1859 and 1860, it is believed that Liberty Church was organized in 1846.

The Presbyterians were ably assisted by the devout Unity Baptists from Switzer, S. C. and the strict Methodists of Gilgal and Mt. Pisgah and there gradually emerged from the rugged pioneer stock a people ambitious, cultured and religious, whose descendants continue to walk in the steps of their forbears, a fact attested to by attractive homes all down Springtown Valley and in Plainville where also you may find a modern School building and 3 handsome brick churches.

But, in 1867, Captain Barney and his Corps of engineers chose to run the new railroad one mile west of Springtown and he named the Village that grew up around the Selma, Rome and Dalton train stop, Plainville, for his home town in Connecticut. After the first train went through in 1870, the little settlement became a popular lunch station and meals were served to the passengers from the "eating house." After the S R and D was sold to the East Tennessee Virginia and Georgia railroad the lunches were discontinued and the eating house became Plainville's first School with Captain Barney's son, Henry, as the first teacher.

Plainville's first storehouse stood where the Boy Scout Cabin is now. Bell and Arnold were the merchants and later Raleigh Bates and J. H. Brownlee ran the store. Lucius Bell, was the Postmaster for the office established in 1871. Before that people got their mail at Pinson Station 3 miles to the south. J. C. and J. H. Brownlee were the Postmasters for 30 years, J. C. when the Democrats were in and J. H. under the Republicans.

Dominating the Village is the beautiful old Brownlee house now owned by Mr. and Mrs. Pete Sutton. Facing the railroad, it stands back from the street on a wide lot set with handsome shrubs and shaded by fine trees.

James Brownlee, with money pouring in from his thousands of peach trees, wanted a home befitting his status as a fruit baron, so in January 1901, he began to build the house. The Calhoun Times carried the announcement in 1901 that "Mr. J. C. Brownlee, of Plainville, will be married to Miss Lee Patton at the home of the bride's aunt, Mrs. S. M. Adams, in Hartwell, Ga., by Rev. Mr. Thomas. The bride and groom will go to Buffalo after the wedding. Mr. Brownlee is a prominent fruit grower of Plainville and his bride is an attractive and cultured young lady."

Mr. Brownlee bought the land and the three room house from Milam Gunn, then had to build a house for Mr. Gunn before he could begin his own. The house built for the Gunns is now the home of Mr. and Mrs. Claud Van Dyke.

The original 3 room house (no one knows who built it but the names of McCurry and Reynolds appear on the deeds) is used as kitchen, dining and den areas and is joined to the main part of the house by a covered passage way.

The main house is four rooms square upstairs and down with a long hall on each floor. The stairway goes up from the back of the hall. The north front room, the parlor, has a handsome carved mantel supported by round columns. It was here in the parlor of the "Hotel Brownlee" that Mrs. Brownlee's sister, Mae Patton, was married to Paul Harrison. The room was decorated with ferns and Autumn leaves. Miss Bessie Anderson, at the piano, and Miss Carrie Mae Brownlee, violinist, played Mendelssohn's Wedding March and Dr. W. H. Darnall performed the ceremony.

The other 3 rooms in the main house are used as bedrooms. The Suttons live in the kitchen ell where they have removed a partition to make one long room across the front. Notable features of this room are the wide-board floor, shining without wax, the varnished walnut ceiling and the handsome mirrored mantel with fluted columns reaching from the floor to the top of the mantel. In here is a lovely picture, in color, of the Suttons charming daughter who was Miss Gordon County in 1954.

Ceilings throughout the house are of beveled wood and the walls are of plaster. Though each room has a fireplace and a graceful columned mantel, the house is heated with gas.

A broad Veranda runs across the front and around the north side of the big house and the former front porch of the little house is pleasant for summer living.

The twelve round pillars of the front porch match the balled spindles in the bannisters which alternate one ball, then two. Dentils are made with one square curved-front block followed by three small ones. The two front windows start at the porch floor. The pointed arcading of the windows is very attractive and the roof line is broken by pediments.

One night, while the house was still under construction, Mrs. Brownlee heard an unusual noise and insisted that Mr. Brownlee investigate. He told her that she was imagining things and refused. She said "I'll go then." Of course, he accompanied her and they found three railroad hobos warming themselves at a fire in the newly built fireplace. They said "Boss, we didn't know anybody was living in this house!"

Following Callie Scott's marriage to T. W. Woods, the Brownlees gave them a reception. The young people played games and danced in the unfinished upstairs rooms. "They were brought up in the church for dancing." Mrs. Woods told me, "and some of them turned out."

Mr. and Mrs. Woods were married after seven years of going together and their wedding was the first in the new Unity Baptist Church. It was in April. Ida Van Dyke and Vesta Floyd did the decorating, using boxwood and potted plants. Mrs. Woods could remember the names of only two of her attendants, Vada Scott and Darnell

Brownlee but she could remember riding to the church in a surrey with fringe on top and two lamps in front and a negro coachman driving two white horses. Here her sister, Mrs. Goswick, broke in with "Callie, you know Norman Miller drove that surrey!" Is a girl supposed to remember every detail of an enchanted evening? Can't she add to the enchantment after fifty years of remembering?

Mr. and Mrs. Woods celebrated their golden wedding anniversary at the home of Mrs. Woods sister, Mrs. Corley.

There were seven Scott girls and all of them are living in 1959. The eldest, Mrs. Corley, is 93. She also observed her 50th anniversary before Mr. Corley died in January 1959.

Mrs. Scott, mother of the girls, was a Hannah and had only one brother. Her father had said to his wife in 1861, "Melissa, I'm going to war and I may not be back. I know you will marry again and I want the children to have the property." He arranged for Frances, the daughter, to have the old home near Plainville, where she spent her life and died at the age of 99. Will Scott, brother of the seven sisters, lives there now. Originally, the house was one big room with an upstairs and a shed room. Frances Hannah's brother was given the place at Reeves Station.

Another interesting Plainville family was the Prough family. Mrs. Hester (Fanny Prough) is still living in the house that she and Mr. Hester built in 1896, a short distance down the Plainville-Rome road from the Sutton home. Mr. Prough was a railroad engineer. "He drove those little engines that they have in Atlanta and Chattanooga," Mrs. Hester matter-of-factly stated and there I was about to fall out of my chair in the excitement of knowing that I was talking to the daughter of a man who was engineer on the Texas and the General!

The new style engine was adopted by the ETV and G in 1881 when the road bought 35 new engines, 28 of them Moguls.

"My father was a rover," Fanny said, "and moved 75 times. When we got to Plainville, my mother said she was through moving —and here we have been ever since."

When the school children would call Fanny a damyankee, she would fight them and the teacher would whip her. Her brother always told her "don't get mad, that's what they want."

One of Fanny's chores was to go to the store for the lamp-burning fuel that the Southerns called kerosene oil, but she always asked for "coal arl." Uncle Jeff, the store keeper, would ask her several times what she wanted and laugh heartily each time. Finally she rebelled and declared I am not going to the store any more. He makes me say " 'coal arl' over and over!"

Scattered about the floor in the dining room and guest room of the Hester home are six deep-piled, odd-shaped small rugs. Mrs. Croff Hayes, now making her home with Mrs. Hester, told me that Mr. Hester raised the sheep and cured the hides from which the soft, wooly rugs were made.

Mrs. Hester's children are Carl of Gainesville, Fla., Talmadge of Atlanta, Max of Chattanooga, Aurie (Mrs. Dodd) of Rome and Lottie (Mrs. Van Atta) of Fla. Another son, Horace, a railroad engineer, was killed in a wreck.

Now, cross the railroad and drive along the saded, paved street that goes up the hill and around the bend to the river. The first house on the right is the home of Mrs. Alma Boswell-Floyd. Dr. Franklin built this house. Across the street, Bill and Aline McEntyre live in the house originally the home of Dr. Floyd. A later Plainville physician, Dr. Bannister, also lived in this house and had a drug store where the Boy Scout Cabin stands.

Next to Mrs. Floyd is Mrs. Climer's house whose neighbors on the other side are the Scott sisters, Mrs. Wood and Mrs. Goswick. It was Mr. Scott who said that Unity Church was in the wrong place, that it should be across the railroad. "If you will move the church" he told the deacons, "I will give the land and $100. So Unity was moved to its present location.

Over the hill and across from the beautiful new Methodist Church is a two-story house, at least 70 years old, built by Than Dodd and Mr. Mostellar. It is now the home of Mr. and Mrs. Henry Boswell and their daughter. Mr. Boswell's parents lived in a log house that stood back of the present one. His mother sold the place for Confederate money while her husband was fighting with the Southern Army. Before the war, they had planted boxwoods and set out 2 cedar trees. One of the trees was blown down in a storm but the other still stands as do the boxwoods, now enormous in girth.

In 1867, the Boswells started to Texas in an ox wagon. Mr. Boswell went broke in Mississippi and his oxen died. He saved one of the ox horns and made a dinner horn of it. Henry Boswell entered the horn in the Atlanta Fair one year and it still bears the Fair tag.

A veranda crosses the front of the Boswell house and curves around the side door. The big square rooms are ceiled and floored with handsome wide boards. Mirrored mantels supported by round pillars grace the two front rooms and the others have fluted ones. The stairway has both round and fluted bannisters perhaps because Than Dodd liked round posts and Mr. Mostellar liked them fluted.

Mr. Mosteller was a trader and owned extensive orchards. He built the house next door to the Boswells and also the original part of the house occupied by Mrs. Woods and Mrs. Goswick and owned by Mrs. Goswick's son.

The Clem Boswell house just beyond Unity Church is another of Plainville's old homes.

Mr. and Mrs. Buford Hopper live next door to the Henry Boswells. Family pieces in their house are Mrs. Hopper's grandfather's dresser and a small square table he made and a 100 year old safe belonging to her grandmother. ("Safe" is the old word for china cabinet.) Then there is a handsome table with Duncan Phyfe legs, made by Mr. Hopper.

You turn to the right around the Methodist church and drive a short distance to the house, made from a barn, that shelters a fabulous collection of antiques owned by a couple who have an almost equally fabulous past, Mr. and Mrs. Charles Meadows. She was Montene Mathis, daughter of Ada Scott Corley by a previous marriage. Like the wonderer who roves the world, tastes the exotics of greener lands then finds that after all, east, west, home is best, Montene returned to her childhood scenes after her husband's retirement from his position as General Supervisor for the Smith Elevator Co., a place he had held for 35 years.

When Mrs. Meadows begins to tell of her activities, you wonder how one small woman could do so much! One of the first settlers in East Ridge, Chattanooga, she organized The Bachman Garden Club and served as its president for six years. She was a member of the Missionary Ridge Garden Club for 8 years, a charter member of the Iris Garden Club and the Rose Society and was chairman of the dining room at the First Christian Church for 18 years.

Mrs. Meadows, a Gray Lady in both World Wars, was the first matron to start feeding the soldiers who guarded the Bachman tubes during World War II. The idea spread over Chattanooga and other organizations joined in giving warm meals to these faithful sentinels. As a Garden Club president, Mrs. Meadows stood in the receiving line at the reception given to President and Mrs. Roosevelt on their visit to the city.

Mrs. Meadows has been a lifetime collector of antiques, hence the extensive collection that she now owns.

LaQuita Dodd led me around to the back of the house across a brick-paved patio (Montene and Charles laid the 13,000 bricks) into the ground floor room ,which was first a shed, then a garage and next a porch. It was finally enclosed and made into a den furnished with comfortable chairs, books, radio, television and a single spool bed on which five generations were raised. As you go up the stair-way, a bust of Hiawatha, painted like the leaves of Autumn, painted like the sky of morning, sits there brooding and does not answer, does not tell you, I'm sure he doesn't know—that he is destined for the Vann House at Spring Place.

Stair-stepped along the wall are pictures of mothers of all the races, mounted on woven reed mats. Mrs. Meadows has toured the 48 states, Cuba and Mexico.

The stall where the stock ate is now the kitchen. Here, Mrs. Meadows has bowed to the modern, for her kitchen has all the pres-ent day conveniences—sink, refrigerator, range, and cabinets galore, built by Mr. Meadows.

One step and this, surely, is the world's treasure room—china from a King's palace, silver from the home of a Philadelphia tycoon, crystal from a Baron's castle—the breath catches on hanging prisms, the eye drowns in a heavenly blue water glass and delight pours from a silver pot or dances on a pewter tray.

Will you have champagne from the Patton Hotel's silver bucket? Let me soothe you with chocolate from the Hershey's silver. Will you sit here in your Gay Nineties frock, with your pompadour crowning your ivory brow, and pour coffee from the Hershey silver, set on coat-of-arms tray?

For the lady who prefers tea, here is the hot water pot, and, of course, sugar, cream and waste containers. This group is valued at $2000.

Over in the corner a flaxen haired princess from Germany might come back from 200 years ago and serve punch with the Kaiser's solid gold, sterling silver handled ladle while small lily of the valley lamps star-gaze from the china shelves lining one side of the room.

The silver butter dish is 80 years old, a round bowl and lid is 200 years old, silver from England and there's a cruet to match.

A glass cabinet sparkles with crystal and glows with hand paint-ed china. The six blue tumblers, in grape design, are from England.

Mrs. Hershey (the Hersheys were Pennsylvania Dutch) served baked beans once a week, from this bowl, in plates of different colors.

The superb milk glass collection is flocked by a red combed rooster cocktail set from Pennsylvania. The hand-painted dinner set has been in the Meadows family 55 years. Glass liquor bottles, a Tom and Jerry punch bowl and cups from Mexico—and here's a small ruby glass bowl, 200 years old, which was picked up in a German Cathedral. The priests drank wine from it.

You'll love the little shell shaped bone dishes—no they are not made of bone, they are set by your plate to hold your chicken bones. (I saw dishes like these at Haney's recently, so they must be in style again.)

Ironstone is of course represented in the china collection along with 2 gold-embossed plates, one red, one blue, from Germany.

The hanging lamp, its prisms flashing diamond lights to every corner, was fashioned two and one half centuries ago and once beamed on beautiful women in the Hershey mansion.

The long room across the front is every bit as exciting as the rest of the house. Are you in love? Then sit here with your sweetheart on the proposal seat. We'll listen from the love seat and two chairs nearby. This corner is mostly German, so twirl your Kaiser mustache and click your Prussian heels while you tell time by the 200 year old clock and finger the 20 carat in-laid gold picture frame. But shudder over this jardiniere, made of 3 kinds of metal, for it was blood-covered when found on Hitler's estate.

Jenny Lind loved the milk glass perfume se tin its tray. The stoppers are miniatures of her hairdo and her face is carved in relief on the bottle sides. Grandma Hershey's breakfast set and Grandpa's mustache cup all gold-embossed are displayed in this room.

One picture frame was in Mr. Meadows' family. It is made of 7 kinds of wood. And there's a picture of Mrs. Meadows' son with his great-grandmother who was 99 when she died. The son lives in Denver, Colo. with his wife and 3 lovely daughters.

The barn was slightly leaning when the Meadows began the work of restoration so the door frame into the bedroom is narrow at the top and wide at the bottom. The bed is hand made from walnut and an 1872 picture graces the wall.

Perhaps we'll have time to go back one day sit at the secretary desk, modeled 200 years ago, and read the 1820 dictionary of the Aristocrats in Europe and to look over the clippings and scrap books that tell the story of Montene Meadows' interesting life in Chattanooga.

On a spring day, you may step down from the living room into a brick paved, screened porch, where ivy grows over a dead tree limb in a walled planted and soft breezes stir the daffodils that dance up and down the sloping lawn and all around the house. For company, you'll have a yellow cat, so big, so much like his jungle cousin that you want to ask tiger, tiger burning bright, may I share your den tonight?

At the foot of the hill is the rest of the house, for this was a house divided against itself—the old Miller house it was. After the death of the parents, the Miller sons removed the top story, set it on top of the hill and made the barn that sat and waited for Montene and Charles Meadows to abacadraba into a home for themselves and their storied heirlooms.

Across the road is the Blankenship house where teacher-historian Miriam lives with her father and mother, and aunt, Leon Autry. The framing of the house is that of the pre-war dwelling probably built by Mr. Parrott and remodeled by Zack Boswell who married a granddaughter of the Parrotts.

Over the hill on the main street that turns into the river bend road, the two Dodd families live side by side, the elder Dodds on the hill, the younger, in the long low house with the painted door.

The senior Dodds were not at home the day I was there but I did see the prized antiques in the C. A. Dodd home. A handsome lamp, round bowl and shade and decorated in big pink roses, from the Sisk home, the Van Dyke egg basket and the flowered mustache cup that belonged to Mrs. Dodd's grandfather are among the treasured keepsakes. Laquita, the Dodds' young daughter, sleeps on an ornate brass bed that is a family heirloom, saved from the forgotten land by Mrs. Dodd. She also salvaged the Unity Church's stove-pipe churn and has it standing by her front door. Three sturdy round dining tables, circa the 20th century, one cut down to coffee height, are used in the kitchen, dining area and living room.

Back in the Unity block, the attractive home of Mr. and Mrs. Frank Salmon catches the eye as you ride down the shady street. Dr. Huffaker built the house for his son after Will's marriage to Dell Hudgins. M. J. Griffin lived here while he was station agent for the Southern railroad. The Oscar Floyds made the place their home for 15 years and the 3 Floyd boys were born in the house. A prized possession of the Salmons is a hand-painted copy of the Floyd Coat of Arms (Mrs. Salmon was a Floyd), done by Elizabeth Norris, a niece of Mrs. Salmon's. The insignia is a black cross, resting upon a silver shield, surmounted by a feathered crest, an olive branch and a unicorn.

We must surely visit the brickyard before we leave this part of Plainville. It is said that the finest brick in the world are made here. Newton Legg, president of the Company, began his career in the brick-making industry while still in his teens. His father, Joel Legg, was running a brickyard, located just across the river on the Sugar Valley road, sometime before 1900. The bricks were molded by hand and dried in the sun. When a sudden shower would come up, everyone would run to cover the bricks.

Newton built chimneys for people all over the country, living with the family while the work was in progress. When only 17 years old, he amazed the citizens of Calhoun by building, for the Haynes House, a chimney with 8 fireplaces laying 10,000 bricks in a record time.

Later, the brickyard was located north of Calhoun on the W and A railroad. Attractive cottages are now scattered over the hills around the clay pits. In the 1920s the brickyard was moved to its present location when a superior grade of shale was found in the Plainville hill.

Newton's brother, H. L. B. Legg, was associated with the Company for many years and Boaz's son, Joel, is now a member of the firm. Horton Gunn, relative of Milam Gunn who set the peachtrees on the mountain, is also a partner. Mrs. Horton Gunn is the former Eunice Legg, daughter of Newton.

Norris Moore, brick-burner, who ran the ferryboat at Moore's ferry as a boy, told me that it takes 10 days to burn a kiln of brick and 12 to 14 days to cool if they do not put in a fan to pull the air out. There are many "bats" in each kiln. Don't some of the cookies break when you take them out of the pan?

Frank Salmon went to work in 1924 as engineer at the brickyard. He ran the steam engine until 2 years ago when the plant converted to electric power. The steam engine used 100 tons of coal a day, so electric power is much more economical. There are 7 kilns and 75,000 bricks can be put in each one. The output is 41,000 a day.

I was there on a Saturday and a brooding silence seemed to hover over the sprawling buildings set against the hill. Not even a train went by to stir the echoes and the 7 huge ovens sat gaping, big enough to bake bread or cookies for the county.

Gordon County owes so much to the Legg family and all the faithful people who have worked hand in hand with the Legg men throughout the years, and to the red old hills of Gordon from whence cometh the shale, the clay, the soil and the water that go into the making of the good red brick.

Cross the railroad tracks—the Selma, Rome and Dalton, the ETU and the Southern all in one—and you are on the Calhoun road again. Here is the house built for Milam Gunn, now the home of Mr. and Mrs. Claude Van Dyke. The Oscar Floyds lived here when I first knew the house. Mr. and Mrs. Van Dyke (she does clerical work at the brick yard) have an unusual lamp, made from a 100 year old flax spinning wheel—and the treadle still works! The wheel has the initials of Mrs. Van Dyke's grandfather, John Wrinkle, and the date 1829 carved on a side. There's a 3 drawer cherry chest, put together with pegs, from the Wrinkle family. Grandmother Wrinkle kept her money in one of the small top drawers, the one on the left. Mrs. Van Dyke has a beautiful yellow glass fruit bowl, done in the buttons design with corners cut in fan shape.

Mr. Van Dyke worked in Gunn's peach orchard and remembers the ten-rail fence that surrounded it. But what is a ten-rail fence to a boy, or two, or three, a hungering for a juicy Elberta peach on a dark night!

Mr. Van Dyke also remembers seeing the ground around the railroad station covered with peaches because the growers could not get cars for shipment. He said that all the doctors and lawyers bought land and planted orchards and the market was glutted.

Other old houses on the Calhoun road are Horton Gunn's father's home and the Talliafero house. New houses dot the country side and line the paved roads and new people, and young people live in them, but theirs is another story.

From Henry Barney's school in the Eating House, to the Academy and Miss Jennie Chandler's school, to a commodious frame building, Plainville has progressed to a modern brick building with up-to-date cafeteria. The school was consolidated with Poplar Springs in 1921 and became the first consolidated school to use a bus to bring the pupils in. It was a Wayne school wagon owned by the county. The principal today is Jack Purcell and teachers are Miriam Blankenship Leo Cagle, Johnnie Gazaway, Mary Blankenship and James Holloran. Mrs. John Allen was manager of the lunch room for about ten years. Succeeding her have been Mrs. Mark Hensley, Mrs. Henry Bowman, Mrs. Raymond Langley, Mrs. Charley Langley and Mrs. N. M. Wright. Bus drivers are Jack Wright and Dean Rogers.

Few rural communities can boast of three handsome brick church buildings such as those that serve the congregations at Plainville, the Methodist, the Unity Baptist and, newest in point of organization, the Fellowship Baptist.

In 1936, a group of about 38 people organized the Young People's

Fellowship Club which met in the homes of members. After much prayer and guidance, the Club felt led to build a church and the Fellowship Missionary Baptist Church was born. One of the members, Mrs. Naomi Hammond, gave a corner lot across the road from hte school property. Mr. T. J. Selders, another member, who owned a well drilling machine, donated a well on the lot. This well, only 36 feet deep, furnished an abundant supply of good water for the church and also for several families living nearby. All of the members thought it to be the handiwork of God to give such an abundant supply of water from such a shallow well in this locality.

Under the leadership of Rev. Burrell Roberts, at that time Pastor of West Rome Baptist Church, the Fellowship Baptist Church was organized on June 2, 1938.

The Plainville Brick Company gave half of the brick, and with other donors, a beautiful brick structure was erected, the auditorium being 40 feet by 56 feet, furnished with new pews and a new piano. Three lovely paintings of Christ, The Baptism, The Crucifixion and The Resurrection, were presented to the church by Mrs. Naomi Hammond.

The Reverend Jimmie Parker was elected Pastor in July 1938 and the deacons were, Ben H. Miller, Ernest Clark, Tom Fowler, Allen Wright and M. H. Hammond (Chairman). J. W. Fowler was clerk, Mrs. T. D. Hester, secretary and Mrs. Naomi Hammond, pianist.

The church grew spiritually and 30 new members were added during the Pastorate of the Rev. H. E. Wright, from 1939 to 1941. Rev. Jeff Moore served the church from April 1942 until June 1943. The material accomplishment of his ministry was the building of a Pastorium in the rear of the church.

Rev. J. H. Holcomb, of Rome, was the next pastor, serving from November 1943 to December 1946. New deacons elected were N. H. Clark, H. K. Cochran and I. W. Fowler.

Rev. Glenn Stairs served from November 1946 to August 1947, when Rev. Holcomb was re-elected as pastor. Cleon Harper and Marvin Webb were the new deacons. Rev. Holcomb served until 1952 and there were 70 additions to the church during his ministry.

By 1949, the church had grown until it was necessary to build a Sunday School Annex, which consisted of 6 rooms and 2 rest rooms. In November 1949 the church membership reached the 100 mark and voted to go into full time work instead of 2 services a month as had been the custom since 1938.

Rev. Charles Moulton was pastor from 1952 to 1954, a member of the church, E. B. Shugart was ordained as a minister and became pastor of the Sugar Valley Baptist Church. Two more Sunday School rooms were added to the annex in 1953 and two attic fans installed in the auditorium. Since 1954, a public address system has blessed the hearts of the community by playing organ chimes for 30 minutes before each service. About 35 members were added to the roll during Rev. Moulton's tenure.

Rev. H. E. Rogers was pastor in 1954-1955 and the present pastor, Rev. W. D. Hunter, came to the church in 1955. The next year, the church started tithing the regular offering, giving 2% to Associational Missions and 48% to the Co-Operative Program. Also in 1956, Celotex was installed overhead in the auditorium and a steeple erected by the Brotherhood.

Hardwood floors were laid in the auditorium in 1957 and Mr. W. E. Dellinger donated runners for the floors. Natural gas and new pews for the church, a heating system for the parsonage, a beautiful oak table and two chairs, the gift of Jerome Webb, and the pulpit stand, table and two chairs, presented by the Brotherhood, were the outstanding achievements during 1957.

R. A., G. A. and Sunbeam groups were organized in 1958, the R. A. chapter being named the Allen Wright Chapter in honor of one of the deceased deacons who had meant so much to the church. The Sunbeams were named the Grandma Brays and the G. A.s, the Jennie Cowarts. The Sunbeams have grown in number from 10 to 21, the G. A.s from 11 to 20 and R. A.s, from 27 to 42.

On July 6, 1958, Brother Clarence Roland, one of the members, was ordained as a minister and elected to pastor Spring Creek Church.

Circle number 2, organized in 1957, meets at night for the convenience of the members who work.

Four new rooms were added to the Annex in 1958 and the WMU purchased a bus. A Hammond Organ was bought with a fund started by Bro. H. N. Poarch who willed the church $500 for the purpose.

Bro. Howard Scott united with the church and was placed on the active list on November 4, 1959, making 14 active deacons of whom the church is very proud. Brother Marvin Webb is chairman of the Board in 1960.

Since Rev. Hunter has been pastor, 107 members have been added, the total membership at present being 330. The church continues to grow spiritually, for which we give God all the praise. Thanks be to God for His unspeakable gift.

A member of the church wrote of Jennie Cowart and Grandma Bray: Jennie Cowart was a charter member of Fellowship Church and was faithful in attendance until 1944 when a fall and a broken hip made her an invalid for 12 long years. She spent these years with her four children staying 3 months at a time with each one. During her stay with her daughter, Mrs. Ben Miller, who lives second door from the church. Mrs. Cowart could hear the church services through the P. A. system with the aid of a speaker set up in the home. She looked forward to these services and enjoyed them very much. Mrs. Cowart died at the home of her son, Carl, in Calhoun.

Mrs. Bray was a faithful member of Fellowship joining after the charter was closed. She overtaxed her strength many times to be in the services. To know Mrs. Bray was to love her.

Plainville may well be proud of her three splendid churches now standing as memorial and testimony to the upright and honorable citizenry that has peopled the community for 100 years and more.

The bend of the river framed the ancestral acres of many of Springtown and Plainville's pioneers. Several of the houses were there before the Civil War. The Cowart house, recently torn down to make way for a new one, was the home of the Earls, Dodds, Hammonds and Cowarts down through the years. All on one floor, the rooms were 20 feet square. Logs for the house were cut on the place, hauled to Kingston by ox cart, sawed and hauled back. The planks, 14 and 20 inches wide, were then hand-dressed and laid horizontally on both interior and exterior walls. The square nails used in construction were made by Blacksmith Smith, in Plainville.

The framing was pegged together.

Near the Van Dyke place is the Champion house. Built before the Civil War, the house, at one time, had a second story. Lawrence Brownlee remembers that the Champion house was always well-painted, a fact notable in a period when most rural houses were a weathered gray. Guy and Pauline Johnson Autry are the present owners.

Thomas Durham, another River Bend pioneer, was one of Spring-town's 1856 Road Commissioners. The family also lived in the Mos-teller-Boswell house in Plainville. Mrs. Mell Hammond is a descend-ant of Thomas Durham.

The Mostellers always kept a Governess, Lawrence Brownlee told me, and other Plainville children went there to school.

David Sisk was the first to build in the Bend. Mr. and Mrs. Cantrell, with their family on nine children, lived in the G. Dodd house and while Professor Putney was teaching the school at Poplar Springs, he lived in the Dodd house.

Enoch Autry and Enoch Floyd bought a 160 acre lot and divided the land, each taking 80 acres.

Other families who once made their homes in the River Bend were Jim Smith, whose sons were John, Ed and George, Ed Dew, Bobby, Orr, the Goswicks, Pattons and Boswells. The Widow Pat-man, William Sisk, Edgar Brown and the Zuber and Woods families were early residents of the community.

When I asked Mr. Woods if he knew any funny stories about River Bend people, Mrs. Woods said "tell her about us. We're the funniest story I know." The present Mrs. Woods was a daughter of Pink Floyd and grew up at Plainville. She married at the age of sixteen and moved to Texas where she lived for 60 years.

"I had a date with her" Mr. Woods said, "on the third Sunday in May, shortly before she married another man. I was sixteen and a half years old."

As a widow, Mrs. Woods came back to Gordon County on visits to relatives. She and Mr. Woods, now a widower, resumed their teen-age courtship, married and are now keeping each other company in their declining years, cheerful, happy and unafraid.

It was in the dead of night that the house fell. The three spin-ster daughters of the late Edward Johnson were awakened by an omnious cracking and rumbling. Snatching their wrappers, they fled from the house just as it came tumbling down in a cloud of dust and debris.

Softened by the rains and snows of many years, the hand-made bricks simply crumbled, reducing the brick walls and timbered rooms to rubbish in a matter of minutes. All the treasured furniture from Grandfather Johnson's home in South Carolina was ruined.

Edward Johnson's father was elected Governor of South Carolina in 1847. At his death in 1855, his son Cheves went to South Carolina home to aid in the settling of the Governor's estate and to ship to Georgia his and Edward's share of the family possessions.

"I shall probably purchase a carriage or traveling wagon be-fore I return to Georgia" he wrote, "in that case I shall be able to bring Selena with me. She is not disposed to leave the country with-out one or two sound whippings."

Selena was the negro slave willed to Edward by his father. An offer had been made for Selena but the brother thought it not enough so advised Edward to buy her husband who was "dirt cheap at $900 and by all accounts a negro of excellent character, not at all unruly."

Edward Johnson had prepared himself to practice medicine but, at his father's request, stayed for a year or two as manager of the plantation in South Carolina. He came to Floyd Springs in 1852.

In his letters to his son, the Governor always concluded "give my love to Betsy and the children." On February 24, 1854 he wrote "I am pleased to hear that your children are in school and hope they have good teachers—it is better to learn nothing than to learn what ought to be unlearned."

Edward evidently became dissatisfied with farming conditions at Floyd Springs for the Governor wrote in May 1854, "I am concerned about the propriety which you suppose exists of your breaking up and leaving your present location from your own report of it, the climate is unprofitious for the production of cotton—the proportion of rich land to the poor is so detached in small parcels that you can never have a population wealthy enough to support churches and schools—notwithstanding some kinks in your head which I have never been able to get out, I have a good deal of confidence in your judgment and providence."

So Edward Johnson did not leave Floyd Springs. His daughter, Anna Virginia, married Shadrach Farmer, from adjoining Springtown District. The Farmer lands, once the property of the Cherokees, had come into the possession of the family in the 1830s, having been purchased from the Government.

On February 7, 1863, Shadrach Farmer about to go into the Army of the Confederate States made his testament: "I will and bequeath to my loved wife, Matthew, a negro about 30 years old and Isabella, a woman about 30 and 1 years old and Emma, a girl about 6 years old—all stock and household furnishings and the plantation on the Oostanaula river, being drawn by me in the distribution of my father's estate." At the death of his wife, the property was to go to the expected child. He also left to the child a negro boy named Alpha, about 11, Frank, about 4, Isabella and a child, with name not known, about 2 years old.

Shadrach Farmer never came home to his 20 year old wife, never saw the expected child. He died of small pox while with the Army in Tennessee. His widow never remarried and the child, a daughter, Talulah, grew up on the Oostanaula river farm. She married John Burney and their only child, Hattie Burney Miller, still owns the farm her great-grandfather bought in the 1830s.

A son of Edward Johnson, David, was Sheriff of Gordon County in 1899 and 1900. David's sister married T. J. Champion and David's daughter, Pauline Johnson Autry now lives in the Champion house in the Bend of the River.

We were at the Fellowship Baptist Church until we digressed to talk about River Bend people. The house across the Calhoun road from the church was built by Mell Hammond on the site of the old John Brownlee home. This old house was one story with an ell and a big room set across the porch from the main building. The Brownlee boys, Carleton, Lawrence and Darnell, slept here after they got big enough not to be afraid. It was called "the rose room" because of the pink roses on the wall paper.

The barn stood across the road on the church lot. One night

the family came home from church or a 'til-bed-time visit to find the barn door swinging open.

"Someone's in the barn!" whispered one of the girls. Lawrence, just beginning to feel that he was grown-up, said "I'll go see who it is." The others tried to keep him from going, telling him that he might be killed. After his brave statement, Lawrence could not back out so strode manfully into the dark recess of the barn and found— nothing. It was only the wind swinging the door back and forth.

The Brownlee grandparents lived at the foot of the mountain across the Rome road from Plainville. On a visit to them, the boys were riding horses. Lawrence was given the colt for a mount. When they came to a puddle in the road, the colt reared and jumped over it leaving young Lawrence sitting in the puddle.

Mr. Smiley bought the Taliaferro house in 1899, coming to Plainville to get the benefit of good water for the invalid mother, Mrs. Wadley. The house was turned around to make the kitchen ell and the four front rooms, two on each floor, were added. Mr. Smiley was working for a cordwood company, buying logs all over Gordon County and having them shipped to Rome.

On a bright Sunday afternoon in January, I rode out the Oostanaula road to Curryville and the house of Bruce Keys. His smiling little granddaughter came to the door and told me that he had gone up North to spend three months with relatives. Bruce is 90 years old and for most of his life, has been a member of Bethesda, the negro Baptist church located on the Plainville road not far from the Rome Highway.

And that is why I do not write Bruce Keys' stories of the church But I shall go again for there is yet to be written the story of Little Row and the Flat Woods.

Martha King was next on my list. Raised at Red Bud, and a Connelly before her marriage, she was a member of Bethesda 20 years ago so could tell me much of the church's history.

Dan and Epsie Gaines, Andy and Maggie Dew, Uncle Dick Garlington, his son, Sam and Sam's wife, Adeline, were among the early members of the church. In the church and cemetery is the grave of Celie Vernon, born in 1818, died in 1918.

Among the 20th century pastors were the Reverends Maxwell, J. C. Campbell and J. S. Zuber, Rev. E. D. Pinkard is the present pastor. Younger deacons were Frank McCullough, Melvin Waters, Frank Engram and Junior Hamilton. Martha's daughter, Daisy Dunehoo, is secretary of the church. There's a piano but no one to play it.

Mr. J. T. Woods, too, gave me historical facts about Bethesda Baptist Church. His grandfather Zuber was a charter member of Mt. Pisgah but the Zubers came from Germany where the name was spelled Zuiber.

Nan, one of the Zuber slaves, stayed with the family until her death. "I didn't like Nan," Mr. Woods said, "because when I would go to visit my grandfather, she would always say 'come here and let me buss you'." (Buss is colloquial for kiss.)

Epsie Gaines always helped the Zubers dry fruit and gather. Dan Gaines cut the wood one Fall and Mrs. Zuber brought out sweet potatoes as pay for his work, Dan asked "got any done 'uns?" It was several minutes before she realized that Dan wanted baked potatoes.

Alf Gaines, son of Epsie and Dan, preached at Bethesda many

years ago. Another preacher, Mr. Woods could not recall his name, said, when the Amens were not coming fast enough from the congregation, "you either have no religion or you are getting more intelligent. I hope you are getting more intelligent."

Then there was the brother who was feeling the call to preach and resisting with all his might. He went to bed one night and found that his feet were too high and his head was too low. He got up, walked around for awhile then went back to bed only to find that his feet were too low and his head was too high. Arising once more, he got down on his knees and said, "Lord, I'll do anything you want me to do." He went to preaching.

Peach blossoms on a mountain 70 years ago—red clay on a Plainville hill being turned into brick for mansions on the hills of Gordon —God looked upon his handiwork and saw that it was good.

No Jean LaFitte was I to go in wearing baggy red pants, cutlass in hand and demand "give me your gold," but armed with note book and pencil, I asked and they graciously showed me their treasures and gladly told me their stories. And no Blackbeard am I to creep furtively onto a sandy beach and bury my pieces of 8 for a 100 years. Happily I open my treasure chest, my money bags have no draw strings and you are welcome to share in all my joyfully gotten gains.

SUGAR MAPLES ON SNAKE CREEK

It was in the Fall of 1831. All day John Baugh had been following the old Indian trail that led across the river and over the hills toward the mountains West of New Echota, the Cherokee Capital. John had come over from England and was looking for a place to establish his home in America. As he trudged up another hill he was thinking "I'll have to camp somewhere. I've come too far to get back tonight."

At the top of the hill John Baugh stopped, weariness forgotten every sense tingling with excitement, wonder and awe filling his heart, for there before him, with the purple mountain reaching around it like the enfolding arm of a tender lover, lay a beautiful valley, a valley of gold! He rubbed his eyes and looked again. No, it wasn't gold but trees, hundreds of trees. They ran through the valley, they gathered in huddles, they raced up the mountainside and it was the leaves of these trees, yellowed by the Falling season, doubly gilded by the rays of the setting sun that gave the Valley the appearance of being covered with gold.

"This is it," John said. "This is the sweetest valley I have ever seen and I am going to call it Sugar Valley."

Such is the legend. Believe it if you like. No doubt, the more practical of you will accept the story that the area was covered with sugar maples when the first settlers arrived.

Edgar Miller tells this story: When Oscar Davis came up from

Picnic at Baugh's Trestle, Sugar Valley, July 4, 1895.

South Georgia he brought ribbon cane and planted it in the fields. It was sweet to taste and made a sweet syrup so people began to call the place "Sugar" Valley.

Not only was the valley beautiful and filled with sweetness of sugar cane and sugar maples but, rich with the promise of fertility, it was watered by many free flowing springs and by a Creek that came out of the mountain, looping and twisting, sometimes playing quietly with the rocks, or lurking in a still, dark pool, then roaring and hissing in flood time, heaving itself this way and that, lying here or moving over there. It was natural for the settlers to call this stream Snake Creek.

As in the Biblical garden, the serpent entered this one-time Eden of the Cherokees for here, in the center of the lovely valley occurred a suicide, two murders and a hanging.

A heartbroken Indian maid named Lucy, jilted by her sweetheart, leaped into a supposedly bottomless pond which today bears her name. The Lucy Pond is located on the farm first known as the Joseph Barrett place, then as the M. B. Abbott farm, and is now owned by Luke Pittman. Lucy's body came up in the Norrell spring about one quarter mile east of the pond.

In 1860, Mr. and Mrs. Johnson were murdered with a butcher's cleaver at their log cabin home on the Jesse Miller place (the Norrell farm). The crime was never solved. Often told in the Bridges family was the story that W. M. Bridges, pastor of the Baptist church in the 1870s and 80s, received a death bed confession to the murder, but no matter how hard the children begged "tell us who the murderer was, Uncle Bill," he never gave up the secret.

When Elias King was Postmaster, the office, established in 1849, was probably located in this house. Later, it was moved a short distance up the Dalton wagon road and used as a tenant house on the Miller-Norrell farm. It was said that a blood spot could be seen on the floor but we could never find it. The house burned in the early 1950s while the Towers family was living there.

The second murder was that of Sara Burns who was assaulted and beaten to death, by a negro named Bill Boaz. The girl and her mother lived in a cabin near the Tannery in the Boaz field on the east side of the Snake Creek Gap road. Bill Boaz was tried, then hanged on a walnut tree that stood in the Baptist churchyard not far from the road. Until well into the 1900s, the tall, fire-blackened stump of this tree, with thick limbs reaching out toward the road, was still there, the sight of it striking terror to the heart of a timid child scurrying homeward in the late afternoon.

Not long before his death, my father told me that a storage house in our barnyard had been built from the logs of the Burns cabin. Had I known this as a child, I am sure I could not have enjoyed the hours of play in the old crib as I did.

When Gordon County came into existence in 1850, Militia District number 1,054 then called Snake Creek, was defined as commencing on the west bank of the Oostanaula river, on the north line of lot No. 82, due west to the northwest corner of lot No. 73, due south with the county line to the river and east with the river to the starting point. The precinct was at the house of John Higginbotham, now the Vance King home on the Calhoun road.

The first road commissioners from Snake Creek were Osborn Reeves, J. P., John Higginbotham and W. H. Black. Others serving during the years 1851 to 1855 were Meshach Boaz, John Baugh, Jesse Miller, D. R. Malone, B. A. Witzell, James Russell, A. E. Fricks and William Akin.

There were also three road reviewers whose duty it was to examine the roads and report conditions to the court. L. D. Cole, Pleasant Frix, J. H. Harbour, John Higginbotham and James Russell were Snake Creek's reviewers.

In 1852, District 1,054 was listed as Sugar Valley.

Among the settlers were the devout people usually found in such groups and soon a church and a three room school were in use. It is thought that the church was built in the 1830s and first used for union services. The only marked grave in the cemetery behind the Baptist Church is dated 1848. It is the grave of Postmaster Elias King.

By 1857 the Methodists had established a church near Baugh mountain about one mile south of the Central Community, and the old log church became the New Providence Missionary Baptist Church, the name still in use when Joseph F. Barrett deeded the land to the congregation in 1887.

According to an advertisement in the March 24, 1859 issue of The Democratic Platform, published in Calhoun, the Gordon County Male and Female Seminary was located at Sugar Valley. Thomas W. Skelly, graduate of Trinity College, Dublin, was the principal. Mrs. Skelly had charge of the Female department when the young ladies were instructed in plain sewing, embroidery in silk, bead and chenille work, tapestry, crocheting, drawing, painting, music and French. The young men were taught Rhetoric, Intellectual Philosophy, Latin, Greek, Astronomy, Navigation, Civil Engineering and Surveying. D. R. Malone, L. D. Cole, John Baugh, J. H. Harbour, J. C. Dowdy, John Malone and G. Winn were the School Trustees.

John Harbor was at Snake Creek in 1849 for Hamilton Harbor bought lot No. 60 from him that year. Jesse Miller sold Lot No. 4, blazed out by D. R. Malone and James Eubanks, to Meshach Boaz in 1850 and Michael Fricks paid John Higginbotham $100 for Lot No. 152. This deed was signed by John Baugh and Osborn Reeves.

We were at John Higginbotham's house, the precinct for Snake Creek Militia District. John had come from Walton County to the North Georgia region soon after the Cherokees were removed. At the time of John's marriage, his wife was only 13 years old, still child enough to go to the woods and ride trees. (To ride a tree, you bend a hickory sapling, sit on it and push up and down. Sometimes the young tree is so strong that it throws the rider like a bucking bronco does a cowboy.)

John and Mary's children were H. O., his wife was Dessie Copeland, Joe, whose wife was Mellie Roe, Sanford, married to Sallie Miller, Sarah (Mrs. Tom Evans), Fannie (Mrs. L. D. Cole) and Molly (Mrs. Taylor Frix).

John Higginbotham must have been much older than his wife for he died when she was young enough for a second marriage and two other children. Her second husband was Washington Lay and their sons were Sam and George. The Lays went to Rutledge to live and the old Precinct House became the home of Taylor and Molly Higginbotham Frix. It is now the home of Mr. and Mrs. Vance King. The house originally faced west and stood to the rear of the present site. When the road was improved, a sharp curve was cut out and the house left sitting in the field. Mr. and Mrs. King decided to build near the new road, with the house facing east. The carpenter suggested that the two front rooms of the old house be used in the new since the timbers were in excellent condition. Accordingly, the rooms were moved to the new site and finished inside with sheet rock and celotex to match the new rooms. Mrs. King said that old residents had told her that more good ham had been fried in the log kitchen than any place in the Valley. The former kitchen is now used as a corn crib.

Fannie Higginbotham married L. D. Cole and their home was the story and a half that stood on the hill where the water tank is now located. This house burned while owned and occupied by the Dacus family. A neat white-painted cottage, the home of the George Faulkenberrys stands there today.

L. D. Cole was active in the country's early life serving as a road reviewer in the 1950s and as a trustee of the Methodist church in 1857. When a piano salesman came through the county, Mr. Cole ordered a Vose Upright piano made of an English wood in a light finish, but for reasons unknown, refused to accept delivery. To the distraught salesman, with a $900 piano sitting in the depot, someone said "Why don't you go up and see M. B. Abbott? He has a houseful of girls." The agent took the advice and Mr. Abbott bought the piano. All of the seven Abbott girls became proficient pianists under the capable instruction of Miss Lida Farris, Miss Annie Bellows and Miss Mary Fite, teachers at Ryals High School.

Each spring the piano was moved to the Baptist church and used during the three day Exhibitions of R. H. S. until the trustees bought one. When Grandma Abbott died, my father purchased the piano. After her death, I took the worn-out instrument, with case still clean and un-scarred, and from it had made five tables and a magazine rack.

"I had the finest fields of wheat and corn in the country" Uncle Hammy was saying, "right here where the depot and the stores and the houses are now." Small of stature and one-eyed (sight in the other eye was destroyed when he bent too quickly over a cotton stalk), Hammy Harbour was yet a power in the community and in the Baptist church of which he was deacon and church clerk. His voice was often the deciding note in a discussion among the Brethren at a church Conference.

John Hamilton Harbour was born in 1823 and died in 1903. He was in the Cherokee country in 1849 for a deed is recorded in his name in that year. His home was the house now known as the Griffin place. Standing just beyond the village among ancient oaks and cedars, the place is still beautiful. Two big springs flow from under a bluff at the back of the house and form a stream of water that is icy cold and quickly numbs the bare feet of those who yield to the yen to go a-wading.

The Griffins were never selfish with their springs and people in Sugar Valley and from other communities often went there for picnics. The Muse family now owns the property and a Sportsman's Club has placed tables and a barbecue pit on the bluff above the springs.

There are two versions of Civil War story about the Harbour-Griffin house. One is that Mr. Harbour, hoping to have his house spared the torch of the enemy, rented it to Union sympathizers and refugees to South Georgia. One of the girls in the family was talking to a group of Federal officers at the front yard gate one day when a bullet from a sniper's gun whizzed by and snipped off one of her curls. Mr. Warren, who was with the sniper, told this story to Mr. Griffin.

The other story, as told in 1936 by Joe Higginbotham, Confederate veteran, to reporters from a Chattanooga newspaper, is this: "there were four sisters, known to be Union sympathizers, who lived across from where the depot now stands" Uncle Joe related, "and as MacPherson approached the Village there was no sign of fighting. A Yanke officer rode up to the house and stood at the gate talking to the girls. A Confederate sharp shooter, a man I knew, named John Allbright, was stationed behind a tree on top of the big hill yonder. Allbright decided that here was a chance to make one Yankee less so he trained his rifle on him and fired. The bullet fanned the officer's hair as it passed without touching him. One of the men in the group raised his pistol and fired back at the tree from where the flash came and the bullet tore the bark from the tree within a foot or two of Allbright."

Mr. Griffin bought the house from Mr. Harbour for $1,000. Since he has been the owner he has built two porches, a latticed well shelter, covered the house three times and finished the upper half story. This house, the Jud Malone house on the Mountain Loop road and the Freeman house on the Oostanaula road were all built on the same plan, before the Civil War.

"I am the oldest man in the Sugar Valley district" Mr. Griffin told me "and Will Walraven is next. There are only two people here now that were here when I came." M. J. Griffin first came to Sugar Valley in 1882, stayed a few months, went back to Plainville and remained as Depot Agent for eight years. He returned to Sugar Valley in 1890 where he was Agent for thirty seven years.

Mr. Griffin first married Stella, eldest of the four daughters of Squire V. H. and Mrs. Emma Davis Haynes. Their children are Maurice, who died in 1957, Jack, Annie Mark and Dean. After Stella's death in the influenza epidemic of 1918, Mr. Griffin married Miss Annie Keith, a noted teacher of Gordon County and Atlanta. She died in 1944.

The big event of the year immediately following the Civil War was the building of the Selma, Rome and Dalton railroad. Work on the road was begun at Rome and at Dalton simultaneously, the two ends meeting at a point a little south of Sugar Valley and here a water tank was erected. The road was completed in 1867. Lulie Pitt's History gives 1870 as the date of the first train's run on the S. R. and D. In it's early years the train was called the Short, Rough and Dirty.

J. H. Harbour must have sold the land for the depot site to the Railroad, but the only deed I could find on rcord was that of September 19, 1873 giving title to one acre of land on Lot 16, commencing at a certain post on the right of way, running back east 105 feet and north 425 feet. The price paid was $25. Y. J. Malone notarized the deed.

In June of 1875, D. B. Freeman, Editor of The Calhoun Times, accompanied Col. W. R. Rankins to the closing exercises of Sugar Valley Academy. They passed wheat fields yellow and ready for the harvest but found the cotton crop poor. Valley people said that as long as they could raise wheat and corn and stock so successfully, they would turn their attention there in the future and leave the cotton to more suitable climes.

"The business section of Sugar Valley" wrote Editor Freeman, "would right now fail to impress the eye of a stranger to any eminent degree. There are only two stores.

"A drive of a mile and we were in one of the best settlements in Gordon County. Peopled by such citizens as Jesse Miller, Ham Harbour, Jud Malone, O. H. Davis, Mehach Boaz and others, the fertile lands will bring about changes in a prominent way."

The young unmarried Editor wrote in one of his columns of the 1870s, "a beautiful blonde from Sugar Valley was in the stores of Calhoun yesterday; but we couldn't find out who she was!" (Lester Frix).

Now the railroad tracks ran through Hammy Harbour's fertile fields and a village began to gather around the railroad depot. A street on the east side ran paralled to the tracks and another broke off from it and crossed the tracks then divided, leading on the right, to the New Providence Baptist Church and Snake Creek Gap and on the left to the Methodist Church.

If the layout of the Village could have been seen from the air it might have resembled an over-sized telegraph pole laid flat on the ground, with the railroad and the streets on each side forming the cross bars and the east-west street making the short and long ends of the pole.

On the south side of the east-west street, the four houses in the block are the Barney Falkenberry house on the corner. The Tarvin family once made their home here as did the Rev. Spencer B. King, Henry and Stella Warren Moss and perhaps others. It is now the home of the Barney Faulkenberrys. Next door is Mrs. Shelton's house, the old Parsons home. Mrs. Parsons was a devout member of the Baptist Church. We always had the greatest respect for her religion. Mrs. Parsons didn't wait for big meetin' time to shout, she shouted at Saturday preaching. In the winter, she clapped her hands in accompaniment but in summer, used a long black folding fan to tap the bench in front of her. If we happened to be sitting on the bench, the fan reached across to our shoulders. When we had been naughty during the week, we felt that this might be the hand of God reminding us of our sins.

Mr. Parsons was Section Foreman for the Southern. The Parsons boys were Jack, Judson and Mack. Judson fell in love with and married the beautiful girl across the street, Clyde Frix. Since he was telegraph operator, they made their home at several stations along the road, their last home being at Hill City. It was my privelege to sing the soprano in a quartet to Judson's pure tenor, Carl Malone's bass and May Dickey's alto. Our most often requested number was "Glory, Glory". Miss May could not pronounce her G's and always sang "Dlory, Dlory."

Third from the corner is the Harvey Everett house, moved many years ago from it's location farther back from the street. The Senior Everett was "Uncle Harvey" and the son "Little Harvey" even when he was grown up and in a home of his own. Uncle Harvey spent his retired years putting new soles on the shoes of the Valley's feet. At this he was a expert. Petite and dainty, with a warm sweetness of character, Dolly was a fitting name for Uncle Harvey's only daughter. Max Falkenberry is the present owner of the Everett house.

Mike and Ann Norrell Hill occupied the last house in the block during the early years of the Valley's history. Dr. Cagle was the next owner and the house is now the home of Mr. and Mrs. Lewis Holsomback.

Across the street is the ancient, weathered Austin house. Here Tom and Clyde Austin grew up with a love of the railroad in their hearts. Both rose to responsible positions with Railroads. Tom was married to Fannie Ellis, of Calhoun, and Clyde, to Gussie Norton of Resaca. Their sister, Beulah, became Mrs. Butler.

The little store building behind the Austin house and facing the railroad, was originally Dr. Frix's office and durg room. Countless merchants since that time have used the office as a general merchandise store.

The top of our telegraph-pole street dead ends at the home of Ralph Chitwood. Three former owners were Dr. Cagle, the Groovers and Dr. Gray. The uppermost bar of the pole developed a curvature of the arm as the street turned to the east and became known as Smokey Row—why, I do not know. Maybe the west wind blew the train smoke over the houses so much of the time that they were a smokegray.

As we move toward Smokey Row, on the right-hand corner is the Graham house where the Quillians lived when they first came to Sugar Valley and later the Tweedells lived here. A. M. Bridges built the house next door which is now owned by Bill DeFoor. The J. Q. Everett house, later occupied by John Hilley, was torn down to make way for two white cottages that are the homes of Lounartha Truman and her brother A. W. Truman.

Mrs. George Lay's attractive home was the Dr. Frix house and here Pet Frix and Curtiss Tarvin were married in 1901. Dr. Frix was born the year Gordon County was created, 1850, and died in 1895. His wife was Amoretta Davis, born in 1856, died in 1903. Their graves are in the cemetery near the Baptist church.

The house was built without studding, the walls being constructed of thick planks set vertically and now covered with wall paper. Originally a hall ran the length of the house but, in remodeling, the front part was combined with the next room to make a large living room. At the same time a half-story of two bedrooms was added. Mrs. Lay, the former Bertie Tweedell, remembers coming to the house as a 6 year old to have Dr. Frix pull a tooth.

The Tweedell family came to Sugar Valley before the Civil War. Their home was in the Methodist community one mile south-west of the Village. Mrs. Lay's mother was a Groover. Grandmother Groover was a widow with small children at the time of the War. When news that the Yankees were coming reached the community, the Groover family hastened to hide the winter's supply of meat that was hanging in the attic. Irving Groover, handing the meat down as his mother and Uncle Joe hid the pieces in the stairwall, said "I've got it all but one piece." "Hand that down too," he was told. Perhaps the little boy thought that if he left one piece the Yankees wouldn't look for the rest. But they found the meat and there was nothing left.

While the Northern Army was marching through, the Groovers and their neighbors were hiding in the woods. A baby began to wail and everyone worked to hush it's crying. After a Confederate soldier died at her house, Grandmother Groover sent his Bible to his mother in California.

Uncle Joe was too old to go to war. With the help of little boys, he buried the soldiers who died as the Armies went through.

Grandfather Tweedell went to school only 3 days but taught himself to read French and make tiny, neat figures on fools cap. He was a Methodist preacher and preached as long as he could stand on his feet.

Standing in the curve of Smokey Row is a house that has sheltered many families, among them, the Parks, Gardners and Lays. It is now the home of the Senior Falkenberrys. Henrietta and George Tarvin live next door in the house their father built. Albert Tarvin was born at new Echota, the Cherokee Capital, where his father was merchant and postmaster, and came to Sugar Valley in 1893. An expert carpenter, he also built the house across the street where the Leonard Faulkenberrys live.

East of the Tarvins, Carl and Genie Strain Malone live in the Alec Wright house. Tillman Johnson built the one next door that was for many years the home of Johnson Everett whose wife was one of the Tarvin girls. The shell of the old Harris house was razed and a small house built on the lot about 1911 for Judson Story. Mrs. Story was a daughter of Rev. and Mrs. W. M. Bridges whose home was the former Dr. Floyd house next door. These two houses burned as did the Dickey house on the hill.

The Dickey Schoolhouse stood across the road from the house and here the youth of Sugar Valley were educated. Mrs. Floyd, wife of the Doctor, was one of the assistant teachers. Professor Dickey sold the house to the Pyroms and moved to the plantation about one mile south of Sugar Valley.

After the house burned, Joe Tarvin built a modern bungalow on the site. Mr. and Mrs. Tarvin were active members of the Baptist church, he serving as Sunday School Superintendent and she as president of the WMU. Both were useful in other phases of church work.

Around the curve, you come to the Davis house, now the home of Mr. and Mrs. Jud Nelson and sons Padgett, Jimmie and Ronald.

Jasper McCrary, of Warren County, drew Lot No. 67, consisting of 160 acres and surveyed by Stephen Crane on June 2, 1832, in the Cherokee Land Lottery. The Lottery deed is in the possession of Leonard Davis, together with the deed made when Jasper McCrary sold the lot to Alfred Barringer, of Murray County, March 1, 1848 for the price of $175. This deed was recorded in Murray County by Wm. C. McCamy clerk of Superior Court.

The Lottery deed is printed and written on a paper 9½ x 8 inches. Around the edge is a narrow border of leaves and flowers and in each corner, a "snowflake" design. In the top center is drawn a square with measurements 40 chains east and 40 chains west, the lot number, 67, and the acreage, 160, printed in the square. The Magenetic Variation east is given in degrees and minutes. The form was entered by Jno-G. Parks, Comp. Gen. and J. Haynes had signed the "received five dollars" line.

The body of the deed read:

State of Georgia

The above plat is a representation of that tract of land drawn by Joseph McCrary, Camp's District, Warren County, situate in the 14th District, 3rd Section of Cherokee County, containing one hundred and sixty acres, which is known and distinguished in the plan of said District by the number 67.

Attached to the paper with pink tape is a replica of the Seal of Georgia, 1799. It is made of wax, 24 inches in diameter, with paper pressed into the wax on each side. Pasted to the back of the deed is a paper inscribed "Grant to Jasper McCrary, Lot 67-14-3-Cherokee.

Secretary of State Office, 17 December, 1832. Registered in Book—(torn) Cherokee 14-3-P. 159. W. A. Terrell Gov."

Oscar H. Davis came up from South Georgia with his sugar cane and bought Lot 67 from Alfred Barringer, paying about $800. Oscar was born in 1820 and died in 1897. His wife, Eliza, was born in 1827 and lived until 1915. Oscar and Eliza Davis were probably charter members of the New Providence Missionary Baptist church, since he is listed as a deacon on the earliest church roll in existence. He was a member of the committee, appointed in 1878 to solicit funds and supervise the building of the present structure which was completed in 1879.

But in 1885, the bretheren of the church "adopted amendments on Bro. Davis" at the August conference, when Rev. J. A. J. Phillips was serving as moderator in the absence of the Pastor. The amendment accused him of persistently refusing to attend church, pay his assessment or help bear the burdens of the church. Bro. Davis pleaded guilty to the charges and though the church earnestly pleaded with him to comply, he persistently refused and fellowship was withdrawn from him in September 1886. However, he was restored to full fellowship in May of 1887 and there is a strong suspicion that he may not have liked the Pastor. There was a new one in 1887. Early Christians withdrawn fellowship or excluded members who did not attend the Services.

Oscar S. Davis was the first son born to O. H. and Eliza. He married Rosa Warren, daughter of a neighbor, on October 31, 1880. His sister, Rhetta, had been married to Adolphus P. Frix on September 16 of the same year.

O. H. Davis had bought a small farm lying immediately north of the present Muse lake and this was the home of Oscar Davis and here his children were born. A long walk lined on each side with cedar trees, silver maples all around and a yard full of blue hyacinths and jonquils are memories we have of this old house, long since torn down.

Walter Davis, an ordained minister, was clerk of the Baptist church and conference minutes of the 1870s are recorded in his beautiful, shaded script. He was principal of the schools at Blue Springs and at Sugar Valley, Sunday School teacher and superintendent. One of my prized keepsakes is a certificate issued by the Georgia Baptist Sunday School Association for a Bible examination and signed by J. W. Davis as superintendent at the Sugar Valley Church. Walter Davis' wife was Emma Fox and they were married in 1875.

Albert Davis lived in a house across the road from the old home. His wife was Florence Everett. Ab Davis, Tom Bridges, Lee Haynes and Doc Lutes attended a school taught by Prof. Cheyne at Decora in 1888.

Walter Davis lived in the ancestral home for a while but Mr. and Mrs. Albert Davis were the last of the family to live there. After Mr. Davis' death, the box known to contain his legal papers could not be found. One day Mrs. Davis was standing quietly in the unfinished upstairs, thinking of where to look next for the papers, when suddenly something flashed by her shoulder and fell to the floor at her feet. It was the box of important papers.

Other children of Oscar H. and Eliza Davis were Emma (Mrs. V. H. Haynes), Nettie (Mrs. Andrews) and Jennie, who never married.

Mr. and Mrs. Warren lived in the house that is now the home of the Ralph Bramblett family. The Warren girls were noted belles. Ida, the younger daughter, was daring enough to leave home and clerk at a store in Calhoun in a day when girls were supposed to stay at home and wait for love and marriage. She and Madison Pate were married in a fashionable wedding at the Baptist Church. They made their home at the Meshach Boaz place until 1902 when Mrs. B. F. Tracey bought the farm and the Pates moved to Atlanta.

Then you come to the Russell Cemetery and the Russell Hill Baptist Church. James Russell, born in 1798, bought the land from Jesse Miller in 1851 and died the next year. Pioneer residents of the community buried in the Russell Cemetery are, Andrew and Nancy Norrell, Robert B. Bandy, E. Roney and America Roney, Rev. Canada Shugart, John T. Warren and Oscar and Savannah Warren Davis.

Across the road from the church, Mary James Harris and her husband, Alec Harris, have returned to Mary's native soil to spend their retirement years. Their cottage home is filled with heirlooms from the James and Harris families. Prized marble-topped tables and chests, a blue sprigged wash bowl, (filled, on the day I was there, with gorgeous zinnias), a sampler done by Hattie Stensbury James in 1927, a picture of Rev. John Wesley, James Hamilton, M. D. and Rev. Joseph Cotel, "sketched as they were walking down a street of Edinborough in 1790, by an original genius who was an expert in sketching with great correctness the figure of every eminent person that appeared publicly in the City," a copy of the Trees of Temperance and Intemperance done by Currier before he went in with Ives are only a few of the interesting possessions of the Harrises.

Sadie Lucinda James, sister of Mary Harris, is building a house nearby. She, too, has come home to rest after many years of work with the Red Cross and several years as head of the organization in Washington. Among the charms on her bracelet is a key to New Orleans presented to her after disaster work done by the Red Cross under her direction.

Tillot, Tillot, Tillot—it is not the highway-man riding, riding, but the hoof beats of Balus James' 2 matched black horses, bearing him and Hattie Stansbury to Gretna Green. She was too young, her parents said, only 17, and, especially, to marry a man 13 years older than she, was unthinkable, so Hattie and Balus eloped, riding away on the black horses in the black of night, and lived happy ever after.

The great-grandmother of the James girls is buried in the Methodist cemetery. On her grave stone are carved the words; Mary McNeely, born in Greenville, S. C. 1797, died at Sugar Valley, 1901, aged 104 years, 1 month and 14 days. A bronze plaque is set in the stone, placed there by the DAR for "a real daughter of the American Revolution."

Ride back down Smokey Row, now a paved street lined with attractive homes. On your right just before you cross the railroad, the hotel once stood. When M. M. Folsom of the Rome Tribune, paid a visit to Sugar Valley, in 1895, he "had dinner at the hotel, run by Mrs. Hill, where everything was done to make the guests comfortable and happy." Joe Higginbotham owned the house when my grandfather, M. B. Abbott, bought it. After my grandmother's death, Aunt Alice Abbott Cleghorn bought the house and made her home there for many years.

The white-washed depot, with its vertical siding and high loading platforms on the front, back and south sides, stood on your left as you cross the tracks. The big freight and baggage room, the waiting rooms, the ticket windows and the sound of the clicking telegraph instruments are never-to-be-forgotten memories. Little engines like the General wood-smoked their way down to Rome and up to Dalton. The 35 new engines, 28 of them Moguls, cinder-peppered over wider tracks with their air-brakes and reclining chairs.

There were excursions to Little Rock and to New Orleans. There were slow trains and the Royal Palm to Florida, pulling a long line of Pullmans, the pop-corn sound of their spinning wheels and the blur of faces at the windows stirring wishes in our seeking minds as we thought of the fairylands to which they were speeding.

But the slow trains were our loves—they took us to Rome for a day of shopping, down at 7:00 A.M. and back at 6:00 P.M. In an hour they ran us north to Grandma's for a week's visit, the efficient fireman, bo-o-a-arding everyone on, the genial couductor punching your ticket, the long, starting huffs and puffs (Oh, did you get a cinder in your eye?), the jerks and finally, the smooth roll of the wheels and the even throb of the engine and the throaty warning of the whistle—the thrill of it!

North of the depot was the Commons. The villagers held ice cream suppers here and sometimes a square dance. We stopped our buggies here on Sunday afternoons after a drive around the mountain loop road and down lovers lane, to watch Train 16 go south and Train 15 come north, 20 minutes apart.

There was the Sunday afternoon when the boys were red-faced and speechless. We had been to The Gap—well-chaperoned to be sure, two girls and one boy in each buggy—and, after comparing notes on the Commons, we learned that each horse, left to his own going, had walked up to the gate of a house and stopped. These were the bootleggers' houses.

The first store in the Valley stood on the corner where Muse's Chenille Plant is now. W. F. Dickey and son began business here. The first Post Office was in this store, Mike Hill was Postmaster and Carl Dickey, Clerk. In 1903, Sugar Valley was the leading shipping point in North Georgia for huckleberries. Dickey and Son bought 300 to 500 gallons a day during the season. So, you might say that huckleberries built the 2 story brick store that was of later years known as the Dickey Store. John Hilley traded his farm near the Baptist Church to B. Y. Dickey, about 1912, for the store and ran the business for several years.

J. Q. Everett's little wooden store building is still standing back of the brick one.

J. Q. Everett's livery barn burned on December 24, 1904. The fire was discovered at 3:00 A.M. as the roof was falling in. Lost were 5 head of cattle, 1 horse, 1 mule, 4 buggies, 2 wagons, a hay rake, a lot of blacksmith tools, $125 worth of hay and Captain Fuller's two horses.

Of a later date is the square 2 story house north of J. Q.'s old store. Mr. and Mrs. Ben Weaver ran a hotel here for several years and here was located the switch board for Sugar Valley's first tele-phone line. The hotel, now owned by Mrs. Lois Malone, has been converted into an apartment house.

Bill Tarvin's livery stable once stood on the hotel lot and Bill's family lived in the first of four houses that zig-zag along the big ditch toward the railroad. Next is Uncle Harvey Everett's and the third house belonged in turn to Mrs. Frix, Mrs. L. D. Cole and the C. M. Muse family. Opal White, J. C. and C. L. Patterson are the owners of these houses today. The last house in the quartet was the home of beloved Uncle Joe and Aunt Mellie Higginbotham.

"Did you ever hear a shell scream?" Uncle Joe asked the re-porters. The Chattanooga news men had followed McPherson's route to Sugar Valley and were interviewing the 88 year old Con-federate veteran. "Well, I'll tell you" he said "I don't believe any man will ever forget the first one. I was 15 years old. McPherson's Yankees had started the flank movement following the failure to route the Confederates at Resaca and started to cross the Oostanaula river at Lay's ferry. Three days before, the battle of Resaca had starte dand when the battle raged around my home, I joined the First Georgia Cavalry on the spot."

"The first Federal detachment that tried to cross the river at Lay's ferry, was met by our command and we made it so hot for them that they withdrew and went further down stream, past the mouth of Snake Creek to Herrington's ferry where they finally started the crossing."

"I was just getting into my first battle when a Federal battery was set up on the high ground commanding Lay's ferry. That bat-tery started firing and when the first shell came screaming over, it was a vivid experience whose memory has stayed with me for 72 years. I could close my eyes today and recall that first shell and how it made the hair of a little 15 year old Confederate soldier stand on end."

"The Confederates were not prepared to meet the Artillery," the Confederate veteran related, "and shortly after the battery began were forced to retire. The enemy then made a pontoon bridge at the ferry and came across."

The Free Press reporters had set out from Chattanooga in a Pontiac to follow the route through Snake Creek Cap, "breezing over the country roads at 30 miles an hour," they boasted.

"You will enjoy speculating" wrote W. G. Foster ,"why the Con-federates could have been so careless as to leave this narrow pass open and how 8000 Federals managed to drill through with their equipment over the one little trail that exists."

Mr. Foster and his companions, Walter Cline and Captain Hi Wenning, found the people of Sugar Valley fine, courteous, hospita-ble folk with only smiles and hand shakes and an invitation to re-turn.

Uncle Joe's house is now owned by Mr. and Mrs. Woods.

A Land Company runs a loading yard on the lot, north of the Higginbotham house, from which logs are shipped over the South-ern Railroad to paper-making plants.

The chief industry of Sugar Valley today is the Muse Chenille Plant, employing over 100 people, where spreads and floor coverings of great beauty and durability are made. Spread-making was intro-duced to Gordon County by way of Sugar Valley and Mrs. Una

Bandy Muse made the first tufted bed spread.

Did the Post Office remain at the location across from the Baptist Church from 1849 until the coming of the railroad? I do not know. Mr. Griffin said that, in 1890 the Post Office was in a store that stood facing the depot on the corner where the Muse Chenille place is now. The next Post Office building was down the street from the first one. Mrs. Nabors and Mrs. Quillian were Postmistresses here. Mrs. Bertie Tweedell DeFoor (Mrs. George Lay) kept the office in J. Q. Everett's old store. Mrs. Curry Roberts conducted the office for several years and the present incumbent is Mrs. Shelton. The Office is now housed in a modern concrete building and contains a number of private boxes.

The Southern railroad sent the mail out on fast trains and how the mail clerk could snatch the bag from its metal post beside the track was always a marvel to me, for he never missed. Fast trains still bring the letters but the heavier mail is brought in a truck.

Merchants have come and gone throughout the years. Lay Bros. had a store at Sugar Valley. Was this one the grandmother of all the Lay stores scattered over Georgia and Tennessee? The Dacus Bros. were in the mercantile business in the 19 teens—and many others. If Dave Freeman could ride through the still fair Sugar Valley he would find more than the 2 stores og 1875. There are now four— Maude Harbor's, Carl Malone's, Barney Faulkenberry's and Danny Thomas'. And there is a cafe, where excellent meals are served in attractive surroundings by the owner, Mrs. Mildred Patterson.

North of the Village is the Muse building that once housed a cotton gin and is now used as a concrete block plant.

Here at the lake was the Walker home. Mrs. Betty Copeland Hill built the house, 3 rooms down and 3 rooms up, with a connecting hall, but never completely finished the upper rooms. As was the case with many houses of the period the original 2 room log house became a kitchen and dining room for the new. A covered narrow passageway connected the back bedroom to the dining room and a raised board walk led from the rear hall door to the kitchen.

Uncle Mac Walker, for 30 years a cripple from rheumatism, would sit in his big rocker under the cedar trees in the summertime and call cheerful greetings to the Valley people as they passed. Almost every day, he drove old Maude up the road a mile or so to visit his daughter, Mattie Dobson. Passing a group of schoolboys, he would call out "hello, boys, howdy!" Led by Ez Alverson, the boys would reply "hello, Mr. Walker, howdy!"

The Walker family of 6 boys and 3 girls was closely associated with the growth of Sugar Valley, always taking an active part in the church and social life and sharing the jobs and sorrows of neighbors, as did everyone in this closely knit community. As the father became more helpless in his affliction, the sons left home to seek employment. But they never forgot the parents and the 2 young sisters at home and often sent gifts to them. On one occasion, two of the latest books arrived. Dotie said "Myrtle, you are the oldest and can have first choice—but I'm going to have St. Elmo!"

Josephine (Dotie) the younger daughter, began her teaching career at the old Ryals High School building and ended that career at the Sugar Valley Consolidated School, as she was stricken one day in her class room.

Myrt, beloved of old and young, Sunday School teacher, Sunbeam Leader, practical nurse to those who needed her, was the Martha of the two and while Josephine sat at the feet of the master of Learing, Myrtis wove a fabric of good deeds with hands that could fashion a beautiful cake or needle an exquisite piece of embroidery.

Aunt Nan, quietly busy with her ducks and chickens—did she think of the time when the Yankees caught her, tied a rope around her neck and threatened to hang her if she didn't tell where Freylach was hiding? She had the letter to him in her stocking foot. Could she still feel the prick of the needle in her hand as she sewed a gray uniform back in the community house at Dalton?

She would allow no reveling or gambling in her house and once threw her Nephew's celluloid playing cards in the fire while he danced around crying "Aunt Nan, you'll burn the house down." (Cliff Bridges was the nephew.)

Now, up the road to the Baptist church and the settlement that was the beginning of Snake Creek and Sugar Valley. Ghosts of the murdered Johnsons, of drowned Lucy and of swinging Bill Boaz may haunt you as you ride along. But let not your heart be troubled with these ancient runes, think of the two houses immediately south of the church.

On the right is the Lutes place which 3 families of beautiful girls called home, first the Lutes girls, then the blue-eyed, fairhaired Moss sisters, Agnes, Alice, Belle and Sally and lastly the lovely Warren girls, Bessie, Stella and Willie. Of course there were brothers in each family, a little brother named Otto climbed up on a shed roof and blew soap bubbles in our eyes.

Mr. Bill Moss, the father, ran a steam corn mill across the road from the church, almost on the site of the Johnson house. When we would haul the bag of corn in our red express wagon, Mr. Moss would greet us with "well here are Mrs. Abbott's little boys!" Finally we refused to go to mill, protesting "grandma ,he thinks we're boys!"

Back in the grove south of the church is the house built by Joseph Barrett, date unknown, but he was county treasurer, 1850-53, and owned much of the land in Snake Creek district.

Genie Strain Maline's grandfather Strain thought of buying the Barrett place but went on into the Gap because it was considered healthier in the mountains. Grandmother Strain died in 1865 and was buried in the mountains. They couldn't get to the cemetery because of the war.

My grandfather did buy the Barrett place. Matthew and Martha Abbott had come from Gwinnett County soon after the Civil War and were living in a divided log cabin facing the Calhoun road on the place now known as the Hilley place.

One day Matthew said "Martha, I've decided to buy a farm. Which one do you want?"

"I want the Joseph Barrett place," Martha replied.

"I can't buy that place, it's too much money!" exclaimed Matthew.

"I don't care" she said, small chin lifting defiantly, "I want the Barrett place and no other."

A few weeks later, as Martha sat in the open hall with her mending, Matthew came by and dropped a paper in her lap. It was the deed to the Barrett place. So the Abbott family grew up at the Barrett house, 8 girls, Alice, Cora, May, Ada, Lois, Una, Myra and

Ethel and one son, Jack who was second to Alice in age. The girls were good, or beautiful or intellectual and all were musical.

The 4 older children probably went to school in the 3 room log school house that stood in the church grove. W. M. Bridges and Mr. Twitty were the teachers. At the Exhibition of 1875, Della Everett and little Anna Williams were featured on the program while a gem of a composition by Sallie Gordon was mentioned. The 2 best speeches were made by John Aderhold and Joseph Jones. Seaborn Harbour, Edgar Dowdy, John Faircloth, P. E. Twitty, Frank Gordon and A. B. Frix acquitted themselves acceptably.

As the Valley gre win population and wealth, M. B. Abbott and V. H. Haynes agreed that the log school house was inadequate. Mr. Abbott gave the land, the timber was cut from his place and the Sugar Valley Academy was built by the citizens of the community sometime before 1890. A few years later, Mr. Abbott advertised in the Calhoun Times that two notes of $400 and $350, paid to him for the Academy had either been lost or stolen.

At a meeting of the Board of Trustees of the Middle Cherokee Baptist Association at Kingston on October 12, 1890, H. F. Ferguson, secretary, recorded; Brethren J. H. Bridges, J. Q. Everett and W. B. Harbour, from the church at Sugar Valley, were present and, on behalf of the church and the community, made a tender to the board of the building and half acre of ground at Sugar Valley church for the purpose of establishing there, the proposed Ryals High School

The donation was accepted and the half acre of land and the Academy were deeded to the Trustees by M. B. Abbott and the sum of $750 paid to him.

H. D. Gilbert, of Cohutta and J. E. Hudson, of Dalton, from the North Georgia Association, W. M. Bridges, of Rome and S. J. Whaley of Nanna, from the Ostanaula Association, Dr. Ayonzo Park and Rev. J. G. Hunt, of Villanow, from the Coosa Association were "affectionately and fraternally invited to co-operate with us in the building of Ryals High School."

The trustees agreed to raise $250 for improving the building, each trustee promising to raise $25 out of the churches allotted him. J. J. S. Callaway had Cassville, Salem in Gordon, Sugar Valley and Bethel; S. E. Smith, Rockmart, Salem and Raccoon; D. W. Peacock, Cartersville and Oak Grove in Bartow; A. S. Tatum, Bethlehem, Mt. Paran, Oothcaloga and Bethesda; W. H. Cooper, Dalton, Tunnel Hill and Ringgold; A. J. Buford, Cross Roads, Cedar Creek, Roland Springs and Oothcaloga Valley; J. H. Bridges and J. Q. Everett, Oostanaula Association; W. B. Harbour, Resaca and Calhoun; Dr. C. W. Mayson, Kingston.

Rev. W. H. Cooper was elected principal and empowered to employ such assistant teachers and music teachers as might be needed to run the school. The school would open on the first Monday in January, 1892. Monthly tuition rates were set at $1 for the Primary, $1.50 for the Intermediate, $2 for the Common school and $2.50 for higher mathematics and languages.

At the next meeting, Dec. 31, 1892, the treasurer reported $96.60 received and $2.65 paid out.

Dormitories were built, a 6 room house for the principal and 2 dormitories of 2 rooms each.

The Academy, as described in an article printed in the county newspapers and the Christian Index, had 2 large rooms on the lower floor, furnished with the best style of patent desks and new stoves and would accomodate 150 pupils. Also on the lower floor were 2 small rooms for the use of the Music Department.

Miss Edna Bell, of Cleveland, Tennessee, was the assistant teacher and came with the most sincere and praiseful commendations from her teachers and pastors in that classic little city.

A more charming young lady was not to be found than Miss Lida Farris, of Cassville, who was head of the music department.

The Baptist Association was congratulated upon their having a school that promised so much for the education and moral benefit of the entire section.

Rev. W. H. Cooper resigned after a term to return to the Pastorate and the Board in Nov. 1892, elected Prof. J. W. Brinson, 50 years old and a graduate of Mercer, as principal.

On May 28, 1894, trustees were asked to appoint a committee to conduct the end of term examinations, that of the High School department to be written, and to include in the curriculum a course in Bible and Church history. J. M. Brittain was one of the teachers.

In September of 1894, Rev. J. G. Hunt was elected principal, Miss Annie Brinson, assistant and Miss Anni eBellows, music teacher.

Treasurer's reports found in the old ledger itemized the money given and days' work donated for the improvement of the building which was 3 stories high. There was a big square room in the center of the second floor with 5 or 6 small rooms on each side opening into the center room. The top floor was all in one room.

At one time in the school's life, a group of young men objected to a disturbance in the school building and wrote to the trustees that they would remove themselves from the premises if the condition was not corrected. Signing the letter dated Nov. 2, 1896 were: J. T. Malone, Jr., L. C. Walker, J. L. Beamer, Paul B. Fite, R. B. England, J. R. McCollum, J. E. Pinion, A. J. Norrell, W. L. Beamer and J. J. Everett.

The May 1897 meeting of the Board was held at Reeves Station when the decision was made to allow only one lemonade stand on the Campus during Exhibition and that to be under the direction of the trustees.

One of the notable Commencements was that of 1893 under Prof. Brinson and his daughter, Miss Annie. Rev. Charles Wright, of Dalton, preached the sermon on Sunday and the following 2 or 3 days were devoted to examinations, songs, recitations and calisthenics directed by Miss Annie Brinson. In the young men's declamation, there was not a bobble, not a break under Prof. Brinson's training. The young ladies contested for a gold medal and the winners were Zella Lutes, Pet Frix, Della Bridges and Johnnie Crawford. Joseph Malone won the declamation medal and Ed Norrell brought down the house with "A Yankee in Love."

The Cherokee Association divided into smaller ones in 1899 and the school property reverted to the original owner, the Baptist Church. The school building was leased to various teachers or the community employed them and the School worked on the 2 teacher plan until consolidation in 1927. The upstairs rooms were used for lodge meetings and occasionally 2 or 3 rooms would be leased and the boys and girls in a family would live there during the school year, doing light house keeping. Sudie, Theodore and James Butler were members of one family of Farmville spending a year in the building.

The dormitories were rented for several years then finally sold and dismantled. In February of 1927, the old building was sold for $177, torn down and carted away.

So ended an era for Sugar Valley. The grove, so long a center of interest in the community was now important only to the Baptists. The new school, with busses bringing children in from surrounding districts, became the focal point. At the old school, boys and girls played town ball, fox and hounds and other active games but basket ball and soft ball took over at the Consolidated school. The many silver cups and trophies, locked in a cabinet, attest to the prowress of the students.

A modern lunch room, electric lights, running water and steam heat are the improvements of today. The 10th, 11th, and 12th grades were moved to Calhoun in 1956 and the 9th. grade after the new building there was finished. The school now carries the student through the 8th grade.

In 1960, William Kelly is principal and the teachers are Mrs. Buford Parsons, Mrs. Frank Edens, Mrs. Joe Ward, Miss Annie Mark Griffin, Mrs. Ralph Bramblett and Miss Genevieve Holsomback. The Cafeteria is in charge of Mrs. Stancill and Mrs. Everett and bus drivers are Mr. George Barnes and Mr. Frank Wheat.

Across the road from the New Providence Baptist Church and the Academy lived Jesse Miller, big land owner of the 1850s, and road reviewer in 1852.

Uncle Jesse was a great horse trader and Edgar Miller says that his mother, Molly, recalled seeing Jesse Miller often ride off leading one mule and return wearing someone else's shirt and leading 6 mules. Peter and Molly Miller, Edgar's parents, were descendants of slaves owned by the Miller family. She was Molly Eliza Betton and came from Carter's Quarter. Molly worked for a family near Calhoun during the War and waited on tables as the Yankees came through. She and Peter Miller met at a church near Resaca and were married on Feb. 20, 1870 by Jefferson Bell.

Jesse Miller, who was probably in the Valley in the 1820s had a brass cow bell that could be heard down in the Valley when the cows were up on Blue Spring mountain. One afternoon while Jesse was working in the big field above the house, he suddenly had a feeling that something was wrong. Stopping his work he stood for a moment listening, then—he had it! The cow bell wasn't sounding its usual musical tinkle from up on the mountain. While he stood pondering the situation, a group of Indians came plodding stolidly down the trail.

As they passed, Jesse heard a familiar sound. "Dratted red skin varmints, you've got my cow bell!" he shouted as he dashed into the group with flailing fists, his feet, booted in raw hide, landing telling blows on unprotected ankles. He soon had the Indians, 7 of them, knocked out. Picking up his cow bell, he went on up the mountain to restore the bell to its rightful place around the neck of the lead cow. Even afterward, if someone said of a thing "that's Jesse Miller's," the Indians left it strictly alone.

Jesse Miller died in 1879 at the age of 76. In 1880, The Calhoun Times reported that Mrs. Jesse Miller's house burned with nothing saved. Annis Miller died in 1889, aged 78.

R. L. Norrell married the Miller daughter, Joann, in 1877, with

Rev. W. M. Bridges performing the ceremony. Mr. Norrell probably built the big yellow house that we knew, after the Miller house burned. The big spring—Lucy's coming out place—down behind the house was always open to the school and the church. Going to the spring was a coffee-break during the all day singings and Association meetings and a respite from the School room during books. At first the spring was a rectangular shape, framed in wood and quite deep. Sometimes a careless boy or girl would fall in—really it was mostly girls who fell in.

One day Vassie Harbour and I went to the springs to fetch a pail of water. Vassie stooped over to fill the bucket and I remember thinking "wouldn't it be funny if Vassie fell in the spring!" The next thing I knew she was standing there dripping wet, crying "wipe my face," and it wasn't at all funny.

When my sister was the one to fall in, Miss Odie put her to bed in warm blankets and sent for me to go home and bring dry clothes.

Miss Odie, the second Mrs. Norrell, was the stern curator of the beautiful willow trees that wept beside the crystal waters, for mischievous boys delighted in cutting the long slender limbs—but never would I have broken one!

Her geese and ducks gobbled around the pond and dived for periwinkles. When she picked the downy feathers from the white birds I could see how the nursery ryhme, always recited during a snow storm, came to be—an old woman in the sky is picking her geese and the feathers are all flying away.

One of my delights was to walk home in the summer dusk carrying a plate on which rested 2 golden cakes of butter, firm and cold from their bed in the spring box, and only Miss Odie could make such beautiful molds!

Uncle Bob Norrell worked on the railroad and left the boys to do the farming until they, too answered the call of the rails and the cross ties. But one or two of his 6 sons or of the 4 orphaned sons of John and Vicky Malone Norrell were always there to tend the big field that stretched in seemingly endless acres from the big road to the woods. With their plows, they made pictures in the tinted soil, color-mixed by a Master hand as no mortal painter could do. And when the little green shoots of corn peeped up at the sun and the two-leaved cotton plants flattened themselves in thick lines through the middle of the smooth-rolled rows of beds, it made a picture of beauty unsurpassed by anything else under the sky.

Ed, Andrew, Russell, Charley, Seab and Alvin—these were Uncle Bob's boys. Daisy, the only girl in this multi-boy family, elected to remain in her father's house, giving years of selfish devotion to her brothers, to the 4 orphan cousins, Joe, Ernest, Barney and Ben, and to her own nieces and nephews.

Miss Daisy had a parlor. A charming room it was, with an art Square on the floor, lace curtains at the windows, a mirrored mantle, a hanging lamp with flowered china shade and glinting prisms, a sofa and 4 handsome white wicker rockers. There was a piano too for Miss Daisy was an accomplished musician and at one time taught a music class.

After taking a course in millinery at an Atlanta store, she joined with Ethel Abbott to establish a millinery store at Sugar Valley which, for a season or two, furnished the women, children and girls of the community with beautiful hats.

Then Uncle Bod died in 1917 and the Norrells, like the Arabs, folded their tents and gradually drifted away. But the memory of their kindness and generosity lingers on in the hearts of all who walked the dusty road to school and church and drank of the cool water that flowed so abundantly from the spring at the foot of the hill.

The first cemetery in the community was the one some distance back of the Baptist church where the graves are marked only with age-blackened stones. The 1867 deed from Joseph Barrett stipulated that no more graves be put in the cemetery, so the hill north of the church was selected as the new burial ground. The first grave in the new cemetery was that of John H. Aderhold born 1816, died 1868. He was pastor of the Baptist Church in the 1860s. Lulie Pitts' history lists the Rev. Aderhold as being the officiating minister at the marriage of H. O. Higginbotham and Dessie Copeland on Nov. 17, 1867.

Among old graves in the cemetery are, Martha Copeland 1812-1883, John Taylor 1817-1879, Lawson Fields 1816-1872, W. B. Armstrong 1810-1880, Mary Armstrong 1813-1881, a confederate soldier, James W. Jamison, 16th Alabama Infantry, Company A, Nancy E. Boaz 1806-1888, Mesha Boaz 1800-1885, Anna Haynes 1806-1877, John Haynes 1800-1879, Thomas Hall 1800-1888, Mary Hall 1805-1887, Dilliam J. Hall 1825-1889, Joel Frix 1816-1898 and Fartha Lynn Frix 1815-1899.

In the triangle, made by the junction of the Dalton Wagon road and the Snake Creek Gap road, is the small 4 room house that was built for Will and Lou Bridges Nelson soon after their marriage. Three of their 7 sons were born here. John and Vicky Norrell lived in the house and perhaps others. Sometime before 1900, John Hilly bought the house and in that year sold the place to Bart and Cora Abbott Bridges.

Four years later Cora died, leaving her husband and 3 little girls. The same year, W. B. Bridges entered the ministry and for 30 years or more, served as pastor of Baptist Churches in Gordon, Whitfield and Floyd Counties. During his retirement of about 15 years, he continued his ministerial duties, preaching when invited to do so, performing marriage ceremonies, in many ways to the community and to Sugar Valley Baptist Church. He died in 1949 still believing that no one could take the place of the bride for whom he waited 10 years and of the companion with whom he lived for only 8 years.

Our telephone was the last one up the road and we were kept busy relaying messages. All the folks above us came to ask us to call the Doctor. At dusk one day, the sound of a galloping horse pounded through the summer air, a white horse dashed over the hill and pulled up in front of our house. With scarcely a pause, Ben Alverson, in white-faced fear managed to get out the words "call the doctor, papa's given mama poison!" then galloped back up the road.

Professor Alverson had accidentally given Mrs. Alverson a dose of laudanum. Home remedies were immediately used and when the doctor's buggy drew up, she was sitting on the porch, smiling.

So, we lived in our house by the side of the road and tried to be a friend to man. We sat on our porch and watched the Valley folks go down the dusty road, to church on Sunday and to the Station or to Calhoun on week days. The school children picked our peaches as they went by or snitched an apple on the way home. Uncle Henry Claridy drove his mule cart down the Hill City road, peace and goodness riding along with him.

Soft summer rain came misting up the mountain from somewhere below the rim and pattered across the field on a thousand little cat toe-nails.

The mountains, Allen Henson said, were named John and Horn for the two sons of the Indian Chief, Blackhawk.

The mountains corralled the Valley, purple on a winter day, or pied in summer with little cloud spots hunting a place to hide, or at night streaked with long rail-fence lines of fire where some one had been careless with a match. Always majestic, ever constant, the mountain beckoned to heights undreamed of while the Valley whispered, "rest, lazy one" and from under the white stones in the cemetery came the echo, "we are the resting ones."

Then to dress up on Sunday and wait for the handsome lad to come driving with romance in his arms, was the crowning joy of the week's ending tasks. Oh, the Valley was sweet and life was sweet and memory is ever gracious, as fancy leads us back to days that are gone forever.

One of our neighbor families that we loved was the Roe family. Mrs. Roe was one of the Warren belles and her daughter Gladys, with her natural curls and winsome manner, inherited the charm of all the Warrens. Gifted in humorous recitation, she delighted her school mates with "Speak up Rastus, and 'spress yo' self." the rhymed story of a young colored girl trying to make her sweetheart propose. Gladys' brothers were Howard and Ernest.

Adjoining our place on the north was the big Tracy farm, reaching from just this side of the creek bridge to our line on one side of the road and to the cemetery and the Abbott line on the other. Meshach Boaz had bought the land in the 1850s. Jesse Miller sold him Lot No. 4, blazed out by D. R. Malone and James Eubanks and he acquired the rest of the farm in 80 acre lots. Born in 1800, he had come from Tennessee to Georgia in the late 1830s or perhaps not until the '40s, and was in Gordon County by 1850.

Meshach was having trouble with his neighbor M. B. Abbott in 1878. Records of the Baptist church show that in March of that year "Bro. Boaz laid a complaint against Bro. Abbott in regard to settlement between them, stating that he had taken Gospel steps to affect a reconciliation and had received no satisfaction." A committee was appointed to investigate but was dismissed in April because they had accomplished nothing. Bro. Boaz made acknowledgement to the church in May. The Brethren bore with Bro. Abbott until 1882, when having received no acknowledgement, the church with drew fellowship from him.

Meshach Boaz died May 4, 1885, aged 85. He was never ill until his last illness and lived only a few hours after being stricken, with seemingly little pain. He was possessed of a broad common sense view of life, in the opinion of the brethren who wrote his memorial. He was successful in business. Having, by wisdom, prudence and industry, secured competency under God, he was able to meet all the demands of a noble and useful existence. His huge sympathetic heart always melted quickly at the mistakes and disorders of his wayward brethren. His house was always a resting place for the ministers of God and he always dispensed charity with a bountiful hand.

The Boaz children were Jasper, Berry, Marion and Elizabeth who married Samuel Nelson. The Nelson children were Charley, Will, Mary and Ola Lee who died tragically in childhood.

The day of the tragedy in 1874, a group of little girls had slipped from school to go wading in Snake Creek, a short distance behind the Academy. Under a bluff, the creek has, through the centuries, washed away at the bank until there is a deep treacherous pool there. Ola Lee Nelson and Alice Phillips waded too far into this pool and were drown. Alice Abbott almost drown in trying to get them out. The two little girls are buired in the same grave with a single stone marking the place.

In many communities, there is one house that excites the admiration and sometimes the envy of everyone. Such was the Meshach Boaz house, up on the hill by the big road to The Gap. The central part of the house was a large hexagonal two story room. On each side a one room wing extended, on the north, a bedroom and back porch and, on the south, the hall and parlor with a bannistered front veranda. The dining room and kitchen joined the big room on the west and a porch reached across the parlor and along the kitchen wing.

After the death of Mesach's daughter, Elizabeth Nelson Black (the daughter of her second marriage was Beatrice Black), Mr. and Mrs. Madison Pate bought the house.

The Calhoun Times in August 1900, reported that "Mrs. Madison Pate and family took the train here Monday for Atlanta, where they will make their home. Mr. Pate recently sold his Sugar Valley farm to Mrs. Tracey, of Rome."

The train stood quietly panting away in little white puffs of smoke as the passengers came aboard and baggage was loaded on. Near the depot, a young lady was attempting to mount a very skittish horse. Engineer Ben F. Tracey was watching from his cab window. "If that girl mounts that horse", he remarked to his fireman, "she's my wife." Fanny Dobson mounted the prancing horse and galloped away as Engineer Tracey's train moved slowly up the track.

How Ben Tracey contrived to meet Fanny Dobson is not known but meet they did and, true to his prediction, she became his wife. They were married in a formal wedding at the Baptist church. Twin sons were born to them but only one lived, Frank.

On Sunday, Jan. 12, 1902, Engineer Travey's train, a mixed passenger and freight, left Atlanta at 11:30 a.m. for Chattanooga. He had orders to meet freight No. 55, at Reeves Station at 3:30. An extra freight was on the siding at Reeves Station and, thinking the way clear, he went on up the track at 40 miles an hour. On a sharp curve, one mile north of Oostanaula, Travey's train met No. 55 and the engines plunged into each other an instant after they came in sight. Engineer and fireman on both trains jumped but Mr. Tracey was caught between two freight cars and lost his life. Guy Connally, engineer on the freight was badly bruised and the conductor and fireman on Tracey's train injured.

The engines were a total wreck and a dozen cars were destroyed. The wreck occurred at a spot where the tracks ran through the Freeman farm. Mrs. Freeman, sister to Mrs. Tracy, heard the crash and knew that it was her brother-in-law's train.

Madame Nordica's private car, Brunhilde, was attached to the rear of the passenger train. The concert singer and Opera star had filled an engagement in Atlanta on Saturday night and was on her way to Nashville for a Monday night concert. She sustained a badly bruised shoulder and strained neck muscles and her accompanist, E. R. Simmons, suffered a badly bruised hand. Madame Nordica's car and 2 other Pullmans were sent over the W & A to Chattanooga and she reached Nashville early Monday night.

Ben F. Tracey, one of the best known of men with hosts of friends, was buried at Rome.

Mrs. Tracey and Frank were living at the big house on the hill. She felt that, for her only child, she wanted a better education than the 2 teacher school provided, so Frank was educated in the Calhoun School and the Dickey School where his mother, too, enrolled as a pupil.

Mrs. Tracey loved young people and many times we sat on the rug in her parlor listening to The Preacher and The Bear and Cohen on the Telephone from her little talking machine with it's blue morning-glory horn. She drove the handsomest rig in the Valley, a high gracefully built buggy with a fringed parasol and a rear platform on which 3 girls could sit and swing their feet. Usually there were 2 other girls in the seat with Mrs. Tracey.

I watched the laughing groups go by and wondered why I was never included. Unable to bear it any longer, I blurted "Mrs. Tracey, why don't you ever ask me to ride with you?"

"Why, honey," she said, "if I asked you, people woul dsay I was after your father!" One of the sacrifices that must be made by the daughter of a handsome widower, who was also a minister.

Fanny Tracey stood over my dying mother that July afternoon in 1904, closed her dead eyes and dressed her body for the casket. She was again in our house on a Sunday in June as I dressed to drive with the young lad to a minister in Calhoun and assume my role, as a wife and mother. She gave me the gray silk gloves that I wore. When she came to her last days, there seemed to be nothing that I could do for her but stand by her hospital bed and tell her of the deep feeling of gratitude in my heart and of my great obligation to her.

The Tracey house burned in the 1940s and Clarence Jones erected an attractive bungalow on the site. Mr. and Mrs. R. F. Jones are now the owners of most of the farm. The old house south of the big house and back from the road was built for Meshach Boaz's son, Marion. Later, Samuel and Elizabeth Nelson lived there. The house across the road was the home of the Boaz negroes, whose ancestors were the family slaves.

Cross Snake Creek and turn to the right. The tall old house on the left was built by Mr. Knight in 1858. S. W. and Sarah Dobson bought the place sometime after they came from Walker County to Gordon in 1887 or eariler. The Baptist church received their letters in June of 1887. An extensive land owner, Mr. Dobson left property to each of his 13 children, and to Tom was given this house.

With 9 children of her own, Mattie Walker Dobson never felt that 2 or 3 more were too many. Spend the night parties, pound suppers, square dances and quiltings were frequent occurrences in the Dobson home and, always, the table was loaded with everything good to eat that could be grown in the fields, on the trees or raised in the pasture.

The next early settlement house is the Haynes place, later known as the Moss place. Mrs. Moss was Malvina Haynes. Very old box woods line the walk to the house which is colonial cottage style.

The Will Strain home stood across the road. Estelle, Belle, Genie and Julia were the lovely daughters of the Strain family, and Pauline, daughter of the second Mrs. Strain. Was this the home of the Rev. J. A. Chastain in 1875 when the road connecting the Pocket Mill road and the Villanow road was laid out? The grand jury reccommended that the road pass by J. A. Chastain's house and connect with the Calhoun-Villanow road near V. H. Haynes.

Up in the Gap is the divide where the water flows one way into Walker County and the other into Gordon. Here Snake Creek begins to flow, gently, quietly, but gathering strength as springs and mountains rivulets join in, he crosses the road 13 times.

When the new road was being surveyed. I wanted to say to the engineer, you, there, with your red and white pole, do you know about Snake Creek? You see him lying there, musical in his soft cadence—but have you seen him when he's bloated with water, foaming here, spilling over the banks there and runing down the road if he chooses? Yes, you do know about him for you have built strong culverts, low ones and high ones. I would like to stand here, on this one, in flood time and watch him throw himself furiously against the concrete only to find himself spl it5 ways with perhaps a part of him sneaking down the ditch searching for an opening in this barrier of asphalt and gravel.

You have conquered Snake Creek with your bull dozers and your giant shovels and henceforth he must be submissive, and content in his old age to accept the guided way.

We are not going to Walker county nor yet to Hill City, so turn around here and drive back to the forks of the road. We'll take the mountain loop road. A private road turns to the left, leading to the Dock Strain and V. H. Haynes farms. The Strain house originally belonged to Marion Boaz who sold it to A. M. Bridges and brother in 1892 and left for Texas. It was the last home of Will and Lou Nelson for they both died here in 1900.

In 1880, John Bridges, of Whitfield County, paid J. B. Stofford $150 for "all that tract of land being lot 216, 14th., district, 3rd., section of Gordon County, except ½ interest in any iron ore or other mineral found on said land." Standing at the end of the private road is the house that was the home of the Bridges family for 20 years. Close by is the house that was built about 1889 for John's oldest son, Alfred, after his carriage to Mittie Hughes. V. H. Haynes bought the farm in 1900 and the Bridges went back to Whitfield County.

V. H. Haynes had become a landowner in 1867, buying from Isaac Bates 280 acres of land, listed as lots No. 70 and 71 in Snake Creek district, for which he paid $35,000.

He was appointed N. P. and J. P. in 1877 and his first marriage ceremony, according to Pitts Gordon County History, was said for W. J. Morelock and Mary Carpenter on July 22, 1877. From then on Mr. Haynes was the marrying squire, even performing one ceremony on top of Horn Mountain. Mrs. Haynes was Emma Davis. Tiny in stature and gentle of manner, she loved her home. Her Cape Jessamines and velvet roses bloomed when no one else' would.

Squire and Mrs. Haynes' children were Oscar, Stella (Mrs. M. J. Griffin), Annie (Mrs. J. W. Nuckolls), Paul, Dora (Mrs. Gus Mullinax) and Aline (Mrs. A. L. Henson). Two sons, Lee and Judson died in young manhood.

V. H. Haynes served 2 terms in the State Legislature, 1915-16 and 1917-18 and was always vitally interested in the Welfare of community, state and county.

Aline Haynes married the boy next door—at least, he lived next door for a time. The Henson family, though not native to Snake Creek, lived at Sugar Valley and left, in the red dust of the roads and fields, foot prints that have not blown away. Two sons have had books published, one is a prominent lawyer another owns a Music Publishing house, still another has been successful in the automotive field and even the little sister is active in the business world, having a dress shop of her own. The adored older sister, Ada, died young.

The elder son, Lucius, friend and counselor to his brothers, comforter to his mother, generously shared his own home with them all. Allen, youthful criterion of feminine pulchritude, lost no time in issuing a writ for neighbor Haynes' pretty little daughter who became his pretty little wife. Clayton, first graduate of the Berry School—he won all the prizes and medals, I think.

The Calhoun Times reported in a September 1907 issue; Professor J. M. Henson of Sugar Valley, who has been in South Georgia since about the first of June teaching singing Schools, has returned home. He had great success in his work while there. Any community would do well to confer with Professor Henson as he thoroughly understands the Science of Music.

Solomon and Paul—what Bible reading mother would not wish for her sons the wisdom of the one and the good works of the other. Last of all, Ruth, symbol of family loyalty.

"The child is father of the man and childhood shows the man as morning shows the day."

Jennie, a negro woman living with Mrs. Malone, at Sugar Valley died in September 1875 at the age of 118 years. She could remember events back to the Declaration of Independence.

The Malone's then, were among the first settlers of Snake Creek. When John Malone first came to Snake Creek, he taught school in a cabin that stood on the Knight (Dobson) place. He died rather early in life and is buried either in the family cemetery on the Y. J. Malone farm or in the old cemetery at the Baptist church. His wife, Mary Jane, was born in 1811 and died in 1895. Her grave is in the new Baptist Cemetery.

Jane's log cabin was in the field just west of the present home of Mr. and Mrs. Buford Malone. This last named house was for many years the home of Lewis and Cornelia Malone Boaz, respected colored citizens. Cornelia and her sister, Jane Clairdy, were the daughters (or granddaughters) of the aged Jennie.

Buford and Mary Malone have re-modeled the Boaz house and furnished it with all modern conveneinces. The exterior is of native field stone.

John and Jane Malone's children were Joe, whose wife was a Baugh, Elizabeth (Mrs. Marion Boaz), Vicky (Mrs. John Norrell), Rebecca (Mrs. Lonzo Ferguson) and Homer, whose wife was Cynthia

Lowe.

Homer and Cynthia Malone's house was on the road recommended by the Grand Jury in 1875 to connect the Pocket Mill and Calhoun Lafayette roads. The upper end of this road was closed so long ago that few of us could remember it. The road we knew extended only to the Malone and Harris houses.

The seven sons of Homer and Cynthia Malone, Carl, Almon, Buford, Maine, Herman, Guy and Ray. All tall dark and handsome and ever ready to squire the girls here and there, added much to the social gatherings of The Valley. Their only sister, and the youngest in the family, was Janie Dell.

Members of the Harris family as we remember them were Wesley, Sam. Mack, Ben and Ella. In 1909, Wesley was principal of the school at the old Ryals High School building. Recorded in the minutes of the Baptist Conference of September, 1909 we find "Bro. Wesley Harris relinquished his lease on the school building."

As a pupil of Prof. Harris, hearing him recite "When Ruby Played the Piano" was an unforgettable experience. The recitation was a dramatic portrayal of a concert given by the eminent Russian pianist Anthon Rubinstein.

"Molly, let's get married before I go to war." "We'll do nothing of the kind, Perry McCutcheon," retorted Molly Chandler. "I want a whole man, not half a man. Wait until you come back from the war and then we'll talk about getting married."

Perry came back from the war still a whole man and he and Molly were married in 1866. For most of their lives, they lived in the house on the hill by the spring, across the branch to the west of the Malones. Molly and Perry's only child, Viola, affectionately called "Dodie," was our Sunday School teacher. She firmly believed that a Sunday School lesson should be studied as carefully as were school lessons and, when we didn't know our lesson one Sunday, she made us get it over! The next Sunday we had two lessons. Many years later, I told her of the incident and she said "Did I do that?"

Viola McCutchen owned one of the few Square grand pianos in The Valley. The piano was probably purchased by B. D. Chandler for his daughter Molly. Other families on the Loop Road who were the proud possessors of Grand pianos were the S. I. Chandlers, the Y. J. Malone's and the J. N. Wrights.

After Miss Dodie had definitely reached the spinster age, she was asked to show the young folks an old time dance one night at a party. Incidentally, the party was taking place in the old home of her grandfather, B. D. Chandler. Miss Dodie, in all innocence, gave a lesson on the dance.

The committee on Discipline at the Baptist Church reported to the next conference that some of the members had been guilty of dancing. I. T. Penn, H. F. Everett and J. W. Warren were appointed to investigate. The matter was tabled for a time and when the committee reported no satisfaction from the dancing members, Miss May Dickey, Mrs. Homer Malone and Mrs. Ludie Strain were added to the committee.

The young people finally made acknowledgements and were duly forgiven but Miss Dodie, overcome by a sense of injustice, refused to attend church. Mrs. Ethel Dickey and Mrs. Homer Malone were appointed to see her. She remained adamant so the church withdrew fellowship from her.

Miss Dodie's former Sunday School pupils felt that the brethren had been a little severe and that the church could have forgiven our dear Miss Dodie for her innocent demonstration.

J. A. J. Phillips, listed on the Baptist Church roll as "Licentiate", lived across the road from the McCutcheons. Bro. Phillips preached when the pastor was absent and often served as Moderator Pro Lem. He was in the chair that day in June, 1878, when after a discussion on the real meaning of the word "Unanimity" in the Decorum, the Conference voted to suspend that point fo rthe present, where upon Bro. Chandler made acknowledgements to the church.

In April a charge of contempt of church had been brought against Mr. Chandler, to which the Rev. J. A. Chastain objected. A charge was then brought against Bro. Chastain for non-fellowship with the church in that he publicly advocated the whiskey traffic as consistent with a sound Christian corality and that he pressed his views in injury to the place and prosperity of the church.

D. B. Chandler was operating a Government Distillery at his home on the Loop Road and was frequently churched for distilling but there is no record of his ever having been excluded. He was the Belv Chandler who rolled the Salt filled drum from Savannah to his home and who, as a baby, had been thrown into the river by the Indians, for his swimming lesson.

The D. B. Chandler farm was purchased by S. W. Dobson for his daughter, Sallie Dobson Copeland and for many years it was known as the Copeland place. Jim Copeland was loved and respected for his kindly nature and nobility of character. A faithful member of the Baptist Church, he was elected a deacon in 1906 and served as church treasurer in 1907.

With a houseful of young people, the Copeland home was one of hospitality and cheer. Hamp, Gordon, James, Dedie, Beatrice, Eolian and Earl were the children of Sally and Jim Copeland. Beatrice died in girlhood and Mrs. Copeland died soon after the birth of her daughter, Florence, named for her Aunt, Mrs. Freeman, in whose home she was reared.

Following the precepts of Forthright parents, the Copeland young people went out to homes of their own to become useful and honored citizens of their several communities.

After the Copelands left The Valley, John and Josie Carter came to live in the old Chandler house. Mrs. Carter's sister, Nancy Ballew, and their widowed mother, "Granny Ballew" to everyone, made their home with the Carters. John and Josie Carter's children were Mary (Mrs. Buford Malone) and Bob. The Chandler farm is now the home of Mr. and Mrs. R. A. Brown.

Tombs Miller's farm adjoined the Copeland place. His son, John and the auburn-haired Nancy Ballew saw each other frequently as neighbors so it was a natural for the two to decide that a life together was their future. Today, they are two of the most contented people I know, living in their lovely little house on the hill, surrounded by whispering pines and a yard full of flowers. As Eolian Copeland married the boy around the curve (Gene Malone), so Nancy married the boy next door. Poet Ernest Neal once told me "for the happiest marriage, choose the girl next door or the boy around the corner."

When John J. Miller, born 1826, died 1873, married a daughter

of D. R. and Cliestia Malone, D. R. gave them a tract of land across
the road from his house and here the young Millers lived in their
house near the spring. But John died at the age of 47 leavin ghis wife,
four sons, Tombs, Tony, Gordon and Johnson and a daughter, Sallie.

The deed, as made to John Miller by D. R. Malone, stipulated
that the land would revert to the Malone Estate in case of the death
of John or his wife. The homeless Miller family then bought the
tract of land next to the D. B. Chandler farm and the young sons
worked for many years to pay for the place. The eldest son, Tombs,
married Mattie Carter and their children were John and Lee, Josie
and Maude.

There's a secret room in D. R. and Cliestia Malone's house. Set
on a hill and facing the east, this house was always considered one
of the fine homes of The Valley. And it has a skeleton, not in a
closet but in a whole room. To reach the secret room, you climb a
narrow enclosed stairway and enter a big square room, walled and
ceiled with wide painted planks, like the downstairs rooms, and
lighted by three windows, one on the front and one on each side of
the fireplace at the north end. Then—step through a door and you
are in the secret room and the secret is out—the skeleton of the house
is built of logs. Bared to the view are wide, hand-cut logs with spaces
between that, surely were filled with clay when the house was new.
How proud D. R. and Cliestia Malone must have been of their big
double house and no wonder it has stood for more than a hundred
years. When I went back in April to read, with Mrs. Cantrell's
magnifying glass, the inscriptions on their weathered tomb stone, I
found the ground around the graves covered with a white blooming
myrtle and brought home a small root of the vine to plant in my
back yard.

The names and dates are, D. R. Malone born 1808, died 1861,
Cliestia Malone born 1813, died 1859. If you go to the cemetery in
the morning, when the sun is at a certain position in the sky, you
can read the inscription at the bottom of the stone, which is according to Mr. Long who lives there now, "When they died, they were
kin to everyone who lived in the Valley."

Judson Malone, son of D. R. and Cliestia, born 1835 and died
1918, inherited the place. All over the Valley, log homes of the early
settlers were being replaced by modern houses of clap board, many
of them painted. So Y J. and Octavia, his wife, born 1850, died 1828,
modernized their home, covering the solid old logs with saw mill-
smoothed timbers, adding porches and perhaps another downstairs
room. Their children were Joe, Claude, Julia, Gene and Tom.

When the young people went to serenade Tom and Zoe Dacus
Malone, on the night after their marriage, we were invited in and
my sister and I played duets on the old square piano in the parlor.

The Malone place is now the property of Patsy Muse Hutchinson. Seaborn Isaac Chandler was born at Newnan, Georgia in January
1827. After his father's death, his mother married John Copeland.
When Seaborn was about 18 years old, he and his step-father and a
younger brother, Belv Chandler, rolled a tobacco drum to Savannah where they boiled sea water to get salt. Belv rolled the salt-
filled drum back home. Seaborn and his step-father took a boat from
Savannah and sailed around the Cape of Good Hope bound for the
gold fields of California. The ship sanded on the Cape and no other

ship came for a long time. All of the crew but six, and James Copeland, died and were buried at sea. Finally, a ship picked up the surviving crew members, together with Seaborn Chandler, and carried them on to California.

Seaborn's mother, a Harbour before her marriage, was a teacher at the Indian village of New Echota. One day the Indians stole her baby, Belv, and threw him in the river to make him swim as they did their own babies. Belv was almost drowned and his back badly scratched, before he was rescued from his Indian swimming instructors.

Seaborn Chandler rode horseback from California to Georgia with his gold hidden in a hollow saddle girth. He came to Sugar Valley, bought a farm on the mountain Loop Road and married Martha Delena Malone. On a visit to Dahlonega after his return from California, Mr. Chandler picked up nuggets as big as a grain of corn and saw a better color of gold than he did in California.

The Chandler story was told to me by Harry Copeland and grandson of the James Copeland who was buried at sea near the Cape of Good Hope. Harry's father was James Robert Copeland and his mother was Margaret Rahm whose great-grandfather came from Germany as an indentured child. The Copeland family lived at Gordon Springs, old home of General Gordon, where Uncle Seab would visit them twice a month, driving 20 miles in his buggy.

Harry Copeland owns many interesting family heirlooms and pictures. His mother's Bible with all the family records in it, is a cherished possession. He once gave Uncle Ceab a knife with dogs' heads carved on one side and horses' heads on the other. When Uncle Seab died, he left the knife to Harry.

In 1886, there was a Sunday School picnic at Perry McCutcheon's and each one that carved his initials on a gourd. The vine was prolific and there was a gourd for everyone but only J. R. Copeland's lived and his son, Harry, now has the gourd with handle several feet long.

"One side shriveled," he said, "and my father cut it out to make a dipper."

Other prized possessions of Harry Copeland are a crank-type record player and a collection of old records and a chest of redwood or mahogany. Best of all is a handmade bed with wood polished until it glows like a red-ripe cherry, for cherry wood it is. The head board, carved in a broken pediment, is supported at each deep scallop by a slender spooled spindle. In the center is a short, curved piece of wood like a square totem pole. There's a mystery about the bed. I promised not to tell. Discover it for yourself.

After their daughter, Mattie, married J. T. McEntyre, Seab and Martha Chandler moved to a small house on the place and left the big house to the McEntyres, whose children were Etta, Seab, Erma, J. T. and Elizabeth. Another little son died and Mattie's only sister, Ettie, died in young girlhood of typhoid as did so many young people of the time.

The McEntyre girls, and even the boys, had such peach-bloom complexions that they were the envy of The Valley. And no Sugar Valley girl felt that she had "arrived" until she had gone for a drive or two in Seab's handsome rubber-tired buggy with its fringed parasol, behind the little red horse named Blanche. Blanche had been Mrs. Tracey's horse. Abbott Hilley's horse, Trixie, was also from the Tracey stable. She was a long-legged, big horse and could trot as gracefully as any Kentucky thoroughbred, while sweet little Blanche just pitty-patted down the road.

Never shall I forget the night we had been to the McEntyre's to a party (they were always having a lovely pound supper or prom party). Fulton Dacus was my beau for the party and since one of his brothers had pre-empted the horse, Fulton was driving the family's big mule, black as the night that sheltered us. On the way home, the mule simply fell down in the road and lay there groaning like a human. Fulton was standing by the poor animal, gently urging him to get up when who should come by but Abbott Hilley and Jewel Meredith driving the high-stepping Trixie. They laughed. I was furious with my cousin Abbott and filled with a deep sympathy for my beau. Seab and Abbott were the first young men to own Model Ts, Abbott's, a run about and Seab's, a brass-trimmed touring car.

The Tracey hill became less steep, I'm sure, because Abbott always came over it so fast he carried the dust with him.

Professor McEntyre was one of the most popular and efficient teachers in Gordon County. No student of his would ever forget verbs, phrases, complements, or clauses after a term of diagramming under Prof. McEntyre. John Edge says he was equally good in Algebra but I never succeeded in learning the first x y of Algebra, so I wouldn't know.

Another beloved teacher was Prof. J. F. Alverson. The Alversons, like my Whitfield County family, were not pioneers of Snake Creek. They came from Walker County. There were always more boys than girls in Sugar Valley (lucky we!) and the four blonde Alverson boys, Earl, Ezra, Ben and Troy, also the two little sisters, Aline and Wynette, had hosts of friends. Prof. Alverson's family, when in Sugar Valley lived at the Snake Creek bridge beyond which the road forks into the Gap road to the right and the mountain loop road to the left. There is a cut-through road by the Alverson place, now owned by Mr. and Mrs. Donald Holsomback, connecting the Gap road and the Hill City road.

Facing this short road is the attractive home of Mr. Will Walraven, his son, Maurice, daughter, Pearl and widowed daughter, Nell McClain. Ludie Watkins Walraven, widow of Fayette Walraven, lives nearby, on the Gap road.

At the February term of court in 1875, the Grand Jury recommended that a public road of the third class be established connecting the Sugar Valley and Pocket Mill road with the Calhoun and Lafayette road. The road would commence near the residence of John J. Medcalf, pass near S. J. Chandler's, to Y. J. Malone's, to D. B. Chandler's, to J. J. Phillip's, via Mrs. Jane Malone's, near the residence of Rev. J. A. Chastain to V. H. Haynes', there intersecting the Calhoun-Lafayette road.

Thus was created the mountain Loop road, so pleasant for a Sunday afternoon drive with your best beau, not too short, not too long. The houses were so close together that there was not room for Madame Grundy to get in a word edgewise. But do not go to the Gap, my dear, nor to the Artesian Well, except with a crowd!

John J. Medcalf's place was the Lay place. In our time it was home of Sam and Sallie Hall Lay and their interesting family, George, Nida, Dock, Kate, Annie and Minnie. Charming, romantic, imaginative and given to figures of speech that no one else would think of—as when Annie, in one of her rare fits of peeve pepper-shook "I don't like nobody no how!"—the Lay young people were unique in the community, admired and loved by every one.

J. J. Medcalf was a member of the building committee for the new Baptist church in 1878. The church agreed to pay him for making a coffin for Bro. Andy Morehead in 1885 and granted him leave of absence in 1888. His wife, she was Nancy Ward, must have died before 1877 for her name is not on the list of church members of the day. His spinster daughter, Georgia, lived with him, as older citizens remember.

The Medcalf house burned and the Lays built the one that is standing today, owned by Marvin and Alma Ward Davis.

T. M. Ward came to Snake Creek in the 1830s, from DeKalb County, and bought the land at the foot of Horn's Mountain which was part of the lot drawn by one of the Smiths. There are four smiths listed in the 14th district of the Cherokee Land Lottery.

The first house was built at a mineral spring that was thought to have medicinal value and near the place are the graves of a young mother and her infant. Joe Ward said that her name was Davis and that she died at the baby's birth. People, seeking treasure, had dug into the graves at some time in the past.

A beautiful wooded lot, near the Sugar Valley and Pocket Mill road, was the site chosen for the new home of the Ward family.

Thornton Ward and his older son, Julian, were active in the Baptist church during the 1870s and 1880s. The Senior Ward was a member of the committee appointed in 1880, to write the church history and of the committee selected to revise the Rules of Decorum in 1884.

Because of the rigid rules of decorum in the early churches, the brethren were frequently called before the Conference. Such was the case with Thornton Ward and his son, Julian. The father would give no excuse but the son appealed for moderation which was sustained by a ruling of Bro. Wright. Despite the moderation ruling, fellowship was withdrawn from the Wards at the August Conference in 1886. (My grandfather was excluded because he didn't like the preacher and wouldn't go to church.)

T. M. Ward was Justice of the Peace in 1865. John Warren and Sarah A. Turner were the first couple whom he pronounced man and wife, the date being September 23, 1865. Other couples united in marriage by Squire Ward were: W. H. Terry and Miss M. E. Harbor, J. W. Nabers and Miss M. C. Strain, David M. Watson and Sarah A. Harbor, R. S. Prichett and Lucinda Miller, all in 1866 and in 1867, J. R. Baugh and Miss G. Miller and W. L. Strain and Miss M. E. Ray. He was appointed Notary Public in 1869. His name disappears from the marriage license list after 1872.

Will, second son of Thornton Ward, spent his entire life on the Ward place. His wife was Liza Thomason. One of the Valley's Queenly matrons, she was loved for her unassuming manner and her devotion to home and family. The adage "Like mother, like daughter," could be most aptly applied to the daughters of Liza Ward. Calm, poised and intellectual, they were like their mother. Alma, an honor graduate of the University of Georgia, devoted her life to the teaching profession, continuing her class room work after her marriage.

In December of 1926, Phil and I were invited to the Ward home to provide wedding music for the first of the Ward girls to leave home. Aline was married to Dr. Olin Newton, of Alabama, in a lovely home ceremony. Two years later, almost to the day, we were back to play and sing for her funeral. She had died, leavnig a small son. Dr. Newton died a short time later and Olin, Jr. was reared in the home of his mother's sister, Alma Ward Davis. Aline was gifted in music and studied at the Atlanta Conservatory. I was so proud of her when she sang "Little Brown Bird Singing" or played Chopin's Valse, in G flat, Op. 70, No. 1. Her son inherited her gift, loved the study of music and became a proficient pianist.

In June of 1927, we were again participating in a wedding at the Ward home, a double wedding this time. Alma was married to Marvin Davis and Eleanor to Clinton Cox. I still have the hand made chiffon handkerchief edged in net and embroidered in tiny roses, that they gave me, and the card which read "from two little brides of 1927 to a little bride of 1917."

The only son, Joe, is married to the former Ella Mae Smith of Newnan, and has lived in the Ward home since his marriage. The youngest of the family, Opal, is married to Gus Jones, of Marietta.

I spent an entertaining Sunday afternoon with Joe and Ella Mae Ward, listening to Joe's stories about his grandfather's day and looking at old pictures of the Ward and Smith families. Ella Mae came to Sugar Valley, from her home at Newnan, to teach in the school. Joe persuaded her to stay and she is still teaching in the school (1960).

The Ward family Bible contains records of six generations, beginning with T. M. Ward's parents and his wife's parents and ending with Joe and Ella Mae's grandchildren. The binding of the Bible, broken at the spine, had been laced together with deer-hide thongs.

Thornton M. Ward bought land lot No. 72 from Smith and built a log cabin of 4 rooms and an attic, the first house built in the Snake Creek section after the lottery, and the place has been in the Ward family for 120 years.

There are a few lots at the foot of the mountain that measure 160 feet long and 80 feet wide. The surveyors lacked one fourth of a mile coming out even when they met going east and west. The present Ward house is located on lot No. 71. Contractors and builders were the Metcalf brothers.

Mrs. T. M. Ward, whose father, Mr. King, owned the Abernathy field west of the Methodist church, lived in the log house while her husband was fighting in the Civil War. T. M. was crippled as the Confederates, hard pushed by the Yankees, were leading the horses across the river bridge at Resaca.

Ann Ward Eskew's son, Sam, was a wheel wright and wagon maker. His shop was located west of the Methodist church. One of the Malones, who was going to drive to Arkansas, contracted with Sam to make a wagon. When he went to get his wagon, Sam told him "I'm sorry, but I have made all four wheels for the same side of the wagon." After Malone had tried everywhere to trade new wheels for old, someone put him wise to Sam's joke.

Another relative of T. M. Ward's, Strawdy Floyd, was a Government distiller but also made liquor for his friends. Every farm in those days had 50 gallons stowed away. Strawdy was arrested and lodged in jail. The Methodist stewards and the Baptist deacons got him out and sent him off to Texas.

Johnny Warren, cousin to the Wards, had lost an arm in the war. T. M. wanted Johnny to run for the State Legislature and needed the support of Y. J. Malone. The road from Wards to Malones was so steep that the wagons couldn't get up it so T. M. gave a right-of-way around the hill to re-instate himself in the favor of Y. J. with whom he had not been on speaking terms because of a law suit.

Seab Chandler and Y. J. Malone were brothers-in-law. They had driven to Calhoun one cold day where they had paid a visit to Ballew's Saloon. They were very much in their cups, perhaps three sheets in the wind, on the trip home. One owned the buggy, the other, the horse. At the steep hill, they got into an argument about who should drive and confirmed by each taking a line. Seab was small and Y. J. was big, so he pulled harder and the horse went off the road, turning the buggy over. Staggering to his feet the portly Y. J. shouted "I can whip you!" to which Seab replied "I can shoot you!" A neighbor came by, calmed irate men, righted the buggy and saw them safely home.

When a man, mistakes forgotten, sins forgiven, can in his mature years be a pillar in the church, enjoying the respect of the young and the comradeship of the old, is he not more to be commended for having surmounted such obstacles? Did not the good father gladly welcome home the prodigal son?

Strong men can resist temptation. Weak men fall, but, with the help of God and friends, may rise again to a place of dignity in the community. The strong look backward with no regret. The weak ones remember in sorrow, the lost weekends.

The old Rome and Dalton road forks from the Gap road at the Pittman place near the Baptist church, crosses Snake Creek and a branch, bisects the Loop road and continues south through the Methodist community to join the paved road a short distance beyond Oostanaula church.

Located on this road between the Pittman place and the crossroads, is the best-preserved of The Valley's ante-bellum houses, the Harbour home.

G. Winn, one of the early citizens of Snake Creek and, in 1859, a trustee of the Gordon County male and Female Seminary at Sugar Valley, began construction of the house, but it was completed by a later owner. John and Anna Haynes lived here for a year, perhaps in the 1860s.

"How far is it to Sugar Valley?" asked a pleasant-faced young man as he stepped from the train at Calhoun one day in the 1850s.

"About five miles as the crow flies" replied the station agent, "but a little father by the road. Don't you want a livery rig? E. R. Sassen has some fine ones at the hotel and you can cross the river at Lay's Ferry."

"No, thank you," the young man said, "I think I'll walk."

From the bluff above the river, he spied a boy fishing from a boat.

"Ahoy, boy" he called, "how much will you charge to row me across the river?"

"I'll take you across for 10 cents" answered the boy.

So Jim Wright crossed the Oostanaula river and followed the trail that John Baugh had walked 20 years earlier. John Baugh had

196   CLIMB THE HILLS OF GORDON

come to establish a home. Jim Wright came to teach in the Seminary.
Soon after the Civil War, J. N. Wright returned to Sugar Valley
and purchased the Winn place. His bride was the former Louisa
Allen, of McMinnville, Tennessee. Their children were Gorda, James
Milton, Viola, Estelle, Essie, Hattie and Farisse.

Mr. Wright was a successful farmer and an influential citizen,
serving as a trustee of the School. He was a member of the building committee, appointed in 1878, for the new Baptist church, clerk
of the conference for several years and on the committee selected
to write a history of the church.

Mr. and Mrs. Wright moved to Rome in 1887 to educate their
daughters at Shorter College.

After the Wright family left The Valley, the eldest daughter,
Gorda, came with her husband and small son to live in the house.
She had married Will Harbour, son of Hammy Harbour who owned
the Griffin place and most of the land around the village. Gorda and
Will's children were Hudson, born at the family's Fairview farm,
"Bunkum," and Psyche, the daughter.

In the family tradition, Will and Hudson Harbour served the
church as deacon and clerk and in many other ways. Gorda Harbour
was active in the women's work and Psyche's lyric Soprano voice
was often heard in Solos at the services.

James and Louisa Wright had installed double French doors at
the front entrance to open on a wide, square veranda. A smaller
porch was added to the end of the south corner room. The handcut
siding is set vertically and a window in the north gable furnishes
light to the attic. All the blinds were made by Mr. Tweedell. An odd
feature of the windows is the arrangement of the small glass panels,
9 in the upper sash and 6 in the lower.

Gorda and Will Harbour built a new porch extending across the
front and the south end of the house, added the dining room and
kitchen, a latticed porch to enclose the well and another porch opening from the dining room and the back hall.

When Hudson and Maude Harbour remodeled the house, the
porches were restored to the original pattern. The new foundation
and the chimney are of native field stone. Lawrence Hillhouse was
the stone mason. There were 8 rooms and a bathroom in this beautiful old house that sits well back from the road in a grove of century-
old oaks. The trees were badly damaged in the ice storm of March,
1960.

James and Louisa's French doors have been replace dby a colonial doorway. If you stand in the square front hall and look down
the narrow back hall, you can see the plane marks in the 12 inch
wall boards. There are wainscotings of narrow up and down planks
in every room. The mirrored mantel in the old parlor is supported
by small Doric Columns. Plaster is used on walls and ceilings of
this room, now used as a bedroom. A carved walnut love seat, upholstered in antique velvet, a chair from James and Louisa's first
house-keeping days, paintings by Estelle Wright, Gorda's little parlor organ, bought at the Atlanta Exposition in 1872 (the blue ribbons
were still on it when the organ arrived), china, silver and many other
family treasures are lovingly tended by the owner of the house,
Maude Quillian Harbour. Elroy, the only child of Maude and Hudson
Harbour, makes his home in Atlanta.

A short distance south of the crossroads is the Copeland place.

The old house was razed years ago to make way for a white-painted cottage. On Christmas Day 1877, Cornelian Halford was married to James Copeland, half-brother to Seab Chandler and Molly Chandler McCutcheon. Rev. W. M. Bridges, pastor of the Baptist church, performed the ceremony.

The Copeland children were, Sonora, Marcus, Delena, Ruby, Lottie and Young. Sonora and her husband, William Campbell, spent several years as missionaries in China and Sonora died there. Ruby married Will Lang whose sister, Hattie, was also a missionary to China and, like Sonora, died in China. Ruby and Will's son, Halford Lang, is an eminent Baptist minister in Tennessee.

Miss Cornelia taught the card class in Sunday School and, since all classes assembled in the one room of the church, we could hear her high sweet voice questioning the little ones. "Who was the first man? Who was the oldest man? Who was the meekest man? Who was the wisest man?" and the answering chorus of children's voices, "Adam, Methuselah, Moses, Solomon."

This indenture, made in 1857 between Joshua Daniel, James G. Gaines, L. D. Cole and Wm. H. Black, trustees of the Methodist church, and the said James Gaines and L. D. Cole as trustees of the Sugar Valley Lodge of Knights of Jericho, for divers good causes and considerations, the said Joshua hath given, granted and bequeathed unto the aforesaid trustees, jointly and severally, for church and Lodge privileges, 3 acres of land situate, lying and being in Sugar Valley, under and around the building known as the Methodist church and the Hall of the Knights of Jericho, now jointly owned and used by the church and the Knights. The land is given with the best of motives, neither party to set up exclusive privileges to the exclusion of the other. The deed was signed by Joshua Daniel, L. S., J. H. Harbour and John Malone, J. P. and recorded in March 1857.

The wording of the deed indicates that the building was there and in use, for how long is anyone's conjecture.

The "old" Methodist church is located on the road once known as the Rome and Dalton road, one of the routes used by Civil War armies. Perhaps the church was used as a hospital since the building was left intact. Churches used as barns by the Federal soldiers were left in ruins.

The Conference of 1871 "opened with prair by Mr. Twedell. Nothing doing for the pore. Conference closed." James Frix joined the church by profession of faith.

Names on the church roll of the 1870s are: Fallins, Gober, Groover, Gates, Harris, Hunter, Hardin, Holsomback, Jones, Kanada, Lowery, Lutes, Moore, Morrow, Miller, McCutcheon, McGinnis, Thomblin, Stansbury, Stephens, Staggs, Smith, Scisson, Tate, Wright, Wilson, Woodruff, Ward, Williams and Woodsough.

Infants baptized by the Rev. W. J. Scott in 1871 were William Marion Harris and Marinda Carolyn Jones. The same year, Rev. J. T. Simmons baptized A. B. Bates and Gidean Gober, Males. Rev. J. D. Myric baptized Charles Luther Gober, Wm. M. Moore, Lorenzo Brand and Wm. L. Staggs in 1875.

S. A. Harris was Sunday School superintendent in 1877 and John Gober, assistant.

M. H. Edwards, P. C. (Pastor in charge) in 1880, added a number of infants to the roll on June 19, Charlie Lee Gober and Maude May Gober. The next day, he baptized 14 infants, though some of them must have been well past the infant stage, since there were several in a family. In the Hardin family there were George Pierce, Aler Susan, Thaddews, Clairer, Edger, Thomas and Allas. Clara H. and Samuel B. Williams, Leila and Archie L. Brown and Minnie Iola and William C. Edge were the other family groups.

N. J. Scott was Presiding Elder in 1871 and D. J. Weems, pastor in charge. Stewards were James A. Tweedell, Churchwell Moore, James W. Brown and Samuel A. Harris. Names added to the church roll in the late 1870s were: Mealor, Baugh, Land, Payne, Black, McEntire, Neal, Simpson, Potts, Phillips, Ray, James, Grubb, Edge, Hyde, Shamblin, Blackstock, Eskew and Weems.

The secretary began to list individual contributions in 1874, these sums ranging from 50 cents to $3.00. None of the men gave under $1.00 and the average for women was 50 or 75 cents. Mary Burch gave $2.50 and Olivia Woodruff, $5.00.

On May 6, the conference secretary noted that a Sunday School of 26 scholars had been organized and from time to time the report read "Sunday School did not go into winter quarters."

Elizabeth Coley and L. J. McEntire, females had "gone to the Baptist" in 1878 and 1893, J. B. Freeman and W. F. Harrow did likewise.

Pastors were W. R. Foote, 1871, F. C. Rankin, 1872 and T. J. Simmons, 1873, with R. W. Bigham, P. E. under D. J. Myric. Pastors were, T. J. Simmons in 1875, H. M. Quillian, 1876, James S. Harkins, 1877 and part of 1878. A. W. Thigpen was P. E. in 1878 and P. L. Stauton, Pastor.

The year of 1883 seemed unfruitful. One report read, "from the church, no report, from the preacher, no report, from the class leaders, nothing doing, from the Sunday School, nothing being done, from the Stewards, assessments not made and nothing doing for the poor." But mission duties were done and literature partially read.

Can the church establish additional prayer meetings and a Church at Sugar Valley, promise to do all in our power to advance the cause of Christ in our midst."

Charges were brought against four of the brethren for drinking and two sisters for dancing and a case made against, Bro. James Stansbury for playing the fiddle in the Ball Room. He confessed his wrongs, said that he wanted to live a better life and asked the church to bear with him. Misses Mamie and Eugenia Edge and Liza Thomason were brought before the church for going to parties.

Pastors from 1880 to 1895 were: H. M. Edwards, Wm. W. Sampler, T. J. Simmons, E. T. Hendrix, J. F. Tyson, H. Murdow, A. Lester, A. H. S. Bugg. M. H. Parks and Thos. F. Pierce were Presiding Elders. Names added to the roll during these years were: Claridy, Crumbley, Everett, Ellis, Gwinn, Joyce, Harbour, Morgan, Roe, Jemmison, Brookshear, Hayard, Gurr, Whittle, Garner. Camil, Passley, Shugart, Damewood, Flemister, Graham, Weaver, Hollingsworth, Johnson, Malone, Davis, Freeman, Austin, Medcalf, Harrell, Carter, Floyd, Neighbors, Dunn, Lawrence, Cooley, Richards and Davidson.

1894 class leaders, Bro. Malone, Harris, Edge and Tweedell, had been inactive. The Sunday School reported favorably but the leaders felt that more good could be done if the parents would accompany their children. The non-attendance of the members at Saturday meetings was to be regretted.

The Sunday School was active in 1895 and the church assessment was $85.00. Some were careless about paying but others did the best they could. There was no Epworth League and the church was not doing her duty for missions. The weather was bad, so Pastor Bugg couldn't visit but he spent his time studying.

Throughout the years, the Methodist church has kept aloft the standard for Christian living. Sunday Services, protracted meetings and Sunday afternoon singings have been shared with all the people of Sugar Valley. The Methodist Young people were active in the Baptist Young Peoples Union, when there was no Epworth League.

In the 1920s, a plan to move the church to the Station was offered but met with vigorous opposition from some of the members. The result was that a new Methodist church was organized in 1928 and a building of native stone erected in the Village. W. F. Walden was pastor in 1928 and Rev. Charles Driggers is the pastor in 1960. Recently a handsome district parsonage has been built on the lot adjoining the church. The pastor serves both old and new churches at Sugar Valley and the church at Resaca.

In the year of 1831, John Baugh had chosen for his home, that part of the Valley near the little mountain that today perpetuates his name and around the section there grew up the Methodist settlement. With the help of the Indians, he cleared his land and built a one room log cabin with a dirt floor and a loft bedroom. His bride came with him and they brought handsome mahogany furniture from England. When Mr. Baugh erected the house that stands today, the log house was used as a kitchen.

Then came the day of tragedy for the Baugh family when the wife and daughter found John Baugh's body at the foot of a pit on the farm. He had been working at the edge of the quarry and the fall into the quarry had broken his neck. His tools were lying on the ground near by.

Jack Abbott, of Sugar Valley and William C. Mitchell, of Alabama, were having dinner together one day in a Tennessee town. William was describing the girl he would like his wife to be. Jack said "I know her."

How the meeting was arranged is not known. Perhaps William come home with Jack for a weekend and was introduced to Miss Mattie Hyde, a neighbor of the Baugh family. And so William Mitchell and Mattie Hyde were married.

They purchased the Baugh farm from Mr. Miller, who had owned the place for a year or two, and remodeled the house in 1904. Of the three owners, two were foreigners, John Baugh from England and William Mitchell whose father, a wholesale furrier had come from Germany.

Mattie Mitchell's parents, Mr. and Mrs. Lewis Hyde, on the hill south of the Baughs. In 1899, Maggie McWhorter, of Calhoun, began a movement to establish a Methodist college for girls on the hill. She and Mrs. Hyde went before the Conference in the interest of the proposed school. The college was never built but for years afterward the hill was called College Hill.

The Baugh Mountain Community School was built on the hill about 1907. After the school was discontinued, the Mitchells purchased the property and converted the building into a summer home. The original house burned and a second one erected on the site has been remodeled by William and Mattie Mitchell's daughter, Wilma, and her husband, Roy Hutchinson. This little gray home on the hill is charming and comfortable, with all modern conveniences.

During the year that Wilma taught school at Baugh Mountain, she held a box supper to raise money for painting the School building. She went away to School and the trustees used the money to dig a well on the School grounds. It is this well that is today providing water for Wilma and Roy's house.

Wilma Mitchell was the first Sugar Valley girl to be graduated from the University of Georgia. She attended the Dickey school at Sugar Valley and Rhinehart College, before going to the University. Sheila Russell, also a resident of the Baugh Mountain Community, is another University of Georgia graduate.

Wilma's husband, the Rev. Roy Hutchinson, whom she met at Rhinehart, is a retired Methodist minister. He served in the pastorate for several years in Oklahoma and was with the General Board of Missions in New York in the office of Superintendent of Missions. From 1946 until 1952, he supervised the establishment of churches on an average of two a day in this country, in Alaska, in Puerto Rico and in other countries.

Old friends, of the Mitchell and Hyde families are happy to have Rev. and Mrs. Hutchinson return to Sugar Valley to live, and Gordon County is fortunate in having them as citizens.

Rev. and Mrs. Hutchinson have two sons. Miles, of Sugar Valley and Jim, of Pittsburg, Penn.

Decendants of the Charter members of the old Methodist Church and of the Knights of Jericho have brought fame to the old names throughout the State and Nation. Ethel Gwin Blackstock's son is a brilliant lawyer and active in church work. Marshall Tippen's son, Ed, who is a grandson of Alec Jones, owns a furniture store in Lafayette. Effie Groover Lemmon's son planned and served the meals for the "Gone with the Wind" premiere. Clyde Austin, who became a vice president of the Southern Railway held his first job with the railroad as lamp lighter at the Sugar Valley Depot. Julius Montgomery designed about 95% of the first bedspreads made in the Valley. Mindell Damewood became a trust officer in the Hamilton National Bank in Chattanooga. Eugenia Edge's husband was a Bank president. Sue Gwinn Sutherland owns an exclusive dress and hat shop at Buckhead near Atlanta.

There are many other sons and daughters of old Snake Creek district, settled by John Baugh, the Malones, Chandlers, Davises, Millers, Higginbothams and Harbours, who have added lustre to the names of their ancestors wherever they have gone.

Now, go back a short distance from Wilma and Roy's house, cross Baugh Creek bridge and turn to the right, we will visit the Dickey and Cooley places before we return to the paved road.

Here on the right is the Dickey house, two storied in big square rooms with a right-angled downstairs veranda. The Schoolhouse was across the railroad on a little hill and the family cemetery is somewhere nearby.

William Franklin Dickey, born Oct. 2, 1849, in Orion, Ala., was the son of James Willis and Burgess Dickey. He chose the profession of teaching and began his life's work in the Schools of Montgomery, Alabama in the 1870s. After coming to Georgia he was principal of schools at Silver Creek, Calhoun and Rome. His first private school was located across the road from his home on "Smoky Row" in the village of Sugar Valley. By 1891, he had enrolled 100 pupils and his school had become widely known and patronized by men and women from many sections of Georgia.

His daughter-in-law, Ethel Abbott Dickey, told me that Professor Dickey considered Viola Wright and Cora Abbott, my mother, the two smartest pupils he had ever taught.

Professor Dickey later bought the farm south of Sugar Valley and moved his school there. After his death, a daughter. May Yon Dickey, graduate of old GNIC at Milledgeville, conducted the School.

W. F. Dickey was married in 1872, to Miss Huldah Yon, daughter of Jesse and Sarah Curry Yon, of Montgomery, Alabama. Each of the Dickey children was given Yon as a middle name — Carl Y. (died 1894), Talmadge Y., Virgil Y., Milton Y. (died in 1901), Clara Y. (died 1881), Burgess Y., Ralph Y., May Y., Blanche Y., Frank Y., Hyrtis Y. (died 1901), Curry Y. and Herbert Yon.

W. F. Dickey opened a mercantile business in one of the first little wooden store buildings in the Village. The firm, known as W. F. Dickey and Sons, was headquarters for shipments during the time that Sugar Valley was the main shipping point for huckleberries. It was in this prosperous period that the two-story building was erected. It is used today as part of a chenille plant.

Following the precedent of the father and grandfather, the Dickey children and grand-children have served with distinction in the fields of education and business. Burgess Y. Dickey represented Gordon County in the State Legislature for the terms of 1925-36, 1927-28 and 1933. He was listed in Who's Who for his courageous stand on a controversial matter.

The Dickey place is now owned by Dr. G. C. Kirkley, of Calhoun.

The Cooley family, long associated with the history of Sugar Valley, are lineal descendants of a Sister of Alfred Shorter, founder of Shorter College at Rome. Devout in their religious life they have contributed much to the work of the church in music and in other fields of service. Alfred and Lee were the Cooley sons who chose to remain in the home community of their parents but their children, like so many of the Valley's ambitious young people, left home to seek employment and establish homes in towns and cities. Twice each year they with other former residents return for reunions, at the Baptist church in May and at the Methodist church in August, to renew friendships and strengthen old ties.

Cross the Southern Railroad and you are not far from Lay's ferry, Scene of a Civil War battle and first crossing place of the Oostanaula river for Snake Creek settlers. The big old house there is the Henry Dobson home. It was owned by the Tanners during the war and was used as a hospital by the army. A blood spot on the floor was scrubbed repeatedly by the Dobson girls but could never be removed. The floor has recently been painted.

"Going, Going, Gone" intoned the auctioneer at the land sale in Calhoun.

"Who is that feller?" The question was tossed from one to another as a be-whiskered man in home-spun jeans walked up and flung a little grip on the auctioneer's stand.

The Tanner farm and one at Oostanaula had just been knocked off to S. W. Dobson, the man in the butternut pants. The little black bag held the money to pay for the newly acquired lands.

"I don't want all the land in Gordon County," S. W. Dobson

often said, "just what joins me."

Since the Tanner house originally stood in the field near the river and Lays ferry, it must have been the Lay home before 1860. Mr. Dobson had the house moved to it's present site. The work was done by Mr. Treadaway, (father of Mrs. John I. Boston and Mrs. Boaz Legg) using log rollers pulled by a yoke of oxen.

S. W. Dobson's father had owned many slaves but the son had only one, for whom he paid $600.

The Baptist church at Sugar Valley received the letters of Bro. S. W.. Dobson and wife in June of 1887, from Fellowship Baptist Church in Walker County. He had given the land on which the Fellowship Church in Walker was built.

S. W. Dobson left property to each of his thirteen children. Henry, the second son, traded his farm adjoining the Tracey place, to Fannie Dobson Tracey for her share in the father's place and here he and his bride, Jessie Roe, daughter of Sam Roe, established their home. Their children were Jewell, Ruby, Goldie, Henry Roe and Sammy Joe.

H. L. Dobson was elected church treasurer in 1922 and held the office for 8 or 10 years. He was always one of the delegates to the association meeting and in 1924, Mrs. H. L. Dobson was elected to represent the church at the Association, the first woman so honored.

When the church was remodeled in 1948, Mrs. Dobson and the children gave a memorial window, dedicated to H. L. Dobson. Later the family's gift to the church was a grand piano. handsome pulpit furniture and, as a birthday honor to their mother, the children installed a set of chimes, with beautiful console in blond wood. As the musical claps of Jesse Miller's cowbell once tinkled over the restful silence of the Valley, the chimes now lift their tones above the noise of motors and wheels and send the beautiful strains of Sweet Hour of Prayer singing through the air, even to the mountain.

S. J. Dobson, youngest son of H. L. and Jessie, and his wife, the former Ora Dell Gentry, have built a handsome brick house facing the Calhoun-Lafayette road and only a few rods from the ancestral home.

The house, with it's white columns, green blinds and colonial entrance, beckons you to swish your hoop skirts through the fan-lighted door way and dance a minuet in the parlor or lean against a column on a moon-light night and pretend you are Scarlet, flirting with the Tarleton twins while longing for your own true love who may be somewhere making love to Malanie.

Across the road is the John Bruce house, in contemporary style, long and low, with a floor-length window that invites you to crunch over the curving driveway in your late model convertible and join the family in a cook-out on the patio.

Nearer the village is the modern brick home of Mr. and Mrs. Billy Muse with it's unusually attractive and convenient interior.

Since our visit to the Russell Hill section, Sadie Lucinda James has completed her artistic house. Standing on a little round hill, the barn-red house overlooks the Harrises lovely lake and the view extends across the Valley to John's Mountain on the West. In her travels about the country as an official Red Cross, Sadie has collected many interesting pieces of furniture, among them a Jeff

Davis sofa, re-upholstered in Aubousson tapestry with small flower design outlined in gold thread and a corner china cabinet from Virginia. The painting over the mantel, she found in Paris. A chair, upholstered in antique green velvet, is a family heirloom as is a small foot stool covered in needle-point done by her mother, Harriet Stansbury James. The den is finished in mahogany with exposed chimney of 100 year old brick, purchased from the builder, Jud Nelson. The kitchen, all in yellow, sports a frieze of small roosters cock-a-doodling across the narrow strip of paper. Six red chinese goblets glow rosily from the top of the window. A carport, patio and extra bath room extend across the north side of the house.

Before we leave The Valley, we must talk about our good negro friends. The Claridys, (Uncle Henry said his name was really Knight, but the Claridys came in and took over.) Henry and Jane, Henry's son Jeff and his wife Ella, the Boaz negroes, who came with Meshach Boaz, the Malones, with D. R. and John and the Millers, with Jesse Miller.

I asked Edgar Miller about Lummus Little, whose wife was Anne Boaz. "Oh, he just drifted in from South Georgia," was the reply. Fortunate for Sugar Valley was the day that Lummus Little drifted in for he was the only man, white or black, who would clean out our deep, cold wells of water, and he it was, who received the Carnegie medal and $1000 for risking his life in the effort to save 3 white men from a gas-filled well at Fairview. Will Hall lost his life while attempting to rescue and today, Hall Memorial Baptist Church commemorates his sacrifice.

On the Fairview road, near The Valley, is the old George Harris home. Mrs. Harris was Henerietta Miller. A large family of Harris boys and girls were popular members of the younger generation in the early 1900s. Mr. Harris loved music and was prominent in the Gordon County Singing Convention.

"Lovely Voices of the Sky" he sang and the pure tenor tunes floated through the vaulted Sanctuary. As my son sang I seemed to hear again the voice of my father singing in the little white church back home. Are ye not singing still on high, lovely voices of The Valley, singing of Hope and Joy and Faith? It is to hear you that we come again in the spring of every year. It is to listen once more to your voices as they whisper from the walls and sing in the blessed sanctuaries of the two loved old churches.

As I left The Valley on a late afternoon, a big moon, low in the sky, rode along with me. Suddenly a wisp of cloud drifted across the face of the silver sphere, as if in sympathy with the mist that filmed my eyes and the veil that wrapped around my heart.

But we shall return, the moon and I, if but for a night, or a day or an hour and sip again the sweetness from the beautiful land of the Chandlers and Malones, the Harbours and the Millers and of John Baugh who came from England to find the sweetest Valley in the world.

OOTHCALOGA DISTRICT, NUMBER 856

Commencing at the west corner of lot No. 98, in the 15th district, 3rd section, thence due north to the east corner of lot No. 299 in the 7th district, 3rd section, thence due south to the southeastern corner of lot No. 40 in the 6th district, 3rd section, thence due west to the west corner of lot No. 98 — just so were the lines drawn on a day in May, 1850 by the Justice of the Inferior Court.

Oothcaloga creek watered the land and Oothcaloga Indian Mission was located in the district, so No. 856 became Oothcaloga, a name derived from the Cherokee word, Ougillogy. The precinct was to be at H. S. Gardner's house.

The first road commissioners from the district were David Morrow, J. P., Uriah Phillips and George Stewart. During the next four years, Matthew Thompson, Thos. B. Shockley, Robert H. Saxon. H. S. Gardner, Henry Cooper, Esq., J. H. Bailey and James Rogers served as commissioners for the district roads.

Oothcaloga was really three districts, Lily Pond, McHenry and Blackwood.

To go to Blackwood, you take this road, U.S. 53, running east to Fairmount, past the church and the spring where once stood the home of an Indian Chief named Blackwood. But some say he was a white man married to an Indian maid. Their house stood on the hill across the road from the Blackwood Springs Baptist Church of today.

Lulie Pitt's history gives the date of the organization of Blackwood Springs Baptist Church as 1872. In the great county-wide revival of 1875, Rev. Tatum and Blanton conducted the meeting at Blackwood and 40 converts were baptized at the close of the services. The revival then moved to Buford's church near McDaniel Station.

I found the church doors open on the day I paid a visit to the community. It was revival week and the wide open doors were a mute invitation to enter here all ye who seek salvation of the soul and peace of mind. I walked through the rooms and stood in the sanctuary, silent you would think but, for me, filled with the echoes of my father's voice as he preached from the book he knew best, the Bible. (W. B. Bridges, pastor of the church for many years.)

A tabernacle once stood to the left of the church as you enter the grounds and here August revivals and summer all day singings took place. The tabernacle is gone now and the church has kept pace with progress by adding Sunday School rooms, gas heat and electric lights, though the handsome swinging kerosene lamp still hangs above the pulpit. The class rooms are furnished with comfortable chairs and lecterns and attractive draperies hang at the windows.

In the sanctuary, there are rugs on the pulpit and altar floors, an excellent piano and new hymnals. The report board showed that the Sunday School has 150 on roll with an attendance of 124 and 125 for the two Sundays reported. An active BTU reported 73 on roll and an attendance of 40 and 35.

The building is of frame structure with stone foundation. You enter the double doors of the church from a rock framed portico with 2 sets of steps. Huge oaks, hickories and pines shade the rear grounds and the spring branch murmurs cheerfully at the foot of the bluff. One can visualize the natural beauty of the spot that the Blackwood family called home over a hundred years ago. Today a paved road passes the church that has, since 1872, served the religious needs of citizens of the Blackwood community.

The cemetery adjoining the church was begun in the 20th century. Names and dates of older residents of the section include: J. R. Waldrip 1871-1934, Lela Goode Waldrip 1870-1921, W. P. Moore 1878-1929, Mary Jane Fouts 1852-1908, Pearl Bell Fouts 1886-1899.

James Fouts 185?-1942, Murphy Stone 1862-1947, Mattie Stone 1869-1943, John J. Ferguson 1861-1934, Dora Curtis Ferguson 1868-1953, John M. Wright 1849-1933, Sudie Putman Wright 1862-1935, G. V. Cooper 1879-1933, Phalba Cooper 1874-1955, Sallie Reece 1882-1938, Debie B. Young 1887-1951, A. J. McEntire 1861-1925, Julia McEntire 1858-1936, Walter M. Payne 1862-1932, Ellen R. Payne 1862-1932, Rev. C. D. Shaw 1873-1957, Martha Worley Shaw 1873-1947, Johnnie Bryant Rockester 1867-1927, J. V. Bryant 1853-1921, Alice Bryant 1861-1937, Susan Anderson 1842-1927, Lela Anderson 1887-1948, Tennessee Anderson 1857-1925, Moses Anderson 1887-1948, Maude Munsey 1854-1922, F. M. Munsey born 1857, M. S. Caldwell 1858-1925, D. W. Caldwell 1857-1939, Gertrude Moore Caldwell 1886-1927, G. W. Caldwell 1882- Arthur J. Barrett 1884-1906, Callie McDonald Barrett 1844-1938, David Barrett 1830-, Myrtle Barrett 1883-1952, Martha J. Bearden 1883-1955, Mary Fox Adcox 1888-1936, Rosa E. Wife of J. C. Fox, died 1889, age 30 years 1 mo., Mary M. Scott 1835-1912, Willard A. Wyatt 1886-1936, William White 1886-1937, J. J. Finger 1875-1934, Dr. Samuel Melvin Harpe 1862-1935, Ida A. Harpe 1869-1939, H. C. Holtzclaw 1875-1940, Lizzie B. Holtzclaw 1878-1919, M. F. Patterson 1879-1938, Etts Patterson 1881-1959, James Edgar Woodall 1871-1945, Esther Murphy Woodall 1877-1940, Mary Ada Payne 1877-1939, L. Frank Payne 1878-1951, Lon Ferguson 1866-1942, Florence Ferguson 1869-1933, Thomas C. Lipscomb 1861-, Mary Lipscomb 1871-1939, Laura Chadwick 1867-1933, J. S. Chadwick 1867-1933, Albert S. J. Brownlowe Co. G. 3rd Tenn. Sp. Amer. War, T. J. Stephens 1864-1923, Sulu Stephens 1867-, W. G. B. Duncan 1843-1917, Mega Duncan 1841-1923, Charles Gulledge 1858-1942, Cansada Gulledge 1860-1942, John Roland Bigham 1862-1944, Lillie Curtiss Bigham 1868-1949, Rev. J. A. McArthur 1875-1945, Cordelia McArthur 1880-, Sam Owen 1875-1957, Flora Abbott Owen 1880-1958. A number of War Veterans are buried in the Blackwood cemetery.

Katherine Barrett was in a fret this morning. She had gone out to feed the peafowls and her pet peacock had flown up in a tree and wouldn't come down. She had coaxed and called and even resorted to tossing a stick at the bird but the lordly fowl merely shifted to another limb and gave her a stony stare from one eye and then the other, at the same time emitting his unmusical cry.

"Stay there then, you naughty bird" cried Miss Kate, stamping her foot, "I don't care if you starve!"

"What's the trouble, Miss Katherine?" a voice spoke from the edge of the yard.

Startled, Katherine Barrett whirled to see Lewis Gaines standing beside his horse a few feet away. So engrossed had she been in her efforts to induce the peacock to fly down that she had not heard the horse's hoof-beats.

"O, good morning Lewis" she spoke confusedly, "I am so exasperated with this silly bird that I am half-mind to send him to the Zoo!"

"Do hitch your horse and come in" Miss Kate invited, recovering her composure.

"They are capricious creatures," Lewis said as he tied the bridle reins to the hitchery post. "We have peafowls too and sometimes they can be exasperating."

"But when he spreads his fan of gorgeous feathers," remarked

Katherine, "you can forgive him most anything."

"Indeed you can," replied Lewis. "Do you know that in the middle ages the flesh of the peafowl was eaten? The bird was carried to the table in all his plumage."

Lewis Gaines had ridden from his home a few miles down the road with the express idea that Katherine Barrett might be just where he found her. More and more often he rode the short distance to call on sweet Kate and soon they were married.

Katherine and Lewis became the parents of Bessie, who married Joe M. Lang and, today lives in her mother's girl-hood home.

A huge magnolia tree grows almost to the front steps and spreads its ancient branches over the yard and leans them tiredly on the porch roof. Mrs. Lang said that she climbed the tree often when she came as a child to visit her grandfather.

When David Barrett bought the farm, long before there was a Gordon County, he rode a mule to South Carolina to see the owner. Through the years, he kept adding land until the Barretts owned hundreds of acres.

Someone told me "Mrs. Lang has an old house." So I went to see Mrs. Lang. She mentioned her grandfather, David Barrett.

"Do you mean that this is David Barrett's house!" I squeled, "am I standing in David Barrett's house?"

David Barrett, whose name heads the list of Justices of the Inferior Court that planned Gordon County and signed the deeds for lots in Calhoun — it was his house. He must have presided over the election of 1852, when the Dawsonville crowd won and the name of the settlement was changed to Calhoun, capital of Gordon County.

It is a lovely place, situated in the curve where two roads meet, one leading to Adairsville and the other to the old Dixie Highway, joining this road at the old Ferguson place. The dreaming silence of the countryside is broken only by the sound of a passing automobile or the dissonant call of a peafowl. To Bessie Gaines Lang, daughter of Katherine Barrett & Lewis Gaines, the place would not seem right without peafowls. And she has them, 20 or more. They roost on the chimneys and knock the bricks off. The cocks strow their argus-eyed feathers over the lawn and fields.

Mrs. Lang receives requests for the feathers from faraway places.

The spots on the tail feathers of the cock, you know, are supposed to be the eyes of Argus. Juno, jealous of Jupiter, gave Argus a thousand eyes and set him to watch her philandering husband. When she was through with Argus, she set his eyes in the feathers of her favorite bird.

Mrs. David Barrett had a fly fan of peacock feathers over her dining table and a little darky to pull the string and keep it moving.

The peafowl hens are drab during the nesting period, but the gorgeous male lifts his small crested head, opens his iridescent feather fan, resplendent with all the jewel colors of Pharaoh's tomb and splits the air with his raucous cry, so out of tune with the perfect harmony of his colors. Golden pheasants and a beautiful silver one mingle with the peafowl under the old oaks and slip beneath the weeping spruce near the house.

The Barrett house has a steep roof with 1 end window upstairs and 2, evenly spaced, downstairs. Verandas need replacing every

so often and, more than likely several have been built throughout
the hundred of the house's existence years. The one there now is
wide with a car port at one end and a low wall at the front edge.
The front door has small-panel glass panels overhead and on each
side. There are 8 rooms in the main house, 6 on the first floor and
2 on the second. A covered passage at the back connects the kitchen
and dining room to the house. A roofed walkway leads away from
the kitchen door to the well. Inside doors are made of 2 long upper
panels and 2 shorter ones in the lower section. The mantels are
all straight line and made of wood.

A long table in the hall is piled with sea shells, coral and other
bits of ocean life. Gaines Lang, son of Col. and Mrs. J. M. Lang, had
made a study of marine life and most of the shells, he had collected.
There is a box of whelk eggs. Gaines had found the Whelk de-
positing the long string of eggs on the sand.

Another son, Sewell, made 3 trips around the world while
traveling for a New York City Bank. Among the interesting articles
he collected on these tours are: an elaborately carved camphor wood
chest from India, a darling little gold-trimmed lacquer table, figurines from Bali, a teakwood table, lustreware and Buddhas of 2
sizes. The Buddhas sit on the mantel and bookcase, immovable and
everlasting as the ages. A peacock feather screen covers the fireplace
opening.

Mrs. Lang once had 7 acres in flowers and shrubs but ill health
forced her to give up her beloved garden and now, she says, it is
dangerous to walk through the overgrown plot. A rattlesnake was
killed in the road in front of the house not long before we were
out there.

David Barrett's house had been out of the family for many
years. Once again it is in the hands of his descendants and, in
fancy, I can see him riding over his acres, noting the changes that
the years have brought and casting a spell of tender protection
over the loved old house while Katherine flits among the trees and
shoos the fowls down for the evening meal.

Mrs. Lang's son, Dr. Lewis R. Lang, lives there with her and
the only daughter, Mary Kate, comes up for weekend visits.

From Mrs. Lang's, follow a narrow dirt road to the old Dixie
Highway and turn to the right by the former Ferguson place, now
the home of Mr. and Mrs. J. E. Scoggins. Suddenly you are there—
at the Oothcaloga Mission house, on your left. A bronze marker,
placed by the Georgia Historical Commission, records that the mission was built in 1821 by Joseph Crutchfield and used as a school
for Indian girls from 1822 to 1830.

John Gambol, born in New York, June 16, 1760, was sent by
the Moravians to the Spring Place Mission and then to Oothcaloga.
George Proske was sent from the Mission at Salem, N. C. to be
assistant. He left in 1825 and John's niece, Miss Polly Gambol,
came to help. Mr. and Mrs. Henry Clayton were sent from Salem
to assist in farm and house-hold work at the Mission.

The venerable house still sits on the log sills laid there in 1827.
The wall logs, some of them 2 feet wide, and badly riddled with
Civil War grape shot, have been covered with weather boarding.
The inside is walled and ceiled with planks, no two the same width.
At first there was no partition in the long front room with its huge
fire-place and one can easily imagine the rows of benches and

black-haired Indian girls busy with their studies in the light of a wood fire. Did Patsy, the Chief's little daughter, have a special corner reserved for her?

Patsy had as her companions the Adair girls, the daughters of Elijah Hix and of Collins McDaniel, of Major Ridge and the Oowatie girls. The Missionaries lived up-stairs and climbed an outside stairway to reach their rooms. For a long time now the stairway has gone up from the kitchen.

The Mission is today the property of Mrs. S. Z. Moore and Mr. and Mrs. Baldwin live in the house.

John Gambold died at Oothcaloga Mission, Nov. 27, 1827. His grave is in the little cemetery on top of the hill, across the road from the house. Other graves are: C. D. Stephens 1817-1874, Carline Stephens 1835-1919, Missouri Ferguson 1812-1913, her daughter, Jessie Lee, aged 1 year, Clarence Stevens 1891-1897, Laura Morrow 1868-1928, and 6 Morrow children ranging in age from a few months to 2 years. What happened to take the lives of these 6 little children? Diphtheria? Typhoid? Or was it that then unknown thing, the incompatible RH factor?

Let's go up in the Look room where we can see all of the Rogers acres. The brickyard out there, the first one in the south, is a busy place, making brick for Gordon County chimneys and for a few houses, Claiborne Kinman's perhaps, or the original part of the Dr. Johnston house on South Wall Street, the one across the street or the Sam Pulliam house on Piedmont Street in Calhoun. There was a brick house next to the Baptist church, owned by Jeffie Fain, one on Trammell Street near the corner of Piedmont and the old Franklin home that stood on the site of the Harlan-Bond house was brick.

B. R. Rogers says that if you're a mind to dig, you can still find brick bats at the site of the old tile and brickyard. The Rogers made ice, too, in the summer time. Indians used a small area on the place for making arrow heads but only small chips were found.

The Leggs borrowed Col. Rogers' brick machine to make their first brick.

James Rogers, born in 1806 of Irish lineage, came to Gordon County in the year 1853, from Sweetwater Creek, where the family ran a cloth factory. They also owned Silver Springs and Homasassa Springs in Florida. Mr. Rogers built the 2 room log house that was not changed until 1900.

Col. Rogers had served as quartermaster in the Seminole Indian War of 1835-1842 and held the same position during the Civil War.

His wife, Antoinette Fleming Rogers, was a belle of New York and owned much fine jewelry. When war came to Gordon County, she and her 2 sons, Newton and Thomas, left their home. As they fled, they could see the Federals on one hill and the Confederates on another.

Newton Rogers moved to Florida when a young man but Thomas stayed on the old place located in the western part of Oothcaloga district, just off US 41 about 5 miles south of Calhoun. The house burned in 1939.

Thomas Rogers learned his math at Fitten School near Adairsville and was graduated from the University of Kentucky. He grew everything that could be grown, on his farm and had a motto made of 100 varieties of seeds, but always hung in the hall of his house.

The motto was displayed in his exhibit at the County Fair each year.

B. R. Rogers, son of Thomas and Josie Bray Rogers, lives in a new brick house on the Blackwood road. He is married to the former Pauline Robertson, of Pine Chapel, and their children are Harold, Julius and Lois (Mrs. S. B. Adamson). Other children of Thomas and Antoinette Rogers were: Antoinette, James N., William N., Thomas D., B. F., Minnie Lillian, Fleming Harold and Stanton J.

Col. James Rogers died in 1893 and Thomas in 1919.

* * * * *

One day in 1960, I stood in the kitchen of the old McDaniel house with Mrs. Payne, her daughter, Mrs. Smith and Mrs. Smith's little girls, Susan and Sheila. Big north windows lighted the pleasant room that was, like any kitchen of today, equipped with all the conveniences.

Suddenly, I found my arms folded rigidly across my chest as I exclaimed "there are ghosts in this house!"

And there were ghosts in the house, though only in my imagination—ghosts of blue-clad soldiers pouring through the front door, crowding into the back hall, issuing a command to the McDaniel slaves, "cook supper for us!"—ghosts of the frightened negroes preparing the meal in the kitchen out back and serving the officers in the dining room.

"Maybe they slept in the attic," Mrs. Payne said and I looked for soldiers on the stair steps coming down to breakfast.

I could see Yankee horses grazing in McDaniel wheat fields and tramping down the corn stalks, and could visualize camp fires of the foot soldiers flickering in the night.

The McDaniel family had refugeed, leaving the slaves in charge of the house, for, after all, had not the men from the north come to free the negroes?

No one remembers when it was done, but everyone will tell you that part of the once 20 room house was moved a little to the north and converted into another dwelling. This house is now the home of Mr. and Mrs. Weldon Burns.

A hundred years ago, a porch extended across the front of the mansion with the colonade formed in pairs, 2 columns mounted on a square base and elaborate grill work at the top. (The roof of the porch was blown away 2 or 3 years ago and the smoke house destroyed in the same storm.) A walk, bordered on each side with boxwood, led down the hill to the front gate and two other boxwood walks stretched catty-cornered each way, one to a garden on the north and the other to the big gates on the south. A picket fence enclosed the entire front lawn.

A row of cedars screened the flower garden and the south lawn from the back fields and the Service yard.

There were fig trees and grape vines and shrubs of all kinds. A climbing rose covered the well shelter and monthly roses bloomed in the flower beds — Marchal Neil, Maman Cochet, the red Velvet rose and Seven Sisters. There were slaves to tend the place and it must have been a garden of Eden.

Mrs. Payne sold the immense boxwoods a few years ago and only a few small ones remain. Several of the Virgin oaks and elms shade the venerable house and some of the cedars still keep a vigil over sweet memories of the golden days.

From the legendary twenty, five rooms are left, really six. counting the small store room behind the kitchen. The hall that divides the house is wide and long enough for two rooms — Mrs. Smith said that she could use two more rooms — and the front door could belong to a medieval castle, so broad and tall it is. The house is pegged together and the windows are so big that special sashes must be made for them. All the rooms and the hall are walled and ceiled with hand-smoothed six inch planks.

The tiles go all the way to the bottom of the well on the back porch. Water is piped from the well to the house now. How long did it take to draw a bucket of water from such a deep well?

Mr. and Mrs. Payne bought the place from Dr. Curtiss.

P. E. McDaniel was a member of the Fulton County Minute Men but was past the age for active service. Perhaps he did get in on the last fighting along with Uncle Henry Hamilton and Ashley Wilkes' father.

After the War, Mr. McDaniel built a corn mill on Oothcaloga Creek and moved his family to the plantation. After his death, Mr. Fields ran the mill. Willalou Nelson remembers Mr. Fields as a very happy man, with his clothes always white with meal.—

A jolly miller on the River Dee
He worked and sung from morn 'til night.

The W and A railroad constructed a depot on the estate and P. E. McDaniel was agent until 1877. The station was an active shipping point for peaches during the period when peach orchards were big business in Gordon County.

Handsome uniformed conductors were always the objects of admiration for young girls waiting at the station to see the train go by. Since her father was agent, Fannie McDaniel had a good reason for being at the depot. Madame Grundy had long ago decreed that no decent girl would ever wave at a trainman.

Conductor R. L. McWhorter needed no waving hand to beckon his attention to Fannie McDaniel, her natural grace and dignity were the charms that drew him to McDaniel Station often during his off hours. They were married and Mr. McDaniel built a house for them near the Station.

R. L. McWhorter became the station agent after his father-in-law's retirement. He served in this capacity for 50 years and was succeeded by P. E. McDaniel's great-granddaughter, Mell Cameron Nelson.

The house that Phillip McDaniel built for his daughter and her husband is now owned by Mr. and Mrs. John I. Boston.

Down the hill a short distance from Fannie's girlhood home and across the road, it is a charming old place. Pairs of posts on a carved base support the roof of a narrow porch across the front and the south end of the house. The Colonial doorway has side panels of 3 colored panes each, one purple, one red and one of white crinkled glass.

In those days, virgin timber was there for the taking and this house, like many others, is floored, ceiled and walled in heart planks, hand planed. Mr. and Mrs. Boston have laid hardwood floors in two rooms.

A huge clothes press stands in Fannie's old parlor with its iron mantel painted white. The press was made by John I., Jr., whose hands are deft in fashioning things of wood and artistic with pencil, brush and easel.

Fannie McWhorter's party for her daughter, Lola, in 1892 was the first to have the gowns worn by the young ladies described by The Calhoun Times reporter.

For the party, Lillie Armstrong was elegantly attired in cream albatross with a blue sash. Aurie Garlington wore an exquisite gown of cream which brought out her beauty to great advantage. Miss Kate Royster was lovely in white wool combined with silk and cord. The lamplight fell gently on pink silk with ribbons and laces and touched lightly on fair cheeks flushed with youth and joy as these young girls of the gay nineties laughed and talked with their handsome young men.

The Kinman house at McDaniel Station, built in 1900, is now the house of the Thurman Bennetts. Weldon Burns' house was once the home of Harry and Abbie Kinman McDaniel.

On the road to Calhoun is the old Terrell house built by Mr. Love. Mr. Kinman bought the place from Mr. Terrell in 1911. Lillie Kinman married Warren Burns and their son, C. L., lives in the old Kinman home with his wife, the former Ruth Holloran and their small son.

C. L. and Ruth are planning to lower the fourteen-foot ceilings of the rooms that still have the original wall, overhead and floor boards.

Much of Mrs. Kinman's furniture remains in the house (she was Rhoda Payne, from Tennessee). Among the interesting pieces are a sofa of unusual design, a hall tree with mirror and seat, a very large built-in quilt chest in the hall and the dining room furniture, a buffet, a side board and dining table with round fluted legs. The corner china cabinet, built in, has a long oval pane of glass in each of the two doors. C. L. has fashioned several handsome pieces of furniture and refinished one floor to a satin gloss.

Several years ago, John North discovered a process of making glass from sand.

"It can't be done," someone said.

Mr. North simply put two electric welders in the sand and made glass there before the eyes of the doubters. Today. buildings of gleaming aluminum stand beside the railroad and here the Glasrock Products, Inc., makes glass for foundry needs. The glass is made, then ground into flour.

C. L. Burns is one of the cooks at the plant. He could not find words that would give my non-technical mind an understanding of the glass-making process so you must talk with him to find out what he "cooks."

Modern homes now line the paved road to Calhoun. The North Georgia Agricultural Experiment Station is located on the McDaniel road at the junction with the Rome road. It is here among new buildings and improved old buildings, located on land that was owned by Jim Lay in 1830, that the State works, through the personnel of the Experiment Station, to keep Georgia farms producing better products for the future. Dean Hayes is the superintendent. He and Mrs. Hayes, a young son, Jack, and a nephew, Eddie Smith, live in the white-columned, remodeled farm house across the road.

Where did the pioneers of Lily Pond and McHenry attend church? Bethlehem organized in 1837, Liberty Presbyterian and

Unity over in Springtown Valley, where not too far away or maybe they went to Calhoun. Riding five or six miles to church, often horseback, was nothing to these sturdy men and women. Their day was from sunrise to sunset, from dawn to dark.

However, as they began to recover from the effects of the War, they felt the need of a church in their own community. P. E. McDaniel gave three acres of land one mile south of the Station and, in 1870, Salem church was organized with thirteen members. Mr. and Mrs. McDaniel from the Second Baptist church in Atlanta. Mrs. Malinda Johnson Bray, Mrs. Elizabeth Abbott, Mr. and Mrs. A. M. Kay, Mr. Jesse Swain, John Swain, Misses Lou and Nannie Swain, Mr. and Mrs. Samuel Walker and Mrs. Adcock.

Salem grew into a prosperous church with a large and devoted membership. On Service days W & A trains stopped at the church for the convenience of the members. A Ladies Aid Society, organized in 1896, met on Saturday mornings at 10 O'clock. Many of the noted ministers of the period and area served as pastor of Salem church.

The building burned in 1927 but not for long was the Lily Pond-McDaniel community without a church. Through the efforts of Mell Cameron Nelson, and others, a larger church soon stood on the site of the old. Sunday School rooms have been added and today Salem church is again shedding "the benign influence (words of Mrs. Julius Jones) of the mother church" over the people.

Fannie McDaniel McWhorter gave the land for a cemetery around the church. To read the names and dates on the grave stones is to know the history of Lily Pond and McHenry.

G. H. Gardner 1838-1904, John T. Aycock 1854-1938, Hettie, wife of J. N. Bray, 1857-1899, Wm. J. Campbell 1824-1892, his wife, Elizabetha, 1824, Annie Lyle Hasty 1878-1908, H. A. Clark 1866-1915, Sarah E. Clark 1869-1921, Joel R. Jones 1841-1906, Vashti Roper Jones 1852-1898. William Wilder 1846. Ann Wilder 1845. Margaret Coley Holloran 1862-1942, James Holloran 1860-1906, Martha Coley 1850-1885, Sarah A. Austin 1793-1885, Lucinda Angeline Coley, wife of J. M. Kay, 1860-1909, James Kay 1841-1882, Ann King 1811-1896. Fannie Augusta, wife of R. L. McWhorter and daughter of P. E. and Caroline McDaniel, 1853-1905. Robert L. McWhorter 1846-1934, Edward Wilder 1880-1911, J. A. Coley 1826. Mary Ann Coley 1825, Mahuldah Kay 1840, A. M. Kay 1840-1905. Fannie Henderson, wife of Stephen Ward Robbins 1862-1948. Amy, wife of J. B. Miles 1857-1887, Cora S. Jackson 1872-1953, Robert N. Jackson, 1862-1904, Charles Jackson 1866-1898, Ida Campbell, wife of A. P. Jackson 1872-1911, John T. Sutherland 1836-1920. Mary O. Sutherland 1848-1906, W. S. Swain 1835-1912, Eliza McDow Swain 1840-1907, Kate Swain 1869-1907, S. J. Bray Rogers 1852-1916, Thomas Rogers 1849-1919, James Rogers 1806-1893. W. M. Steele 1840-1926, Nancy Rebecca Steele 1846-1893, Jesse W. Aycock 1852-1930, Linea Aycock 1850-1916, John Herbert Bradley 1878-1947. Antionette Rogers Bradley 1877-1947, Ella Hill 1870-1935, Rod Hill 1862-1932, A. M. A. L. Johnston 1877-1941.

*   *   *   *   *

The name of the Liberty Community dates back to the organization of a Cumberland Presbyterian Church over a century ago. Recorded deeds show that the land was acquired from V. H. Cain in 1859 and from Joseph Cameron in 1860.

Bernard Franklin says that a church was there much earlier, probably about 1847. The uncertainty about dates of organization of Gordon County's first churches may arise from the fact that one of the pioneer land owners would say "you can build a church on my land and pay me when you are able."

Such was the case at Sugar Valley Baptist church where a building was on the site two decades and more before Joseph Barrett deeded the land to the church.

Trustees of Liberty in 1860 were John Phillips and David W. Neel. The church, called The White Church by older citizens, is located a short distance east of the Rome road, Ga. 53, three miles southwest of Calhoun.

Rev. Z. M. McGhee was pastor for twenty five years. The Calhoun Times of August 1880 reported Rev. Z. M. McGhee has resigned as pastor of the Liberty Presbyterian church of which he has been pastor since the building's dedication 10 years ago.

Other early pastors were J. H. Miller. Walter Swartz, Rev. S. Mann and George Danley. Herbert A. Daniel was pastor in 1933, Rev. R. C. Templeton succeeded him and Rev. Snipes served the church for five years. Elder Carl Drake, of Chattanooga, is the present pastor.

Famous Divines who were guest ministers at Liberty were Dr. W. H. Darnell and Mark A. Matthews. M. L. Matthews, father of Mark, was an Elder at Liberty for many years.

Liberty was one of the County's greatest institutions in the late 1800s. Camp meetings and revivals attracted great congregations and the people worshipped there regardless of creed.

Families began to move away and church services were discontinued. Trees and bushes grew almost to the doors and windows and the White Church was almost forgotten except as a building there in the edge of the woods, its walls barely visible through the trees.

Then, in 1925, new life came with new people, the church was re-organized and a regular pastor installed. The Elders in 1933 were W. N. Rogers. clerk, M. B. Overton, J. C. Overton, B. R. Rogers and Carl Fox. J. L. Turk was Sunday School superintendent.

Names of pioneer members include Burns, Leavitt. Garlington. Rogers, Thompson, Matthews, Barrett, Stewart, Colston, Duggar. Tomlinson and Abbott.

Rev. Z. M. McGhee was married to Miss Sarah Cameron in 1862 and the two lived to celebrate their golden wedding. The McGhee children were W. S., J. O., John, W. C. and Lillie May. The Camerons lived in the house that faces the junction of the Rome and Reeve Station roads.

Today, Liberty church is again a power and influence in the community. The building is always in an excellent state of repair, the trees and bushes are kept at a distance and Liberty is once more the White Church just off the Rome road.

Mrs. J. C. Overton (Totsy Payne), scrapbook chairman for the Community Club, has included activities of the church in the records. Pictures and newspaper clippings giving accounts of meetings and special service are among the scrapbook items.

Mrs. Snipes, wife of Pastor Snipes, organized the Woman's Auxiliary of the church, which was named in her honor, the Lydia

Snipes Auxiliary. Frequent workshops and Study Courses for the women are sources of information and means of instruction in all phases of the church's work.

The good wishes of all the people of Gordon County go with this famous old church and it is the prayer of all alike that the membership will remain active and continue to grow in numbers.

On order of the County Board of Education in September of 1924, the school districts of Reeves, Savannah and McDaniels were consolidated to form the Liberty Consolidated School district. Dolph Fuller, Walter Brandon and M. B. Overton were elected trustees. An $8000 bond issue was floated, a four acre site secured and a four room with auditorium building erected. One of the first school busses in the county was purchased at the same time.

Many teachers have come and gone during the 37 years since the School's consolidation. Miss Willalou Nelson holds the record for the longest tenure, having received several years ago, recognition for 25 years of teaching at Liberty. To date, she is still a member of the faculty. Principal of the School is J. T. Acree, teachers are Mr. Dendy, Miss May Fuller, Miss Blanche Gardner, Miss Johnnie Rickett and Miss Nelson. Lunch room supervisors are Mrs. A. L. Shaw and Mrs. J. T. Acree. Robert Reese and Truman Webb drive the orange busses with their precious load of the future.

Sometime later, a smaller building was erected on the school grounds and used as a cannery for a while, then as a work shop. It is this building that is now the Club house for the Liberty Community Improvement Club and the Home Demonstration Club.

One hundred citizens met at the school on February 5, 1957 to organize the Community Club. J. T. Acree, principal of the School, was elected president, Dewey Braden, vice president, Mrs. Raymond Roach, secretary, Jack Overton, treasurer and Mrs. Frank Overton, reporter.

County Agent John Gunnels presided over the organization meeting. Miss Kate Calloway, County Home Demonstration Agent and Lewis Weaver, Assistant County Agent, were also present to aid in forming the new club. Marlen Holcomb was president in 1958.

The Club was very active from the beginning, presenting interesting programs on the various phases of community life at each monthly meeting when a covered dish supper was served. Members were active in the Community Chest Campaigns, TB and Cancer films were shown, district boundary markers erected and a weekly news letter, Liberty Chimes, printed.

The Club won first place at the Coosa Fair in Rome and a prize of $300 the first year a booth was entered. Another year the Club's exhibit won, third place and a prize of $75. The president in 1961 is Mr. A. L. Shaw who has been elected for his second term.

The Home Demonstration Club was formed on January 29, 1958 with Miss Maude Fuller as president. Representatives of the Club have entered the County dress revues, winning awards in all classes.

Mrs. Jack Overton is retiring after two years as president of the H. D. Club and is beginning a term as president of the Gordon County Council of H. D. Clubs.

Mrs. Overton, as Scrap Book chairman for the CTC, has included pictures of attractive homes in the Liberty district in her book and her own home is an excellent example of community improvement.

The house is the old Stevens-Harkins place, a building strong in structure and needing only modern touches. The natural gas line was run between the house and the barn, so piping it to the house was a simple matter. Set on a little hill, overlooking the Rome road, with a background of pines and other trees the Overton place is one of the most attractive in the community.

* * * * *

The road turns away from McDaniel Station, climbs hills and wonders around through fields, branching off to the right or left so often, that someone with a poor sense of direction can soon be lost — as I was.

Albert Kay's house is on one of these roads. James and Fielding Kay, brothers, came to Gordon County in the 1850s. James married Miss Ann Lovelace and they reared a family of nine children.

Huldah Nix came as the bride of Albert Kay to the house that was built of timber cut on the place — split pine logs for the sleepers, round poles for the rafters, heart pine for the floors and ten inch planks for the inside walls. Succeeding owners, C. P. Nelson and Willalou and Roy Nelson have made changes, such as building new porches, installing present day conveniences or adding another room.

Albert and Mahuldah's children were James, John, Frank, Mattie and Reuben, who married Miss Adeline Wood and lived at Fairmount. Ben died while serving the Confederacy in the Civil War and Mary died in youth. Josephine married first, Dock Lyles and second, J. W. Kinman. James' first wife was Martha Coley. After her death, he married her sister, Lou Coley and the companion of his last years was Minnie Hudgins.

After losing one daughter, Albert and Huldah Kay doubly cherished the one left to them. No doubt, Mattie Kay attended the best schools and, certainly, she studied music for her name appears on the lists of organists at meetings of the Gordon County Singing Convention.

Perhaps it was at one of these Conventions that Charley Nelson met Mattie Kay.

Charley and Will Nelson, grandsons of Meshach Boaz, lived at Sugar Valley. Very sporty young men they were, driving handsome rigs, dashing about the county to gatherings and meetings and making trips to the Exhibition in Atlanta, as Will did, or to Texas, Charley's trip.

Some jealous young swain put a black snake in Will's buggy one night at church service.

Will married Lou Bridges, of Sugar Valley, but Charley had met Mattie Kay, of Lily Pond. Lewis Boaz, descendant of slaves who came to Sugar Valley with Meshach Boaz, in 1850's or earlier, served as coachman for Charley Nelson. Behind two beautiful horses hitched to an elegant buggy, Lewis would drive his young master the ten or eleven miles to Lily Pond to call on Miss Kay.

Charley P. Nelson and Mattie Kay were married in December of 1891, at a quiet home ceremony with Rev. J. J. S. Callaway officiating. Mr. and Mrs. Nelson lived for a time in Texas but soon returned to make their home at the old Kay place, where Mr. Nelson had large peach orchards. Later, the family moved to Calhoun and the Nelson children are still residents of the town and county, making constructive contributions to the life and growth of Calhoun and Gordon County.

Will and Lou Nelson died within the same year leaving a family of seven young boys and one girl. Four of the children, Roy, J. D., Willalou and J. B., today live on the Kay-Nelson farm. One of the most beautiful lakes in North Georgia has been developed on the place and friends of the Nelson, Brown and Spink families are privileged to enjoy fishing, boating and picnicking at the spot.

I took the wrong turn and was lost among the hills of Oothcaloga. The house on my right was the home of Herbert and Antionette Rogers Bradley. I stopped at the next house to ask my way and found Mr. and Mrs. Ballard living at the old Gillespie place. They sent me on the right path and round and round I went and came out at the home of Cousins J. D. and Esther Nelson. Esther and her young nephew went along to show me the way to the Jones Floral Farm.

* * * * *

"May your skies be arched with brilliant Stars and your pathway fringed with the sweetest flowers." These words inscribed on the inside cover of a little brown book in 1880 to the owner whose name is written in scrolls and swirls on the fly leaf.

The little brown autograph album once belonged to "Miss Minnie Bray" and was graciously loaned to me by her nephew and niece, Mr. and Mrs. Bynum Rogers, Blackwood Road.

On the inside of the title page, Minnie Bray had penned in shaded letters and swirling lines "To My Friends

"Here is a place
For you to trace
A pleasant word or two
If hard to find
Your name alone will do."

In copy-book hand writing with blue ink the opposite page reads "Presented to Miss Minnie Bray for good conduct and proficiency in her studies, by her teacher,

Nora Neel
Mount Lion Academy October 1, 1880."

Page after page of sweet sentiment and witty sentence follow. A sincere and honest wish for the cares of life to rest lightly on Minnie Bray from her instructor Wm. J. Neel, is there. Another old teacher wrote "You are so good and kind and true, your friends ought to be good to you," Signed "J. W. W.," this teacher could be no other than John W. Swain, one of Gordon County's first settlers.

A. W. Moss, of Adairsville, wrote in January 1882," Omnes Vincet Armor." Her true friend, John E. Swain, pinned "In life's tempest when each needs an umbrella, may yours be upheld by a handsome young fellow." Della Toliver, Austin Female Seminary. February 8, 1881, requested, "If ever you a husband get, and he these lines should see, relate to him your school day life and give him a kiss for me."

From Kate Swain, "Minnie Dearest, May your witness ever shine like the blossoms on a pumpkin vine" and, Cousin Minnie, "we parted there as true friends part-yours to command, F. D. Bowdoin."

Jennie Lee Erwin, teacher, contributed "Loyez dans la joie awec duex qui pleurent" — your gentle and tender heart, dear Minnie, will make it easy for you to do this."

In a heavy black hand, H. F. C. wrote "Remember this and bear in mind that a jaybird's tail sticks out behind."

Other well-wishers were; F. L. Dyar, R. A. McCollum, E. B. Earle, Mattie Kay, George M. McDaniel, Alice Dyar, A. P. Colston, Charlie D. Hopkins and Della Abbott.

"Dear Minnie, Carrie Swain wrote on the last autograph leaf, "When on this page you chance to look, Think of me and close the book." Adairsville, March 22- 83."

Thomas Roger, who was to marry Minnie's sister, Josie Bray, wrote at Rosedale Farm, March 5, 1883 — "To write a few lines in your album, my friend, shall engross a few moments, my thoughts and my time. But in these few moments, oh what shall I say? Where shall I begin to leave off. I pray? In the first place, I'll speak of the wind, and the weather, with its clouds and its streams and its sunshine together. "Tis a picture of life and all a moral may gleam from each withering flower and murmuring stream."

And, on the very last page of the little brown book is written "Miss Minnie, accept the best wishes of your friend, J. P. Jones."

Little did I dream, when I parked my car in the edge of the grove at the Bray place on an October day in 1960, that my feet would take me up the driveway into such a treasure trove. I rang the little brass dinner bell at the door on the side of the house that faces the springs and Mr. and Mrs. James Wellborn Bray invited me in.

I had last visited the place when Minnie Bray Jones was living. The outside of the house is still hers but the inside belongs to the present. New floors of wood sawed from trees on the farm, pale green glass curtains, long flowered draperies, a green rug, modern furniture and a grand piano have moved into the room and hall, now one big space, that once was cluttered with Miss Minnie's papers, books, magazines and her pitcher collection. The old kitchen is inviting with paneled walls, sunny windows and den furnishings.

On the opposite side of the house two bedrooms, one in blue, one in pink, are divided by a charmingly fitted dressing room.

"Walk slowly across the room while keeping your eyes on the picture," Mr. Bray told me. I did so and the eyes of the man in the frame followed me.

"You can't get away from him, can you?" I marveled.

This remarkable and handsome portrait of J. W. Bray was done, in color from a small photograph, by Mr. and Mrs. James Wellborn Bray's son as a birthday gift for his father.

"Our son, Roddy, who is a ministerial student at Yale, has made an extensive study of the Bray family history," Mrs. Bray said. "I will call him and ask him to send you some of his notes."

The next week, I received a special delivery, air mail package from William E. Bray, Yale University, New Haven, Conn. He had sent me his entire script with generous permission to use it all.

I give you his story of the Bray family.

THE BRAY ESTATE

Six generations of the Bray family have enjoyed the fine old colonial house and gardens of the Bray Estate in Gordon County. From the present owner's great-grandfather who first owned the estate down to his grandchildren who play around the century-old boxwoods, which grace the yards surrounding the ante-bellum house, on weekend visits, the estate has enjoyed a romantic history difficult to match in the annals of Georgia history.

When northwest Georgia was still wilderness and Indians lived at New Echota, a young Methodist minister with his wife and five children traveled to the land of red clay hills. Rev. Bannister R. Bray settled five miles south of what is now Calhoun in 1837. There near a grove of oak and cedar trees surrounding three springs he built a house of logs covered with white clapboard and faced with a row of six majestic white columns. The roof of the old home still is supported by wooden pegs, and some of the original glass panes remain. Even the six white columns were cut from trees on the farm itself, and different from most columns, thety are solid and sturdy oak.

The minister was like many other Georgians of that restless period in the state's history. He had been born in Virginia in 1800 and had come to Georgia as a child settling with family in Elbert and Madison Counties. There he was married and had four children by his first wife; William A., James S., Bannister O., and Mary Ann Bray. In 1832 he married a second time, his young wife being Nancy Mitchell. And in 1835 in Henry County, a fifth child, Wellborn Mitchell Bray, was born. It was from Henry County that the family moved when they ventured into this unsettled part of the state.

For ten years the Bray family made the colonial house their home. Bannister Bray made additional land purchases until the estate grew to a size estimatetd at almost two thousand acres. It covered the area between the Liberty and Lily Pond communities and stretched south almost to what is now the Bartow County line. Gordon County deed books are filled with records of transactions made by the versatile minister.

But in 1847, Bannister Bray felt compelled to answer a challenge in Atlanta, so he moved with his family from the estate and sold some of his land. One of his friends, Benjamin H. Bailey, moved to the main house after the family departure. In Atlanta, the various interests and activities of Bannister R. Bray increased, and he soon became "one of the wealthiest men" in the city. His love and compassion for northwest Georgia never ceased, however, and it was in Gordon County that he died in 1863.

The sons of the Rev. Mr. Bray, recalling the wonderful years of their youth at the Bray Estate, returned to make it their homes. In 1857, William A. Bray, then 35 years old and the eldest of the four brothers, officially purchased the main house of the estate and surrounding lands (consisting of 140 acres). By 1860, with the help of his father, William Bray had accumulated 535 acres of the original estate. Meanwhile, his three younger brothers had also returned to Gordon County. Acquiring land once owned by their father, James S. Bray settled in the southwest corner of the old estate, while Bannister O. Bray settled in the southeast corner.

The youngest of the brothers was Wellborn Mitchell Bray. While his older brothers had planned to return to the old estate with the intention of farming, he had become interested in law. He studied for two years at the University of Georgia and was graduated from Emory College at Oxford, Georgia in 1855 with an AB degree. He studied law with Col. James Milner of Cartersville and was admitted to practice in 1858 at Cassville. He then moved to Calhoun, where he was living at the outbreak of the War between the States.

When war broke out, all four of the Bray brothers were living in Gordon County, and each one fought for the cause of the Confederacy. William Bray enlisted in Gordon County in September, 1862 in Company I, 63rd Georgia Regiment. Bannister O. Bray had enlisted earlier in 1861 in the 4th Georgia Infantry and later fought in Virginia, returning to Georgia from the battle there at the close of the War.

Early in the War, Wellborn M. Bray was elected captain of the Toombs Volunteers, which was organized at Calhoun, but severe illness prevented him from accepting the command. In March of 1862, however, he joined Company D, 40th Regiment as a private. He served for six months and was then authorized to raise a siege artillery company by the secretary of war. This company was organized near Savannah, and Welborn Bray was chosen First Lieutenant, which he remained until 1865. In that year it was changed into an infantry company, and he was made captain of it. He was in this position at the end of the war.

Wellborn Bray fought with honor in the following battles: Dalton, Resaca, Rocky Ford, Kennesaw Mountain, Atlanta, Franklin, Nashville and Pulaski, Tenn., and at New Hope Church. At New Hope Church he was wounded by the explosion of a shell.

Returning from an extensive campaign in the war, **Wellborn Bray established the first school in Atlanta after the war.** There he worked, teaching many of Atlanta's most prominent sons, until the public school was founded. He then became principal of the Ivy Street Grammar School and taught there until 1873 when he resumed the practice of law. In 1886-88 he represented Fulton County in the state general assembly. He was appointed to the finance, educational and corporations committees and was widely known for his vehement opposition to the convict lease system. His arguments were described as "able, eloquent and masterly." His memorable words before the general assembly are as true today as they were in 1887: "No man is utterly irredeemable. But if you extinguish within him the light of hope, you educate him in crime. The lease system is an educator in crime, denying all the principles of humanity. Treat the convict as a human being and you may reform him."

Captain Bray was a member of the Atlanta Board of Education from 1887 until 1897. He was very active as a Mason, a member of the Atlanta Pioneer Society, and a member of the Atlanta Camp of the United Confederate Veterans. According to his own wishes, the latter group conducted his funeral following his death in 1903. He lies buried in Atlanta's Westview Cemetery.

Describing Wellborn M. Bray as "a practitioner of zest, earnestness and superior worth at the Atlanta bar," "his biographical sketch in the **Memoirs of Georgia,** Vol. I, copyrighted in 1895, concludes: I "He is a city father, who has guarded Atlanta's welfare faithfully." It is appropriate and fitting that the present owner of the Bray estate, James Wellborn Bray, should have been named for an uncle who had become such a distinguished Georgian.

While the War between the States had scattered the Bray brothers across the battlefields of the South, their homes had remained intact despite Sherman's destructive march from Dalton to Atlanta, which passed through the eastern portions of the estate. The family of William A. Bray, living in the Estate House, hid the silverware and china in the spring branches behind the house, and many of the family valuables were hidden in the cellar. Prior to the warm, William Bray's family consisted of his wife Malissa and their eight children. But during the war, Mrs. Bray died, and within time William Bray married again. His second wife was Malinda Johnson, a true Southern lady of distinction. As the South sought to bind its wounds, there was a period of hope in the future. It was in this period, on April 21, 1866, that a daughter was born to the family. She was named Minnie Lillian Bray and was to have a profound effect upon the history of the estate.

Being the "baby girl" of the family, she felt especially close to her mother, and adopted her mother's passion for planting and growing beautiful flowers, and even as a little girl, she would spend hours day by day working in her mother's flower garden around the old house.

William Bray was a rather quiet man, but a good farmer, and he developed and cultivated the lands of the Bray Estate with care. The period of the ownership (from 1857 until his death in 1888) passed without many outstanding events, with the exception of the strains of the war years and the rigors of the Reconstruction period. He willed the estate be divided among several of his children, except for the original 140 acres of the House and gardens, which he left in the care of his wife, who, three years later, passed it on to Minnie Lillian Bray who had become the wife of a Baptist minister, Rev. Julius P. Jones. The other sons of William Bray either sold their land or died without wills. At any rate, only the House and gardens and the surrounding land remained in the Bray family. Even the family cemetery (in which is buried William A. Bray, Bannister O. Bray and countless other relatives in unmarked graves) is on land which left the hands of the family. It is on the farm now owned by Mrs. P. H. Holloran. The late Mr. Holloran, always a friend of the Bray family, carefully preserved the cemetery until his recent death.

Meanwhile, the children and grandchildren of James S. Bray grew up and moved away from Gordon County. The last of his descendents living in the area was a son, William Bannister Bray, who died in July, 1956 in Plainville. A great-granddaughter, Mrs. Lemon Awtrey, Jr. (formerly Miss Jane Bray) lives in Acworth.

Bannister O. Bray married Susan Rud in 1849, and after moving back to Gordon County in the late 1850's, lived on his farm at the southeast corner of the estate until his death in 1905 at the age of 77. He had four children: Indiana, James W. N., Roxana, and Bannister Rufus Bray. The younger son, Rufus, moved to Texas where many of his descendents still live, while J. W. N. Bray remained in Gordon County, however, for 49 years. Having married Hettie Pitman of Texas, he raised a large family and was active in Liberty Cumberland Presbyterian church. Following the death of his wife, he later married her younger sister, Jennie Pitman, and in 1903 moved with his family to Dalton 25 miles away. There the following year, a son, James Wellborn Bray, the present owner of the estate was born.

Thus, around the turn of the century, countless cousins, uncles and aunts, of the Bray family either died or moved away one by one, until Mrs. Minnie Bray Jones, owner of the House and grounds, became the only member of the family to remain at the estate.

Minnie Lillian Bray married a young Baptist minister fresh from seminary in 1884. He was Julius Peek Jones, a distinguished young man of 26, who had been graduated from Mercer University at Macon, Georgia and Southern Baptist Theological Seminary in Louisville, Kentucky. They came to Gordon County the following year, and his ministry there with his faithful and lovely wife has become almost legendary. For fifty years he devoted himself to the ministry in this county. He served at many churches including Bethesda, Salem, West Union and Brooks Chapel.

Rev. and Mrs. Jones presented a fine picture. They were indeed a credit to the community. From a fine distinguished family with roots in Pennsylvania, Julius Jones had an education which was truly outstanding in his day or this. Many older citizens of the county remember his eloquent sermons and the fine gentleman he was. And his charming wife was reared as a true Southern lady. But there was always in Minnie Bray Jones a love for the soil and the earth which she had loved as a girl in her mother's flower gardens.

When she and her husband became owners of the Estate House and grounds in 1891, she immediately set out to improve the already well-cared-for gardens. The three springs in a little glen behind the house made the perfect setting for bulbs and rock gardens, so she immediately set out spending her free hours on her favorite pastime of raising flowers. Working around the old oak trees (one of which is now more than 200 years old), and the majestic tree-boxwoods which were brought from Virginia before the war, she developed one of the finest gardens in North Georgia. With rock walls around the springs (the earliest of which dates 1914), and fields of daffodils, her interest flourished throughout her life. In the setting of the gardens near the estate House, the Rev. Mr. Jones performed countless wedding ceremonies. Today passers-by continually visit the contemporary owners and say, "We were married by Rev. Jones with Miss Minnie witnessing the ceremony in these gardens." Rev. Julius Jones performed "more marriages than anyone else in Gordon County."

As his ministry continued, the Rev. Mr. Jones was stricken with crippling disease and it soon became necessary for him to discontinue his work at the church, and he became an invalid confined to the house. He would often enjoy walking in the garden while his health was better.

Faced with the necessity for providing for her husband and herself during his illness, Minnie Bray Jones resorted to her favorite pastime as their livelihood. She knew that the market for daffodil flowers and bulbs was good, so she set out to grow them for a profit.

Within a few years she had the fields and hills near the Estate House covered with a yellow blanket of flowering daffodils, and annually she would gather the cut blossoms and bulbs to harvest them. Her markets included stores in Washington, New York, Cincinnati, and Atlanta. At one period of crisis in her enterprise, she was made her own stationmaster at McDaniel Station from which she shipped her flowers, so she could continue her sales.

Though the farm itself is rather secluded (between the main thoroughfares: the Atlanta and Rome highways out of Calhoun), many people heard of the rolling hills of yellow blossoms, and soon scores, then hundreds of people traveled from surrounding cities and states every spring to witness the spectacle. Today, fifteen acres of flowers. which bloom annually there, are a living memorial and reminder of the efforts and devotion of Minnie Bray Jones.

In 1931 an article appeared in the Atlanta Journal Magazine entitled "Daffodil Farm Prospers," and the crowds of visitors each spring grew to enormous sizes. Many people still recall visiting the place, which became known as "Daffodil Farm" or simply "the flower farm." The commercial name which "Miss Minnie" (as she was affectionately called) adopted was Jones Floral Farm.

After the death of Mr. Jones in 1932, "Miss Minnie" continued to be the "flower lady," and the familiar memory of her standing with her bonnet shading her eyes in the fields of daffodils still can be recalled by hundreds who paid her a visit. She and a cousin, Miss Lilla Alexander, became the official hosts of the many travelers who stopped there. "Miss Minnie" would often invite the guests into her house, which was decked with her pitcher collection and picture albums of all the old Brays who used to live around the familiar valleys and hills. In a prominent place in the hallway hung a portrait of Wellborn M. Bray, of whom she was very proud. On a visit in 1940 of her second-cousin, James Wellborn Bray of Dalton, she proudly showed him this portrait of the man for whom he was named.

Loved by her neighbors and friends as a "wonderful lady of noble character," "Miss Minnie" died in 1947. With her death passed the last member of the Bray family from the estate which had born their name for more than a century.

Since Rev. and Mrs. Jones had no children, and she had left no will, the farm was sold at public auction in May of 1950. For six years the House was owned by Mr. and Mrs. Jesse H. Payne, and it was while living there during that period that Mr. Payne passed away.

But just as the sons of Bannister R. Bray had returned (from Atlanta) to the family estate a century before, so a great-grandson returned in 1956. Remembering his visit to see his cousin Minnie, James Wellborn Bray, who was living in Dalton, consulted Mrs. Payne about the purchase of the place. With the memories of visits to his father's homeplace, his grandfather's grave nearby, and the Estate House itself while "Miss Minnie" was living there, J. W. Bray made several visits to the old house and gardens.

On May 17, 1956 with the official purchase, the Bray Estate returned once again to the family, and James Wellborn Bray became the fourth successive generation of his family to be its owner.

J. Wellborn Bray was born in Dalton the year after his family moved there from the lands of the estate. On August 16, 1920 he and Thelma Louise Day were married at Calhoun. Also born in Dalton, Mrs. Bray is the daughter of Mr. and Mrs. Homer P. Day.

Having established himself in business as the owner of a shoe wholesale and repair store before, during, and following the depression years of the late '20's and '30's on Dalton's Hamilton Street, Wellborn Bray became well known and made numerous friends. His father had often encouraged him to "get into politics" and run for the office of Whitfield County Tax Collector, which was then an influential and highly respected position in county affairs. But his business was doing so well he neglected the challenge. But following the death of his father in 1935, he was again confronted by the possibility of seeking office in the 1936 primaries. This time his decision was positive.

His opponent in the office of tax collector was a distinguished and respected office holder, who had held the post for eight years of faithful service. J. W. Bray's first attempt was not successful, but even the most keen political observers were amazed at how close the election was. Refusing to be discouraged by the narrow failure of his first political venture, he ran again in 1940 and was elected this time overwhelmingly. He was re-elected to the same position in 1944 and 1948. Thus twelve years he commanded a political and civic post of importance, and his influence in the political life of Whitfield County was felt years after his retirement from the political scene in 1952.

While serving the people of Whitfield County as tax collector, Mr. Bray had been continuing his interests in business. In the early 40's, in addition to his shoe store, he expanded into the production of bedspreads and bath sets on a small scale as a subsidiary endeavor, and action spurred by the already booming chenille industry in Dalton. Still his business ambitions were not satisfied, so he set up a small machine in the attic and another in the basement of his home experimenting with his major interest — shoe manufacturing. In 1945 his interests converged in the founding of the Bray Company, which produced the first chenille house shoes in the country. The company has continued to grow and prosper, and today it is the largest house slipper manufacturer in the South and among the top five in the country. As a further measure of progress it was incorporated in March, 1960. Today the plant is located one mile south of Dalton on the U. S. 41 Highway, and its modern architecture drew from the classification as a model small plant recently in a publication of the Dalton Chamber of Commerce. Thus, the small experiment of J. W. Bray in the attic and basement of his home in the early forties has grown within 15 years into a plant presently employing more than 50 people.

Despite his success in business, J. W. Bray has in no way lost his political acumen. Even in the 1960 primaries in September, political aspirants from United States Congress to state representatives were dropping by his office in Dalton to get his advice and to try to encourage him to give them a prediction on the election's outcome. His wife patiently sighed in August, "Well, you can tell it's election time again, The phone is ringing constantly." Much of this is due to experience and his long time association with the people of Whitfield County. While carrying cne of his campaigns in the 1940's to Dalton, the late Governor Eugene Talmadge once called on Wellborn Bray for his prediction on an election in which all of his friends and political advisers had predicted he would carry Whitfield County. Sitting in the governor's room in Hotel Dalton, J. W. Bray told him he would lose the county by 400 votes. When the election was over, Talmadge failed to carry the county by 420 votes, breathtakingly close to the prediction. After that, the governor always made it a point when he came to Dalton to check for reliance upon Wellborn Bray's political insight.

In his early years, while still owning his shoe store in Dalton's business district, Mr. Bray, constantly seeking new ventures, sought in new avenue of business to be an amateur real estate invester and contractor. He recalls that during this period he must have built at least 20 houses in and around Dalton. Still fascinated by this prospect, he was still buying, remodeling and selling old farms and houses as late as 1953 as a sideline.

In many ways, James Wellborn Bray is the embodiment of the Bray family in one generation. Possessing the versatility, venturesome spirit, and leadership of Wellborn Mitchell Bray, his famous great-uncle, he also is blessed with a keen sense of concern for other people, which makes him right at home immediately with a stranger. It was this aspect of his personality, which helped win for him such an overwhelming support in the election in Whitfield County. But there is within him another element which even more identifies him with the life of Georgia, and this is a phenomena rapidly vanishing from the state scene — a keen **awareness** of the past, a sense of direction in the present, and a constant eye to the future — the combination of qualities which has always madet and kept the state strong. One does not have to be around Wellborn Bray long to hear him relate some incident of his political career, or some story about his father (who is a legend within the Bray family), or some little saying or truism passed down from generation to generation. The past heritage is so deeply rooted in him, it would be difficult for him to speak or reflect without some reference to it. But at the same time here is a man full of conviction about where he stands at the present time, ready to speak freely about the major political, social, or economic positions of the day. At the same time, he is constantly developing new and ambitious ideas for his plant and the new venture which he has devoted himself to — the restoration of the Bray Estate.

For when J. Wellborn Bray bought the estate in 1956, he bought with him a wealth of experiences from his background. He immediately set out to restore the grandeur of the House and gardens which they had enjoyed in the past, but which were neglected after the death of his cousin Minnie. As he sought to clear the bushes and undergrowth from the front yard which had been accumulating for the years, many of the older neighbors moaned, "He's going to ruin that place." Some even called him about it. But today, no one has any complaints, for he has replaced undergrowth and weeds with sprawling lawns and freshly planted flowers. And in every case, he has sought to revitalize the flowers and shrubs which once bloomed luxuriously under the generous care of Minnie Bray Jones.

The House itself, one of the oldest and best preserved antebellum houses in Georgia, has been restored in an effort to preserve its finer qualities, but also to keep it livable. The main body of the 123-year-old house is basically the same (used as a living room and bedroom), but the old kitchen built on the northwest side of the house before 1898 has been converted into a den, and the room at the back of the House built for Julius Jones around 1920 is still used as a bedroom.

Mr. Bray has replaced the 50-year-old secondary house with a modern brick one, and on the hill behind it has built three chicken houses. He has remodeled the barn, added a three acre lake, and revitalized all the pastures on the farm for his cattle. In addition, he has expanded the area covered in the flower gardens, so that the total area slightly exceeds the one time 15 acres. Even though

Minnie Bray Jones might not be at ease around the new swimming pool near the house, she would surely be pleased to see her fields of daffodils bloom into the familiar yellow blanket each spring.

Despite the new improvements, it is always the daffodils which people remember and which, even today, scores of people travel to see in the early Spring. And to many people the estate will always be to them the "Daffodil Farm." The hospitable and friendly manner of the Bray family extends to these many friends and visitors, for Mr. and Mrs. Bray are generally happy to show guests around the garden while Mr. Bray will entertain them with some political opinions or stories about an interesting experience he has had. Visitors who were there 2- or 30 years ago, who compare Wellborn Bray to Mrs. Jones, will consider him a just heir to the grounds. No less hospitable is his wife, Mrs. Thelma Bray, who has faithfully stood by and supported each venture and experience with a surprising consistency. Indeed, her sons claim she is as much of a Bray as any member of the family. She is also the perfect hostess, making a stranger feel like a friend, and if you're a relative or especially close friend of the family and have enjoyed a meal with them, you may have experienced what may truly be called "southern cooking" at its best under her supervision. It is worth noting that her recollection of Brays in the past, and family matters and affairs are no less inclusive than those of her husband or any member of the family.

But what of the future of the estate?

The Wellborn Brays have two sons: James Wellborn Bray, Jr., born in 1930, and William Elrod Bray, born in 1937. J. W. Bray, Jr. is a graduate of the University of Georgia where he received his BA degree in journalism, and he recently earned his Masters degree in Education at the University of Chattanooga. He is married to the former Miss Emily Adams, and they have two children, Laura Lynn and James W. Bray, III. He is general manager of the J. W. Bray Company, Inc., and the family lives in Dalton. But on weekends and holidays, the entire family assembles around the table at the old House on the Bray Estate, and as generations before them have done, offer prayers of thanksgiving to their Lord.

The fifth and most recent generation of the family to make the Estate home is in the person of William E. Bray, known by his friends as Roddy Bray. He was graduated from the University of Georgia majoring in history and philosophy and is currently preparing for the ministry by working toward the Bachelor of Divinity degree as a student at The Divinity School of Yale University in New Haven, Connecticut. All of the family are members of the First Church in Dalton.

Thus the future of Bray Estate appears to be well rooted in memories and proud heritage; it is in a real sense inseparable from the history of the Bray family in Georgia. For here just as they have done for twelve decades, Brays come and go. Indeed, there seems to be almost an element of fate, that on two occasions the family would leave, but always return. But the new generation of Brays do not speak of leaving. They returned and here, they will tell you, they plan to stay. In this resolution and in this history, one may recall the words of Ecclesiastes: "One generation passeth away, and another generation cometh: but the earth abideth forever."

In 1929 when one and two teacher schools were disappearing

from Gordon County, five of these schools in Oothcaloga district, Belmont, Blackwood, Spring Hill, Union Grove and Watsonville, were consolidated. The name chosen for the new school was Belwood, from the first syllable of Belmont and the second of Blackwood. The first trustees were C. W. Fox, W. N. Rogers and J. L. Turk.

Today, the Belwood Community Club is known throughout the North Georgia for its outstanding, contribution to community life. The Club's booths at Gordon County 4-H Fairs, the Coosa Fair at Rome and Whitfield County Fairs win almost more ribbons than can be carried home.

The attractive 1960 book of the club features the history of the community which dates from Indian settlements along the trail that became the Great Tennessee road of the 1820's and the Dixie Highway of the 1920's.

Goals for the Belwood Club at the beginning of 1960 were increased attendance at Club meetings; continued sponsoring of the Boy Scout troop, improvements to Club house, school roads, health standards and living conditions; cooperation in Soil Fertility; sponsor an annual farm Work Day; forestry and field crop demonstration; plan youth activities; promote home improvement and beautification; purchase piano, song books and silver for the Club room.

Officers who steered the Club to completion of this monumental project were, A. B. Richards, president, W. E. Barrett, first vice-president, Mrs. John Hurd, second vice-president, Mrs. Gene Nix, secretary and Mrs. Rayford Hall, treasurer; Program and planning committee, W. E. Barrett chairman, Mrs. John Hurd, Mrs. Frank Richardson; Survey, Mrs. Max Baker, chairman, Mrs. Ernest Tally, Mrs. Horace Bigham, Helen Barrett; School and church, T. E. Cornelison, chairman, Clarence Garren, M. L. Johnson, Rayford Hall and Jewell Ray; Finance, Mrs. Rayford Hall, chairman, Mrs. Allice Sutherland, Mrs. Virgil Avery, Mrs. W. E. Barrett, Mrs. Wiley Patterson; Agriculture, Poultry and Livestock. M. L. Johnson, chairman, Horace Bigham, Claud Walraven, Ernest Tally; Nutrition and Food Preservation, Mrs. Durham Richards, chairman, Mrs. W. E. Barrett, Mrs. Claud Johnson, Mrs. M. L. Johnson and Mrs. Clayton Henslee; Community Beautification and Home Improvement, Mrs. Frank Richardson, chairman, Hilda Rickett, Mrs. Mack Serritt, Mrs. A. B. Richards and Max Baker; Publicity and Scrapbook, Mrs. Gene Nix, chairman, Mrs. Frank Richardson, Mrs. Charles Holcombe; Youth Activities and Recreation, Mrs. Jewel Ray chairman, Virginia Fuller, Gail Richards, Johnny Rickett and Sue Hensley; Health and Sanitation; Durham Richards, chairman, Virgil Avery, Trammel Robinson, John Hurd and Ed Chitwood; Attendance Committee, Mrs. Ed Chitwood, chairman, Mrs. Ralph Gray and Mrs. Jewell Ray; House committee, Rayford Hall, chairman, Virgil Avery, Wyley Patterson, Gene Nix and Erwin Rickett.

Program subjects for the year were; January Religious Emphasis, February, Gordon County History, March Gardening, April, Youth Activities, May, Food Preservation, June, Ice Cream Supper and Nutrition, July, Picnic and Planned Recreation, August, watermelon cutting and Fair Booth Discussion, September, Health, October, wiener Roast and Community clean up, November, Thanksgiving, December, Christmas Party.

County Agent John Gunnels, Assistant County Agent Milton

Stewart and Home Demonstration Agent, Miss Ann Sims are Club advisors. Meetings are held on the third Friday night of each month with, usually, a covered dish supper.

Mrs. Frank Richardson edits a monthly news bulletin to Club members. A yard of the Month is selected by committee of judges. Among the first winners of this award were Mr. and Mrs. Frank Richardson, Mr. and Mrs. Max Baker and Virginia Fuller.

One of the first things I noted when I entered the Club room Friday was a large placard on the wall bearing the caption, "Goals for 1960." Under this headline were listed 18 separate tasks which the Club had set for itself to accomplish during the year.

I thought surely this is too much for any community to undertake in a single year. However, when some of the 12 committees had submitted, their reports, it was astonishing and inspiring to note how many of the 1960 objectives had been achieved — Mack's Column in The Calhoun Times, Nov. 24, 1960.

Editor and Mrs. McGinty were guests of the Club at the Thanksgiving, and end of the year meeting when the retiring president, A. B. Richards, handed the gavel to the new president, W. E. Barrett.

During the year members of the Belwood Club assisted in organizing a Club at Oakman and others attended a party given by the Liberty Club.

The Gordon County News of November 29, 1960, printed an announcement that the Belwood Club had won an honorable mention award in the Chattanooga area Improvement contest and was presented with a gift of $15.00 at a banquet at the Read House in Chattanooga. Mrs. Frank Richardson, Home Improvement and Beautification chairman presented as the Club's Contest entry the yard of the month project.

I needed a guide on my trip over Oothcaloga district Number 856, so I stopped by the Fuller Home on the Blackwood road to enlist Virginia Fuller.

Jim and Rhetta Coffee Fuller lived for 25 years in the old J. A. Mims house a short distance back of the present Fuller home. They bought the place from Dr. C. F. McClain. The Mims house is empty now. The dirt road runs so close to the front door that the place is envetloped in a cloud of dust with every passing automobile

A tornado ruined the frame house that was the home of Will and Sally Holsomback Fuller, parents of Jim, leaving intact only the back section which was made of field stone. A new brick structure now joins the stone part of the house and timbers from the tornado wreckage were used to build a barn.

In the Fuller living room there is a room divider, ceiling-high, on which is displayed an interesting china collection — a pitcher from Minnie Bray Jones' collection, a plate in cream and gray with big white roses, from Germany, one from Mis' Clyde McDaniel's with painted roses in the center and deep scallops in blue, a fruit plate from the State of Virginia, one from California, a Fields of the Woods plate, another is a pink willow from Mt. Vernon and there's a green plate from Warm Springs.

Virginia Fuller said "we'll go in my car" and we did, stopping to pick up Bea Richardson who lives over on the Old Dixie Highway. The two had been planning a jaunt over the hills and through the woods of Oothcaloga since last summer and both agreed that this lovely Autumn Saturday afternoon would be as good as any time.

Virginia should have been a jeep driver in World War II. She raced along narrow rutty roads, drove straight up one mountain and round about another and had to stop on one of them while Mattie Johnson moved a good sized tree limb that had fallen across the road.

Our objective was ancient private cemeteries and family estates of ante bellum days. The first mountain we climbed a foot (all the cemeteries were located on top of mountains) was to the Abbott cemetery, a short distance east of Ga. 53. Here, we found the graves of all the Abbotts. How restful and peaceful it was! Only a small cleared spot on top of the hill with the silent woods surrounding the eternal sleepers. Our foot falls made no sound on the pine needles carpet and only the muted hum of a motor on the highway disturbed the stillness.

Jacob Abbott, born 1802, died 1863, his wife Elizabeth Young, born 1809, died 1891 —" A. Abbott and M. J. Campbell was married July 23, 1857," inscription on a stone. A. Abbott 1830-1903, Mary 1835-1905, Robert A. 1833-1862, Edith H. 1866-1915 and Ambrose 1856-1915. Then, there were the Wyatts — James D., 1845-1921 and Cassie L. 1866-1919. Was Roxie Thomas 1868-1909 a kinswoman? Laura E. Fox born 1877, married to R. E. Bennett 1887 and died 1888. Ella, a daughter of Wyatts, 1874-1901. Mamie L. wife of J. L. Faith 1884-1904. Bessie Greeson born 1886 died 1912.

Harvey E. son of A. H. and C. C. Greeson born 1886, died 1912. Infants of the Faiths, the Greesons and the Foxes — so many baby graves everywhere.

At the lower edge of the cemetery was a low moss-covered stone marked Boss Scott, died 1938. My companions said that he was a respected colored man of the Community. We surmised that a number of unmarked graves near by could be those of the family slaves.

We tramped across a ploughed field (hoping that Jim Fuller wouldn't see us) and climbed a hill to the Fuller cemetery. A carpet of creeping myrtle, showing green through the new fallen brown leaves, covered the hill top and sent its small evergreen-leafed vines trailing down the slope. We found unmarked graves of infants and adults and the grave stones of Edgar Milton 1883-1905, son of W. A. and Essie Fuller. Roxie Fuller, 1891-1893 and William Lewis Fuller 1877-1885.

We must see the new colored sub-division, they said, so, away we went over new-cut roads, up and down hills and around the new houses, some of them frame, others brick. Ida Scott. widow of Boss Scott, lives in one of the houses. The old homes of these colored folk, who had lived for so many years in this section, were in the way of the new super-highway and must be moved. The owners, were paid for their property and the sub-division was opened. The second generation of Poarches are residents of the area, Uncle Joe, son of Mose who was the ancestor of the family, and Aunt Malinda. The Poarches bought the land from John C. Garlington. Richard Varner, retired school teacher, lives in his house beside the old Dixie Highway.

Straight up the mountain, Virginia drove, to the Curtiss family plot. Here lie the Curtiss ancestors; James M. Curtiss 1825-1912, Elvina Cobb Curtiss 1825-1892, William Marian Curtiss 1847-1934, Anne Maria 1848-1915, Robert Battey 1879-1916, James M. 1884-1899, son of Dr. and Mrs. W. M. Curtiss, Walton Henry Curtiss 1874-1924, N. C. Curtiss 1856, his wife, Marie Hubbard, died 1891, Sarah, 1856-1929, daughter of L. N. and Serena Smith Curtiss, Nancy Surrey Curtiss 1834-1862, John M. 1827-1902, his wife Cathron 1829-1905, William Curtiss 1804-1887 and his wife Martha Bonn 1799-1876.

The Ferguson, Owens, Campbells, Binghams, Fowlers and Jones are buried here among the Curtiss, and Margaret Chambers 1855-1918. W. E. Ferguson 1832-1908, Frances 1835-1890. M. Wiley 1832-1906, Salina Owen 1840-1922, T. C. Owen 1840-1922, Henriett, 26 years old, died 1898, J. W. Owen 1864-1902, and Emma Mertie Owen 1894-1909.

Elizabeth Campbell 1858-1903, Sallie A. Bigham 1854-1927, Vashti Bigham 1823-1916, Josiah Bigham 1822-1898. Josephine Jones, wife of J. R. Jones born 1859, Charles T. Fowler 1870-1922 and Elizabeth Fowler 1877-1924.

The graves covered with rocks are those of Federal soldiers.

James and Elvina Curtiss were very proud of their fine new house, finished shortly before the Secession. Cut from virgin timber, the thick log sills would last a hundred years, they were sure. There were 6 large rooms and a hall. Two double chimneys in the main part and one in the ell made it possible to have all the rooms warm if company came in cold weather.

The front veranda had four square columns made of wide heart planks lined with stout rough boards.

Facing the Tennessee road—once the Indian Trail to Augusta— the house was set on a slope so that the back section had a ground-level cellar.

The march through Georgia had begun and the Yankees were at Calhoun, a mile or so north of the Curtiss home. William Marion, the 17 year old son, had joined the Confederate army as the enemy approached. At home with James and Elvina were James, 14, Cicero, 9, and Joe, 4 years old.

Many of the county families had refugeed to other parts of the State, but the Curtiss family remained at home to accept the fortunes of War as they came.

It was May of 1864. James and Cicero hurried into the house, pale and trembling, crying "Ma, Pa, the Yankees are coming! We saw them on the road right above the curve!"

James Curtiss, in his work as a doctor, was accustomed to crisis and spoke quietly to the boys and his frightened wife, "now, sit down and try to act as usual. The soldiers will not bother us."

Elvina picked up little Joe and ran for the back stairs. "If there's a battle," she cried" the brick walled cellar will be a safer place!"

Cicero followed his mother but James stood with his father at a front window and watched the troops pass by.

Suddenly, there was a fusillade of gun fire. Dr. Curtiss went to the south window. A few yards down the road the Federals were running for the shelter of the trees or dropping to the ground. Three or four lay still where they fell. The advance patrol sent out from Calhoun had been ambushed by the Confederates. The sound of shots from the other side of the house drew the Doctor to a north window. As he stood there, a minie ball cracked through the pane above his head, splintered a plank in the wall over the mantel and lodged in the chimney. Confederate soldiers were firing from the hill to the northwest.

Then, the shooting stopped and the skirmish was over. The Confederates withdrew and the Union soldiers came out of the woods to bury their dead and care for their wounded.

Dr. Curtiss walked down to the group of Soldiers.

"I am a doctor," he told them and began to examine the men.

"This man is still alive" he said, "bring him up to my house."

Federal officers came out from Calhoun and found the soldier, perhaps several, being cared for by Dr. Curtiss and his family. And that is why the house was spared on Sherman's march to the sea.

James Curtiss was not a Northern sympathizer. His young son was in the Southern Army. He was a Christian, and a physician dedicated to the healing of his fellow man, friend or enemy.

William and Martha Curtiss came to the Cherokee country some time before 1822. Charley Fox remembers a log house that stood in the field north of the Dr. Curtiss home which must have been William and Martha's. Or, it may have been the Schoolhouse for, in those days of no public schools, the school building was a part of every country estate.

William and Martha, James and Elvina, together with Mr. and Mrs. John Ferguson, and Mr. and Mrs. Alfred Wright, organized a church in the Curtiss Schoolhouse, a church that was the mother of the First Baptist church of Calhoun.

This years passed, William and Martha, James and Elvina were gathered to their faters in a letter land and are buried in the cemetery where lie seven generations of the Curtiss family.

William Marion, son of James and Elvina, attended schools at Sonoraville and Calhoun and studied medicine in Louisville, Ky., and in Atlanta, he received his degree in 1871 and came back to minister to his own, the people of Gordon County. He married Anna Maria Hauk, of Sonoraville, daughter of Berry Hauk, of Tennessee and Mary Sanders Hauk. Their children were Alfred Lee, David Clark, Walton Henry, Anna Valeria, Robert Battery, Daisy Marian, James Berry, Howell Cobb and Pinkie Myrtice. Robert, James and Myrtice died in youth.

Dr. Curtiss moved to Atlanta while still a young man, where he established a chain of drugstores. He was on Atlanta's Board of Health, a mason, Woodman, Red Man and a member of the Knights of Phthias.

Anna Maria died and Dr. Curtiss married Delilah Fowler. Their daughter is Willie Mae (Mrs. H. L. Byrd).

Dr. Curtiss health failed and he returned to Gordon County to spend his last years at the old home.

Bea Richardson called me one day in January 1961 to say, "they are tearing down the Curtiss house. I thought you might want to see it."

The north was marching through Georgia again and the South was marching back. The Old Tennessee Road, the Dixie Highway and US 41 were all out-moded. A Super-highway that would cut through the hills, by-pass the towns and stretch its 4 lane length up and down the State was the only solution to the traffic problem of the Century's sixth decade.

"Mrs. Curtiss, your house is in the way," they said, "it must be moved."

Move the old house all the way across the field to the other side of the farm? impossible, the task and the financial consideration were too great. So the house must be dismantled.

The two front rooms went first—and the veranda. The thick log sills lay exposed to air and sunshine after 110 years of holding up the floor that echoed with countless steps of Curtiss men and women and their children.

The columns, lined with rough planks and faced with smooth painted ones, fitted, nailed and joined together by the hands of men of another century, could not be torn apart.

As the timbers came down, the best of them were trucked across to the pine-shaded hill where the new home of Delilah Fowler Curtiss is being erected.

I found two bedrooms and the kitchen still standing, roof intact but weather boarding gone. We sat, Delilah, Willie Mae and I, in the warm kitchen, fragrant with the aroma of food being prepared for supper, and talked about the Curtiss family. Two big Bibles were open on the table and we read the entries made by James and by William—James Marion Curtiss, born August 20, 1825, Elvina A. Curtiss born January 17, 18?6, James M. Curtiss and Elvina A. Cobb were married November 26, 1846; their children, William Marion, born November 6, 1847, James Alford, April 3, 1850, N. Cicero, December 27, 1856 and Joseph Elton, December 9, 1860.

William and Anna were married in Gordon County June 15, 1869 by Rev. Alison Wilson, witnesses were H. B. Hauk and Margaret Hauk Addington.

Names of all the grandchildren and great-grandchildren, births, marriages and deaths, are carefully recorded.

"See what we found in one of the columns this morning," Mrs. Curtiss said as she untied the string around a cardboard box. When the box was opened, History began to sing. Her song ran down the Scale of Time a hundred and 60 years for in this box was a little book, its lower edges black and with age, and frayed, but the print on its pages clear and plain. It was a copy of the minutes of the 6th Annual meeting of the Cherokee Baptist Convention, held at Marietta, May 18, 19, 20, and 21, 1800. Edwin Dyer was moderator of the Convention, W. A. Mercer, secretary and T. H. Stout assistant secretary.

Page 9 records a request that the trustees make out a statement of the indebtness of the Cherokee Baptist College (at Cassville) together with an urgent plea for a plan to endow the College for $50,-000.

There is a report on Sabbath Schools one section of which reads "if you have no Sabbath School in your church, come to the Sabbath School Convention (to meet in Rome, July 1800) and learn how to get one up and keep it going."

On page 12—"We the colored members of the Marietta Baptist Church send you $11.05, collected from our congregation to send to African Missions."

Included in the find was a copy of the Democratic Platform, published in Calhoun in April 1860, by W. V. Wester, a copy of the Atlanta Intelligence of 1860 and an 1858 copy of the New York

Mercury.

And there was a letter, illegible in all the important parts, but it seemed to be describing the building of the house.

William and Delilah were married December 29, 1916. Much younger than her husband, Delilah has survived him for more than 30 years. Now she has moved across the field to her new home on the Fairmount road and Willie Mae and M. L. have returned to their home in Jacksonville, Florida. We say good bye to another land mark as we read, with great respect and admiration, of the contributions made to the growth of the county and State by the Curtiss family. We are sure that the descendants of these strong Christian people will always look with pride at this period in the family's life and will find in the lives of their ancestors, inspiration and encouragement for many generations to come.

Now, you go past the old Morrow place, through the Haney ancestral acres to Gardner's. The springs, flowing from under a bluff, were once a favorite picnic place for Gordon County people. These little walled-in pools are beds of water cress. And here is the Gardner house, home of H. S. Gardner, Oothcaloga District's road commissioner of the 1850's and early settler of the county.

Sherman's headquarters were in the Gardner house while he was in Oothcaloga district. It's a wonderful old house — big double doors, alike at front and back entrances, with glass panels overhead and on each side, hand-planed planks of uneven widths on walls, ceiling and floors and two double chimneys at each end. The house was begun in 1850 and the Gardners moved in two years later. As was customary in those days, the kitchen stood apart from the main house. The passageway has been enclosed and now forms the dining room, a step down from the main house. A stairway rises from the back hall to a half-story of two rooms, one of which, still unpainted, is a store room.

The doors throughout the house are simply fascinating in their construction of up and down planks nailed to cross pieces and inside button fasteners—one door was made of only three wide planks.

Claud and Mattie Johnson—she was the daughter of Melvin and Mina Orr of Orr's Mill—have made the old kitchen into a modern cooking, eating and living room, cheerful with many windows, growing plants and colorful furnishings. It's only a step out the back door onto the granite slabs and a walk across the yard to the long chicken house. (A little grandson was chasing hens around the house.)

Out at the barn, a 2000 pound registered Holstein stood munching a bunch of hay at the trough.

"He's a pet," remarked Mattie Johnson.

"O! a Ferdinand" quipped Bea Richardson.

However, no one volunteered to pat the pet or eat daisies with Ferdinand. When Virginia decided that we wouldn't have time to stop for a closer look at the Holstein Aristocrat, I breathed a sigh of relief.

So, up a mountain again—here's where we found a tree limb blocking the way—to the Gardner cemetery, penned in by a new concrete wall and carefully tended.

Sarah H. Gardner, 1814-1895, was a kind and affectionate wife, a fond mother and a friend to all; Sara E. 1847-1869, wife of John A. Matthias—"O wife how I miss you—from letters 10 & 14 June," the almost undecipherable carving read. We did not know, we could only guess that the quotation was from the letters of John Matthias to Sara, who died 4 years after the War. A John Matthias is listed in Lulie Pitt' roster of Confederate soldiers, in Littlefield's Volunteers Co. B, Gists's Grigade, organized in September 1861.

Elizabeth Ann, 1842-1930, wife of Seincon Stephens, Mary A. Gardner 1868-1885, Annie L., daughter of M. E. and M. C. Gardner, died 1889, William E. Gardner, 1837-1915, Miles A. Thedford 1819-1903, Annie Gardner Thedford, 1850-1930, daughter of H. S. and S. N. Gardner.

The tall slender monument towering over the other graves is that of H. S. Gardner 1816-1910.

The graves of Gardner slaves, one an infant of 1887, are at the back of the cemetery just outside the wall.

The legend is that a black-face man is buried in the Gardner cemetery—not a negro or a minstrel end man. He and another man, both nameless in the legend, were bitter enemies and this man had sworn to kill him on sight. Knowing that his enemy was the conductor, our man of the legend, thinking to disguise himself, blacked his face and boarded a street car in Rome, Ga. His enemy the conductor, recognized him and shot him dead there on the street in Rome. He was buried with the black still on his face. Did his family want him to face his Maker as the black sheep of the family?

"There's a stone on top of the mountain inscribed "this man was killed a few feet from where he is buried," I was told, we set out to verify the report but this was the highest mountain that I couldn't climb. Half way up the bellows began to wheeze and the pumping station was slowing down, Virginia, Mattie and Ivey Owens were out of sight and Bea Richardson went on after a short rest. I returned to the car, followed by two beautiful black and white calves crying "Maa, Maa." If I had not been selected as a mother to man, there is nothing I would like better than being mama to a soft-eyed black and white calf. (How can anyone enjoy eating beef?)

When my companions, looking fresh and unweary, came down from the mountain, they told me that the grave we were seeking was that of D. A. Odum, killed there on the mountain near where he is buried, on May 16, 1864. He was a member of Company A, Mississippi Calvary.

The Kinmans, Claiborne and Wesly, one born in 1805 and one in 1807, are buried near the soldier.

The small pink house stood on a high spot of ground, looking to the mountain. Around it were green fields where fat cattle grazed and a little spring branch gurgled its way through the meadow. Ivey and Bob Owen who own the place were cited in a farm magazine for home and farm improvement.

The pink house is built on the site of Wesley Kinman's log house. Claiborne and Wesley Kinman came to Gordon county in 1832. They lived for 2 years in one of the Oothcaloga mission buildings, then moved to farms of their own in Oothcaloga Valley where they spent the rest of their lives. The farms were pillaged by Union soldiers and all the livestock killed.

Elisha and Talitha, children of Claiborne Kinman, married into the family of Thomas Hall, son of Jesse Hall, soldier of the American Revolution. Both had large families whose descendants are still prominent in Gordon County affairs.

We drove down Trimble Hollow road to the Trimble places, two in Gordon County and one barely over the line in Bartow. Three proud old houses reminders of Gordon County's period of well-to-do county Squires. The house nearest the county line was Will Trimble's. This house had somebody in it, but sat there among the ancient trees looking rather sad and lonely. Mayhap, in the memory of Will Trimble's children, the house is filled with joy and laughter and the light of the parlor lamp still gleams through the triple windows and the veranda yet echoes the footsteps of dear ones while shadowy forms pose on the ornate bannisters or sit serenely in cushioned porch chairs.

"Oh, John Gray lives here," they said, Bea and Virginia, "he went to school to me."

The house looked deserted and empty and we saw no person until we walked to the back and found a group of people busy in a cotton field. Virginia and Mattie went one way while Bea and I chose a small out building to explore. The floor was clean swept and the room empty except for a few pieces of discarded furniture and an oxen yoke hanging on the wall.

Some steps led down to a cavernous gloom.

"I'm afraid to go down there," I kittened.

"Come on I'll go first," said brave Bea.

We descended warily and found a queer-looking table almost filling the room. It was a chicken brooder, long out of use and piled high with chairs, the high-backed, cane-bottomed chairs that I have wanted, to go with my old-time dining table.

"Come and look in the window," Virginia and Mattie called, "it's beautiful in there and there's a well in the middle of the living room!"

Standing tiptoe on a rock, we peeped into a dining room to see rich red wall-to-wall carpet, newly papered walls and handsome antique furniture.

As we stood in the yard, admiring and discussing, a young colored man walked up and said that he was born on the place and that his name was Ulysses Grant Reynolds.

"Are you a Yankee?" Virginia teased.

Ulysses smilingly said "no" and asked if we wanted to see the inside of the house.

John Gray Trimble, Jr. and his wife, who was Sidney Barton, daughter of Mr. and Mrs. R. B. Barton, of Adairsville, are carefully and lovingly redecorating the house that was, until recently, the home of Miss Ella Trimble.

Restoration of this fine old house was begun with the back section, of later date than the main part. The "Well" in the middle of the living room is a cistern and the family room actually grew around it, for the cistern was on the back porch. One side of the room is all windows and the concrete floor is painted red. The brick walls of the cistern, its windlass still in place, are also painted red and the small square trough, through which waste water was once poured to run out and down the hill, held a pot of snake's tongue (some people call it mother-in-law's tongue).

Comfortable chairs, gas heat, lamps, a handsome secretary desk, old prints and many collector items make the room a most inviting place. In the passage leading to the kitchen, there's a wash stand and bowl and pitcher.

Light and sunshine pouring through the tall windows, warm red wallpaper and the open fireplace made us feel that we must sit down to the round dining table and have a cup of coffee, though the master and his lady were not there to invite us.

Ulysses Grant told us that he made the hearth which looks like red brick but isn't. Was this Miss Ella's little churn sitting there, dasher ready, at the window by the fireplace? It is small and tapered toward the top, then flares out to hold the lid and dasher.

A hunt table, its legs shortened, stands on one side of the room, holding a copper kettle lamp, the bowl filled with red berries. A line of varied-size pitchers marches across a narrow shelf over the sink. Built-in oven and cabinets of modern design fit in beautifully with the old furnishings and the comfortable rockers that invite you to rest awhile. A baby's play pen sign-marks the fact that youth is at work here.

The oval banquet table and accompanying chairs, that belong to the Trimbles, a linen and silver chest of three big drawers and two small ones and a chimney-side cabinet filled with china and silver, complete the dining room furnishings. Eye-catching is a small side table of odd construction—a closed center section underneath the top. The open space on one side held a beautiful clear glass cake stand.

A bed with massive headboard, from the Barton family, dominates the bedroom and the dresser and chests are marble-topped. The baby's bed is there and the soft red carpet is kind to the bare feet of sleepy parents who must see to a baby's needs at 2:00 a.m. The painted, prism-hung lamp from the parlor of 50 years ago, now an electric fixture, is the central light for the room. The china clock on the mantel is embossed in gold and black. I had never seen one like it and Ulysses and I picked it up, looking for a date and manufacturer's name, but there was none.

A narrow passage between the bedroom and the main house opens onto a small, square porch. By the inside door is a row of shelves filled with books and such. I saw an Elizabeth II Coronation plate.

We wondered through the silent rooms of the main house, peered up the stairway and wondered what stories the shuttered rooms could tell. Dishes, chairs, bedding and other things lay about, mute reminders of the dismantling. A huge clothes press was still in the hall. Pictures that once hung on the walls, now leaned, backs out, against the wall. We turned them—Faith and Love and The Three Graces—how much the pictures on the wall do tell of the characters of the room's occupants!

Quietly we left through the wide front door and across the long veranda where once, when Agricultural families were the cream of the county, the Squire of the plantation could sit on summer afternoons, family and friends about him, look over his growing crops and offer a prayer of gratitude for the bounty that was the result of his plans and labors.

We had been curious about a tall, mysterious tower located a few yards below the house. It once supported a water-tank, Ulysses said. A piece of rusty pipe was sticking out of the ground beside the driveway and a lily pool with seed pods thick on the lily pads was not far away. The little house at the end of the drive is a wheat granary.

As you leave the Trimble estate, you have in your heart a great admiration for John Gray in his task of restoring the home of his ancestors to its onetime elegance, and for Sidney, his lovely wife, who is a Ruth in her Whither thou goest I will go.

Oothcaloga District, east and west and down to the Bartow line, knee-deep in history, teeming with life today, this is your story.

MOLLIE'S LETTER TO SUSIE
JULY 13TH, 1866

Susie, Darling

I have just received your beautiful present. Please receive my best Thanks. I can't keep from admiring it—so much like you dear self. How can I ever repay you for your kindness. As pleased as I am with it don't think that it is not appreciated when I say I am sorry you have put yourself to so much trouble and expense or that I wished you had of sent that hat instead. None loves a pretty bonnet more than I. ("O Rhett, you know I've just got to have this bonnet"! —1961 quote) Some of my Grandma's pride about me in that respect. So I have on my head and feet something nice I don't "care much else. But comfort would adopt something more suitable for the long rides that we are compelled to take and that in an open Buggy. To ride 14 or 20 miles these hot days with nothing to shield the eyes is not very pleasant. I saw the Seaside (evidently the style name of the bonnet—JBR) and liked it better than anything that I had seen and as there was none in the Country I wrote to you and I suppose that you concluded that I could not be without one of your nice Bonnets and I was so much trouble you would send me one and get rid of me. Now don't be angry. I have written just as if you were by my side. Won't I cut a dash riding with a preacher or have him waiting on me while I am doing up my hair to put on my Love of a Bonnet, keeping him waiting so to be behind his time as the last time I did go. Then to ride with an old slow mule with patched Harness, a wooden spring (seat?) won't I look fine. Newt" says you know that he is tired of mowing Timothy Hay as he has more than he can save. Offering to mow mine—alluding to the heads in my Bonnet—for half.

So much for the Bonnet which are rare things up here, there are four being all in the country 2 you have sent. I have not seen the 2 from Atlanta. Mine is so becoming John Henry says makes me look "mighty Sweet" which is enough to flatter anyone and make them satisfied. Dick B. will conclude that I just got it to please him as I said I had sent for a hat. He said why don't you get a Bonnet they look so much better. I am waiting with much patience to hear from the P. O. to get that Long Letter. I will wait for it to finish this so with love many many kifses ever yours. Susie, Darling it is Sunday evening—Being all alone having written a long letter to Uncle Tom I can't keep my thoughts from turning to you. If the long letter has not come I will write anyway. There was not any preaching around save the Hardshell Mr. Thompson and I know that Mr. Sykes will not blame me if you do for staying home writing to you instead of going there even if I did have a new Bonnet to display—I have read Harvey "On Night. But I wished to put in my plea for you to be at home by the 21st of this month as they are all anticipating a grand time at a Picnic at the spring—I don't care anything about it tho" I have been so selfish as to go to none this year. Can't you come— Before you have I want you to find out if Mrs. Sykes will take me to

board next year and at what and if you can give me employment for
I don't think that I can let you leave me again for the love bird pines
for his mate and you have been mine so long that I miss you so much.
I don't have the Blues so bad when you are near As all the evil
spirits fly before your sweet smile—I can't enjoy life and be as
happy as anyone if I would. I have many kind friends who seem
anxious to have me with them and it is always pleasant to be with
them Tho" it is not profitable For I am always on expenses compelled to appear so as not to disgrace them. I think that I would
rather do something that would support me and which I could find
pleasure. I sometimes fear that I cannot stand confinement tho" my
life has been one of denial yet I have had the will to say when, or
how I should go or what to do. You have stood so can I and if
Mother's health does not prevent I will go with you. I know that I
had rather be with you than to be a cook or any old widower. I will
wait and take my Yankee yet when I will get someone to wait on
me go North and live happy—for these poor subjugated people will
never be able to live easy again—that is in the country all the negroes
flock to Town and there you can get them cheap enough—But in
truth I would rather have negro labor than all the white help you
can give me. I know when you come Susie that you will think we
live in a wildernefs and that the green grass will be quite refreshing to your eyes after gazing on Ribbons and artificials so long but
don't grow fastidious and get shocked if your friends are not so
citified their hearts beat warm and true for you and only await
with the patience of Job your coming. Kate spent the day with Mrs.
Veach yesterday — were all well and George fell in love with
"Soody's" niece and thinks her prettier than his ma's he wishes to
see you I am afraid I won't get to see much of you for you will want
to stay with Ma and I won't be able to stay with you. I received a
long letter from Charlie the other day was coming home and coming
to see us. I must write to him—I owe so many letters—and here I
am writing to you when I might answer them. I told Mother that I
could write to all as easy as I could write to you I would not mind
writing. I thought of offering to put up some fruit for your sister,
any kind that she would wish if you will bring me the jars and
sugar I suppose she has plenty of them. I will if she would like to
have it and think that it would be done nice enough to suit her. But
it would give me pleasure of putting up either Peaches, Pears,
Quinces or Aooles—if I had made anything this year so as to afford
to give—I merely suggest this thinking that it might be cheaper for
me to do it for her as we have such an abundance of fruit. I have
put away one Bottle of Honey for her knowing that you don't have
such am saving Fried chicken for you make haste or it will be
spoilt. Love to all and I will quit my nonsense promising if you will
come soon not to trouble or weary your patience no more. All send
love and ever believe me to be your affec.-friend

                                                                    Mollie.

Home of Robert C. Saxon
Ante Bellum

Home of Colonel James Rogers

WALL STREET HOUSES
(THROUGH 1910)

Could I be an artist for a day, I would set up my easel on the grass plot in front of the Civic Center take by brush in hand and paint pictures of Wall Street.

Shaded mall of the town's memories, graveled lane of the Model T, paved route of the Diesel motor, Wall street runs backward in tender retrospection, forgetting the dust and the mire, disregarding the creeping threat of Commercialism, remembering only the beautiful and the good. It speeds forward on the rolling wheels of Time, scarce seeing the now—transit is too fast—intent only upon the morrow and the mysteries still unexplored, whether of mind or of space.

Fit a canvas to the frame for the decade of 1870. Wall street has long since erased the foot prints of Indian Moccasins and only Talitha Kinman Hall can remember the chief's little daughter riding her pony through the woods. Still raw in the hearts of men are the echoes of the tramp, tramp, tramp of the boys in blue marching through Georgia.

But Wall street weeps not in cemeteries nor yet holds past mortems over mummified remains for it has looked into a crystal ball and knows its destiny.

Cover the crystal ball and save it for a future seance. Look to

Mrs. A. B. David on College Street, 1906.

the north as we picture 1875. The two small white churches in the foreground are the Baptist, facing east and the Methodist, on the corner across the street, facing west. Church street is perfectly beautiful on this May day. The little elms set out by the council and the trees beyond the churches are emerald green in new leaf. White picket fences sentinel around the little houses of worship and the people go in and out the doors and up and down the street, the women in Shepherdess bonnets and long, full skirts and the men in broad-brimmed, flat-topped hats and frock-tailed coats.

Dave Freeman, bright young editor of the town's newspaper, thinks that the odd-looking cupola on the Baptist church should be replaced by one more suitable for the commodious building and that the Methodist steeple isn't inviting either.

Rev. Mr. Wilkes is pastor of the Baptist church and preaching days are second Sundays and Saturdays before. This is the third building for the Baptists. The first one, after the organization in Curtiss School house, stood near Chandler Hill. The second was at the intersection of Piedmont and Wall streets (the home of Mr. and Mrs. John Mote is there now). It was a shell of a wooden building with loose boards laid across the rafters for a ceiling. One Sunday morning a mischievous boy climbed into the loft, waited until sermon had begun, then lifted a board and dropped it yelling "the house is falling!" Preacher and all made a scrambled rush for the doors. This building was destroyed by the Federals in 1864.

The organ used by the Sunday School which has been meeting in the Courthouse, was moved last week to the Baptist church where

Home of Mrs. A. B. David North Wall Street

the Sunday School will now meet. In 1878, the worn out instrument was to be replaced by one of Mason and Hamlin's finest organs.

The Methodist church glows at night in the light of two new hanging lamps. The church needs a sexton. Someone passed Sunday night at 11 O'clock when both doors were open and the lights still burning. Rev. A. C. Thomas is the pastor sent by the Conference last November. He is an earnest and eloquent preacher and Calhoun is fortunate to have him.

This is the year of the great revival. It began in the Methodist church, was continued for 3 weeks in the Baptist and spread all over the county. Barrooms disappeared, Sunday Schools were doubled, the town's worst sinners converted and one hundred and twenty five members were added to the churches.

The Methodist congregation is worshiping its second structure, erected in 1874 on a lot given by E. J. Kiker. John P. King gave the lot in 1850 for the first building on the corner of Court and River streets.

Next to the Methodist church is the home of Calhoun's most prominent lawyer, Col. E. J. Kiker. He always dons a beaver hat for court week and, on the eve of a difficult case, rides his pony around town all night.

The house is Dutch colonial with two gabled front windows in the second story. Green blinds and a gracefully bannistered front veranda add to the attractiveness of the house and the front walk to Wall street is bordered on each side by double rows of daffodils and jonquils. A wire fence encloses the yard. It is cheaper than a picket fence, Col. Kiker says.

Just behind me as I sit in the shade of the Virgin forest trees between Col. Kiker's and town is the square, big-roomed house that is

Home of Judge and Mrs. T. W. Harbin

Mrs. Fields School. Asbury Reeve's carriage and wagon shop is next. Stop by and look over the new buggies and wagons displayed on the front porch.

Across the street in a grove of trees is the big rambling house, with barn in the rear, that is the home of Judge T. A. Foster. Men from out in the country always hitch their ox wagons and horses in Judge Foster's grove, when they come to town. Mrs. Foster, (she was Susan Garlington) a daughter, Flora, and son, Fall, are the other members of Judge Foster's family. Two children, Mary and Oswald, died young.

Judge Foster, (the title was acquired during his service as Justice of Inferior Court 1860 to 1868) was born in Gwinnet County in 1834 and came to Calhoun in 1856 where he entered the hardware business. The next year he joined J. M. Harlem to form the mercantile firm of Foster and Harlan, which was to be the towns leading store for many years.

It is June 1876 and Judge Foster is making brick for a new store building on the corner of North Wall and Courthouse streets. By June of the next year he is having the old wooden store building torn down but it is not until August of 1880 that the new store, costing $5000 and extending 20 feet on Courthouse street and 78 feet on north Wall, stands finished two stories high, ceiled inside and roofed with slate.

Another decade begins and Judge Foster has bought T. M. Ellis' Livery Stable, enclosed the burnt lot, where Hightower's hotel stood, for a horse lot and finished a 65x75 foot addition to the stable. Like many another man who has assumed too many business interests, Judge Foster finds the burdens of life too heavy and one day in September of 1881, he comes home from town, kisses his wife and Florrie, his daughter, walks out to the barn and fires the bullet that takes his life. So the book is closed on the story of one of Calhoun's finest citizens.

In 1917, Ferdinand King, M.D., of New York, was writing articles of reminiscence to the Calhoun Times. Ferdinand was the son of the Dr. King who owned a plantation in Springtown Valley, near what is now Scottsville, on the Rome road.

One of his letters to the paper described a ride rivaling that of Paul Revere or the Highwayman or Ichabod Crane. It happened in 1867.

Ferdinand's father had made a bumper crop of wheat that year and had orderetd one of Foster and Harlan's reapers. The new-fangled machine would not cut the wheat but simply chewed it up. So the reaper was pushed back against the fence and farm hands with scythes went to work on the wheat field.

The next morning, young Dr. King was sent to town with a note for Judge Foster. After reading the note the Judge said to Joe Barrett, his chief clerk, "this is a fine mess, isn't it? There's not a machinist in this town that knows anything about that reaper. I'll have to go myself. I'll get it going in 15 minutes."

The two men proceeded to Boaz's livery stable where Judge Foster ordered his horse saddled and secured a stubble-tailed mule of the Jack rabbit variety for his companion. The Judge's horse, Job, was of immense size and had hoofs as big as sea turtles. Judge Foster was large of body and short of legs and when astride the horse his legs stuck out at an angle of about 50 degrees.

"As we passed the depot" Dr. King wrote, "the train waiters waved. George Ransom was at the depot and later told us that the circus was so good that he was tempted to follow it to the end.

"Before we reached the Pine Thicket, I found I was on the wrong side of the Judge. He was an inveterate tobacco chewer and at short intervals, discharged an enormous shower of tobacco juice, which I had to dodge. I changed places and became the leader.

"Judge Foster wore white linen pants, a white vest and a wide-brimmed straw hat. His cotton socks were flopping over his shoe tops. One hand held the reins and the other divided time between his flapping straw hat and a big silver watch with which he insisted on pounding the pommel of his saddle as though marking time for the riders.

"By the time we had reached Oothcaloga Mills, his pants had slipped up to his knees. As we passed the Young farm we flushed a large body of barnyard fowls and one hen lost two thirds of her brood under the feet of the Judge's charger. As we passed Squire Neal's a large, unfriendly dog dashed out, seized the loose end of my trousers and made a lunch of it. The Judge's horse knocked a fat slow-moving hog out of a mud hole and crushed a black snake that, disturbed by the commotion, was squirming across the road.

"As we approached the white church, I suggested that we stop at the creek for the horses to take water. 'Couldn't think of such a waste of time' replied the Judge, 'we've got to get to your daddy's by noon.'

"I drew reins at the Creek. The Judge figured to clear the stream at one bound but his horse had other plans. He stopped at the brink, set his feet firmly and the Judge took an involuntary header into the stream.

"Ye gods and little fishes! Picture the Judge sitting there, somewhat dazed, in the middle of that creek. The water was clear, so his linen did not suffer so much from the water bath but it clung to him like the paper on a wall."

Dr. King and Judge Foster remounted and proceeded at a slower pace, stopping at each stream for the horses to take water. After they reached the farm, Judge Foster spent two hours on the reaper but coundn't make it work.

*   *   *   *   *

The Malone's live in the house on the north corner of Wall and Trammell streets. With gables at each end, formed by the steep-pointed roof and three windows breaking the front roof this is almost a house of seven gables. Green blinds against a white wall and a picket fence made the home of Dr. J. H. and Sara Dickson Malone one of the most attractive on the street and a perfect setting for the interesting young people of the family, Sallie, Lou, Alfred, Frank, Paul, Orrie and Nell. Many are the balls, dinners and sociables held in this hospitable home.

It was in the Malone house that Harris Reeve dressed for her wedding and walked on a white cloth laid across the street to the church for her marriage to Col. F. A. Cantrell. Lou was an attendant in the wedding and Alfred and Frank were ushers. Prominent in the social life of the town, the Malone children also excelled in School work. Frank received honorable mention for his declamation Spartacus and the Gladiators, Lou's contribution to the closing program of the Gordon County University was a recitation, Literature, and Orrie's sweet singing often charmed the commencement audiences.

Dr. Malone spent the war years as physician to Anderson prison, came to Calhoun after the war and entered the drug business with Dr. W. J. Reeves. Until the fire of 1888, the southwest corner of Court and Wall streets was known as Reeves and Malone's corner. Dr. Malone was county school commissioner during the 80s. After Sara's death in 1889 at the age of 37, the drug store was sold to Dr. Chastain and the Malone family moved to Atlanta. But the aging doctor was not happy away from his old home and soon returned to live for a while at the Calhoun hotel. He was serving as country treasurer at the time of his death in 1899.

North of Dr. Malone's is the home of J. B. Boyd. Sometime later, the Pricketts would own the house and the Prickett daughters, Mary and Cornelia would live here until their deaths. The small was then to be razed and P. C. Dunnagan and A. B. David, neighbors to the right and left, would buy equal parts of the lot.

Just where Wall street narrows and curves lightly to the east, Line street, once the county line, comes down to intersect the north-south lane. One day this would become Heartbreak Corner for Sallie Kimbrough. She was to see her beloved trees cut to make way for a paved throughway and the side walk come up to her window. She did not live to see her house torn down and the part of it left, moving down Wall street on a truck, nor to see her loved spot become Gasoline Corner.

The house was the home of C. O. Boaz and Dr. Harbin and T. W. Harbin. H. J. Doughty died here. When Mark Matthew's horse ran away that day in 1899, through the business section and two blocks to Rock street, he stopped at C. O. Boaz's fence, left the wrecked buggy there and ran back to the Livery stable with one shaft hanging.

Claude and Vera Erwin bought the house, did extensive remodeling and sold it to Roy and Helen Richards. But for so long it has been home of Sallie Kimbrough and, as such, it bowed to progress.

* * * * *

A deep ditch runs along each side of Wall street and another cuts diagonally across to empty Mt. Pisgah's waters into the fields beyond the railroad. A wooden bridge spanned the big ditch for a time until the City Council eventually put in a brick culvert. The Cantrell home is the only house on the east side of this block in my picture of the 1880s. Lawrens Hillhouse is building across the street and has the framework up and ready for the weatherboarding when the cyclone of 1888 lays it flat. Undaunted, he begins again and in 1890 the work is finished and Idalette Hillhouse comes up from Cartersville to keep house for her brother. Laurens has set a circle of elm trees from his place to the A. S. Tatum home and to this day the trees give shade to the houses later built on the Hillhouse lot.

Laurens Hillhouse, from the windows of his soul, could see beauty in a wooden ring from a pineapple crate. That's what they are, the rings in the ornamented gables at each end, and on the front of his house. Pineapples, shipped to Augusta, were held in place in the crate by wooden rings. Laurens picked them up, brought them to Calhoun and carved delicate spindles for the center of each ring.

Four rings are set between two then scallop-trimmed strips of wood with a center strip connecting the point of the gable and the lower stripes. A semi-circular piece of wood in which six of the spindles radiate from the center support is placed over this line arrangement.

An old picture of the house shows a narrow veranda, almost hidden by a vine and by tall-growing shrubs — J. N. F. Neal purchased the place from Mr. Hillhouse in August of 1907. He made improvements, probably by building a wider veranda and installing two little windows with blinds to size and diamond panes, in the front. Mr. Neal sold the house to C. L. Moss in 1913 and seven years later, Mr. and Mrs. Henry Dorsey became owners of the property. Only the four families have lived there, Laurens and Idalette Hillhouse, the J. N. F. Neal family, Lum and Madge Moss with their children and Henry and Annie Dorsey with their daughters.

The Dorseys immediately began to make changes that have serialized through the years as the owners planned and worked to make the staunch old house conform to newer patterns of living. A chimney was removed to make the living room larger, a pantry jutting from the kitchen wall on the north was made into an entrance way and the big south porch became a bathroom and a latticed summer living room.

Originally the roof of the front porch was a sun deck "and it never leaked" Mrs. Dorsey said. A White Columned Stoop now frames the handsome Colonial doorway and the deck is edged with ornamental iron instead of the frame wood bannisters. The upstairs door is recessed and two big windows from the side walls. The interesting figures carved over the door and around the outside of the pediment were most likely done by the hand of Laurens Hillhouse.

In the spacious living room, the rose-flowered draperies harmonizing with the soft green of the rug, and Empire sofa, Duncan Phyfe end tables, comfortable chairs, lamps, and a card table near the window tell the story of an old house that lives on in peace and contentment, knowing that it is loved for its homeness.

A drop leaf cherrywood table, now Katherine's, was bought many years ago by Mr. Dorsey's mother from Mrs. Hubbard, and used as a kitchen table. The needlepoint covers on footstools and chair were done by Katherine and by Frances during her long and successful conflict with a serious illness.

But the dominant feature of the pleasant room is the reproduction in oils of a photograph of Annie Dorsey and her two young daughters, Katherine and Frances. The lovely pose, the delicate skin tints, the white of the children's dresses against the sky blue of their mother's lace and georgette gown all suggest a Madonna by Raphael or Rembrandt. Perhaps only a Titian could have caught the subtle shades in Annie Dorseys auburn hair.

The wide opening between dining and living rooms was once close by French doors, "I took them down and stored them in the garage," Mrs. Dorsey said, "because it was too much work to care for them." A former tall-boy Majestic radio has been remodeled to make an attractive open-front cabinet which holds a milk glass

WALL STREET HOUSES
247

collection and flowered china pieces. The space formed by the double chimney has been utilized for built in cabinets one in each room.

Up in Katherine's room is a walnut dresser hand-made by Bob Collins' ancestor. A whiff of lavender scent from a handkerchief drawer, a glimpse of a merry face in the oval mirror and a rustle of taffeta as a girl of the 80's leaves for the Ball — you feel it as you stand in this lovely room with its antique bed, low white-painted chest set by the little window and a pine-branch wall paper.

Mrs. Dorsey's room, the hall sitting room and a bath complete the upstairs arrangement of the house.

The untimely death of Henry Dorsey in 1935, at the age of 48, was the tragic chapter in the life of his family. Joining the A. R. McDaniel Co., in young manhood he went on to a partnership in the firm. Erect of cariage, handsome in appearance. Henry Dorsey is remembered by everyone who knew him for his smiling face and friendly greeting.

* * * * *

Col. and Mrs. O. N. Starr will go to housekeeping in the new Wright house on the upper end of Wall Street. The year is 1886. The house was later the home of A. S. Tatum. Baptist minister known to have been a pastor of Unity Baptist church at Plainville. He was the author of a book, Gems of Short Sermons.

By 1893, L. D. Hillhouse, of Palm Beach, Florida, has bought A. S. Tatum's residence up in Gilt Edge, the most beautiful and desirable section of the City. Mr. Hillhouse sold the place to Dr. C. F. McClain in 1899.

Dr. McClain had come to Calhoun from Acworth in May of 1895, but moved to Tilton in August of the same year. He returned to Calhoun and purchased the house that was to be his home for the rest of his life. Pleasant, courteous, always ready to answer any call night or day, Dr. McClain was the beloved physician. He and Mrs. McClain, the former Fannie Orr, of Acworth, were devoted members of the Methodist church and among the town's most civic-minded citizens. Mrs. McClain was a charter member of the Woman's Club, a member of the Cabin building committee and president of the Club in 1919-20. Active in the woman's Missionary Society, she organized the Young Woman's Missionary Society that later became the Business Women's Circle and then the Wesleyan Service Guild. With her daughter, Lois, she was in charge of the Beginner's department of the Methodist Sunday School. On each October promotion day, she tearfully gave her six year olds to the Primary department.

Then Dr. McClain was gone and Mrs. McClain too and only Lois was left. She could not live alone in the house on North Wall street, so left to make her home with relatives in Acworth and Atlanta.

Mr. and Mrs. J. H. Hobgood bought the house in 1934.

The great-grandfather of the Hobgood family came to Georgia from North Carolina. His sons and grandsons lived in Bartow, Pickens and Whitfield counties before coming to Gordon.

The son of the migrating great-grandfather married Miss Mitchell and their children were Frank, Bill and Joe. Frank and Mary Jane Bennett Hobgood were parents of Annie, (Mrs. Joe Tarvin, of Sugar Valley and Calhoun) and H. M. who died at

Resaca.

Joe's children were Mary, John, Skid, Penny, Genie, Bell and May. Genie married a Hughes and became the father of Frank Hughes, distinguished in Georgia Educational Circles.

Bill moved to Pickens but his son John returned to Gordon and it was John's son, J. Hollister, who became the owner of the McClain house.

Mrs. J. H. Hobgood was Dell Sutherland, daughter of Jim and Leona Green Sutherland. The Sutherlands, too, lived in Bartow and Pickens before coming to Gordon.

Tom, a brother of Jim, was the father of Carl Sutherland whose latest achievement (1960) was that of being elected president of the Reserve Officers Association of the United States after a colorful career in the Army and its Reserves.

A talent for music runs through the family of Hollister and Dell Hobgood, probably inherited from Leona who was able to play several instruments without any music study.

Perhaps the outstanding musicians of the family are Gene, a cousin, and son of Gene and Ruby Sutherland and Betty Hobgood (Mrs. Clayton Doss). Both are proficient in piano and organ and both are ministers of music in large churches. Gene is gifted also with a beautiful tenor voice.

The two younger Hobgood sons are married to talented musicians, Jack, to Gloria Gay and Billy, to Shirley Hall. The eldest son J. H. Jr., is the owner and editor, of the Gordon County News. His wife, Mary Lou Nevin, daughter of a Dalton newspaper editor, is also a graduate of Journalism and is at present a member of the City School Board, the first woman ever elected to this position. Another son, Trammell, died a few years ago. He had married the girl next door, Helen Beamer.

The Hobgood house on North Wall, now a duplex, has been added to and remodeled until there are, Dell said, "three rooms across the front, three rooms in the middle and three rooms across th back." Two kitchens have been made from the big south porch and there is still plenty of porch.

The front of the house is ell-shaped and the extending room ends in a shingle-surfaced gable with lattice work at the top. The porch roof is supported by slender Doric Columns.

Two wide windows light the front rooms and are fitted inside with old venetian blinds, louvered in six sections. The short slats are fastened to a dowel rod that is moved up and down to open or close the sections.

There are seven fire places in the house each with handsome pillared mantels and tiled hearths in brown or green. Double sliding doors connect the parlor and reception hall and all rooms have the original chandeliers.

Dell Hobgood's cherished heirloom is a love seat from her first house keeping days. The back bed room that was Dr. McClain's, has recently been furnished with a bed from the old Kimball House in Atlanta. The horizontally panelled high headboard and slightly lower foot-board are in solid cherry.

*   *   *   *   *

Mr. Ed Jackson has bought an interest in the furniture business of Jackson and Griffin, the new firm that bought J. S. Hall and Co. This was in September of 1899 and in December of the same

year Mr. and Mrs. E. L. Jackson moved into the Henderson house,
corner of College and Line streets. The Jacksons at another time
lived in the Dr. Reeve cottage on College, now the home of Mr.
and Mrs. Homer Bailey. The furniture store was located in the
brick building south of the Doughty building and was purchased in
1903 by Mr. Jackson and Mrs. Anna King.

The house on North Wall Street, now the home of Mr. and
Mrs. Oscar Stewart, was built by Mr. Jackson in 1905, on a lot
acquired from Laurens Hillhouse. Its lines are simple, the nearest
thing to ornamentation are the gables of the north room which are
faced with double edged shingles.

Florence Jackson was noted for her beautiful flower garden
and her charm as a hostess.

Mr. Jackson added a Funeral Directors Service to his business
and was the first to use regular funeral hearses. Wagons had been
used until Mr. Jackson bought his black-painted vehicle. Pictures
of the hearse in the Jackson advertisement show the high body set
apart from the driver's seat, the coach's glass windows draped in
fringed curtains and carriage lamps decorating the front.

Of Mr. Jackson's two sons, Thurman carried on the Jackson
tradition of Furniture Dealer and Carl continued the Funeral
Service. He was the first in town to have his own Funeral Home.
The Funeral Service was sold to J. W. Thomas after Carl's death.

I sat on the steps of the Doughty cottage to write about the
Johnson house across the street. Mrs. Story, who has lived in the
house for many years, was not there. She was ill at a hospital in
another town.

Mrs. H. J. Doughty had built the house next door to her own
house in 1899 for her adopted son, Eugene, and his bride. It was
describetd as an "elegant cottage, one of the most neatly finished
and elegant homes in town." Finished in hard oil, all the rooms
were wainscoted and fitted with elegant mantel and grates and
elegantly furnished by Mrs. Doughty.

A. R. McDaniel bought the cottage in 1904 from Mr. Harbour
and in 1909 the little house was moved across the street to make
way for the new house that S. C. McBrayer and a strong Corps
of men were to build for Mr. Jesse Johnson.

                              *   *   *   *   *

The Johnson house is one of the most beautiful of the older
houses on Wall Street. Two tall, white chimneys rise from the
hipped roof and an elaborately ornamented gable projects from the
center front. The same delicate spindles found in the Dorsey house
are used above the three windows in the gable. Diamond panes in
the upper sash over a solid-paned lower one make the tri-window
the taller one in the center, a shorter one on each side, eye-catching. The pediments are made of small square blocks.

The colonial doorway is framed by an entrance porch with two
Ionic columns. At first, the house had the popular front and across
one end veranda which was later replaced by the present arrangement of a bannistered porch at the end, opening from the living
room, and the entrance portico.

Mrs. Johnson had wept heartbrokenly when she learned that
the carpenters had built the roof too low, making it necessary to
cut two feet from the base of her Columns.

A handsome fan light over the door, glass side panels with

leaded insets — four squares in the center, two above and two below the center ornament-and a lacing of tiny panes at the bottom and top of the panels are the features of the beautiful doorway to the Johnson house.

The marriage to Miss Mattie Hill and Mr. Jesse Johnson had occurred in January of 1901 at the bride's home in Resaca and for a time, the couple had lived in Atlanta where Mr. Johnson held the position of Dispatcher for the W & A Railroad. The illness of Mrs. Johnson's mother brought them back to Resaca for about a year and, since 1909, the house on Wall Street has been the family home.

Tragedy struck the family with shocking suddenness when, Jack, the only son was killed in an automobile accident only hours after his marriage to Elizabeth Sloan.

Son of Dr. J. A. and Mary Barnett Johnson, Jesse had a deep bass voice and his singing enriched the music of the Baptist choir throughout the years.

Mattie Hill Johnson, gentle, kind and beautiful, was a belle in her girlhood days and one of Calhoun's loved and gracious matrons. Crippled by a fall, she spent her last years in a wheel chair. A sweet memory of Mrs. Johnson is the smiling greeting she gave to friends and everyone who passed her shaded porch on a summer day.

Like mother, like daughter, Mary Johnson was a charming hostess on my Sunday afternoon visit to the home of her parents where she now lives alone.

When the house was built a hall extended through the center and was divided midway by two columns, matching the veranda colonnades and red vetlvet portieres. After the front hall was combined with the south room, the columns were placed at each end of the former partition.

The usual arrangement in the days of the long hall, placed the parlor, dining room and kitchen on one side and the bed rooms on the other. The four fireplaces have mirrored mantels, corinthian columns reaching from floor to top, except one which has broken columns, and tiled hearths in white, blue or green. The living room mantel formerly in the parlor, is mahogany. The others are oak. Two small cabinets built into the top of the dining room mantel hold cut-glass goblets and small wine glasses that belonged to Mary's great-grandmother. Other prized inheritances from the mother of the grandmother are a bone china plate in bird-of-paradise design and a fruit compote in exquisite blue glass. Great-grand-mother brought the set of six bone plates in her lap from her mother's. Only two are left the other being in the possession of a cousin, the former Louise Sheats, of Kingston.

Standing under a small service table placed against the wall, are two child's chairs, the blue one was Mattie's, the red one, Jesse's.

On the service table, among other pieces, are a handsome blue chccolate pitcher, wreathed in gold, a low glass bowl iced in white and a cookie jar that looks as if it had come from a Persian Mart, but Mary said, "I think mother got it with Arbuckle coffee coupons."

Mrs. Johnson took her parents' banquet lamp with its colored glass shade and prisms, removed the bowl and wired the shade to

the chandelier. I wish I might have been invited to dine in the
rainbow glints that must have suffused the table and its setting
from this unusual central light.

Julia Cleghorn Hill's drop leaf table in solid cherry stands in
the back hall. It is part of great-grandfather Hill's banquet table
which would seat a large number of people when assembled.

Two fine antique beds, a marble topped dresser and family
pictures, one of the Hill family and house at Resaca, and of Mr.
and Mrs. John Hill in their youth and one of the boy Jesse Johnson
are in the south bedrooms.

When Mr. Johnson was living as a young man in a boarding
house full of ladies who were always embroidering, he remarked
one day "I believe I could do that." The ladies dared him to try
and the result of the dare hangs framed in the bedroom — perfectly stitched red rose buds on a green leafed stem with Jesse's
and Mattie's pictures set in small open ovals in the white cloth.
The embroidery work was exhibited at the Gordon County Fair
and would have won first place except for the fact that it was
done by a man!

Back in the living room, past the two beautiful columns, we
stand before a crayon picture of Aurora, the Dawn, sipping nectar
from a blue morning glory. This work was done by Mattie Hill while
she was a student at Mary Sharp College in Murfreesboro, Tenn.
Aurora's lovely, calm face might have been a self-portrait and the
flowing grace of her white robe bespeak the pure mind of a sweet
girl of the nineties.

An unusual lamp with tall alabaster stem, its round ruby-red
glass bowl decorated with a painted sea horse in a strip of sea
weed, was a gift from one of Mattie's beaux. A parlor table with
red marble top, a settee upholstered in leather and a glass bell
holding a natural-looking bunch of flowers were Mrs. John Hill's.
She was Mattie Cox from S. C. and came to Resaca with her family
during the Civil War. John Hill came from Tennessee.

The modern beds in Mary's room (the old parlor) are nothing
loth to hold as coverlets, two gorgeous quilts made by Mrs. Hill.
One is the Irish Chain design using tiny diamond shaped pieces,
striking in pastel colors from an age when red and green were
the quilt colors. Infinetismal stitches form the pineapple pattern in
the white squares and fresh rose leaves were used as models for
the quilted ones. The other quilt follows the red and green color
plan and is made in the Cherokee rose pattern. Mattie L. Hill's
name and birth date are quilted into the white center blocks. A
delicate Dresden China Clock sits on the mantel in Mary's room,
tick-tocking its memories of the lovely lady who reigned as queen
of the beautiful home filled with loved traditions.

As I left this Calhoun home of the early 1900's. I glanced
back to the mahogany mantel and the bronze clock that had
measured the hours for Mattie and Jesse Johnson and to the tall
candelabra on the hall table, that came with the clock as wedding
gifts, I wished that Time could roll backward and bring again the
charming people who lived in the Wall Street houses.

* * * * *

When the Baptist church realized the need of a home for the
pastor, they began in January of 1905 to raise money for the
project. By February $1100 had been pledged and the house that

is now the home of Mrs. F. C. Bolding was built on a lot given by W. L. Hines. Notable is the unusual facade of the house. On the north side a long roof salt-boxes to the rear and rises steeply at the front to form a high gable. Three narrow windows in the upper story are slightly projected and above them is a small arched ventilator. The roof extends over the front porch and a narrow frieze of block spindles ornaments the roof line. The room over the veranda has short windows, set out from the wall and trimmed with small square posts to match the larger ones on the porch. Uneven lines on the south side break the monotony of a straight wall and three large windows welcome the warm south breezes.

Then the Baptist pastor's family was provided with another home near the church and the big Wall street house went into other hands.

In May, 1905, The Calhoun Times recorded the death of Mrs. F. M. Bolding at the age of 90. She was born in South Carolina and had come to Gordon about 1839. Grandma Bolding had been living with her son, F. M. Jr., at his home near Fairmount.

F. M. Bolding's eldest son, Mark, excelled in oratory during his college years and became a successful lawyer in Atlanta.

The second son, Fred C., insisted that farm life was not the one that he desired, that he must have a profession. He chose the profession of dentistry.

One day, over in the north Georgia town of Dahlonega, Fannie McGuire, came out of her house and walked across the street to the hotel to use the telephone. The Proprietor greeted her with "come in, I want you to meet the new tooth doctor."

So Fannie McGuire and Dr. Fred C. Bolding met and were married. They came to Calhoun in July of 1917 where they shared the J. B. F. Harrell house (the old E. J. Kiker home) with newly-wed Rob and Annie Mae Bolding. Their first house-alone living was in the Doughty cottage. At that time, Lucile Ballew Hopper owned the former Baptist Pastorium, then a duplex. Colonel (his name, not a title) Dorsey lived in one apartment and Mrs. Johnnie Gordon, the other. Colonel's lease ran on for several months after Dr. Bolding bought the house but Mrs. Gordon moved out and Dr. and Mrs. Bolding with their children, Fred and Frances, lived in two rooms of their new home.

The Carter family had lived in the house. Exzene Carter was married to Ralph Haney in the room that is now Mrs. Bolding's den. Kate Royster (Mrs. John Littlefield) lived in this room when she first came to town.

The Boldings joined the army of remodelers and went to work on the interior of the house. Down through the years, their ideas have united with the good features of the house to make one of the most charming and comfortable homes in town.

A wall was removed and French doors installed across the rear hall where the stairway begins and turns and rises to the second story. Three rooms have handsome mirrored mantels and tiled hearths. In the dining room and former parlor, the round columns are floor length and in the living room, short ones support the mantel top.

The pride of the breakfast room, once a butler's pantry, are the beautiful walnut table, made by Cap McEntire, the four ladder-back, splint-bottom chairs from the parlor of Fannie's girl-hood home and a utility cabinet made from the base of a side board, also a family heir-loom. Two long ripple front drawers and two short ones hold linens and a glass upper section reveals shelves full of china and crystal.

Two of Fannie's water colors hang in the breakfast room, one, a pair of storks and the other a redpepper plant.

Among the many beautiful pieces of china displayed in the dining room is a tiny chocolate set that belonged to Fannie's sister. The two little cups are set in petaled saucers and there's a tiny bowl for lump sugar and a toy-like pot. Other pieces of note are a cake plate in quaint design and seven cutglass dessert dishes.

Water colors done by Fannie during her School days at Dahlonega, are one of pale lilacs, another of nasturtiums and a bunch of brown-eyed susans in a little Brown jug. The Young artist found the susans growing along a ditch and took them to art class.

Over by a window in the living room stands a beautiful love seat "Doctor and I sat here when we were courting" Fannie told me. The settee is covered in pale green tapestry and its high curved back is framed with carved mahogany.

The pie crust telephone table and a slender three-legged table are from Fannie's girl-hood home. "The Knights of Honor met upstairs" she said and the little table and another like it were lamp stands." No longer needed to hold the light, the little table sits pertly beside the piano holding a handsome strawberry-wreathed vase.

Three old paintings in the living room, Cane Creek Falls, The College and Campfire Scene, were painted by an "Old Maid" in Dahlonega and given to Dr. Bolding in payment for dental work.

A flowered chocolate pot with three of its six cups and saucers, sits on the coffee table. The set was a gift to his mother by the young Fred C. Bolding in his first years away from home.

The old pastorium parlor has long been the family sitting room for the Boldings. The warm red tint of the walls, matching the maroon tiles in the white-manteled fire place, the Doctor's easy chair in place, other comfortable chairs and the lamps synchronize the heart beat of the home. Fannie's water colors in here are a seascape and a snow scene.

"I've decided something," said Mrs. Bolding one day to her son. "What now?" he asked.

"I'm going to get rid of this house. It's too big" was the reply.

But will she get rid of her house of memories? Memories of Little Sister who died there. "Who are the smartest ones in your grade?" her mothetr asked. Frances replies "Me and C. P. Reeve." Memories of the tall blond Doctor and his bird dogs and his cabin at Dew's. The young son following his father's profession. The lawn with its formal garden, and roses and myriads of flowers. The plot behind the fence where the tuberoses grew — I think Fannie Bolding will manage some how to keep her big house and her green and flowering yard.

*   *   *   *   *

Col. F. A. Cantrell had bought the lot across from J. B. Boyd's and next to C. C. Boaz in 1891 but sold it to W. F. King the next year. It was on this site, considered the prettiest in town, being on the line of beautiful water oaks running north from the Baptist church, that Mr. King erected his elegant residence in 1892.

W. F. King had come from Cave Spring in 1880, just in time to be an attendant in the Wilson-Hines wedding in February of 1881. He was also a member of the Reeves-Cantretll wedding party in 1885. Mr. King was first married to Mrs. Crawford and their home was the house on lower Court street later known as the Tinsley place. He was in business with Mr. Hines, for a time, ran a store of his own and later joined Mr. Haney in a partnership that was dissolved September 13, 1892.

Mrs. King died not long after the new house on Wall street was built.

Loneliness is not a fit companion for a man and empty rooms are never any solace. So, W. F. King began to think of a new companion and Mistress of his house.

Someone said "Why don't you go down to the tabernacle meeting this week and meet Miss Lyda Saxon?" It was Anna, the auburn-haired sister, with whom W. F. King fell in love and they were married. Mr. and Mrs. Logan Pitts gave a reception, at their lovely new home down the street, for Mr. and Mrs. King.

Mr. King's health failed and he died a young man, only 49 years old.

Robert C. Saxon, a native of Laurens, S. C., moved to Gordon in 1850, the year the county was created. His first home was one of the Indian log cabins but he soon built a small frame dwelling. With slaves to till the almost virgin soil, Mr. Saxon was successful from the start. A growing family needed a larger house. The gravel house was the outcome.

In an article written for The Atlanta Journal, Lilie Pitts tells the story of this unique and historic house which was located in Gordon county, very near the Bartow county line.

"My father drew the plans himself," Manie Saxon told Miss Pitts, "skilled laborers were employed and, after many months, the job, representing so much thought and labor, was completed. It was a beautiful structure of octagonal design, two stories high, each showing the same floor plan, that of four large rooms supplied with double windows, and four small triangular rooms, arranged to preserve the octagonal contour. These latter served as front and rear entrances, butler's pantries and stairway landings. The concrete walls were a foot or more in thickness. The chimney, which was located in the center, contained eight fireplaces, and they never smoked!"

"For two years," Lucile wrote, "this dream house of Mr. Saxon's sheltered a large and happy family. The gray of the pseudo-stone walls blending with the green of grass and foliage, the fagged paths, the background of virgin forest, appealed strongly to their sense of beauty; passers-by paused to wonder and admire, guests were welcomed, friends and neighbors enjoyed the cordial hospitality and life flowed smoothly."

But there were no schools in the neighborhood, so Mr. Saxon moved to Cassville to take advantage of the fine male and female Academies there, leaving his Gordon County home in the hands of a caretaker.

When war was declared, Mr. Saxon joined the confederacy, where he served as Adjutant, quartermaster of General Lucius Gartell's brigade, Captain of a Company of Georgia Reserves that he himself assembled and Lieutenant Colonel.

As the enemy approached, Mrs. Saxon and the children fled to Hawkinsville, picking up the two older girls as Wesleyan College, Macon, and taking with them the slaves and necessary equipment.

The octagon house was used as a fort and on May 24, 1864, was the scene of a sharp skirmish during which the concrete walls, designed for permanency, were crushed to pieces by the enemy's artillery.

Accompanied by Anna Saxon King and Lyda Saxon, Thomas Spencer, of the Daily Tribune News at Cartersville, paid a visit to the site of the octagon house on July 25, 1950.

According to Mr. Spencer's story, written for his paper, a confederate battery, just west of the Saxon house and in the middle of the road, was playing havoc with the attacking Federals. So accurate was the fire that the Federals brought up thirty six guns to silence this one battery.

"But" wrote Mr. Spencer, "lets let the historian of the First Tennessee Regiment, Company H. give his description of the house."

"The house was of fine brick, octagon in shape and a perfect fort. There were windows upstairs, downstairs and in the basement. There were fine chairs, sofas, settees and Brussells carpeting, fine lace and damask curtains. Fine bureaus and looking glasses. Beautifull pictures in gilt frames and a library of fine books."

"More than one Federal report mentions the house and how it withstood the bombardment of shot and shell and minie balls. The Federals paused to pour solid shot and shell into the house and, today, not one scrap remains of this magnificent pre-war home. A plaque now marks the spot, placed there by the Georgia Historical Commission.

Robert C. Saxon, a lawyer who began his practice at Cassville, was Road Commissioner for Gordon county's 856th. district (Lily Pond) in 1852 and superintendent of Bartow County Schools for sixteen years. He was first married to Martha Elizabeth Glenn Crocker and second to Mrs. Georgia Whitaker.

One of the precious heirlooms in possession of Lyda Saxon, is a lock of her mother's hair cut from the young girl's head by her mother, Malinda Crocker, on the eve of Elizabeth's marriage to Robert C. Saxon, son of Charles Hugh Saxon, on February 9, 1843. Other mementoes are Elizabeth Saxon's silver thimble and two or three legal papers handwritten by Malinda Crocker in 1840 and 1842.

Bell was the oldest, Orie was the fattest, Manie was the tallest, Clara was the goodest, Anna was the prettiest, Kathleen was the smartest — this is the way Lyda, the youngest, described the Saxon sisters "and," she twinkled, "since none had been called the sweetest, I decided I would be the sweetest."

To the people who have known Lyda Saxon through even a few of her 94 years, "the sweetest" is the title that any of us would have chosen for her.

Mr. Saxon had bought Grassdale with Confederate money and put the slaves out there. After the war and the freeing of the slaves, he made a school house of the slave cabins. A Mr. Tomlinson had begun the building of Grassdale, but war came and he could not finish the work. Mr. Saxon bought the property and completed the white-columned brick house. Grassdale burned and again the Saxon family had lost a beautiful home.

Five of the Saxon daughters married but two elected to remain single, Manie, to teach School and Lyda to become a nurse.

An oval framed miniature of the young girl, Lyda, pictures a lovely face, the abundant hair coiled on the back of the head and lying in loose waves over a patrician brow. Another photograph shows her in a gown she wore as bridesmaid in a friends wedding, a part she played so often that one was tempted to say "Fie, Lyda, didn't you know three times a bridesmaid never a bride!"

Happily married sisters are sometimes eager match makers and to Kathleen Mavourneen (the smartest) the seeming complacence of the pretty little sister in her spinster state was the inspiration of a story entitled "To Wed or Not To Wed."

Kathlen names her heroine Malinda Mitchell who because of the war, had been deprived of many privileges, both social and educational that had been the heritage of the ante-bellum Southern girl, Malinda's type was rather that of the Grecian, with clear cut features and dark sparkling eyes. Her disposition was sunny and cheerful, an eye always for the beautiful and a pleasant word of greeting for the old as well as for the young."

The happy carefree days of farm life, as the sisters, the brother and Malinda grow to maturity, are recalled, the searching of field and wood for the first spring fruits, the riding of the tree horses, finding birds' nests, wading the cool, rippling brook and many other events of those character-building years.

Malinda (or Lyda) was ever the magnet around which flocked a bevy of girls for stories and conundrums. The boys gathered around too, but in vain, Malinda would say, "I can't love you boys other than friends. You would not wish an unloving wife" or "I am too generous with my affections to concentrate on one."

One by one the girls fell out of line and took on the matrimonial yoke, even Katrina, who joined the band of matrons and faced the future bravely.

"It is no mean sacrifice that a woman makes," wrote Kathleen, "When she takes the marriage vows — giving up her friends for his friends, adjusting the household machinery to his convenience. A woman does not mind adversity so much if it is garnished with love and appreciation."

"Malinda," the story continues, "compared the happiness of her mated friends and decided to tread the winepress alone. The father and mother she humored, smoothed and nursed through their declining years and then she stands alone. Could we call her a misspent life? No, the hand that has steadied the old and the weak, the life that has been spent in ministering to parents is as much honored as hers that has been given to replenishing the earth."

Lyda remained a bachelor girl. She went to West Ellis hospital in Chattanooga to study nursing and was graduated there in 1912. During her stay at West Ellis, she wrote poems to all the doctors and nurses and wrote the story of her training days in rhyme, concluding —

> "But the busiest day of them all
> I now so vividly recall
> Patients many, nurses few
> And, oh, so much to do
> Duty hours six 'til ten

Thermometer stood 100 then
July fourth, nineteen eleven
Only time I wished for Heaven
That strenuous day I'll never forget
For, really, I'm tired yet."

Not too tired, however, for a year's work in a hospital at LaGrange, then in the Red Cross field to teach classes in nursing to both white and negro women. Her retirement years have been spent in Anna Kings house with Manie, who died first, then with Anna alone until Anna's death in 1950 and now with Lizzabel and Eva.

Eunice Gunn Adams, in her "You Know What" column in a Cartersville paper wrote, "a trip to Calhoun would not be perfect, as delightful as it is, if it did not include a visit to Miss Lyda Saxon. Tiny and fragile as a Dresden doll, Miss Lyda is as vivacious as I remember her as a girl. Busy as ever and still going about doing good. Miss Lyda belonged to the era when trained nurses did twenty four hour duty. She stayed with us a month during the serious illness of a beloved sister. Still fresh in my memory is the joyous night whten Miss Lyda said 'she is better.' "

On Miss Lyda's 94th birthday, she was a patient in Gordon County hospital. Mrs. Warden, superintendent of nurses, and her staff had prepared a surprise birthday party. Alvin brought up her candles lit tray and including members of her Sunday School Class, the little room was jammed with people singing Happy Birthday.

Posed with cake, candles, flowers and gifts, Miss Lyda's picture was in the local papers. Afterwards she received letters from two former patients, one a baby case in 1912 and the other a woman whose brother she nursed in 1913. The brother is still living at 91 years of age.

Miss Lyda's nieces, Lizzabel and Eva Saxon, came to live with her a few years ago and both are teachers in the Calhoun Schools. Daughters of Clara (the goodest) who married her cousin, Robert Louis Saxon, Lizzabel and Eva believe the adage that marriage between cousins is not wise, for they each received a double gift of the Saxon intellect, as did their brother, Harold, who was a teacher and secretary of the Georgia Education Association for eleven years.

It is not surprising that Kathleen could write a story and Lyda could write poetry, that Lizzabel and Gene can stand up in the Sunday School class or the Wesleyan Service Guild and speak easily in a discourse about the lesson or any program subject that Manie, Lizzabel, Eva and Harold could excel in School circles — All of this is understandable when you read Robert Cristwell Saxon's story, written at Grassdale Farm in 1905 when he was 84 years old.

From the Cabin To the Mansion or True Worth Rewarded, by Robert C. Saxon, is a narrative about South Carolina people who lived in the early part of the 19th century "When Christianity was at a heavy discount and implied social ostracism, if not persecution, as illiteracy and immorality dominated the people."

Rebecca, wife of John Hoppkins and mother of 12, was not ashamed of her allegiance to Christ. To the narrator of the story, 15 years old at the time and imbued with the idea that "all religions were the result of ignorance, tradition and priest-craft," she presented a radiant countenance and possessed a cheerfulness that inspired the skeptical young man with a desire to be a christian of her type.

The youngest child of the Hoppkins family was designated as the survival of the fittest and made the hero of the story. In chapter four, he (Jack Hoppkins) meets a stranger who is to be the prime influence in his life. The story proceeds in a deep religious vein, at times dramatic in its episodes and again sparkling with wit and humor. Of one character, Robert Saxon wrote, "God will have to relax the iron bands of the covenant and let her in for she is certainly one for whom Christ died and the devil has no use for her."

"Please tell me' Jack Hoppkins begged," the difference between a moral and a Christian character."

"Moral character resembles reputation, simply what others regard us to be," replied Mr. Williams, "While Christian Character is what we know and God knows us to be."

Mr. Williams recitation of his experiences in the Wilderness of North Carolina with an Indian half-breed, Joe Scott, makes exciting reading. How they killed bears and snakes and climbed over hills and through cataracts to establish a colony in the wild land is a thrilling story.

Mr. Saxon carries his hero, Jack Hoppkins, through his marriage to Mary Williams, daughter of his benefactor, to financial and social affluence and, finally to the beautiful Christian death of the beloved Mary.

Robert C. Saxon died at Grassdale in 1908 at the age of 87. His second wife, the former Mrs. Georgia Whitaker, of Etonton, died a few years later.

An aristocracy of intellect vaunts not itself and is not puffed up but humbly and joyfully shares its broad inheritance with all alike and humanity is the better for having brushed elbows with the intellectual.

The King-Saxon house is one of three tall gracefully proportioned houses that are neighbors to each other on the west side of Wall street in the block north of the Baptist church. For many years the show block of Calhoun, these three houses have been the nucleus of the social life of the town. Though similar in basic structure, each has distinctive architectural features. One difference, is the bay set in a corner of the King-Saxon house, where the front porch steps fan-spread to fit the four-windowed nook.

Turn back the pages of time and come with me into the parlor of the King-Saxon house. We will sit on the love seat in the bay window on a winter night. The fire light falls on the deep red Persian rug and the soft lamp light caresses the wall and peep-eyes from the drapery folds. Because of the bay window, everything is catty-cornered in the room — the mantel directly across in the corner and the rug laid diagonally, so we will not talk of common place things tonight. You tell me your dreams and I'll tell you mine.

We had dinner for two across the hall in the rich walnut-wainscoted dining room. Here, too, the fire light glows from a corner chimney and the double French doors are closed against the cold of the long hall. The big china cabinet is handsome in deep toned varnish to match the wainscoting. Fitted with drawers for flat silver and linens, solid doors for plates and such, and glass upper doors for display of treasured pieces, this built-in feature is a complement to the charming room.

The bedroom will be warm, too, for there's a fire place in every one. Across a little downstairs cross hall is the kitchen. A latticed porch runs down the south side with a well house at the end. Stepping stones radiate to the garage to the well house and to a shady backyard garden plot, closed in by the hedge that Lyda planted.

* * * * *

"What are you going to wear to the wedding?" This was the question on the lip of every woman and girl in town in the first days of June 1890. Invitations were out to the marriage of Flora McDaniel, daughter of County School Commissioner, W. J. McDaniel, To Logan Pitts, only son of Mrs. N. E. Pitts.

The wedding was to be the first in the new Methodist church, completed and dedicated in 1889. The Pitts, of course, were Presbyterians but the McDaniels were Methodists and the bride may choose her own church for the scene of her wedding.

The altar was banked with flowers and the handsome mahogany chancel rail twined with graceful vines. The lamp light fell softly on the pale green walls of beveled ceiling, laid in geometric designs, and on the light summer dresses of the ladies, assembled with their men in the church.

The front pews, reserved for the family, were marked with ribbons and here were seated Julia and Nettie McDaniel, sisters of the bride, and Lulie and Mamie Pitts, identical, twin sisters of the groom, lovely in their pink, yellow, blue or white dresses of silk mull or organdie. Mrs. N. E. Pitts, mother of the groom, probably wore her best black silk for in those days, a widow, never got out of black except for a calico dress, which she wore at home.

The newspaper reporter failed to mention music, but, more than likely, Mrs. W. L. Hines played the wedding music at the reed organ. Music teacher and church organist from her girlhood Lizzie Wilson Hines was the musician for many occasions.

At 8:30, the father and mother of the bride came down the aisle and took their places at the right of the ministers. Then came the ushers, Mr. J. W. Logan and Dr. R. M. Harbin, who stood on either side of the center. The flower girls, Lucy Freeman and Virgin McDaniel, entered next, then the bride and groom came down the right aisle.

Rev. Mark Matthews, pastor of the Presbyterian church, performed the ceremony, assisted by Rev. L. P. Winter, pastor of the Methodist church.

There was an elegant reception after the wedding at the home of the groom's mother.

In February, 1891, The Calhoun Times carried the announcement that "Mr. L. P. Pitts will, in the near future, begin the erection of a handsome and costly residence on the corner of Rock street and College avenue." Mrs. N. E. Pitts had purchased this lot where the Locklear, J. M. Fite and Pate houses now stand, from L. L. Reeve.

Logan Pitts, however, did not build on this corner lot but chose the beautiful site north of the Baptist church, where in April of 1893 Contractor A. B. Gregg, of Dalton, began work on a two story residence. The house completed in June, was described as one of the handsomest in the City.

Flora McDaniel Pitts loved entertaining and her hospitable home was often the scene of pleasant social gatherings. Almost the entire town was invited to a reception for Mr. and Mrs. W. F. King after their marriage in 1896. An annual spend-the-day party for the grandmothers was one of Mrs. Pitt's favorite social affairs. Mrs. Pitts was a charter member of the Calhoun Woman's Club, organized in 1902, the Club's first recording secretary and president in 1910. It would be necessary to go through all the records of the Club to list Mrs. Pitt's many activities.

She was president of the UDC Chapter in 1905 and on July 4, 1917, organized the Gordon County Chapter of the American Red Cross, serving through the War as Vice Chairman. In her farewell address at the close of the War, Mrs. Pitts said "It has been a labor of love, a seeking for results, with no thought of self and, because of this spirit, which has pervaded the American Red Cross throughout the War, a French Statesman said recently, that, although France has known long of America's greatness and enterprise, it remained for the American Red Cross to reveal America's heart."

Logan Pitts, only son of Lizzie and Tom Pitts, came as a child to Gordon County. He was educated at the Calhoun Academy and the University of Georgia.

One of Calhoun's pioneer merchants he was first in business with Mr. Hicks then with W. F. King. He was cotton buyer for Crown Cotton Mills, from 1899 to 1932 and a member of the Mill's board of Directors.

Mr. Pitts served as Mayor of Calhoun in 1904-5, was a member of the City School board and an Alderman when the City Public Schools were inaugurated. He served as Gordon County Representative in the Georgia Legislature in 1923-24 and as a State Senator in 1909-10. Mr. Pitts died in 1932.

Logan and Flora Pitts' only son and only child, Henry, never married and the illustrious Pitts heritage died with him.

Unlike the other two houses in the block, the Pitts house lacks the angles and varied lines seen in its neighbors. Straight lines, unadorned gables and the absence of pediments characterize the simple dignity of the residence. Seven Ionic Columns support the roof of a wide porch that extends across the front and the south side of the entrance hall. Glazed tiles form the floor of the bannistered veranda and a narrow open terrace runs the width of the north corner room, under a large plate glass window that forms the shallow bay.

The Logan Pitts house is now an apartment, owned by Dr. and Mrs. J. E. Billings.

*   *   *   *   *

In 1884, Gabe Hunt purchased the house next to the Baptist church. He had sold his house across the railroad to Mr. W. G. Fuller, of Rome, because Mrs. Hunt did not like to live out there. She considered the place too far out in the country. Mrs. Hunt's "country" home was the original house on the corner now occupied by the one known as the Anna Lewis Blackwell home. The present owner is H. G. Bagley.

The Hunt home on Wall street stood where the Pure Oil Gas station is located. When Mr. and Mrs. John Neal moved the Ballew house from downtown to the Hunt lot the little house was moved to the back and later, removed to be used as offices by Dr. George C. Kirkley dentist.

"I could have built a completely new office for the cost of remodeling," Dr. Kirkley told me, "but Pop (Dr. G. C. Kirkley, Sr.) would not hear to it. He insisted that the house be preserved."

And there it is today, facing south, to the Baptist Church. Modern in every detail, the old Hunt house proudly wears its veneer of red brick and stores it's memories of bygone days in the old timbers and boards of the framework.

Gabe Hunt came to Calhoun, from North Carolina, as a boy and for 30 years was a familiar figure about town. He planted the young wateroaks on Wall street and watched them grow — 3 rows of trees, one on each side and one in the middle — that were the admiration of all who rode down the street that was to become one of the nation's main arteries of traffic, the Dixie Highway and U.S. 41.

Residents on Wall street went to bed that Saturday night of June 5, 1915, with no thought of anything but the restful day to follow — Sunday and church services.

Suddenly, in the pre-dawn period, when all the world seems balanced on peace and repose, the air was rent with explosions, one after another, until the third one left the echoes rumbling into silence and the people stunned and shocked with the unexpectedness of the blasts. Until well into the morning, only Wall street home-owners knew what had happened.

Three of the trees in front of the Baptist church had been dynamited.

A new road to Florida was being built and would run through Calhoun the length of Wall street. That the center row of trees must come down was a foregone conclusion. But the Women rose up in arms to prevent the cutting of the trees. What can five men do against a score or more of women, some of them ably abetted by their husbands? Whose idea it was no one knew then or knows now, but someone decided there was a way to get around the women — dynamite in the night.

I wonder if there was a Sunday School or even a church service, on that disturbed Sunday morning.

Jessie Adams Robinson who was telephone operator in 1915, says that people kept her busy all morning, calling to ask if she was all right. Residents in other sections of town thought that the Bank had been blown up. The telephone office was then in the second story of the Bank building.

The front page of The Calhoun Times of Thursday, June 10, carried the Story — Trees Dynamited, Sleepers Excited, Calhoun Citizens Awakened Sunday Morning by Dynamite, Destruction of Trees object and Not Money.

In the opinion of the editor, it was a poor way to celebrate the coming of the Dixie Highway or clear the way for it.

"There is no excuse for lawlessness" wrote Editor Tribble, the parties may have thought this the way of progress. The City officials had every right to cut the trees in broad daylight. Threats or illegal interference do not justify illegal Acts."

Columnist Gus Hall, in a lengthy front page article wrote — "Early last Sunday morning, someone dynamited three beautiful trees in front of the Baptist church. Had the trees been blown down the city light plant would have been put out of commission by the falling trees — the trees were destroyed to spite certain people who did not want the trees down and to force the Council to cut the trees. If any man thinks the trees should come down. let him do it in broad daylight. The veneer of civilization that covers the inate savagery and lawlessness of human nature is a thin fragile thing."

Gabe Hunt, thinking only of the beauty of Wall street and the comfort of its people in the 1860's could not visualize the event of fifty-five years later.

John Hunt, son of Charley Hunt and grandson of A. M., told me that he was on his way home about 11 O'clock on Saturday night June 5, 1915, when he saw two men, using an old-fashioned auger, boring holes in the trees on Wall street. He hurried home to inform his father of what he had seen.

"Lord a'mercy, son," exclaimed Mr. Hunt, "don't tell that! A man that will dynamite a tree will burn your house down!"

So the Hunts, Charley and John, kept the secret until, presumably, it was safe to reveal the names of the men, one a city employee, the other, one of the town's prominent business men.

From 1890 to his death in 1897, Gabe Hunt had been associated with Dr. J. H. Malone in the Drug Store. Dr. Malone said of him "I have never known a man who had a higher sense of honor than he."

Charley Hunt, only son of G. M. and Mollie Freeman Hunt (she was a sister of Dave Freeman, 1870 editor of Calhoun Times) was an inventor and a mechanical genius. In 1896, he invented a slot machine that was the wonder of Atlanta. Exhibited on the sidewalks of the city, it drew crowds that blocked the street until the Mayor ordered it moved. Charley's invention was called a vending machine. Brilliantly lighted and 8 feet tall, the machine would give a choice of 7 articles in cubicle boxes. If a box was empty, the nickle would be returned. Charley spent $1000 and a year and a half on his invention. D. H. Livermore, W. W. Ballew and Charley Hunt formed a company, with an investment of $11,000 for making the slot machines but nothing came of it and someone else got rich on the patent. Charley Hunt was wont to say, "I could always make everything but money."

After the construction of Calhoun's Water Works, Charley Hunt opened a bath house over J. M. Ballew's store and advertised baths at 15 cents. A special night was reserved for the ladies. His mechanical genius was evident in his bath house sign, a wagon wheel, lighted in such a manner that it seemed to be in perpetual motion.

Charley Hunt sponsored a bicycle race after bicycling became the rage. A track was built on the Commons north of the depot (now the Cabin Park) light strung through the trees and refreshment stands placed here and there. Cyclists from Dalton and other places came to take part in the race. Mrs. G. M. Hunt gave a reception for the bicycle enthusiasts at eleven o'clock.

Charley Hunt was proprietor of a 10c store in 1904. When the School children were trying to raise money to improve the old school building for use as an auditorium, he generously gave 10% of a Saturday's sales.

H. C. Hunt, brother of G. M., was living in the little house on Wall street in 1882. A note in The Calhoun Times during that year read "H. C. Hunt has been ordered to move his fence back and open the street by the Baptist Church."

Hunt, of Rockingham, N. C. (Dr. D. G. Hunt, of Rome, was another Ann Hunt, of Rockingham, N. C. (Dr. D. G. Hunt, of Rome, was son.) H. C. enlisted from Gordon County in 1862 and became Second Sergeant in R. M. Young's Company, 40th Regiment, Georgia Volunteers. He remained in service throughout the War.

When General Barton wanted to send a message to General Pemberton during a battle, 20 year old H. C. Hunt volunteered to take the message. He rode a magnificent Kentucky thoroughbred horse, belonging to a member of Gen. Barton's staff and made a two mile dash parallel to the enemy's lines under continuous fire. Miraculously, he escaped the bullets and delivered the message. For his bravery he was promoted to the position of Aid-de Camp on Gen. Barton's staff.

H. C. Hunt was a charter member and leading spirit in the Confederate Veteran's Union and Commander for many years. Lulie Pitts wrote, "he was accustomed to write loving obituaries in memory of his Gordon County Comrades as one by one they pitched their tents on the other side."

He volunteered to fight in the trenches in 1917, but the President wrote, "you can do more good at home." Mr. Hunt had served as clerk of the Inferior Court until it was abolished in 1868, was clerk of the Superior Court in 1866-1871 and County School Commissioner.

* * * * *

The year was 1864 and, for Calhoun, the battle was over. The Army of the North was leaving. Behind them, the sky over the little village was murky with the smoke from blazing houses and the air smothery with the smell of burning wood.

As the dreadful cry "the Yankees are coming!" had sped from mouth to mouth down the six miles from Resaca to Calhoun, Martha Beavers Young and her little girls, Mary, Nannie and Sallie, had left town, taking along the little food and clothing that was left to them in this third year of War and privation. They may have gone to the home of Martha's father, General John Fluker Beavers, at Summerville.

Robert Young, the husband and father, was fighting with the Confederates at Resaca. He had been elected Captain of Company D, 40th Regiment, Stovall's Brigade, when it was organized at Calhoun in March of 1862. Wounded in the battle of New Hope Church, he came out of the War a Lieutenant Colonel.

Robert M. Young was born and reared in Walker County and began his career as a merchant at Villanow, on the other side of Snake Creek Gap. A vry old brick store stands there now, in a corner where the paved roads cross.

Old deeds at the courthouse furnish some information about the activities of Robert Young in the years immediately preceding the Civil War.

A deed of partnership with James W. Jackson "for the purpose of buying and selling merchandise usually bought and sold in Villages and the country," is dated 1857. Included in the deed was a business at Villanow under the name of John G. Jackson and Co. The total investment was $10,000, each partner to advance $3333⅓, to assume one third of the losses and share one third of the gains. Rent for the houses and lots at Calhoun and Villanow was listed at $300.

However, this was not Robert Youngs first business venture in Calhoun. When the first land sale took place on July 16, 1850, he purchased lot number 2 in the 1st section of the newly laid out town, then known as Dawsonville or Oothcaloga, for Young, Sims & Co. The price paid was $317.

In 1857, he sold two lots in Section 22 to E. W. Brown, with the stipulation that the north 50 feet of Lot 1 would be reserved for an east-west street. At the same time, he deeded lots 28 and 39, originally part of the Chandler Estate, to Mr. Brown, including all improvements except the barn built by A. B. Edwards.

Mr. Young was living in Cassville in 1860 and from there he sued I. M. C. Dunn for lots 2 & 14 in the 22nd Section and recovered the property at a sheriff's sale. These lots were named as the residence lots of R. B. Young (father or brother?) E. W. Brown was the administrator and the property was sold to James N. Carter for $2400.

E. J. Kiker purchased from R. M. Young. in 1868, Lot No. 6 in the 4th Section, 200 feet front and 150 feet back. This is the lot later deeded by E. J. Kiker to the Methodist Church.

By 1870, R. M. Young was operating a Department store, employing 15 clerks, located in a two-story frame building on the south corner of Wall and Court streets.

His son had died in boyhood and Mary, too, died in youth. Nannie attended College Temple at Newman, Georgia and Sallie was graduated from Rome Female College. She never dreamed that her classmate, Ellie Lou Axson, would one day be First Lady of the land as Mrs. Woodrow Wilson. Mattie Young married Mr. Reed.

Not too occupied with his own affairs to be interested in the welfare of his State, Col. Young represented Gordon County in the Legislature in 1872.

Financial troubles came to the family and the Young building was sold at auction in November 1875.

Col. Young died in 1878 and is buried in Chandler Cemetery.

The Young lot was purchased from E. J. Kiker in 1874 and a church erected. The Methodists of Calhoun worshipped in this building until it was leveled by a cyclone in the Spring of 1888.

Sinclair and Ophelia Mims built their first home, a neat four room cottage, near the Gin on Mill street in 1890. The Gin, operated by Gray and Mims, was on the corner where the Sutherland and Strickland houses are today on the Street now called Oothcaloga.

Ophelia was a member of the Bonner family that owned Bonner Spring and the farm that was once a part of New Echota. The Elks Club now occupies the site of the Bonner house.

Sinc Mims was clerk of the Superior Court from 1895 to 1907, at one time County Administrator and an Elder in the Presbyterian church. Ophelia was a charter member of the Calhoun Woman's Club and active in all organizations for women.

The couple never had any children and were much in demand as chaperones at the picnics and social affairs of the young folks. Their new house on Wall street was always open to friends and Sinc and Mis' Ophelia are remembered as pleasant, public-spirited people ever willing to give of themselves and share whatever they had with others.

Sinclair Mims died in 1924 and Ophelia a few years later.

Julia Cleghorn Hill and her aunt Mrs. J. W. Hill, after the death of Mr. Hill, decided that the home on the Sugar Valley road where they had lived for so many years, was too far out for two women to live alone. And, in flood time, the Oostanaula river would spread its back-waters wide between their house and town, cutting them off for days and, sometimes, weeks. They purchased the Mims place and moved to Wall Street.

James W. Hill had died in 1931 and his wife, Ann Norrell Hill, followed him in death the next year. Julia, left alone, converted the house into a duplex, adding an ell opposite the kitchen wing with a paved patio between the two extensions. She made a lovely flower garden there on the corner of Piedmont street, in the one-time church yard, where Henry Brogdon, years ago had planted Old Maids, Four O'clocks and Johnny-jumpups behind the picket fence.

Julia with her innate charm, her talents and her gift of friend-liness, should have lived to enjoy the mellow years, but she died a comparatively young woman.

John and Ida Boston, who in a year of Calhoun's "phenominal growth," had built a mansion on one of the hills of Gordon, moved down in the Valley to Julia's house to spend their retirement years.

No more loving hands could have fallen heir to Henry's flower beds and Julia's garden than Ida Boston's. The flowering peach trees have been tended with care, the weeping cherry was replaced when it died and the pink dogwood, the first to be set set on Wall street, still blooms in the front yard.

Julia's big yellow iris, also a first in town, was the nucleus of an iris and bulb border that causes people to exclaim to one another each spring, "have you seen Mrs. Boston's bulb garden!"

The house, following the architectural lines of the period, has a four-sided roof with two double chimneys and gables at north south and west. Slender Daric Columns parade with the porch around a curved corner to the Trammell street side. Perhaps, when the Diesels move over to the new super highway, porch-sitting may again become popular — But, now, closed, air-conditioned rooms are quieter and cooler, so the porches are deserted.

The front door, of plate glass with wide matching panels, once opened to the customary center hall but the front part has been combined with the north room to form a spacious reception salon with dining area in the rear hall.

Handsome draperies at the triple window, soft carpets, to hush the foot steps, divans, chairs and lamps for conversation groups, all in blending tones of sandalwood and beige, bespeak the excellent taste of the Bostons, in choosing home furnishings.

Prized possessions are a Victorian chair of carved walnut done in Mulberry antique velvet, with tufted back, and a marble-topped table from the home of Ida's grandfather Hamilton.

Along with the Chickering piano and the birds in Mis' Ophelia's old parlor, I found my gargoyles! I had looked in vain for the grotesque little faces on Wall street's columns and here they were!

Mrs. Boston came to see and to touch and she said "I have dusted these columns dozens of times and I had never noticed these faces!"

Columns may have acanthus leaves symbolizing heaven, or gargoyles carved in the capital.

The mantel is painted white and the oval mirror set above the lower shelf, reflects a set of beautiful Italian China ornaments, Ida's loves, two covered urns and a footed oblong compote in a persian-like design with a small round picture in the front of each piece. A fat white china cat crouches on the top shelf of the mantel, all ready and waiting to pounce.

"You must see my birds," Mrs. Boston had said.

I had not heard chirping or trilling, so I thought "the birds must be asleep."

We walked into the music room and over in the corner stood a cabinet, its shelves filled with the most amazing collection of china, glass and pottery birds that I had ever seen.

There was a gorgeous pheasant brought from Jamaica by Tommy Brown, there were cockatoos, a blue parakeet from Hitler's Barchtesgarten, in Germany, a pair of precious blue birds, a pert cardinal, tiny baby birds and birds of all kinds in every pose imaginable.

Cock Robin in his red breast perched sedately on a china tree stump as if he were king of all the winged creatures around him. Was that a sparrow near by? I didn't see a bow and arrow.

An identical pair, two love birds cooing on a limb, were given by different people. One was purchased in Washington, D. C. and the other in Chattanooga. A pair of saucy jays called "thief, thief" and two little birds in a flower clump might have come from my lady's chamber in Trianon. Pink flamingos arched their slender necks in princely disregard of the feathered folk about them.

On the lower shelf of the cabinet was a slipper collection, not so large as the bird collection but quite as entrancing. One black pottery slipper is a relic of the Hamilton family and there's an ivory swan that belonged to Jo Alexander's mother. Pearl Hill brought the green glass swan from Mexico where she saw it made. A slipper-was it Cinderella's? — made entirely of blue for-get-me-nots and trimmed with a pink rose is romantic, and the boudoir slippers with fluted ruffle tops are dreamy.

Aldine Brock sent the pair of tan pottery lace-shoes from Newberry's antique shop in Gadsden, Alabama. A little cat sits in the arch of each boot staring intently at a hole in the toe while the wily mouse sits on the top of the boot looking down on his would-be tormentor.

Ida Boston's idea of collection birds in china, glass and pottery must have been born of her years of residence on the hill above town where she had for her daily companions, the feathered ones of the air who made their nests in the trees and the vines about her home and sang their happy tunes from morn 'til night.

"Attention is called to the card of Dr. J. H. Boston, dentist, who has located in Calhoun with office at the Rooker Hotel. He has recently graduated from dental college and is thoroughly competent in his profession." This was the notice that Calhoun people read in The Times of June 1908.

J. H. Boston's father was Fred Boston, of Whites, Georgia and his mother was Mary Connor, both of English-Irish ancestry. Mrs. Boston was Ida Hamilton whose family was living in Dalton at the time of her birth. Her mother was Leila Longley.

The Boston and Hamilton families moved to Atlanta where John Boston and Ida Hamilton attended the same school.

They were married in June of 1908 and came to Calhoun to make their home, living first at the Rooker Hotel then located in the Rankin-Norton house, west of the railroad.

Their next home was on River street at the Lawrence Brownlee house and then the move to the bungalow on the hill.

At the time the chenille industry began in Gordon County, the Boston family became interested in the business. Many of the large plants of today were started in a family garage or basement. The Boston's Mt. Alto plant expanded rapidly, joined a nothern firm and today is one of the largest plants in the section, manufacturing rugs, bedspreads and other articles.

The Boston children, Willie, Edna and Jack, all live in Calhoun and own three of the town's most beautiful modern homes. Mr. and Mrs. T. J. Brown (Willie) live on College street. The ranchtype home of Mr. and Mrs. Luke Spink (Edna) overlooks Oothcaloga Creek, east of the Rome road and Mr. and Mrs. Jack Boston (she was Foy Legg) live on Mt. Alto, the beautiful hill-top residence section of Calhoun's younger citizens.

Dr. and Mrs. Boston have five grandchildren, Tom and John Brown, Jack and Joy Spink and John Boston III.

When I ride on the Wall street road, I often look back to the time when the Dunnagans lived on the corner at Line. The house was shut and still and the dark green shades were drawn to keep the strong, westing sunlight from fading the flowered rugs.

Mr. Dunnagan died, and Mrs. Dunnagan too. Before she went she said to her good friend and neighbor on the other corner of Line "I want you to buy my house."

So she did — Tennie Moss Combs and her husband, Harvey Combs, owners of the Combs Funeral Home on the North corner of Wall and Line, purchased the Dunnagan house.

The steps were still there and the porch had not fallen on a rotted sill, but the house needed paint, and light, and air in the rooms, dark and silent to some, but, to the friends of Mrs. Dunnagan, lighted by her gentle smile and turned with echoes of her soft voice.

We missed the Dunnagans, quiet unassuming people though they were, going about their own affairs, Mr. Dunnagan to the store and, on Sunday both attending church services.

The new firm of P. C. Dunnagan, on the corner opposite Malone's Drug Store, have started business in a rush. They have a complete new stock of dry goods, notions, shoes and furniture—The Calhoun Times, December 1900.

With such an auspicious beginning, life in Calhoun was full of promise to the Dunnagans, but in September 1903, grief came into their home, to walk beside Mrs. Dunnagan for the rest of her life.

Baby Agnes, eleven months old, the only child they ever had, died of cholera infantum, in September of 1903.

After Mrs. Dunnagan's death, a niece had come to dispose of the house furnishings. She stopped in her task to phone the Combs.

"Tennie," she asked, "will you come over here? I've found something I'm afraid to touch."

A little excited and rather curious, Tennie went across the street to the Dunnagan house. The niece led her to a closet and pointed to the top shelf and a stack of small packages, wrapped in newspaper and tied with old-fashioned red-striped wrapping cord.

When the packages were opened, they were found to contain ashes, fine soft ashes.

The two women gazed in preplexed silence for several minutes. "Have you found any baby clothes?" Tennie asked.

"No", replied the niece.

"One time when I was here," Tennie said "Mrs. Dunnagan showed me baby clothes, two or three drawers full of long dresses, petticoats and other things."

They decided, then, that Mrs. Dunnagan, unable to endure the thought of another child wearing her darling lost baby's clothes, had burned them and tied the ashes in the packages, perhaps thinking to have them buried in the family plot at the cemetery, as she had done with Mr. Dunnagan's clothing after his death.

The relatives had come and gone and the house had been turned over to the new owners.

Vera Erwin, next door neighbor said "Tennie, lets go see the house you've bought."

Tennie agreed and the two friends walked through the rooms, seeing them as they would look with the Combs living there and discussing possible changes.

They were standing in the hall when they heard Mrs. Dunnagan's voice ask "What are you girls doing in my house?"

There was a frantic rush for the front door and both tried to go through at the same time but were unable, in their disturbed state to unfasten the screen latch. Tennie says that to this day, she bears a scar where part of her caught in the latch hook as they scrambled out of the hall.

Houses aren't really haunted, but they might not be so lonely if they had a ghost or two. The ghost in the Dunnagan house was only Harvey Combs, who had slipped in the back way and secreted himself in a closet. He gave such a good imitation of Mrs. Dunnagan's voice that Tennie and Vera were thoroughly ghosted.

To relieve the somberness and bring a bit of life and color to the long-quiet rooms, walls were papered in a gay rose pattern, with pink ceilings, and white paint went on the wood work. Partitions were removed and all the front thrown together.

The hall colonade, once hung with velvet portieres and dividing the length, was moved to the ends of the opening between the north front room and the hall.

The latest change to the house was the removal of the porch and front door. An entrance, with portico, was made on Line street. The inside recess of the former front door was filled in with shelves to hold decorative articles of various design, and a cabinet space at floor level.

A large sectional sofa in the living room turns its back to the draped and corniced window and faces the fireplace, graced, as are all of Calhoun's early 20th century houses, with a beautiful cabinet mantel. Soft carpet to walk on, comfortable chairs to sit on and numerous lamps to light your way are waiting for you, and Tennie and Harvey love entertaining. The base of the lamp over by the fireplace is part of the Logan House table leg.

The dining room furniture is Early American in maple.

I peeped in the guest room and it had an occupant—Santa Claus, made of a man's union suit stuffed with a bale of hay and dressed in the traditional red, white-trimmed suit, he had stood beside the front door during Christmas and had been moved to the guest room to await dismantling.

The twin beds and chests of drawers in the other bedroom had gone through the fire that almost destroyed the Funeral Home a few years ago. Tennie refinished all the pieces in an antiqued brown. A wash stand, made from the dresser, holds an old bowl and pitcher, flowered in pink dogwood on white.

This little passage way was a part of the Dunnagan's back porch. A maple chest and a cedar knitting bucket on legs stand against one wall and around the corner is an oldfashioned wall telephone. Don't look now and I'll tell you something—it isn't a telephone, it's a radio! you turn it on and control the volume with one bell and select your station with the other. And here is a 125 year old extension table from the Tinsley family. The fruit-filled bread tray was Laura Reeves'. Tennie said "I guess it belongs to your family."

Mrs. Dunnagan would say "Well, Tennie, you haven't changed my kitchen very much. Why, there's my old kitchen cabinet!" and sure enough it is her old cabinet. The base, given a new counter top and fresh paint, sits beside the stove and the upper part has become a wall cabinet.

The Combs' refrigerator, damaged in the fire and re-finished in bronze enamel, along with the cabinet sink under the windows.

You have seen new houses looking idle and foolish, like a hat on the shelf at the store. Now, Tennie's new room wasn't going to be sad for the lack of something in it. A woman wants something new now and then, doesn't she? If it isn't a whole new house, it is a new room. Knowing nothing about feet and inches—few women do —she stepped off the size on the lawn.

"Mrs. Combs, that's an awful big room," the contractor told her.

"I want a big room," she replied.

Take two steps down from the areaway and there you are, in a big room, new, yet old for it is filled with American retired in furnishings and surrounded by American modern in windows, walls and tiled floors. On your right as you step down, is an exotic fountain from Somewhere, or Anywhere, its water flowing from one to another of four green bowls stair-stepped among the green vines that grow all around and climb the green painted lacy iron work framing the entrance to the main house.

A black iron pot on one side and a black iron kettle on the other side of the hearth remind you that once Georgia women cooked in just such a fireplace as this and you throw a grateful look over your shoulder to the gas range in the kitchen. Reproductions of hutch cabinets stand on each side of the fireplace and a sofa that is used for sitting is over against the wall.

The coffee table with the short, fat legs was cut down from a banquet table from the Logan Hotel. Surely this was the table that groaned with the food served by the Young Men's Dining Club to the young ladies SLD Club seventy years ago.

There's another sofa by the corner windows perfect for a reading spree—and a round oak dining table that Gene Moss was using to mix his paints on, until Tennie rescued and refinished it.

"Where did you find your spinning wheel?" I asked.

"Oh, it came from three different places," Tennie answered.

She wanted a spinning wheel, so she and Harvey drove out a country road looking for spinning wheels.

"Stop here, Harvey," she would say "this house looks like it might have a spinning wheel."

Some did, but the owners would not part with the prized relics. Finally, they found the bench of one in a tumbled-down smokehouse. Another house had a spinning wheel in the barn but only the wheel was usable.

"I am not going to stop at another house," Harvey declared, after he had drug portions of wheels out of the debris of fallen walls and roofs," people will think we are crazy!"

The next morning, Tennie started out in the opposite direction and found a spindle. She assembled the parts as she thought a spinning wheel should look. Perhaps the ghosts of three great-grandmothers slip in to softly finger its ancient wood. In the still of the night, the sound might be the purr of a smooth-running automobile on Wall street or it could be the hum of the old spinning wheel in the den as its three former owners try it out to test Tennie's workmanship.

Here in this room, during the Fall and Christmas of 1960, Tennie and Harvey Combs entertained the Garden Club, the Red Bud Community Club, members of the Gordon County Hospital Staff, officials of the City of Calhoun, two Sunday School Classes, Tennie's Baptist Class, the Methodist class of which Etta Dobbs is a member, and a family Christmas dinner.

This house did have a broken heart when Mrs. Dunnagan lost her little girl and, years later, her companion. Could she come back now, I am sure she would feel that Tennie and Harvey Combs have mended the heart break in the old and filled the new with something in it.

*   *   *   *   *

P. S. The story of the Dunnagan-Combs house has been framed around an original poem by Tennie Combs, The House With The Broken Heart, which she has read many times at church Homecomings in Gordon County and on other programs.

Two Calhoun matrons were walking north on Wall street one afternoon in 1897. They had passed the corner of the Foster building when their conversation was interrupted by the sound of shrieks, a chorus of excited feminine voices and a queer rattling noise.

The two women stopped and looked up just in time to see two bicycles bump down the steps of the Ballew house and catapult into the street before the wheels could be turned back to the sidewalk by their riders.

"If that isn't just like Maude and Julie Ballew!" exclaimed one of the women.

"Did you see what they had on?" Bloomers, black sateen bloomers!" said her companion.

"What is this world coming to when Southern girls will come out in a garb started by that—that Yankee woman—What was her name?"

"Amelia Bloomer, I think. Maude Ballew isn't afraid to try anything. She has always driven any of her fathers horses no matter how wild they were."

"Yes, and you remember she sprained her arm about five years ago when she jumped out of the buggy after her horse had become frightened at a fast train."

"Must have been Charley Barrett's train. He always went through town so fast it was dangerous to be anywhere near the railroad with a horse and buggy."

The two matrons resumed their walk and Maude fell off her bicycle in front of the Harbin house. She usually had two or three falls on every ride, but Julia never fell. Later, the girls explained that someone had dared them to ride their bicycles down the steps, so they had mounted in the back hall, pushed through the portieres and pedaled out the front door.

This is the story of a Wall street house that isn't there but was there. In fact, it was in two places on the street and was twice almost destroyed, once by a cyclone, once by fire and finally did burn.

The first location of the house was on the site of the Martin Theatre, where it stood in the path of the 1888 cyclone. On a Sunday morning, the service at the Methodist church was broken up when smoke began drifting through the windows. The congregation rushed out to find the Ballew house a blaze. Not too badly damaged, the house was repaired and remodeled.

John and Maude Ballew Neal moved the house, sometime in the late 1920's, to the lot now occupied by the Pure Oil Station and here, about 10 years later, it was burned to the foundations.

The Ballew and Davenport families were living in Gordon County in the 1850's and 60's. J. M. Ballew, Sr. bought three farms of 150 acres each, in 1850, from E. D. Hudgins, paying $1400 for the property. H. S. Davenport is listed in the Medical directory of The Confederate Flag, Calhoun's 1861 newspaper.

The Davenports lived in a small house on Piedmont street (Lay-Hall Grocery Co.). Joe Davenport, as a small boy, made the fires in the courthouse for Col. Dabney and the other lawyers. His mother stood on the porch each morning with a lighted lamp until Joe had crossed the street. He was afraid of the dark. Did it take even more courage to enter the empty courthouse? His mother had lighted the way and his duty was there. How comforting the blaze of the first kindled fire must have been to a scared and lone little boy!

Kate the red-haired sweet member of the family, married Mr. Branch and lived in Cedartown. Stately, handsome Helen was wed on April 8, 1866, to Tom G. Jones who became Atlanta's first licensed policeman.

Mollie, the dark-haired beauty, writer of our letter to Susy Darling, married her yankee, C. J. Thayer, but, alas, he did not take her north and hire someone to wait on her. He stayed in Calhoun and went into business. Thayer and Ferguson was a grocery store of 1877.

Mollie had five babies, but only one survived infancy, a son, Carl. Her family was furious with her for marrying a yankee and Carl was always bitter towards his father's northern relatives.

Curtiss J. and Mollie Davenport Thayer and their four babies are buried in the Ballew lot at Chandler cemetery.

Jack Davenport, witty and very smart, ran away to join Barnum and Bailey's circus and became one of their top-notch clowns.

Hal, youngest of the Davenports, was one of the first Atlanta Constitution Newsboys. The papers, sent up on the train, were sold to the public at a news stand. The young boy Hal was almost drowned when he fell from the deck of an Oostanaula river steamer. He was rescued by a colored man who dived in after him. The young man Hal was with the State Revenue Department, stationed at Ellijay.

Dora, named for an army captain, Travis Van Dora, married J. M. Ballew, Jr. and it is with her family that Calhoun is most intimately concerned.

The Ballew children were Maude, Lucille, Julia and the baby boy who survived his mother only a few months. Dora died in 1894.

Maude was born in the little house that has stood on the same spot since it was built in the 1850's by Uncle Dick Adams—across Line street from the end of King street. The Ballews moved from this cottage to the house on Wall street.

Hoop skirts were in style again and Mrs. Ballew's little girl, Maude, decided that she wanted a hoop skirt because everyone else was wearing one. Mrs. Dunn, who lived near Fain Cemetery, made the hoop skirts but didn't like to make little ones.

"I ran everyone crazy until I got my hoop skirt," Maude Neal told me, "and there's no telling what my father had to pay for it."

The well in front of the Wall street house had a curb around it and took up half the sidewalk. When Mr. Ballew made an addition to the back of the house, he had this well filled and dug another in the rear.

The elm trees in the middle of the street never much because the oxen gnawed the bark. Farmers hitched their wagons to the trees and the oxen, with nothing to do, stood and chewed elm bark.

At one time, J. M. Ballew was the biggest tax payer in Gordon County. He owned a number of cottages and houses in town, some he built and others he purchased and remodeled. One piece of property, sold to J. M. Kindred in 1883, was the Calhoun Hotel.

With his brother, Wiley, he bought the Boaz Mill on the Rome road for $8,300 and sold it to J. T. Black in 1897. J. M. Ballew, born in 1858, died in 1915 and is buried in Chandler cemetery.

Maude was a pianist at the New Episcopal church on South Wall for several years. The rector, Bishop Craighill, gave her a beautiful Bible and wanted to confirm her. Mr. Ballew objected. "He was afraid I would marry Percy Howard," she said.

Percy Howard, his sister, Mrs. Ed. Parrott, the Boisclairs, Roffs, Jacksons, Camfields and the family of Nellie Peters Black were all active members of the Episcopal church.

Maude Ballew was married to John Neal at a fashionable wedding in the Methodist church that was built after the cyclone. Hollyhocks were the principal decoration and Charley Hunt made a letter B for the bride's door and an N for the newly married couple to pass under as they left through the other door.

The couple never had any children, but their house was always open to the young people of town.

Both were musicians, Maude a pianist and music teacher and John a member of the Calhoun Band, playing the Alto horn. Maude is a talented artist and at one time maintained a studio on the second floor of the building now occupied by The Calhoun Hardware Company.

Lucile's marriage to Tom Hopper was a home wedding. Mr. Ballew had bought the lot north of the Methodist church from Dr. Malone and here he built a house for Lucile and Tom. This is the house that was the home of the R. R. Owens from 1917 until it was razed to make way for the Drive-in Bank.

Julia was also married at home to Charles Wagner and left immediately for her new home in Winder.

Dr. Davenport had given to his wife, Sara Kilpatrick Davenport a negro girl named Cilla. She was expecting her first baby, and the baby girl named Roxie, was born in a back room of the Davenport home. Roxie married Jim Bennett and their children were Pete, Helen, Fannie and Jim Jr.

Pete lived with Maude and John Neal until Julia's son Charles was born, when he went to live with the Wagners.

Jim, Jr. died with a heart attack on the steps of the Calhoun Hotel after it became the Bus Station. Fannie, 75 years old, lives in Chattanooga.

Lucile and Tom Hopper rest at Chandler's near Molly's family. Charles Wagner died and Julia is at home with her son, Charles, in Atlanta.

Maude, left a widow several years ago, has since lived in the old Black-Byrom house, now a duplex facing Trammell street. A fall and a broken hip have not dimmed her spirit, nor stopped the work of her gifted hands for they still fashion works of art, a letter basket made of Christmas cards, or a flower arrangement in a bubble glass. Her brown eyes still sparkle and her ready laugh yet tinkles. Her memories of Calhoun's life since she became a part of it, are fresh and accurate.

We bid farewell to another Wall street house, now only a phantom of misty memory, its occupants only names on a tomb stone. But, here in recorded events, the Davenports, Ballews and Neals leave behind them the mark of a useful and constructive part in the history of Gordon County.

Late one afternoon of a summer day, two women, friends and neighbors on College street in Calhoun, were returning from a drive out the Sugar Valley road. The handsome pair of black horses trotted smoothly along, raising scarcely a drift of dust while the two friends chatted gaily of this or that.

Claud Silvey and Belle David made a charming picture on that summer afternoon. Beautiful women they both were and happy in the way of young womanhood, Claud, because she was just being a friend and Belle, because she was soon to experience the joy of becoming a mother.

Suddenly the stillness of the afternoon was broken by the sound of furiously pounding hoofs and the rattle of an empty vehicle. Claud quickly drew reins and the women looked back to see a run away horse rapidly overtaking them as they were about to enter the covered bridge.

"Get out of the buggy and out of the road, Belle", commanded Claud then turned her attention to her own horses. The terrified runaway dashed by and through the bridge leaving the women to calm each other and their excited horses. Years later, Belle David was to say "We were almost killed at the bridge!"

A. B. and C. E. David, brothers, had come from Comer, Georgia, soon after the turn of the century, to accept positions in the Calhoun National Bank. At that time, the Bank was located on the North Corner of Court and Wall Streets, facing the Courthouse, In 1907, A. B. was elected president and cashier and C. E., assistant cashier. At the death of the bank's president, O. N. Starr, in 1922, the two David brothers were advanced to the positions of president and vice president-cashier, which they held for the rest of their lives.

Austin Banks David was a member of the City Council in 1917-1920, and honorary member of the Woman's Club, a charter member of the Civitan Club organized in 1921, a stewart in the Methodist Church, where he held various offices, twice state senator and a member of the Committee to solicit funds for the building of the New Methodist church in 1916 (now the Civic Center). Having always a deep interest in town and county affairs, Mr. David was chairman of the American Red Cross during the second World War.

In every family there are oft-told Civil War stories and others continue to come to light. even a hundred years after the famous conflict.

J. T. Baker, of Danielsville, told this story to Gertrude Ruskin, who passed it on to me.

"My wife's mother", related Mr. Baker, "married Major R. H. Bulloch, who was ordinary of the County at one time. Her sister, Betsy Freeman, married a Mr. David, of Madison County. Mrs. David's house was set afire by Sherman's men during the Civil War and her husband shot off his horse. Mrs. David's family were spectator's to the tragedy. After her husband's death, Mrs. David married a Freeman."

"The phenomenal growth of Calhoun continues," wrote the town's Editor in July of 1909, "Mrs. R. S. McArthur is giving the finishing touches to Cr. and Mrs. A. B. David's Colonial residence next to Dr., Mills. This is perhaps the most artistic home yet built in Calhoun." The Davids had bought the lot from Dr. Mills in July of 1908 for the price of $1000.

The house is a square two-storied structure with veranda extending across only the lower front and down the south side to join a room extension. An interesting feature of the north Wall is a half octagon formed by four windows. The kitchen joins the dining room on the west side and the upper story of this ell forms the back stairway enclosure. A simulated widow's walk crowns the hipped roof from which rise three white chimneys. Windows to the left, windows to the right, every where two-sashed, solid-pined windows flood the big beautiful rooms with light.

Four Ionic Columns support the roof of the veranda and the wide colonial doorway, always so artistically decorated at Christmas tipifies the spirit of true Southern hospitality.

"Toot, toot," "honk honk," or maybe it was "Ooogah, Ooogah," that I heard on an afternoon in 1918, when I hurriedly pushed my baby buggy off the side walk into the weeds and looked up to see Bill David flying down from Hunt's corner on his bicycle. He whizzed by and I moved back to the walk, muttering imprecations on all little boys.

Several years later, I stood on a creek bank at Gray, Georgia and watched Bill David grasp a thick muscadine vine that hung from a tree beside the creek, swing through the air and drop into the muddy, deep water. He always came up though I was always sure he wouldn't.

Bill swung on his mental grape vine through badge after badge until he acquired the wings of an eagle and became the first Eagle Scout in Calhoun.

Perhaps this keep the way clear, this swing through the air, this eagle spirit was the build-up for that day when Bill flew a plane across the English Channel.

We were listening to the radio, Phil and I, as we did almost every minute of the day and half the night, hearing Gabriel Heater say "it's good news tonight" or "it's bad news tonight" and hoping on hope for a hint of how the Navy was doing in the Pacific or how the PC's were faring in the Mediterranean. The newscaster, (not Gabriel Heater), began to tell a story. He mentioned the name of a plane and we were galvanized in our chairs as I cried "that's Bill David's plane!"

And we listened to the story of a pilot flying back from a bombing mission, with German bombers on his tail, flying low over the English Channel, wounded crew members inside his bomber — a nameless pilot who sat at his controls, wiping flames from the back of his hair and landing the plane safely in England. We heard the pilot, nameless because of War security, extolled for his Courage and skill and we knew it was Bill David because we knew his name for the plane that was to him a living thing.

Oogah, German bombers, didn't you know that was Bill David?

In August, 1957, the Weisbaden Post, a weekly newspaper, published by the Air Force in Germany, carried the announcement that Col. W. B. David had been named Commander of the 7100st. Air Base Group. Graduate of the University of Georgia and of the Flying School at Randolph Field, Col. David had held a succession of assignments prior to World War II and, early in 1943, had formed the 388th Bomber Group and the same year, the B-17 Group became operational under the 8th Air Force in England.

Col. David completed 25 combat missions over the European Continent. His decorations include; the Silver Star, Flying Cross with two oak leaf clusters, Air Medal with three oak leaf clusters, Purple Heart with one oak leaf cluster, American Defense ribbon, American Theater ribbon, ETD campaign ribbon with four campaign stars, World War II Victory medal and the French Croix de Guerre with Palm.

Co., David's wife is the former Pauline Marshall, of Tennille, Georgia. Polly and Bill met when she came to Calhoun to teach in the City Schools.

She spoke so quietly as I started down the steps that the purport of her words did not register in my mind and I stood there puzzling "did Mrs. David lose two babies?" Belle David had said "I had two other sons, you know." Indeed, I knew it well for I had watched them grow up.

How like a mother! no matter how high on a star one child may climb, the others, whatever the number, are just as dear and just as important to her.

Since we began with the youngest, we will turn backward with ages, to the second son, C. B. (Claude Barker). Tall, erect, with waving dark hair and a graceful swing to his walk, he was the Adonis of the family. School, Scouting, Swimming, Sunday School and all other boy activities filled C. B.'s growing years. One day, he and Ruth McConnell, daughter of Hackett McConnell and granddaughter of Captain Joseph McConnell, slipped away to a minister and were married. Together, they continued their studies at the University of Georgia.

The David boys never had a greater admirer nor stauncher

friend than Phil Reeve. He boy-scouted, fished and hunted with them and many are the tales he told of their antics and daring-do. He and C. B. were duck hunting at Dew's pond on one occasion when C. B. shot a duck. It fell with a broken wing and ran off through a corn field with C. B. right behind it shouting "Stop duck, I'll shoot!"

When C. B.'s college days were over he went to work in the Bank in Calhoun. His death when a young man was a great shock to his family and friends.

There is something about being the eldest son or daughter in a family that sets one apart in certain ways. One may have the defiant don't expect me to set an example for the young ones attitude or another may be the stabilizing influence, the steady, sedate leader in a family group.

Tom Banks, eldest of the three David boys would certainly be in the second classification. Setting the place for his brothers, he preceded them through all the tomsawyer years and was the first Calhoun boy to earn the badge of First Class Scout. He added to his hobbies that of wood work and the initial building erected on his Hall hill lot was a big workshop which he has often shared with the boys of the Methodist Vacation Bible School, helping them with their hand work projects.

Sunday School teacher, alderman, member of the School board and Director of Civil Defense, T. B. David has ably demonstrated his willingness to serve in the up-building of Calhoun and Gordon County. Emory University and Harvard were the media of Tom's education. He joined the personnel of the Calhoun National Bank, after a year or two of residence in Atlanta, and, today, is president of the bank, one of the town's oldest institutions. His wife is the former Minnie Nelson, daughter of Charles and Mattie Kay Nelson.

I stopped my car on Piedmont street at the rear of the David home opened the picket gate, walked under the pergola—this year blue with morning glories—and went up the path to the back door. Conventional in the front with lawn and trees and shrubs, the house presents its intimate side to Piedmont street. Passerbys may peer over the fence or peep under the trellis and catch glimpses of triangular flower beds smiling with pansies in the spring and rosy with verbena in the summer, of smooth walks and grass plots, a lily pool, comfortable seats and big fat cats sunning on the back steps or keeping a vigil at the pool to take care of any little fish that might get too curious about the outside world.

"Come into my old-fashioned kitchen," Mrs. David said, "I have angel pie and coca cola for you." So, I sat in an old fashioned chair at an old-fashioned table, treasured possessions from Belle Barker David's girlhood home at Molena, and tasted food for the angels—a base of delicately browned meringue (you bake it for an hour) a mere kiss of lemon and a light frosting of whipped cream.

Food of the gods to sustain the physical, then a share of the beautiful to delight the eyes of the mind—this was the menu for my visit to the David home. It was not my first visit, by any means, for I had often been there to circle and missionary meetings, had even played the Steinway piano. But, this time I was there with note book and pencil to question, and to ponder whether the mantel columns in the dining room were modified Ionic or were called by a name I didn't know.

A house such as this one never needs improvements, only changes now and then for the pleasure or convenience of the occupants. One change made was the enlargement of the downstairs bedroom by taking in part of the wide back porch. The bathroom, only a step around a corner from the bedroom, is the model for all family showers—taps on three walls, at the top for the 6 foot members lower down for the shorter ones and on to the reach of a small grandchild.

"I was born by this clock and I hope to die by it," Mrs. David told me as we examined a tall clock, patented by Fashion in 1875, standing on a mantel as it had for 80 years in the Barker family, still bearing the date of purchase written in by her father. The lower half of the clock face is a circular calendar, patented in 1876 by the Southern California Clock Company.

There is a hymn transcription that I like to play on my little organ, "How Can I Be Lonely?" and this song came to mind as I entered Mrs. David's living room for here is all the family, in pictures everywhere. On the top shelf of the cabinet mantel stand pictures of the three sons, each made at the age of 21, pictures of the grandchildren and great-grandchildren line the walls of the door recess and a German-made large photo of Colonel W. B. David hangs over the desk. A glassed in frame holding Bill's badges, ribbons and medals, from Eagle Scout to Purple Heart, stands on the desk under the photo.

The smoker's set on the desk is done in tones of cream, orange and brown, so skillfully blended that the eye can scarcely separate the tints. The set includes tray, cigar holder, a lighter in the form of a Greek lamp (you fill it with alcohol and light the little tip), and containers for ashes and matches. Each piece is monogrammed with a D in English black letter type. The small round clock, set in a block of polished wood, on the mantel came from Germany, perhaps made of wood from the famous Black Forest.

The Haviland China, in pieces of twelve, is hand-painted with gold in wild carrot design. Pearl Steadman Reese, a cousin of Mrs. David's, did the painting on the china. There's a graceful vase for flowers—and such cute stemmed salt cellars, like tiny Sherbets—a huge tureen and a special tea set. Glinting with diamond points of light from many crystal facets, the chandelier radiates a shimmering brightness over the handsome French period dining room furniture and multi-mirrors its rays in the rich brocade of draperies.

The modern console piano changes the parlor of 1909 into the music room of today, but, at Christmas, when all the family gathers for the Christmas tree party, the interior-decorator music room becomes again the old-fashioned parlor of special occasions. Two mahogany love seats, upholstered in dove gray antique velvet, face each other in front of the beautiful white mantel with its four Corinthian Columns, mirror and black marble fire place, complemented by brass fittings. Round tables at the fire place ends of the seats hold lamps modeled after the rayo parlor lamps of 50 years ago.

When the Decorator, employed by the Davids to re-do the interior of the reception hall, parlor and dining room, had finished the work he haid, "we need two figurines for the mantel in the music room.

"I have them upstairs," Mrs. David replied. She had relegated the little statuettes to the upstairs rooms, thinking they were, perhaps, out of date.

The Decorator was delighted and, to this day, the little French boy and girl, their provincial dress delicately molded in china, stand on the white mantel as if to say "no matter how you boast of your American Colonial, our country has had her share in your plan of furnishing." And no one can make wall paper such as the French do, which fact is evidenced in the handsome paper used in the David house.

Several large crayon portraits, one of Mary Magdeline at the foot of the Cross, hang on the walls, all done by Belle Barker David while she was a student at Southern Female College (LaGrange).

Tie-back draperies in the reception hall, music and dining rooms are alike of rich brocaded silk in a soft green with ecru silk fringe on swag, cascades and panels.

The stairway is unusual, beginning in the back hall with three steps to an open landing framed in square railings and newel ponts. The enclosed second flight is joined by the back stair steps to form the single third flight to the upstairs hall.

The remodeled bathroom on the second floor has aqua fixtures and is almost big enough for a bedroom. The heavy, elaborately carved hall set, two high backed chairs and a console table, once stood in the reception hall down-stairs, with two matching lamps, lighted at dusk of an evening, ever reflecting a moon-beam ray of cheer to night travelers. I remember telling Mrs. David that we would miss the lamps and she said, "Oh, there will be a light in here!" and there is, but-some-how there's a nostalgia for the old ones.

The green bedroom, just over the dining room, has the same four windows on the north. The mantel is white, with mirror and green and brown tiles. The hightop bed, the wardrobe and dresser are of heavy oak and the rug is green. The adjoining room is pink and ivory and a youth bed in one corner is ever ready for the spend-the-night great, granchild. The rug is persian tan and black and the hearth tiles are tan and white.

The informal front-hall sitting room is furnished with a Duncan Phyfe sofa, a comfortable much-used leather easy chair, needle-point foot stools and smoke stands. A glassed in sleeping porch opens from the hall.

The guest room has twin beds and vanity dresser. The wall paper is gray with ivory roses in scattered pattern and the rug is gray chenille. The crayon portrait here is of the angel Gabriel, holding a child as he flies over a sleeping city. Gabriel never came for a child in Belle David's house but waited until the child became father to children before he made his soul-flight.

We see a house as others see it, but to know the heart of it one must seek the inner recesses to find the memories stored there, such as those of three generationsof David children who have rocked in the little wicker chair standing by the stair entrance.

So, if the David house is two-faced, the blame must rest upon Dennis Johnson and the other 1852 surveyors who made this block only one lot deep. Why? Perhaps the lay out began with the court-house square, parallelling to line and tapering to a point where Piedmont joins South Wall.

As I walked down the path to the picket gate and my car, two gorgeous water lilies—pale pink, sky blue or orchid, I could not say, smiled Aloha from the pool.

The words of the 1909 Editor—"perhaps the most artistic house yet built in Calhoun," still apply to the stately home and we can but send up a fervent petition that, in the progress of commercialism, the David house will be spared.

* * * * *

It was moving day on Wall Street one August day in 1898. Mr. and Mrs. Tom Brown were taking possession of their elegant new residence, just completed. Tom had bought the lot from Dink Offutt in 1897.

For about five years, there had been only three houses in the block north of the Baptist church, the old Gabe Hunt house, the Logan Pitts, built in 1893 and the W. F. King house, erected in 1892.

Flora McDaniel Pitts had been very much opposed to Tom's building next door, fearing that he would put up a "cheap" house. Tom, slightly nettled at Mrs. Pitts' subtle hint that he was not able to finance a house that would harmonize with the other two, proceeded to erect the most elaborate of the three.

The house is two-story. The north three-room length end faces Wall street, the high gable being formed of diagonally placed planks and ornamented in the center with a small louvered opening. The straight line front is broken in the second story by a small room set at an angle from the south corner. The gables here and on the south room have the same facing as the one on the north.

The long windows have single-paned sashes except the front hall window which is a pre-modern picture window. A transom over the front door gives extra light and air to the rooms. A porch extends across the front and around to the south bedroom. The posts are squared at top and bottom with round-columned mid-section and the bannisters are miniatures of the posts. A balcony opens from the up-stairs front hall.

Tom Brown was a "drummer," a traveling salesman for Peeples and Trotter, Wholesale Grocery Firm of Chattanooga and, later for the Reynolds Tobacco Company. His wife was Mary Humphries of Ramhurst.

Tom and Mary had five children, two of whom died young. The three surviving were Effie Lee, Jake, named for his grandfather Humphries, and Robert.

With such a big house, Mary Brown could not sit with folded hands nor live with no one for company but little children while her husband was traveling so she kept paying guests. Professor Fulton, principal of the Calhoun Academy, boarded with her, and widower Robert Mizell. Lovely brown-eyed Myra Hopper, from Petersburg, lived at Mrs. Brown's and attended the Academy.

Tom's younger brother, Gus, had come from his home out in Dry Valley to stay with Mary and go to School.

Gus Brown today lives on the old Belv Chandler place on the Mountain Loop road at Sugar Valley. His wife was Minnie Harkins, daughter of John S. and Hannah Kiker Harkins.

Mr. Gus, now retired, has many interesting and amusing memories of his stay at Mary Brown's on Wall Street.

One night, he said, they were seated in the living room when Tony Bandy, the cook, came in laughing so hard she couldn't speak.

"Tony, what in the world are you laughing at?" Mrs. Brown asked.

"Mis' Mary," Tony answered, between gasps, "you know that high-up window in the kitchen where we throw out the bones and the dogs fight over them? Well, I thinks I'll see what this ole bone-eatin' dog will do, so I throws a pan of boiling water out the window."

"Why, Tony," Mrs. Brown exclaimed, "aren't you ashamed to be so cruel to a dog!"

"No'm, Mis' Mary, them dogs aggrevate me, always gnawin' and growlin' under the window."

"What did the dog do, Tony," asked Gus.

"He just run plumb head-on into Mis' King's board fence"—and Tony left the room still delighted with her trick and unaffected by any criticism of her deed.

Henry Pitts, only child of Logan and Flora, would often come over to visit the Brown children and one day he was invited to stay for dinner.

After the blessing, Mrs. Brown asked, "Henry, what will you have to eat?"

Henry looked over the bountifully supplied table (Mrs. Brown was noted for her good cooking) and said, "I don't see anything that I like."

"What do you eat at home?" he was asked.

"O, Papa doesn't come home and mother and I eat a biscuit and drink some milk," replied the little boy.

Tom had borrowed money from Mr. Smith, a wealthy railroad man, to build his fine new house. Mr. Smith demanded payment and Tom couldn't pay, so the house was sold at a sheriff's sale. It went to J. T. Black for the sum of $1,750.

Tom Brown did not return from one of his trips and his family never knew what happened to him. A body, that might have been his, was found in the back-waters of a river in Alabama, but positive identification was never made.

His widow grieved bitterly for many months, but not in idleness. She went to work in Hall Bros. department store and it was here that she met Mr. Walling, a salesman, from Texas. After several trips to Hall Bros. and talks with the attractive widow, Mr. Walling walked in one da yand, in the presence of everyone in the store, said to Mary Brown, "I've come for you."

She might not have gone that very day, but Mary did become Mrs. Walling and moved to Texas. She is living today (1961). Mary Humphries Brown Walling, 92 years of age, lives in a nursing home at Carrollton, Georgia, still alert and interested in life.

Ben Brown, brother of Tom and Gus, also 92, makes his home in Oklahoma.

Mary Brown West, of Carrollton, sister of Tom and Gus Brown, was a guest in the Brown home the day of my visit and was an interesting participant in our discussion of the family.

J. T. Black, a prominent land owner, had lived at Crane Eater, where he operated a grist mill. His home was the beautiful place that is now the home of Minnie Roe.

He was married to Mary Fannie Kimbrough, January 22, 1870. She died in 1896 and he was later married to a daughter of Mrs. David Barrett.

J. T. and Mary Fannie's sons were Alec and Fain. Alec was very much in love with Sallie Kimbrough but she did not accept his proposal. "We are too near kin," she said. Alec carried someone else. Like Alec's brother, Fain, Sallie Kimbrough remained unmarried to the day of her death.

J. T. Black represented the county in the State Legislature for the year of 1886-1887. He purchased Oothcaloga Mills from J. M. Ballew in 1897 and worked with Charley Hunt to secure an electric light plant for Calhoun in 1903. He died in 1917 at the age of 68 and is buried in Fain Cemetery.

Mr. J. C. Garlington has sold his farm at Reeves and will move to Calhoun if he can find a house. He and his sisters would be a valuable addition to Calhoun.—The Calhoun Times, December 1904.

A week or two later, John Garlington, his sisters, Robbie and Aurie Garlington, and Mrs. Mary Darnall, her small daughter, Aurie Will, and Dr. W. H. Darnall had moved to Calhoun and were occupying Major Roff's house on otuh Wall Street. (Major Roff had died in November 1904.)

Rev. W. H. Darnall, eminent Presbyterian minister, served as Pastor of the Calhoun Presbyterian Church for 21 years.

William H. Darnall, 1865—a name and a date written in ink on the front binding of a little brown book. The pages of the book were mostly blank, except for the first few and two or three at the back. It was begun as a diary by a young man whose life became so filled with the duties of a husband, father and minister of the Gospel that there was no time to write on the clean white pages of the little brown-back book.

His first entry was this: my wife's first spinning was a hank of cotton yarn on the 3rd day of February 1878 near Pinson's store, Floyd county Georgia. I preserved a small bit of the yarn as a token. —W. H. D.

The next entry: William Henry Darnall was born December 21st, 1841, in the town of Decatur, DeKalb county Georgia.

Mrs. Mary Ann Darnall was born October 17th, 1835 near Dahlonega, Lumpkin county Georgia.

On the third page: Wm. Henry Darnall and Mary A. Cabot were marrie dat 7 O'clock P.M. March 6th, 1867, at the "Indian Castle" Newtown, Gordon county Georgia, by Rev. Z. M. McGhee, Cumberland Presbyterian Pastor, near Calhoun, Gordon county, Georgia.

At eleven O'clock P. M., we knelt and inaugurated family prayer in our household, dedicated ourselves to God afresh, implored His blessings on our union, His guidance through life, His fatherly providence for us for time and eternity and sanctifying grace that we mighet discharge our duties to Him and to each other and ultimately be saved, with our loved ones in Heaven.

We read as our Consecration chapters, the 57th Psalm and the 5th Chapter of Jeremiah. The 5th Chapter of Jeremiah was read because upon it solemn vows were made in 1866 in fulfillment of a strange dream had by my wife.

Thus began the long and fruitful life, no blank pages there, of W. H. Darnall, grandfather of Aurie Will Darnall Starr (Mrs. J. H.), who so graciously granted me permission to read the little brown book and another precious possession, the medical journal of her father, Dr. William Clement Darnall. Like his father's diary, the pages of William C.'s book were never filled with written prescriptions and medical notes, for he died young. Between the pages of his book, his daughter had stored her memories of her grandfather.

From a clipping found among the letters written by W. H.

Darnall.

Rev. Henry Darnall, D.D.
By W. R. L. Smith.

It was about the beginning of 1866 that, in Calhoun, at the home of Mrs. Cabot, I first met the young lawyer, Henry Darnall. Soon afterward, he married that attractive lady. His gifts were brilliant and there was promise of a distinguished career like that of his uncle William H. Dabney.

However, there was a complete reversal of his life. He made a profession of religion, joined the Cumberland Presbyterian Church and announced his purpose of entering the ministry. He had intellectual culture and oratorical grace and immediately became popular as a preacher.

While Dr. Smith (author of a book on the Indians of New Echota) was at Cumberland University at Lebanon, Tennessee, a teacher in the law department asked him if he knew a young preacher named Darnall in Gordon County, Georgia.

"I have received a letter from Rev. Darnall," said the teacher, "and I am much impressed by the elegance of the hand writing and the intelligence of expression."

W. R. L. Smith did know the young preacher.

"It was my joy" he wrote so many years later, "to see my dear friend installed as Pastor of the University church at Lebanon. In three years, he was on the throne of power in the finest pulpit of his people. He went to a church in Mississippi in the 1870's, then to Chattanooga in 1887. I saw him last at Calhoun in 1914. His saintly form advances the credit of Gordon County."

Continuing from Henry Darnall's diary:

At 2½ O'clock Saturday, April 6th, 1867, at Sumach Church, Murray county Georgia, I was *licensed* by the North Georgia Presbytery of the Cumberland Presbyterian Church to preach the Gospel, Bro. James W. Ramsey acting as moderator. Rev. A. Templeton conducted the examination on Theology. At eleven O'clock A. M. the same day, I preached my first and trial sermon from Ecclesiastes 9th chapter, clause of the 10th verse, "Whatever thy hand find to do, do it with thy might."

At 9 Oclock Saturday, October 5th, 1867, at Bethany church near Tunnel Hill, Whitfield county Georgia, I was *ordained* and thus set apart to the whole work of the ministry by the Georgia Presbytery of the Cumberland Presbyterian church. Bro. J. L. Milburn preached the sermon and Bro. A. Templeton presided and gave the charge. At eleven O'clock the same day, I preached my trial sermon from Matthew 7:21, "Not everyone that saith unto me Lord, Lord, shall enter the kingdom of Heaven but he that doeth the will of my father which is in Heaven."

Oh! the dignity and solemn responsibility of an Ambassador of God, a preacher of the unsearchable riches of Christ! Lord, help my weakness, make me faithful!

Children born to William H. and Mary A. Darnall—

On the 16th of December, 1867, at precisely 8 p.m., a son was born. He was named by his father and mother, Henry Thomas— Henry for its father and mother and Thomas for an uncle on the mother's side—Thomas for a grandfather and an uncle on the father's side. He was born in the south front room of the old missionary house at Newtown (Old Indian town) near the junction of the Conncsauga and Coosawatee rivers in Gordon County, Georgia.

On January 4th, 1869, W. H. Darnall left to take charge of the church at Lebanon, Tennessee and arrived there January 5th. He took charge immediately and went to work.

A son was born the 24th day of November, 1869, in the north room of the house formerly occupied by Dr. Miles McCorkle, in the town of Lebanon, Tennessee. The second son was named William Clement.

A daughter was born July 21st, 1872, three minutes before 12 O'clock at night. She was named Mary, one of its mother's names. The baby was born in the north room of the lower story of the house owned by Mr. W. Z. Neal and on the lot adjoining that of John A. Lester in the town of Lebanon, Tennessee.

Henry T., William C. and Mary Darnall, children of Wm. H. and Mary A. Darnall were dedicated to God by baptism September 8th, 1872, the ordinance administered by Rev. Richard Beard, D.D., in Lebanon, in the south room of the lower story of the house owned by Wm. Z. Neal. The children of Dr. A. F. Claywell, Andrew B. Martin and Thomas Norman were baptized at the same time and place by W. H. Darnall (myself).

The last page of the little brown book contains the family tree of the Darnalls.

Only the ones directly connected with W. H. Darnall are mentioned here.

Thomas Mauzy Darnall was married to Ann Harris Dabney (sister of Will Dabney, Calhoun pioneer), June 22, 1837.

Ann died May 27th, 1854 and Thomas married Martha Elmira Hayden December 31, 1857. Martha Elmira was born September 25th, 1819.

There were nine children in Thomas M.'s family. Wm. H. was a son of Thomas and Ann Dabney Darnall.

The diary records a bit of interesting news about distant relatives of the Darnalls.

Charles Carroll, of Carrollton, married Mary Darnall, daughter of Henry Darnall, Jr. in June of 1768. This Henry Darnall, Jr. was the son of Col. Henry Darnall who acted as land agent for Lord Baltimore.

Col. Henry Darnall, Sr. was judge and registrar of the land office in 1691 and was succeeded by Charles Carroll, father of Charles Carroll, of Carrollton.

By 1895, Rev. W. H. Darnall was back in Gordon County as pastor of the Presbyterian church at Calhoun. His home was at Center (he always spelled it Centre), Alabama, but he spent much of his time in Calhoun.

In June of 1891, The Calhoun Times printed this announcement: Dr. Will Darnall and Miss Mary Garlington will be united in marriage at the home of the bride's mother on June 25. Dr. Darnall is a successful young physician from Center, Alabama and Miss Garlighton is one of Gordon County's most popular belles.

Dr. Will Darnall, young physician of Center and Huntsville, Alabama, died in July, 1904. He left a ledger, its pages blank except for a few notes and it was this book that his daughter used as a keeping place for her treasured memories, letters from the grandfather who was also father to his dead son's only child.

Sometime in early life, Aurie Will Darnall acquired the pet

name of "Spot" and it is to the little girl "Spot" that Dr. Darnall's first letters, each a poem or a bit of beautiful prose, are addressed.

For "Spot" he wrote—
> Dear little Miss
> I send a kiss
> As sweet as sweet can be
> And all the love my little dove
> That I can give to thee.

On December 6, 1900.
> Earth is our night
> We do but dream
> But God in love
> Shows to the dreamer, glory's gleam
> Bright from above.

And for Aurie—
> I have a doll
> Her name is Poll
> In her blue eyes
> There mirrored lies
> The image of grand-dad
> No other boy can claim the joy
> For I am just the "fad"
> She is my pearl
> My bestest girl
>
> And grandma is her name.

As he was beginning to feel the advancing years of grandfatherhood—
> Dear little Spot
> Forget me not
> A sinner old and Shattered
> Whose sun sinks low
> Whose step is slow
> And garments soiled and tattered.

Will and Mary Darnall were living in Huntsville, Alabama and to "Tarpon" and "Spot"—

Some might think the aged bundle is a snowdrop in this brisk weather, peeping out beautifully in the winter blast, some and old-fashioned pink, giving out its sweet life to the chill winds: but he is of the opinion he's laughter's lovely laurel, the same dear ever-green in summer's heat and winter's snow.

And then, he would a-fishing go—
> The parson with hook and line
> (The lovely old Divine)
> Went to the river with a wish
> To catch a mess of fish
> His noble soul with lofty pride
> Down by the river side
> Defeated by a terrapin
> Alas! it was a sin.

He caught no fish, so his mind turned to—
> A chicken pie is surely good
> To give new life to Daddy's blood
> And Mammy sure can fix the dish
> To suit an epicure's fond wish.

In the way of all Adams—
>When ordered dad tries to shirk
>Your Grandma makes him work
>When he would eat and sleep
>She takes a gentle creep
>And gives him such a whack
>It makes him rise and shine
>A halleluia line.

Your Grandma says it requires genius to provide such verse as this.

Perhaps thinking of the "whack" he wrote—

Dear little "Queen Bee"; when we left, your mammy rode in a big boat and did not fall in the river. If she had, do you think Grand-dad would have jumped in after her?

For "Spot" in 1903—
>Dear little feet
>O may you meet
>Along the way to Heaven
>The Savior's love
>All ever above
>In countless mercies given.—Grand-dad.

And—To the Bestest—
>Dear little Aurie
>Like Annie Laurie
>With eyes of sweetest blue
>Whose light is springing
>From glad heart singing
>Dear heart loving and true.

At Christmas his letter was to—
>Dear little "Spot"
>Lies on her cot
>Expecting old Kris Kringle
>And in her dreams
>To her it seems
>She hears his sleigh bells jingle.

To his son:

I am amiable and lovely until this mother of yours wants me to part my hair in the middle and wear a button-hole bouquet. Then I stand on man's inalienable beauty and swell up of dignity.

From Center Alabama, 1905—

We are in rocking chairs on the piazza of The Palace, surveying the multitudinous sights and listening to the marvelous hum of the city's vast population. (Center was a village). Your Grand Mammy wants me to get up and cakewalk—not without a ginger cake first.

One of Dr. Darnall's favorite pastimes was poking fun at himself—
>Now I doubt not
>That little "Spot"
>Is thinking of grandmother
>And that dear boy
>Who is her joy
>The handsome Parson brother.

In a letter of sympathy to the Garlington family after the death of the young girl, Aurie Garlington in 1911, he enclosed a seven verse poem, "written in Rome, Monday, while returning to Centre"—

One verse is quoted—
        For those that sleep
        Our heart shall keep
        The sweet faith of a better land
        Beyond the tomb
        Is Heaven's bloom
        The child is in the Father's hand.

Now, the little granddaughter was a college girl—

To "Spot" at Brenau College—

While you are under human teachers in your college life, let the blessed fact abide in your thought that the Divine Teacher, the Savior and Friend is with you always, caring for the training of the soul.

Through the College years, the inspiring letters continue. With a discourse on the great poets, he sends a bunch of violets gathered in January.

Often, the letters are signed "Polly's errand Boy" and sparkle with a humor that would never die as long as the illustrious Doctor of Divinity lived—"Centre is still ahead of New York, has prettier weeds in the street"—and "walk right up to your mirror and kiss yourself 2½ times for your Grandmammy and about 40 times for her Dude who has on his French slippers tonight."

Items of interest about his daughter's family in Center and friends were not omitted—"Mrs. Carden is visiting in Alabama, went in her Chalmers auto."

In May—"Spring is a symbol of resurrection and the angel's song. Two Oceans of love for Spot from two spring blooms."

To Aurie Will, visiting a friend at Eastman, Georgia—Some lines to wish well to you and your friends, right out of the heart of two sweet young things—we trust and believe you will have a delightful stay with your friend. That "light fantastic toe" (who is the author of that quotation?) tell me now and do not hesitate to speak your mind—is Grandmammy's "light fantastic" as light as mine?

And, in a March letter from Center—
        You'd scarce expect a boy like me
        To try to write as you can see
        A letter to a college girl
        Whose blue eyes make two old hearts twirl.

As the man grew old, the beautiful script of the young Darnall became smaller in size and not so clear, but the great creative mind still produced words and phrases and lines of elegance, fraught with meaning as in the poem written at the Garlington lot in Fain Cemetery, "Where my boy sleeps"—
        We go our way
        Our little day
        With hearts that look above
        Till we shall meet
        Reunion Sweet
        In Heaven's life of love.

From The Calhoun Times of April 14, 1921:

Dr. W. H. Darnall has passed to his final reward. The beloved Minister died at a Milledgeville Hospital, Sunday night, April 10, 121 at the age of 79. As pastor of the Presbyterian church for 21 years, he was one of the most beloved ministers who ever served a pastorate here.

Dr. Darnall retired from active service something over a year ago on account of failing health, bringing to a close a distinguished and useful ministerial career. A man of brilliant mind and gentle heart, he won the esteem and love of the people among whom he labored and of all with whom he came in contact and his going away will bring sorrow to thousands.

Interment was at Center, Alabama Wednesday, Mrs. Mary Darnall, Miss Aurie Will Darnall, Mr. John Garlington, Mr. S. Mims and Mr. Logan Pitts attended the funeral. One daughter, Mrs. Frank Savage, of Center, survives Dr. Darnall. Mrs. Mary Darnall is a daughter-in-law.

In his Random Remarks Column, J. A. Hall, former editor of The Calhoun Times, describes the house in which Dr. Darnall was born, December 21, 1841 in Decatur, Georgia.

The house was built by Dr. James C. Calhoun and stood on the east side of the courthouse in Decatur. Known as The Calhoun House, it was constructed of the best lumber, with all the framing hand-hewn and the ceilings wide and thick. The stair was of polished Walnut.

Dr. James C. Calhoun married a sister of Col. Will S. Dabney. It was to Dr. Calhoun's home that Will Dabney came as a young lawyer, 19 years of age. Col. Dabney was born in Jasper County. His mother and father died young, leaving several children. One of them married Dr. Darnall's father.

Thomas M. and Ann Dabney Darnall, married in 1837, were at the home of Ann's sister for the birth of their son, William Henry Darnall.

Col. Dabney's health failed and the Doctor advised him to seek lime water. He came to Gordon County to become one of the pioneers, a trustee of the Calhoun Academy in 1852 and State Senator in 1853-1856. He was present at Milledgeville when the Georgia Legislature voted to secede from the Union.

Col. Dabney's home was somewhere near the New Echota Methodist Church of today.

The Garlington family was living in this section before the Civil War. Earliest dates on gravestones in Chandler Cemetery are those of Christopher Garlington, born 1792, died 1866, his wife, Eliza Aycock, born 1801, died 1892 and John William Garlington, born 1842 and died 1866. Mrs. Thomas A. Foster, who was Susan Garlington, is buried in Chandler Cemetery.

An Editor of the local paper, published in the 1890's, mentions "Uncle Dick Garlington, one of the most interesting darkys in the county, came to this region with the first settlers." He would come often to town and loved to talk of his life here before Gordon County was created.

The Garlingtons lived on South Wall Street for about two years, then, in 1906, purchased the J. T. Black residence on North Wall which was their home until the death of Robbie Garlington, the last of the family.

Personal Column notes in the local papers of the 1880's made frequent references to visits of the Garlington family from their home at Reeves to friends in town.

Mrs. L. A. Foster and Miss Flora Foster often visited Mrs. Garlington.

Aurie Garlington was one of the guests at Mrs. McWhorter's party for her daughter, Lola, at McDaniel Station in 1894, when the

gowns worn by the young ladies were described in detail by a reporter to The Calhoun Times, Aurie wore "an exquisite gown of
cream which brought out her beauty to great advantage." John and
Jeter Garlington were among the young men attending the party.

Robbie Garlington had entered College in Rome in the Fall of
1894.

In 1889, John was appointed, by examination, to a scholarship
in the Technological School in Atlanta. Jeter stood the examination
at the same time and applied for a place in the school.

Jeter died in 1901 and Aurie in 1911.

John Garlington was one of the incorporators of the Peoples
Bank in 1905 and served the institution as president and director. He
was charter member of Civitan Club of the 1920's and was elected
to the City Council in 1923. After a three year term on the Council,
he was chosen as the City's mayor in 1926.

During his administration, extensive improvements were made
on the streets, especially Wall Street. The Dixie Highway had been
routed on College Street with a turn onto Line and another at Wall.
These sharp curves were eliminated and the highway re-routed directly north, on the only north-south street extending the length of
the town.

Wall Street was narrow in the block north of Line, and there
were deep ditches on each side. The necessary widening and grading
cut steeply on one side and raised the side walk above lawns on the
other. In the business section, the block south of the Court square
simply sloped down hill. The street was leveled and concrete steps
leading to the sidewalk built along the length of the business houses
located on the east side.

Naturally, there was much opposition and angry words dominated the conversation of many people—and there were a few law
suits, we'll admit—during the progress of the grading and paving of
the highway that was to become US 41.

The growth and progress of a town depend upon men who can
peer into the future and are fearless in their determination to prepare the way for the generations to come. As we, through these 35
years, have watched the traffic on the National highway grow into
a constant stream of huge trucks, vans and private cars, until a four
lane through way has become a necessity, we can at least, evaluate
the far-sighted planning of these men who were at the helm three
decades ago.

John Garlington died in 1927. Mrs. Darnall and Robbie continued
to live in the house on North Wall Street. Gentlewomen they were,
and faithful in the support of their church, the Calhoun Presbyterian.

Memories of these ladies of the Wall street houses bring a non-
talgic wish that once again we could stroll down the walk under the
old Oak trees, with the silence broken only by the now and then
putt-putt mutter of a Model T or the clip-clop of horses hooves as
Matt Byrd's or Roach Bros'. grocery drays went by, and see them
sitting on the Verandas, clad in light summer dresses, languidly
waving a painted fan as they chatted with afternoon callers and
bowed politely or called a friendly greeting as we passed.

And the days were filled with laughter and the parlor lights
burned late as the beautiful young daughter of the house, Aurie Will
Darnall, entertained her friends and dressed for the afternoon parties

and auto rides and evening balls. Her wedding at the Presbyterian church was exquisite in every detail.

"Are you going to save your wedding dress for your daughters? I asked.

"Oh, no," Aurie Will Starr replied, "I am too economical for that. I am going to have it dyed and wear it now."

So, Mary Jeter had a new wedding gown for her marriage to Bob Horsley at the Methodist church on Wall Street. Perhaps Bobbie wore Jeter's dress when she was married to Bill Matthews in the new Methodist church on Line Street. Both weddings were "Out of this World!"

"We bought the house from the Garlington Estate in 1945", Josephine Billings told me.

Dr. J. E. Billings, a native of Wautagua County, North Carolina, came to Fairmount, in Gordon County, as a young Doctor just out of Medical school in 1933. He joined the Staff of the Johnston-Hall Hospital on South Wall street several years later. He was the chief Medical examiner for World War II draftees when there was only one other doctor in Calhoun. (Dr. W. D. Hall).

Dr. and Mrs. Billings were married in 1940. She was the daughter of John and Carrie Keefe Miller.

John Miller came to Gordon from Catawba county North Carolina. He was the first agent at Fairmount for the new L & N railroad completed in 1905.

The Millers lived at Bull's Gap, Johnson City, Bristol and Knoxville, all in Tennessee. Carrie was her husband's assistant in the office.

Neal and Jane Elizabeth Waddle Keefe were living in Calhoun at the time of Carrie's birth, "in a house somewhere near the present Post Office" she said. It may have been the Foster house, or J. M. Ballew's new cottage in the rear of C. C. Harlan's. Both houses were torn down long ago.

Jane Waddle was going to the school that Neal Keefe was teaching. As is often the case, the young teacher fell in love with one of the older girls in his class room. Their marriage was a teacher-pupil union.

After John Miller's retirement, he and Carrie came to make their home with their only child and daughter, Josephine Miller Billings.

It would seem that tiny, dainty Carrie Miller was meant only for someone's pet, but she is a dynamo of energy. In addition to being, wife, mother and assistant Depot agent, she has held numerous offices in church organizations.

As president of her Sunday School Class in Calhoun, after she was grand mother to a teen-age girl, she would call the members "dear", often say they were "sweethearts" and always threw a kiss for good bye until next Sunday. She was Neal Keefe's own daughter, for, to him, everyone was "Darling" or "Sweetheart."

"He and Bill Dew and Phillip Tate ran the Democrats," said Carrie Miller.

The house that Tom Brown built remains much the same in outside appearance. The Blacks, Garlingtons and Billings in turn rearranged and redecorated the interior each to his own taste.

The hall chandelier was discovered in the attic of the Pitts house next door which was purchased by Dr. Billings a few years ago. The stained glass in the shade was broken but a man in Rome, Georgia restored the chandelier with glass from Chattanooga, Tennessee, and the Billings added prisms. The shade is hexagonal with brass fittings and chains.

Two victorian chairs without arm-rests, in wine velvet, stand one on each side of the walnut chest of drawers against the stair wall. A little girl picture of the Billings daughter, Ann, is on the chest.

A brass wall Sconce and mirror and lovely, permanent flower arrangements make the hall a pleasant greeting place to visitors.

The sofa over by the three windows in the living room belonged to John and Carrie Miller and will seat four people without crowding. Two Victorian chairs, one upholstered in needle point and the other in tapestry, complete the seating arrangement.

An enlarged picture, in color, of Ann hangs over the console piano and a little French boy and girl in bisque form the candle stand on the piano. Against the wall paper background in soft rose with blue forget-me-nots and pink roses, the mantel mirror reflects lustre candle holders formed of a pink bowl on a floral base with tear-drop prisms. The pictures in this room are all in washed-gold old family frames.

The dining room is furnished in walnut, the draperies are rose-flowered and the white mantel has scroll-top columns. A handsome silver coffee service on the buffet is every ready for coffee time guests.

The old butler's pantry is now the refrigerator recess. Since the house was erected before the day of built-in cabinets, these were a must-do after the Billings bought the place. Yellow and white are the warm colors for this north side kitchen. The oval table, painted white, belonged to the Garlingtons. A majestic evergreen of the Spruce genus just outside by the picture window provides a screen for family breakfasts. An oversize pantry serves as ample storage space.

The back hall is a den and library and behind this is a bedroom and bath that was used by Dr. Billings' father who came to spend the last of his more than 90 years with his son.

The south side bedroom that was Mary Darnall's has a beautiful white mantel with a row of short spindles under the shelf. A bath tiled in rose and pink connects this room to new one added for Carrie and Ann. This room is dainty in pink and the twin beds are high posted in walnut.

The first stair flight begins at the wide front window, two or three steps, to a landing, a turn and another flight brings you to the up-stairs hall. The huge wardrobe there against the wall was the Garlington's.

"I guess it was just too big to move," Josephine said.

Was it carried up in sections and assembled in the hall?

"We have not re-decorated the upstairs rooms," Josephine told me, "they are as the Garlingtons left them."

Three big square rooms, one for Aurie, one for Robbie and one for John.

Perhaps Drummer Tom Brown kept his sample cases in the little angle room, but the last two owners have used it for a rumpus room.

The south bed room was Pop's (Mr. Miller) and is furnished in maple. Ann's baby bed is kept here with the furniture that was Jo's first bedroom suite. The wall paper is blue, striped in bands of pink roses and the rug is blue.

There are ample closets in all the rooms, which is surprising for older houses were usually lacking in this convenience.

The mantel and woodwork in the front bed-room are in handsomely grained walnut, the paper is pink-flowered and the rug is wine colored. The same grained wood work is used in the back bed-room and the furniture is green-gold. Pictures of Josephine as a young girl and as a College girl are on the chest and the dressing table. She laughingly called attention to the "hair-do."

The bed was heaped high with a froth of billowy skirts—Ann's formals, each carefully protected in cellophane. There was the dress she wore as Sweetheart of the Senior Prom and the exquisite Creation that she wore. as Miss Gordon County of 1960, to the Pageant in Columbus.

During her High School years, Ann was Editor of the Annual and represented Calhoun School in declamation and the one-act play. She studied music through Elementary and Junior High School, served as Sunday School pianist and sang in the choir of the First Methodist church where her mother has been soprano soloist since she came to Calhoun. Ann also played the piano on graduation night for her High School Class.

Three generations of petit women. But a list of their activities would fill pages. Each has held offices in church and civic organizations since she was old enough to assume such responsibilities. One is reminded of the adage "the most precious things come in small packages."

Carrie sees to the welfare of her family and bakes Ann an angel cake. Josephine is a member of the High School faculty and Ann is a student at Shorter College in Rome.

The service that a doctor gives to humanity as well-known. Because of ill-health, Dr. Billings was forced to give up his practice at an early age. He smokes his pipe, goes to the Rotary Club on Fridays and to church on Sundays and thinks about fishing in his off hours.

We ponder it's future—the future of this loved house that has stood for many years in the shade of the Oaks on Wall street. Will it be left as a momento of Wall street's golden days? Or will it be the victim of progress and come down to make way for a supermarket or some other commercial building?

Whatever it's fate, the house will live on through the people who have called it home, the Browns, the Blacks, the Garlingtons and the Billings, from 1898 to 1961.

The two red brick house on North Wall street were the doctors' homes, Dr. Mills' on the corner of Trammell and Wall and Dr. Richards' between the Civic Center and the business block.

Dr. Mills first acquaintance with Calhoun was in 1883 where he was here as a salesman for a patent churn with a self-revolving dasher, but it was not until 1900 that he came to live in Calhoun.

G. W. Mills' father owned extensive property in Faywood Valley, near Subligna. Dr. Mills built a large house at Subligna but never quite finished it. He married a daughter of Mr. and Mrs. Ramsey whose home was at Dry Creek near Subligna.

Subligna is across two mountains, John's and Horn's, from Gordon county.

To be near their daughter, Mr. and Mrs. Ramsey moved to Calhoun. Their home was the Juan Fields place on the corner of College and Chandler streets. Nine houses are now located in the block that J. M. Reeve sold to Juan Fields about 80 years ago, and in the Ramsey pasture that was for so long a playground for the neighborhood children.

Dr. Mills was elected president of the newly organized Baptist Young People's Union soon after he came to town. He bought an interest in a Drug Store and by 1907 was full owner.

In 1908, Mary T. Whitson wrote a story about Calhoun's business men for The Calhoun Times. Of Dr. Mills she said; Dr. G. W. Mills, one of the leading physicians, is proprietor of a very handsome, perfectly appointed Drug Store—everything glitters. to the lofty ceiling.

Dr. Mills was born in Chattooga county in 1932, was educated in the County Schools and graduated in medicine in 1887. He practiced one year in Chattooga County and eleven in Whitfield before coming to Gordon.

The Mills house is glazed brick with simulated windows, walk roof top. A gable, faced with cement in which bits of colored glass have been imbedded, extends from each of the four sides. A wide porch across the front, plate glass in the door and big windows of solid lower sash, with narrow colored glass panel at the top, form the facade.

The hardwood floors in parlor and dining room are laid in an intricate pattern. Mantels are cabinet form in rich grained wood.

"There was not a closet in the house," Birdie Mills Dyer told me, "Papa said they were not healthy."

All the electric switches were in the halls, a very convenient arrangement—no one need walk into a dark room.

Birdie Mills created almost a sensation in town in 1903—she married the pastor of the Baptist church.

Edwin M. Dyer was the third minister in the family to serve (1901-1903) as pastor of the Calhoun church. His grandfather, Edwin Dyer, was pastor in the 1870's and his father Wylie M. in 1879 and 1890.

After the wedding, the church gave a reception for Rev. and Mrs. E. M. Dyer and presented them a silver service.

"Our house at Marietta burned" Birdie said and a soup ladle is all that is left of the silver."

Captain W. M. Dyer always prayer with his eyes open and, on one occasion, the Mills children, Birdie, Gene, George and Reese were a little late for the service. Gene was leading the others down the aisle. He stopped and waited for them to enter the pew, but they were no where to be seen.

"Well, if they ain't gone!" Gene said aloud.

The congregation laughed, whereupon Captain Dyer said "I don't know what happened, but I'll wait until everyone is quiet."

Birdie, Gene and Reece had realized that Captain was praying, not preaching, and had quietly slipped into a back pew.

W. M. Dyer, son of Edwin and Nancy Austin Dyer, was born at Social Circle, Ga., in 1837. The Senior Dyer was pastor at LaFayette and W. M. attended Academy there until he was 18 years old. He received his degree from Cherokee Baptist College at Cassville in 1857 and a choir in Mathematics at the College. He received his law degree in 1860 from the law School at Chapel Hill, North Carolina. In 1861, he joined the Confederate Army and was made an adjutant-general with the rank of captain.

After the battle of Resaca, Captain Dyer led his brigade safely over a burning bridge across the Oostanaula river. For this courageous act, he was recommended for promotion to the rank of Major but was captured in the battle of Atlanta July 18, 1864 and spent the remaining years of the War as a prisoner on Johnson's Island.

During the War, Captain Dyer married Miss Louise Erwin of Fairmount and returned to Fairmount when the war was over to become principal of Salacoa Academy. After 10 years residence in Texas, he returned to Gordon County in 1891 to serve the Baptist Mission Board. He died in 1917 and is buried at Fairmount.

Mrs. Mills remained in the house after the Doctor's death and opened her big house to roomers. Banks and Claude David stayed at Mrs. Mills' when they came to town to accept positions in the Bank.

Rev. Edwin Dyer died and Birdie came home to live with her mother an deducate her children in the Calhoun Schools Edwin M. Jr., Louise, Frances, G. Wylie and James are the Dyer children.

Birdie Mills Dyer lives with her son now and often returns to Calhoun to visit friends.

Dr. W. A. Richards and family arrived in Calhoun, Tuesday night, January 10, 1899 and moved into the house vacated by Dr. Hightower.

A few weeks after his arrival, he had purchased the Calhoun Hotel and at once began to have the building overhauled and made into a practically new structure of 30 rooms, fitted in style.

In 1901, Dr. Richards traded the hotel to J. W. Logan for his house and farm on the Rome road and a cash difference of $3600.

Of pleasant address and making friends easily, Dr. Richards soon became one of the busiest doctors in town. He purchased a lot on Wall street and, in February of 1910, began the construction of a large brick house. The house, described as one of the handsomest and best finished building in North Georgia, was completed in December and the family took possession.

Dr. Gardner, son of G. W. Gardner, tells this story about Dr. Richards—his car and a farmer's mule and wagon met in the covered bridge over Oothcaloga Creek. The mule was practically on top of the car.

"Get your mule off of my car," commanded the Doctor.

"I didn't put him up there," retorted the farmer, "you get him off!"

Dr. and Mrs. Richards' children were; Minerva, (Mrs. L. D. Neal), Luther, Annabel (Mrs. L. M. Boaz) Ethel (Mrs. C. D. Dyar) Roy and Harry.

William and Samamtha V. Richards died in 1921 and are buried in Fain Cemetery.

All of the Richards children established homes in Calhoun except Luther, who lived in Oklahoma.

Roy followed his father in the medical profession and was, for many years, one of Calhoun's leading physicians. His younger son, Charles, carries on the tradition and is at present one of the town's popular young doctors.

Elected to the City Council in 1922, Dr. Roy Richards served in his capacity through 1926, becoming mayor after the death of Mayor J. C. Garlington in 1927. He remained in office through 1929 and was again elected mayor in 1932.

He was an officer in World War I and a charter member of the Paul Gwin Post of the American Legion, organized at Resaca Confederate Cemetery May 10, 1919, and was Commander in 1919-1921.

Harry Richards also a World War Veteran, and his family lived in the Richards house for a few years following the death of his parents.

It was acquired by the Methodist Church to be used as a parsonage but was sold after a short time to Dr. and Mrs. W. R. Richards. Subsequent owners of the property were, John Hunt, Glen Harris, Ben Goldman and Leo Copeland, of Dalton. In 1946, J. W. Thomas, successor to Jackson Funeral Directors, leased the house and established his Funeral House there. He became sole owner of the house in 1951.

A beautiful Chapel, seating 185, was added to the north side of the house in 1959. From the family room (the Richards dining room and parlor) you enter the chapel through a double doorway. The handsome gold-embossed draperies, soft side-lights, lamps and comfortable chairs make the room a serene and consolatory setting for the last service given to loved ones. A piano and an organ are there to be used as the family wishes.

The flower room is back of the chapel and the embalming and display rooms are in the older part of the building. Sixteen adult caskets in soft gray and in copper or bronze were on display in the two rooms.

The dominant feature of the reception hall is the white mantel. Ionic columns are carved in acanthus blooms and leaves and are finished with square tops and bases. The arch between the columns is elaborately carved. Other mantels in the house are constructed along the same lines.

The Seth Thomas clock was bought by the Calvin Wright family in 1860 and another upstairs, in 1840. One of Estelle Wright's paintings hangs on the stair wall. The love seat and chairs to match, two tables and two other chairs are from the Pitts-McDaniel home.

The ceiling are handsomely paneled or finished with wide, curved moldings. Draperies and wall paper on the lower floor are in muted shades of green.

Living apartments for the Thomas family are on the second floor. Six rooms that were bedrooms for the Richards girls and boys are now bedrooms, dining room and kitchen for Evelyn, J. W. and Bruce Thomas.

The long roomy hall is furnished as a living room. The large family room at the end of the hall is a recent addition.

Mrs. Thomas was Evelyn Hammeth of Atlanta. J. W. Thomas, whose mother was Sunie Wright, is descended from the Shelor, Wright and Thomas families of Springtown district. J. W. and Evelyn only child is Bruce, age 14.

Floyd Whittemore resigned, after 8 years with Thomas Funeral Home, to become County Clerk. Brady Anderson, stayed 10 years and M. L. Dale, 4 years. (he was recalled to Service). Men now with J. W. and their length of stay are, Fred Caldwell, 8 years, Roy Hammontree, 7 years and Jack Hughey 12 years. Three ambulances answer the call bell at Thomases.

The exterior of the house is glazed brick. Brick pillars support the arched veranda roof. The floor of the porch is red tile and the steps and underpinning are granite. A car port was built after the Funeral home was established. The double brick garage of the Richards is at the back, on Piedmont street.

The roof of the house has wide eaves and a widow-walk top. A gable over the north room is faced with geometric paneling and 2 little windows are formed in the same design. A small square off set has 3 like windows.

Boxwoods border the walk to the chapel and azaleas, spring bulbs and camellias bloom in season.

Carry my easel for me, will you, across court square to the corner, where I will sit to finish my painting of Wall street.

Or should I sit on the courthouse lawn? It was here that the very first settler built his lean-to and lived in it, with his bear dogs, until another man settled at Cassville.

Talitha Kinman Hall loved to tell the story and Julian Fain passed it on to me. The settler moved on after the other man had built his lean-to at Cassville saying that people were getting too close, he didn't like neighbors.

My first picture is not a very pretty one. This is Bull Neck, in the block south of the courthouse. Please stand guard beside me for here are the saloons and the livery stable and, anytime, a reeling man or a galloping horse might come out of Bull Neck.

A row of trees down the center of the street and one on each side never let the sun in to dry up the mud holes. The wagons bog down and the men must carry the guano sacks on their shoulders, from the warehouse. The stores in this section are all sorry-looking wooden buildings. All were cleared out in the fire of 1888.

The first four lots are business houses. David S. Law, Justice of Inferior Court 1850, paid $201 for lot 5 in section 10. He may have built the brick house that stood on the lot until the 1930's. It was the home of the Skellys and of Mrs. Ida Roach who kept her Millinery shop in the house part of the time and, at another time, in the brick store next door.

David S. Law, his wife Nancy and a baby, are buried in Chandler cemetery.

The old brick house was torn down when Dr. Z. V. Johnston built his hospital. The Rooker Hotel now stands on the site.

Robert S. Patton paid $150 for lot 6. A two story white frame house was erected on the lot sometime in the dim past. It was the home of the Hines family. Maude Ballew Neal says that Dr. W. J. Reeves was residing in the house when she was a little girl, for she went there often to play with Eva Reeves. Cynthia, Beulah, Lee, Fred and Virgil were the other Reeves children. Maurice Thompson was deeply in love with Cynthia Reeves and it was to her that he wrote his poem entitled "Cynthia."

Mrs. Dorsey, mother of Henry Dorsey, lived in the house and others, too, who are not here to tell the story.

Lot 1, Section 11 was the home of General Charles H. and Ruth Dawson Nelson. Mr. Dawson ran a store down near the railroad and it was for him that the village was named Dawsonville in 1846, or earlier. Could the Nelson house have been the Dawson home?

General Nelson, whose ancestry dated back to Lord Nelson of England, served in the Seminole Indian War and helped move the

Cherokees from New Echota. He bought a plantation at Big Spring after the removal of the Indians.

General Nelson went to the Mexican War in 1845 and came home a Brigadier General but with health broken by exposure in the tropical climate. He died in 1848 and is buried in the family cemetery at Big Spring (Dew's Lake).

Charles and Ruth Nelson's daughter, Hannah, married William H. Morris and was living in the Nelson house at the time of her daughter Julia's marriage to Joseph McConnell on September 12, 1870, T. M. Pledger, minister.

According to The Democratic Platform, Calhoun newspaper of 1861, Hannah was the music teacher at the Calhoun Male and Female Academy and W. H. Morris was in the grocery business. He served as County treasurer in 1863-1864.

Then, in 1874, Ruth Amanda Nelson sold the house to Berry Boaz and, for 19 years, it was the Boaz home. Berry was often seen driving his handsome phaeton up and down Wall street. His wife, Bessie Fain Boaz taught music on the very organ that her husband purchased in 1878. The rich-toned instrument had 12 stops and chime of bells.

In 1893, Louis D. Hillhouse, of Palm Beach, Fla., bought the place for $1500 but stayed in Calhoun only a few months. Mrs. Hillhouse was unhappy in the North Georgia Country.

J. M. Kay rented the house in 1897 and bought it in 1901.

The original structure was of 4 rooms and hall, a square front porch, square columns and green blinds at all the windows. Ethel and Minnie Kay told me that the old columns and blinds are stored under the house.

"We wish they were back," one of them said.

The kitchen was set apart at the north corner and connected to the house by a breeze-way.

Identical colonial doorways open at the front and back and the 4 doors into the hall have transoms. The walls are plastered and ceilings are planks of various widths. Hand-cut logs in the foundation are pegged together.

From the house on the hill top, the lawn sloped gradually to the street but changes through the years have left sidewalks at two levels, one at the rock wall edging the lawn and the other at the pavement.

A Virgin oak shades the north lawn and five gnarled cedars, three of them dead, are all that remain of the fragrant, evergreen trees that once bordered the walk up to the front door.

Many of the Kay household furnishings were lost in a fire but Ethel has a handsome banjo clock that belonged to the Engrams. The large roll-top desk in the hall was used by J. M. Kay in his store and the hat rack and wardrobe were in the John Gordon family. Noah McGinnis started housekeeping with the beautifully finished spool bed that is hand made and joined with wooden pegs. Noah was a big man, so the bed is extra wide and long. The oak side-board, table and chairs were Mr. Kay's last gift to Lucinda, his second, wife. He was first married to Martha Coley, Lucinda's sister. The companion of his last years was Minnie Hudgins Kay.

J. M. Kay, brother of A. M. Kay of Oothcaloga district, was reared at the Barton place in Sonoraville district. He was manager of the Peters farm for several years then moved to Calhoun where he engaged in the mercantile business for the rest of his life.

On the night of the big fire of July 13, 1901, Dr. Richards dashed up on the porch calling for Mr. Kay, not knowing that he had already gone to town.

"Good God, Mrs. Kay," he exclaimed, "the town's burning up!"

The little girl, Minnie, walked up to the window as she had seen the good doctor do and parrotted "Good God, Mrs. Kay!"

May be the town was burning up, but Minnie got a whipping.

After the fire the men's clothing stock at Kay's in the Doughty building was spread to dry on the courthouse lawn.

Ethel Kay Engram-McClellan and Minnie Kay occupy the house that their father rented 64 years ago and bought 60 years ago. The four big rooms are let to young men temporarily away from their home towns while Minnie and Ethel are cosily established in the two south rooms.

"Don't you envy us?" Minnie asked, and pointed to a coal-burning heater with a pot of beans cooking on top. I did experience a moment of envy as the memories came flooding for I once had a heater just like it—and a pot of beans.

Across Nelson street and north from the Kays are the Watts and McGinniss houses.

The McGinniss farm lay around the river bridge on the Sugar Valley road.

"Granny McGinniss kept the bridge" Arva said.

A bridge was swept away in the flood of 1861, so the bridge that Mrs. McGinniss tended, probably a toll bridge, must have been the covered one that fell during a storm in the spring of 1916.

Noah McGinniss was a contractor in the 1880's and built many of the older brick stores of Calhoun. He was elected sheriff in 1885 and held the office until his death from bullet wounds received in a gun battle with outlaws in 1892.

"Mother and I were picking cotton in a field near the railroad and north of Plainville," Nancy Ballew Miller told me. "We did not know that one of the outlaws was hiding in a house near by until the shooting began. We left the field," she concluded.

The Inferior Court of Gordon County deeded lot No. 2 in section 11 to Stephen N. Jones on February 13, 1850. Stephen sold the lot to James M. Orr, July 13, 1854 and bought it back from James, with appertanances, for $500, on October 19, 1859. Did Stephen build the house? or James? It was there during the Civil War for when the house was remodeled in 1921, a front column was found to be all greasy inside where the meat had been hidden. We wonder if the Yankees found it.

Mary Ann Cabot, widow of F. M. Cabot, dry goods merchant at Calhoun in 1861, was occupying the house in 1866. Two of her frequent callers were W. H. Darnell and W. R. L. Smith. She married Mr. Darnell in 1867 and went with him to live at New Echota.

Sometime after this, John H. and Susan Arthur moved into the house in lot 2. John Henry Arthur and Susan Lane were married November 19, 1867 by Rev. Z. M. McGhee, pastor of Liberty Presbyterian church.

Susan concealed her letters in the wall of an upstairs room where they were found in 1911.

"Why did she put the letters in the wall?" some one asked.

The last years of the 1860 decade were days of reconstruction and the Arthurs might have feared reprisals had the letters been discovered.

One of the letters to Susan is included in this story.

The Millinery Store at which Susan was working belonged to Vadilia Loveless in Adairsville. It was the only one in this section in 1866 and people severely criticized Vadilia for being in business. She was the grandmother of Mrs. Alice (Topsy) Howard, now of Adairsville.

The John Henry of Mollie's letter was Mr. Arthur and "Dick B." was Dick Bowdoin. The Bowdoin family home was 2½ miles north of Adairsville, now the Bennett place.

Mrs. Veach was Julia Echols before her marriage. She became one of Adairsville's most beloved matrons and her children and grandchildren are still prominent in the town's life.

John Henry and Susan, with their daughter Jennie, moved to Texas and the house on lot two saw many families come and go.

J. C. Campbell bought the place in 1904 from T. M. Ellis, administrator of the Frix estate, Successive owners were R. H. Land, Henry Brogdon, T. M. Boaz, L. D. Neal and Dr. Z. V. Johnston.

Henry and Jessie Jagoe Brogdon purchased the property in 1911 and it was Jessie who saved Mollie's letter from the heap of papers that a workman had piled on the ground.

"I wish I had saved them all," Jessie said, "but I had no place to keep them."

Young Henry Brogdon owned a beautiful stallion named Red Skin which he gave in part payment for the house and lot on South Wall. The horse was sold and resold and finally wound up in Alabama. Rumors were that the fine animal was eventually shipped to France.

After many years of business in Calhoun. Henry Brogdon retired to his farm north of town. Left a widow, Mrs. Brogdon moved back to town and now lives in an attractive cottage on Willard Street.

Deeply interested in family history, Jessie Jagoe Brogdon keeps in her cedar chest, priceless family momentoes, among them daguerrotypes, like pictures on tiny mirrows, resting on velvet in exquisite frames of gold-scalloped walnut. These were the first I had ever seen and I was charmed with the delicate images produced on a silver plate treated with iodine. Louis Daguerre presented the invention to the public in 1839.

A pistol box that belonged to Jessie's grandfather, Dr. Samuel R. Nisbitt, of Kentucky, is the repository for treasured old letters. One letter, written by Dr. Nisbitt to his son, William Kemp Nisbitt, is marked "not to be opened as long as I live."

When the letter was opened it was found to contain the formula for a cancer cure.

"Handle this with greatest caution," Dr. Nisbitt wrote, "use it right and it will make you a fortune. And keep it to yourself."

The skin cancer was to be sprinkled with a little arsenic, then covered with a poultice of onions. After 12 hours, the poultice was to be removed and the sore greased with sweet oil, then a salve of mutton suet and beeswax applied.

"See that the patient is in a good fix before you begin and make him take iron while he is under the influence of the arsenic—and study metdicine before you use it" were the doctor's final instructions.

"We have always had great confidence in her judgement" wrote W. E. Jagoe and Jennie Jagoe from Madisonville, Kentucky on May 22, 1910 as they promised the hand of their daughter in marriage to Henry Brogdon. Naturally, Jessie Brogdon prized this letter above all.

The handsome round dining table and chairs were acquired by the Brogdons when they moved into the Wall street house.

"I don't see why anyone would want pictures of sheep on a china lamp," remarked Mrs. Brogdon as we examined the unique lamp that once belonged to Mrs. Samuel Harlan. Did not the Master say "feed my sheep?"

Two small ladder-back chairs and a marble-top parlor table also were in the home of Mrs. Harlan, grandmother of Henry and Lula Brogdon.

Henry Clay Brogdon's Engraved Knights Templar Sword hangs on the wall near a picture, in color, of Mike and Linda Brogdon, children of Kemp and Virginia Burdette Brogdon.

Linda's christening dress, delicately embroidered and fashioned of fine cloth and lace, made by her grandmother Jessie, is carefully preserved. A cousin of Linda's, Charles Clements, and Gary Ralph Bullard, child of the Presbyterian pastor also wore the dress for the christening service.

The Brogdon men were prominent in town and country affairs from the beginning. Wiley Brogdon was a road reviewer from the 24th district and Justice of the Peace in 1853 and a member of the town Council in 1861.

G. W. Sr., Elsworth and G. N. Brogdon joined Company C, 8th Battalion, Gist-Walker Brigage when it was organized in October of 1861.

Extensive changes were made to the Brogdon house by Dr. Johnston. The kitchen ell was torn away, two rooms upstairs and down were added at the rear and the entire building venered in new brick. A terrace across the front is centered with a square portico supported by the ante-bellum columns.

The side walk was once level with the lawn but was lowered with the street paving. Twelve steps now lead up to the front walk.

Mrs. Z. V. Johnston (Arva Tolbert) made one of the towns first formal gardens and her flowers were fabulous. At one Garden Club meeting, her house was decorated with 500 regal lily blooms. The covered terraces and lily pools are still there in the back yard and many of the fine shrubs remain. A little log cabin with shutters and a rock chimney is tucked away in one corner under the trees. I thought it may have been mammy's cabin but Mrs. Brogdon said that it was some little girl's play house.

While I was prowling the premises, in company with a lordly rooster who was strutting his priority, Arva Watts Johnston came in with her groceries. She said the rooster took up residence uninvited and crows them awake at 5 o'clock each morning.

Zeb, Jr. stayed on in the old home after the death of Dr. Johnston. He and Arva are custodians of the Watts and Johnston heirlooms. Two straight-backed chairs, upholstered in tan and gold tapestry, are from the McGinnis family as are two chests one of solid walnut and one of cherrywood.

Minnie Bennett, one of a family of orphaned children, was adopted at the age of three by the McGinnisses. At her marriage in 1902 to Claude Watts, the procedure was reversed. The reception came first and the Wedding afterward.

The attractive lamp with round china shade, its thistle blooms looking real enough to float on the breeze, was a gift of the groomsmen—a delicately formed little clock and a sea shell were brought from New Orleans by Mr. and Mrs. Watts when they returned to Calhoun after several years residence in the Louisiana City.

No more beloved couple ever lived in Calhoun than Dr. and Mrs. Johnston. Public-spirited and co-operative in every way, they were generous with their talents and possessions.

Dr. Johnston, in partnership with young Dr. Wilbur D. Hall, built Calhoun's first Hospital in 134-35. There were only three beds at the start, with offices and reception room on the lower floor—later, a second story was added and Dr. R. D. Walter and Dr. J. E. Billings joined the Staff. Miss Arminda Haney, who had been Dr. Johnston's assistant, moved on the hospital as the efficient office manager.

Doctors and nurses came and went and the hospital continued to serve the public until the Gordon County Hospital was constructed. It is now operated as the Johnston-Hall Clinic, by Dr. Hall, Dr. Walter and Dr. J. L. Rabb.

Dr. and Mrs. Johnston's children are, Zeb Jr., Mary Arva and Tom. Billy died at the age of six months and James, young husband and father, 1960.

Next door to the Johnston house, once stood a long house of one room width. The front porch was 56 feet by 14 feet. Three small shed rooms were attached at the rear.

Jessie Robinson says that Callie McConnell Barrett was a guest in her home in 1920 and told her "I visited here 50 years ago. The house is just like it was then."

In 1864, Callie and her mother learned that their brother and son, Joe McConnell, was encamped with his Confederate unit near Red Bud. Mrs. McConnell and her daughter, Callie, walked about 10 miles to visit their confederate soldier.

Col. and Mrs. J. M. Lang lived in the house at one time and the Bryants, who sold the place to Henry and Annie Dorsey, Mr. Dorsey sold to the Brewers, then G. F. and Jessie Robinson purchased the place from Mr. Brewer. Carleton and Doris Fite were the next and last owners of this 1870 house. It burned to the ground 25 or more years ago.

Across the street from the Cabots and Arthurs were the Lanes. Ileys and Hicks. The Episcopal church, a one-story, wooden building, of chapel design, was built on a lot donated by John P. King. The Sinclair Service Station is located on this lot.

A brick house stood on the site of the Gulf Service Station. It was the home through the years, of L. P. Roebuck, Mrs. Talitha Hall, the Reeds, the Holcombs and the Tom Cantrells.

The Hicks home was in this block. Henry K. Hicks, son of Alfred and Harriet Dover Hicks, was born in North Carolina in 1837. The family moved to Whitfield county in 1845 and then to Gordon. He was associated with many of the town's early business firms, Sams, Arthur and Co., of prewar days, Hicks and Thayer, Grant Hunt's Drug Store and H. K. and F. L. Hicks.

Henry Hicks and Pamela Ivey were married in 1857. Their children were, Georgia (Mrs. G. W. Hamrick) Alfred (died in youth) Elizabeth, Ophelia and Fitzhugh Lee. Henry and Pamela are buried in Chandler Cemetery.

F. L's first wife was Ella Johnston; children, Henry, Ernest and Hugh. The second wife was Linnie Byrd, of Fairmount and their children are Frank and Bessie (Mrs. Melvin Langford).

F. L. Hicks and W. M. Hughey established Calhoun's first garage and automobile business in 1915. They sold Overland cars and accessories and supplies for Fords.

A director of the Fair Association in 1906 and a member of the building committee when a new Methodist church was erected in 1916, Mr. Hicks was active in many phase's of the town's growth. He served as Mayor in 1923, 24, 25, 1930-31 and again in 1934. He was president of the Peoples Bank, a private Bank organized in 1905.

F. L. Hicks built the spacious house that is now the studio and offices of WCGA, Calhoun's Radio Station. Used cars sit on the spot that was Linnie Hick's flower garden. She was flower chairman of the Woman's Club where her artistic arrangements brightened the Cabin on second Thursday afternoons.

The Lane house was between the Hicks and the Ransomes. John Lane sold his house in 1873, to S. R. Ivey for $1000. Mr. Ivey deeded it to his daughter, Permelia H. J. Hicks in 1879.

Mary Hall Alexander lived in the Lane house at one time. The lot extended from street to street and Mrs. Alexander's cow pasture was at the back. Her husband, James Alexander, Co. G, 12th South Carolina Regiment, was a casualty of the Civil War. His young widow never re-married and lived to an advanced age, still true to the memory of her soldier in The Lost Cause.

George and Lou Wyatt Ransome built the house next door with money that Lou inherited. A one-story structure at first, it was raised to second story height by Mr. DeJournette, a later owner, who purchased the place from the Scotts. Mr. DeJournette sold to the family of Rosa and Noami White. An apartment today, the house is leased by Mrs. G. F. Dillard.

George and Lou's first house was on Railroad street, across from the Calhoun Hotel.

Lou fed the train crews and her little girl, Mollie would swing the trains as The Texas and The General, famous engines of the Civil War locomotive chase, as they switched from the main tracks to sidings to load wood.

Robert Ransome, father of George, came to this section from Monroe, Georgia. He helped move the Indians and served in the Mexican War. For his service, he was given extensive land holdings in the West.

Lou's father was Lonzo Dow Wyatt, a Methodist preacher from East Tennessee and her mother was Edith Swaggerty Ransome.

Mollie's sister, Edith (Mrs. C. H. Barnes) was assistant postmaster with Mrs. Ida Johnson. Another sister, Ada, married W. N. Dorsey and the only brother, George F. was married to Miss Elizabeth Jones in a brillant wedding at the Presbyterian church.

Down the street from the Ransomes was the home of the Camfields and later, of Major Aaron Roff whose second wife was Rebecca Camfield. The first Mrs. Roff, married to Aaron in 1837, was Mary A. Glascock.

Aaron Roff helped to build Dawsonville (Calhoun). He ran a lumber mill and sawed the timber for most of the houses in the village, among them the Hotel and Oothcaloga Mills.

After Rebecca's death, Major Roff turned to gardening. His rose garden, of 50 varieties, was one alone in its day. When you pass Bea's Beauty Box and the Barton home, picture a white picket fence and an old time Southern gentleman walking in his garden in the early morning when each unfolding flower is dew-diamonded and a mocking bird sings in a tree—say with our poet, Mabel Hall Poole -

Have you ever looked down in the heart of a rose?
Do you know why one is a dainty pink
And another a brilliant red:
God makes all these things for as to enjoy
And he dwells in the heart of a rose.

Members of the Boisclair family mentioned in the old newspaper are Amelia (Mrs. T. R. Harkins) L. V., honor student at the Calhoun Academy and Mrs. Lydia Boiscliar who died in Augusta, June 11, 1884.

The house at the end of the long street was the house of Dr. W. W. Wall. It was a story and a half structure with a kitchen and small porch at the south front corner. Dr. Wall was a justice of the Inferior Court in 1850 and a grand Juror in 1859. (Mr. W. T. Wall, native of Calhoun and son of Dr. Wall, died in Atlanta in 1899.)

Mr. and Mrs. James W. Jackson owned the place at a later date. Mrs. Jackson was deaf and did not like to be alone in the house while her husband was away on business. Will Brown, young son of Dr. E. W. Brown, a neighbor, would come up every night and sleep at Mrs. Jackson's.

Dr. Brown came here in 1851 from Forsyth County and entered the Mercantile business with Wiley Brogdon. Their brick store was on the site of the Bearden Provision Co.

Elbert Washington Brown son of Jesse Brown (1810-1894) and Sarah Kendall Brown was born in Pike County, March 28, 1828. The family moved to Forsyth county in 1834 and then to Gordon.

Dr. Brown was educatetd in the Common Schools and received his Medical degrees from Vanderbilt University, the Atlanta Medical College and Pennsylvania University. He served through the Civil War as assistant field surgeon. Dr. Brown was also a graduate Pharmacist. The Brown home was the house on the south side of Roberts Electric brick building.

E. W. Brown was married in 1856 to Sarah Nelson, daughter of General Charles H. Nelson. Their children were Sarah and Charley. Betty Tanner was the second wife and children of this union were Odessa (Mrs. Ben Chastain) Mary Elizabeth (Mrs. J. M. Murphy) and William. Dr. Brown died in 1899.

Young Will Brown fell in love with Dr. Wall's house and after, Mrs. Jackson's death, while still in his teens, purchased the property. He raised the half-story to full height and added square columns reaching to the top story.

Will Brown went to work at the Depot as messenger boy and advanced to Station Agent, an office that he held until ill health forced his retirement.

When he and Ruby Haulbrook were married she, like all new homemakers, wanted to change the house. The columns, but of proportion, she said, were removed and a low terrace built across the front, with entrance portico and porch at the north end of the house. The two front columns and the four at the porch are Doric.

The solicitors mother in Ruby Brown could not endure the thought of four little boys sleeping in any of the four big rooms upstairs, so a large sleeping porch was added at the rear of the south corner room downstairs. Before the day of elaborate motels, Ruby Brown's house became a popular spend the night place for tourists.

The sleeping porch has been, for 13 years, a kindergarten School room. Furnished with piano, tables, chairs and cabinets, it is a perfect setting for the excellent pre-school training Mrs. Brown gives to Calhoun's five year olds.

The kindergarten's Lilliputian Wedding is always one of the high lights of the Spring season in Calhoun.

W. C. and Suzanne Mayson Haulbrook came to Gordon from Maysville in Banks County, in 1892. The family lived for a time at the Laurens home, built by Larkin Haulbrook, on the Rome road and in the old brick house, then a white-columned mansion, on the A. P. Beamer farm.

Children of W. C. and Suzanne Haulbrook were Clyde (Mrs. A. R. McDaniel) Mabel (Mrs. Peterson,) Myrtle (Mrs. Blair) Paul Mayson, Hugh Lawson, Hallie (Mrs. Meinung) and Marian (Mrs. Boem).

Will and Ruby Brown's sons were William, who died in 1956, Kenneth, of Louisville, Ga., Austin, of Atlanta and Dr. Coleman Brown of Emory Hospital.

Across the street was the Huey house. Too large for modern small families and falling into ruin because of the absence from Calhoun of all the family, the house was dismantled several years ago. The site was purchased by Dr. R. D. Walter and is now a beautifully kept lawn adjoining the Walter home. A rock wall keeps down erosion and two flights of steps lead up to the plot.

W. M. Hughey was in business in Calhoun in 1884 when he was serving cold drinks at soda fount and hot goobers from his new peanut parcher. In January of 1885, he wrote an advertisement in verse for his store next door to Hines and King.

Mr. Hughey was a member of the City Council in a period of years from 1889 to 1918, serving as Chairman in 1891, as treasurer in 1892 and again in 1907 and a Marshall in 1908-09.

He was married to Miss Jimmie Prickett in 1885 and their children were Bessie, Willie, Emmie, Paul and Parks.

Wall street, called Main, and Broad, and Church runs from Rock street (Line) to Dr. Wall's house. Berry Boaz drove his phaeton up and down Broad street and wagons mired to the hub in its mud holes. Oxen chewed bark from the elm trees on Main, and Church street was perfectly beautiful on a May morning in 1880.

Flora Pitts is no longer here to entertain the grandmothers once a year in her Wall street home. The Garlington and Saxon ladies no longer dress for an afternoon of visiting on the front porch. E. J.

Kiker is no more seen riding his pony in the moon light as he ponders a court case. Only in memory does Dr. Mills come down the steps, black bag in hand, to drive many country miles to a patient's home (he was my little sister's "pill doctor"). Dim forms of the Richards family move under the brick arches and flit through the rooms perhaps to pause in the new Chapel and breathe a prayer of gratitude that the Doctor's home is now a place of dedication to the dead.

There she goes. There goes Old Wall street. Say goodbye to Old Wall street, ladies and gentlemen.

The End.